PORTABLE EDITION | BOOK 3 | FOURTH EDITION

ART HISTORY

A View of the World
Part One: Asian, African, and Islamic Art and Art of the Americas

MARILYN STOKSTAD

Judith Harris Murphy Distinguished Professor of Art History Emerita
The University of Kansas

MICHAEL W. COTHREN

Scheuer Family Professor of Humanities
Department of Art, Swarthmore College

CONTRIBUTORS

Frederick M. Asher, David A. Binkley, Claudia L. Brittenham, Claudia Brown,

Patricia J. Darish, Patricia J. Graham, and D. Fairchild Ruggles

Prentice Hall

Boston Columbus Indianapolis New York San Francisco Upper Saddle River
Amsterdam Cape Town Dubai London Madrid Milan Munich Paris Montréal Toronto
Delhi Mexico City São Paulo Sydney Hong Kong Seoul Singapore Taipei Tokyo

Editorial Director: Craig Campanella
Editor-in-Chief: Sarah Touborg
Senior Sponsoring Editor: Helen Ronan
Editorial Project Manager: David Nitti
Editorial Assistant: Carla Worner
Editor-in-Chief, Development: Rochelle Diogenes
Development Editors: Margaret Manos and Cynthia Ward
Media Director: Brian Hyland
Media Editor: Alison Lorber
Media Project Manager: Rich Barnes
Director of Marketing: Brandy Dawson
Senior Marketing Manager: Kate Mitchell
Marketing Assistant: Craig Deming
Senior Managing Editor: Ann Marie McCarthy
Assistant Managing Editor: Melissa Feimer
Production Project Managers: Barbara Cappuccio and Marlene Gassler
Senior Operations and Manufacturing Manager: Nick Sklitsis
Senior Operations Specialist: Brian Mackey
Manager of Design Development: John Christiana
Art Director and Interior Design: Kathy Mrozek
Cover Design: Kathy Mrozek
Site Supervisor, Pearson Imaging Center: Joe Conti
Pearson Imaging Center: Corin Skidds, Robert Uibelhoer,
 and Ron Walko
Cover Printer: Lehigh-Phoenix Color
Printer/Binder: Courier/Kendallville

This book was designed by
Laurence King Publishing Ltd, London
www.laurenceking.com

Commissioning Editor: Kara Hattersley-Smith
Senior Editors: Melissa Danny/Sophie Page
Production Manager: Simon Walsh
Page Design: Nick Newton/Randell Harris
Photo Researcher: Emma Brown
Copy Editors: Tessa Clark/Jenny Knight/Robert Shore/
 Johanna Stephenson
Proofreader: Jennifer Speake
Indexer: Sue Farr

Cover photo: Two equestrian figures. Tang dynasty, first half 8th century CE. Molded, reddish-buff earthenware with cold-painted pigments over white ground, height (male figure) 14½″ (37 cm). Arthur M. Sackler Museum, Harvard Art Museum, Cambridge, Massachusetts. Gift of Anthony M. Solomon (2003.207.1-2). Imaging Department © President and Fellows of Harvard College.

Credits and acknowledgments borrowed from other sources and reproduced, with permission, in this textbook appear on the appropriate page within text or on the credit pages in the back of this book.

Library of Congress Cataloging-in-Publication Data

Stokstad, Marilyn

Art History / Marilyn Stokstad, Michael W. Cothren; contributors, Frederick M. Asher … [eg al.]. —4th ed.

Includes bibliographical references and index.

ISBN: 978-0-205-74422-0 (hardcover : alk. paper)

ISBN: 0205-74422-2 (hardcover : alk. paper)

1. Art—History. I. Cothren, Michael Watt. II. Asher, Frederick M. III

2011

2010001489

ISBN 10: 0-205-79093-3
ISBN 13: 978-0-205-79093-7

CONTENTS

للاسلام ممهدا وللملة موطدا ولادلة الرسل موكدا وللاسود والاحمر مسددا

وصل الارحام وعلم الاحكام وقسم الحلال والحرام ورسم الاحلال والاحرام كرم الله

8–1 • Yahya Ibn al-Wasiti THE *MAQAMAT* OF AL-HARIRI From Baghdad, Iraq. 1237. Paper.
Bibliothèque Nationale, Paris. (Arabic MS. 5847, f. 18v)

ISLAMIC ART

The *Maqamat* ("*Assemblies*"), by al-Hariri (1054–1122), belongs to a popular literary genre of cautionary tales dating from the tenth century. The manuscript's vividly detailed scenes provide windows into ordinary Muslim life, here prayer in the congregational **mosque**, a religious and social institution central to Islam. Al-Hariri's stories revolve around a silver-tongued scoundrel named Abu Zayd, whose cunning inevitably triumphs over other people's naivety. His adventures take place in a world of colorful settings—desert camps, ships, pilgrim caravans, apothecary shops, mosques, gardens, libraries, cemeteries, and courts of law. Humans activate the scenes, pointing fingers, arguing, riding horses, stirring pots, and strumming musical instruments. These comic stories of trickery and theft would seem perfectly suited for illustration, but of the hundreds of surviving manuscript copies, only 13 have pictures.

This illustration **(FIG. 8–1)** shows a mosque with the congregation gathered to hear a sermon preached by the deceitful Abu Zayd, who plans to steal the alms collected from the congregation. The men sit directly on the ground, as is customary in mosques (and traditional dwellings). They look generally forward, but the listener in the front row tilts his chin upward to focus his gaze directly upon the speaker. He is framed and centered by the arch of the niche (**mihrab**) on the rear wall, his white turban contrasting noticeably with the darker background. To the extent that he represents any specific individual, he seems to stand in for the manuscript's reader who, perusing the illustrations of these captivating stories, pauses and perhaps projects himself or herself into the scene.

The columns of the arcades have ornamental capitals from which spring half-round arches. Glass mosque lamps filled with oil hang from the center of each arch. All the figures wear turbans and flowing, loose-sleeved robes with epigraphic borders (*tiraz*) embroidered in gold.

The sermon is delivered from a pulpit (**minbar**) of steps with an arched opening at the lowest level. This *minbar* and the arcades that form the backdrop to the scene and define the mosque's interior are unnaturally reduced in scale. The painter has manipulated the sizes so as to fit the maximum amount of detail into the scene, sacrificing natural space in order to make the painting more communicative. Likewise, although in an actual mosque the *minbar* would share the same wall as the niche in the center, here they have been separated to keep the niche from being hidden by the *minbar*. There is little modeling to represent volume: Instead depth of field is suggested by the overlapping of forms.

LEARN ABOUT IT

8.1 Discover Islamic art's eclecticism and embrace of other cultures.

8.2 Compare and contrast the variety of art and architecture in the disparate areas of the Islamic world.

8.3 Interpret art as a reflection of both religion and secular society.

8.4 Explore the use of ornament and inscription in Islamic art.

8.5 Recognize the role of trade routes and political ties in the creation of Islamic artistic unity.

HEAR MORE: Listen to an audio file of your chapter **www.myartslab.com**

ISLAM AND EARLY ISLAMIC SOCIETY

Islam arose in seventh-century Arabia, a land of desert oases with no cities of great size, sparsely inhabited by tribal nomads. Yet, under the leadership of its founder, the Prophet Muhammad (c. 570–632 CE), and his successors, Islam spread rapidly throughout northern Africa, southern and eastern Europe, and much of Asia, gaining territory and converts with astonishing speed. Because Islam encompassed geographical areas with a variety of long-established cultural traditions, and because it admitted diverse peoples among its converts, it absorbed and combined many different techniques and ideas about art and architecture. The result was a remarkable eclecticism and artistic sophistication.

In the desert outside of Mecca in 610, Muhammad received revelations that led him to found the religion called Islam ("submission to God's will"), whose adherents are Muslims ("those who have submitted to God"). Many powerful Meccans were hostile to the message of the young visionary, and in 622 he and his companions were forced to flee to Medina. There Muhammad built a house that became a gathering place for the converted and thus the first Islamic mosque. Muslims date their history as beginning with this *hijira* ("emigration").

In 630, Muhammad returned to Mecca with an army of 10,000, routed his enemies, and established the city as the spiritual capital of Islam. After his triumph, he went to the Kaaba **(FIG. 8–2)**, a cubical, textile-draped shrine said to have been built for God by Ibrahim (Abraham) and Isma'il (Ishmael) and long the focus of pilgrimage and polytheistic worship. He emptied the shrine, repudiating its accumulated pagan idols, while preserving the enigmatic cubical structure itself and dedicating it to God.

The Kaaba is the symbolic center of the Islamic world, the place to which all Muslim prayer is directed and the ultimate destination of Islam's obligatory pilgrimage, the *hajj*. Each year, huge numbers of Muslims from all over the world travel to Mecca to circumambulate the Kaaba during the month of pilgrimage. The exchange of ideas that occurs during the intermingling of these diverse groups of pilgrims has contributed to Islam's cultural eclecticism.

Muhammad's act of emptying the Kaaba of its pagan idols instituted the fundamental concept of **aniconism** (avoidance of

8-2 • THE KAABA, MECCA
The Kaaba represents the center of the Islamic world. Its cubical form is draped with a black textile that is embroidered with a few Qur'anic verses in gold.

MAP 8–1 • THE ISLAMIC WORLD

Within 200 years after 622 CE, the Islamic world expanded from Mecca to India in the east, and to Morocco and Spain in the west.

figural imagery) in Islamic art. Following his example, the Muslim faith discourages the representation of figures in religious contexts (although such images abound in palaces and illustrated manuscripts). Instead, Islamic artists elaborated a rich vocabulary of nonfigural ornament, including complex geometric designs and scrolling vines sometimes known as **arabesques**. Islamic art revels in surface decoration, in manipulating line, color, and especially pattern, often highlighting the interplay of pure abstraction, organic form, and script.

According to tradition, the Qur'an assumed its final form during the time of the third caliph (successor to the Prophet), Uthman (r. 644–56). As the language of the Qur'an, the Arabic language and script have been a powerful unifying force within Islam. From the eighth through the eleventh centuries, it was the universal language among scholars in the Islamic world and in some Christian lands as well. Inscriptions frequently ornament works of art, sometimes written clearly to provide a readable message, but in other cases written as complex patterns simply to delight the eye.

The Prophet was succeeded by a series of caliphs. The accession of Ali as the fourth caliph (r. 656–61) provoked a power struggle that led to his assassination and resulted in enduring divisions within Islam. Followers of Ali, known as Shi'ites (referring

to the party or *shi'a* of Ali), regard him alone as the Prophet's rightful successor. Sunni Muslims, in contrast, recognize all of the first four caliphs as "rightly guided." Ali was succeeded by his rival Muawiya (r. 661–80), a close relative of Uthman and the founder of the first Muslim dynasty, the Umayyad dynasty (661–750).

Islam expanded dramatically. In just two decades, seemingly unstoppable Muslim armies conquered the Sasanian Persian Empire, Egypt, and the Byzantine provinces of Syria and Palestine. By the early eighth century, under the Umayyads, they had reached India, conquered northern Africa and Spain, and penetrated France before being turned back **(MAP 8–1)**. In these newly conquered lands, the treatment of Christians and Jews who did not convert to Islam was not consistent, but in general, as "People of the Book"— followers of a monotheistic religion based on a revealed scripture —they enjoyed a protected status. However, they were also subject to a special tax and restrictions on dress and employment.

Muslims participate in congregational worship at a mosque (*masjid*, "place of prostration"). The Prophet Muhammad himself lived simply and instructed his followers in prayer at his house, now known as the Mosque of the Prophet, where he resided in Medina. This was a square enclosure that framed a large courtyard with rooms along the east wall where he and his family lived. Along the

Islamic art delights in complex ornament that sheathes surfaces, distracting the eye from the underlying structure or physical form.

ablaq masonry (*Madrasa*-Mausoleum-Mosque of Sultan Hasan, Cairo) juxtaposes stone of contrasting colors. The ornamental effect is enhanced here by the interlocking jigsaw shape of the blocks, called **joggled voussoirs**.

cut tile (Shah-i Zinda, Samarkand), made up of dozens of individually cut ceramic tile pieces fitted precisely together, emphasizes the clarity of the colored shapes.

muqarnas (Court of the Lions, Alhambra, Granada) consists of small nichelike components, usually stacked in multiples as successive, nonload-bearing units in arches, cornices, and domes, hiding the transition from the vertical to the horizontal plane.

wooden strapwork (Kutubiya *Minbar*, Marrakesh) assembles finely cut wooden pieces to create the appearance of geometrically interlacing ribbons, often framing smaller panels of carved wood and inlaid ivory or mother-of-pearl (shell).

mosaic (Dome of the Rock, Jerusalem) is comprised of thousands of small glass or glazed ceramic tesserae set on a plaster ground. The luminous white circular shapes are mother-of-pearl.

water (Court of the Myrtles, Alhambra, Granada) is a fluid architectural element that reflects surrounding architecture, adds visual dynamism and sound, and, running in channels between halls, unites disparate spaces.

chini khana (Ali Qapu Pavilion, Isfahan)—literally "china cabinet"—is a panel of niches, sometimes providing actual shelving, but used here for its contrast of material and void which reverses the typical figure-ground relationship.

south wall, a thatched portico supported by palm-tree trunks sheltered both the faithful as they prayed and Muhammad as he spoke from a low platform. This simple arrangement inspired the design of later mosques. Lacking an architectural focus such as an altar, nave, or dome, the space of this prototypical **hypostyle** (multicolumned) mosque reflected the founding spirit of Islam in which the faithful pray as equals directly to God, led by an imam, but without the intermediary of a priesthood.

ART AND ARCHITECTURE THROUGH THE FOURTEENTH CENTURY

The caliphs of the Umayyad dynasty (661–750) ruled from Damascus in Syria, and throughout the Islamic Empire they built mosques and palaces that projected the authority of the new rulers and reflected the growing acceptance of Islam. In 750 the Abbasid clan replaced the Umayyads in a coup d'état, ruling as caliphs until 1258 from Baghdad, in Iraq, in the grand manner of the ancient Persian emperors. Their long and cosmopolitan reign saw achievements in medicine, mathematics, the natural sciences, philosophy, literature, music, and art. They were generally tolerant of the ethnically diverse populations in the territories they subjugated, and they admired the past achievements of Roman civilization and the living traditions of Byzantium, Persia, India, and China, freely borrowing artistic techniques and styles from all of them.

In the tenth century, the Islamic world split into separate kingdoms ruled by independent caliphs. In addition to the Abbasids of Iraq, there was a Fatimid Shi'ite caliph ruling Tunisia and Egypt, and a descendant of the Umayyads ruling Spain and Portugal (together then known as al-Andalus). The Islamic world did not reunite under the myriad dynasties who thereafter ruled from northern Africa to Asia, but the loss to unity was a gain to artistic diversity.

EARLY ARCHITECTURE

While Mecca and Medina remained the holiest Muslim cities, the political center shifted to the Syrian city of Damascus in 656. In the eastern Mediterranean, inspired by Roman and Byzantine architecture, the early Muslims became enthusiastic builders of shrines, mosques, and palaces. Although tombs were officially discouraged in Islam, they proliferated from the eleventh century onward, in part due to funerary practices imported from the Turkic northeast, and in part due to the rise of Shi'ism with its emphasis on genealogy and particularly ancestry through Muhammad's daughter, Fatima.

THE DOME OF THE ROCK.   The Dome of the Rock is the first great monument of Islamic art. Built in Jerusalem, it is the third most holy site in Islam. In the center of the city rises the Haram al-Sharif ("Noble Sanctuary") **(FIG. 8–3)**, a rocky outcrop from which Muslims believe Muhammad ascended to the presence of God on the "Night Journey" described in the Qur'an. It is the site of the First and Second Jewish Temples, and Jews and Christians variously associate it with Solomon, the site of the creation of Adam, and the place where the patriarch Abraham prepared to sacrifice his son Isaac at the command of God. In 691–92, a shrine was built over the rock using artisans trained in the Byzantine tradition. By appropriating a site holy to the Jewish and Christian

8-3 • AERIAL VIEW OF HARAM AL-SHARIF, JERUSALEM
The Dome of the Rock occupies a place of visual height and prominence in Jerusalem and, when first built, strikingly emphasized the arrival of Islam and its community of adherents in that ancient city.

8-4 • CUTAWAY DRAWING OF THE DOME OF THE ROCK

faiths, the Dome of the Rock is the first architectural manifestation of Islam's view of itself as completing the prophecies of those faiths and superseding them.

Structurally, the Dome of the Rock imitates the centrally planned form of Early Christian and Byzantine martyria (SEE FIG. 7-20). However, unlike its models, with their plain exteriors, it is crowned by a golden dome that dominates the Jerusalem skyline. The ceramic tiles on the lower portion of the exterior were added later, but the opulent marble veneer and mosaics of the interior are original (see "Ornament," page 264). The dome, surmounting a circular drum pierced with windows and supported by arcades of alternating **piers** and **columns**, covers the central space containing the rock **(FIG. 8–4)**. These arcades create concentric **aisles (ambulatories)** that permit devout visitors to circumambulate the rock. Inscriptions from the Qur'an interspersed with passages from other texts, including information about the building itself, form a frieze around the inner and outer arcades. As the pilgrim walks around the central space to read the inscriptions in brilliant gold mosaic on turquoise green ground, the building communicates both as a text and as a dazzling visual display **(FIG. 8–5)**. These passages of text are especially notable because they are the oldest surviving written Qur'an verses and the first use of monumental Qur'anic inscriptions in architecture. Below are walls covered with pale marble, the veining of which creates abstract symmetrical patterns, and columns with shafts of gray marble and gilded capitals. Above the calligraphic frieze is another mosaic frieze depicting thick, symmetrical vine scrolls and trees in turquoise, blue, and green, embellished with imitation jewels, over a gold ground. The mosaics are variously

thought to represent the gardens of Paradise and trophies of Muslim victories offered to God. The decorative program is extraordinarily rich but, remarkably enough, the focus of the building is neither art nor architecture but the plain rock within it.

THE GREAT MOSQUE OF KAIROUAN. Muslim congregations gather on Fridays for regular worship in a mosque. The earliest mosque type was the hypostyle, following the model of the Prophet's own house. The Great Mosque of Kairouan, Tunisia **(FIG. 8–6)**, built in the ninth century, reflects the early form of the mosque but is elaborated with later additions. The large rectangular space is divided between a courtyard and a flat-roofed hypostyle prayer hall oriented toward Mecca. The system of repeated bays and aisles can easily be extended as the congregation grows in size—

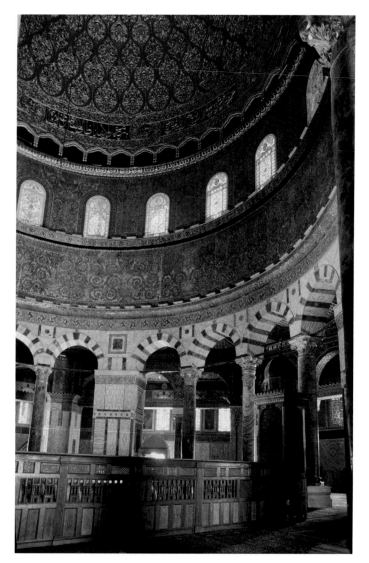

8-5 • DOME OF THE ROCK, JERUSALEM
691. Interior. The arches of the inner and outer face of the central arcade are encrusted with golden mosaics, a Byzantine technique adapted for Islamic use. The carpets and ceilings are modern but probably reflect the original patron's intention.

EXPLORE MORE: Click the Google Earth link for the Dome of the Rock www.myartslab.com

The Five Pillars of Islam

Islam emphasizes a direct, personal relationship with God. The Pillars of Islam, sometimes symbolized by an open hand with the five fingers extended, enumerate the duties required of Muslims by their faith.

- The first pillar (*shahadah*) is to proclaim that there is only one God and that Muhammad is his messenger. While monotheism is common to Judaism, Christianity, and Islam, and Muslims worship the god of Abraham, and also acknowledge Hebrew and Christian prophets such as Musa (Moses) and Isa (Jesus), Muslims deem the Christian Trinity polytheistic and assert that God was not born and did not give birth.
- The second pillar requires prayer (*salat*) to be performed by turning to face the Kaaba in Mecca five times daily: at dawn, noon, late afternoon, sunset, and nightfall. Prayer can occur almost anywhere, although the prayer on Fridays takes place in the congregational mosque. Because ritual ablutions are required for purity, mosque courtyards usually have fountains.
- The third pillar is the voluntary payment of annual tax or alms (*zakah*), equivalent to one-fortieth of one's assets. *Zakah* is used for charities such as feeding the poor, housing travelers, and paying the dowries of orphan girls. Among Shi'ites, an additional tithe is required to support the Shi'ite community specifically.

- The fourth pillar is the dawn-to-dusk fast (*sawm*) during Ramadan, the month when Muhammad received the revelations set down in the Qur'an. The fast of Ramadan is a communally shared sacrifice that imparts purification, self-control, and kinship with others. The end of Ramadan is celebrated with the feast day 'Id al-Fitr (Festival of the Breaking of the Fast).
- For those physically and financially able to do so, the fifth pillar is the pilgrimage to Mecca (*hajj*), which ideally is undertaken at least once in the life of each Muslim. Among the extensive pilgrimage rites are donning simple garments to remove distinctions of class and culture; collective circumambulations of the Kaaba; kissing the Black Stone inside the Kaaba (probably a meteorite that fell in pre-Islamic times); and the sacrificing of an animal, usually a sheep, in memory of Abraham's readiness to sacrifice his son at God's command. The end of the *hajj* is celebrated by the festival 'Id al-Adha (Festival of Sacrifice).

The directness and simplicity of Islam have made the Muslim religion readily adaptable to numerous varied cultural contexts throughout history. The Five Pillars instill not only faith and a sense of belonging, but also a commitment to Islam in the form of actual practice.

---

one of the hallmarks of the hypostyle plan. New is the large tower (the **minaret**, from which the faithful are called to prayer) that rises from one end of the courtyard and that stands as a powerful sign of Islam's presence in the city.

The **qibla** wall, marked by a centrally positioned *mihrab* niche, is the wall of the prayer hall that is closest to Mecca. Prayer is oriented towards this wall. In the Great Mosque of Kairouan, the

qibla wall is given heightened importance by a raised roof, a dome over the *mihrab*, and a central aisle that marks the axis that extends from the minaret to the *mihrab* (for a fourteenth-century example of a *mihrab*, SEE FIG. 8–12). The *mihrab* belongs to the historical tradition of niches that signify a holy place—the shrine for the Torah scrolls in a synagogue, the frame for the sculpture of a god or ancestor in Roman architecture, the apse in a church.

8-6 • THE GREAT MOSQUE, KAIROUAN, TUNISIA
836–875.

EXPLORE MORE: Click the Google Earth link for the Great Mosque of Kairouan www.myartslab.com

The Great Mosque of Cordoba

When the Umayyads were toppled in 750, a survivor of the dynasty, Abd al-Rahman I (r. 756–788), fled across north Africa into southern Spain (al-Andalus) where, with the support of Muslim settlers, he established himself as the provincial ruler, or emir. This newly transplanted Umayyad dynasty ruled in Spain from their capital in Cordoba (756–1031). The Hispano-Umayyads were noted patrons of the arts, and one of the finest surviving examples of Umayyad architecture is the Great Mosque of Cordoba.

In 785, the Umayyad conquerors began building the Cordoba mosque on the site of a Christian church built by the Visigoths, the pre-Islamic rulers of Spain. The choice of site was both practical—for the Muslims had already been renting space within the church—and symbolic, an appropriation of place (similar to the Dome of the Rock) that affirmed their presence. Later rulers expanded the building three times, and today the walls enclose an area of about 620 by 460 feet, about a third of which is the courtyard. This patio was planted with fruit trees, beginning in the early ninth century; today orange trees seasonally fill the space with color and sweet scent. Inside, the proliferation of pattern in the repeated columns and double flying arches is colorful and dramatic. The marble columns and capitals in the hypostyle prayer hall were recycled from the Christian church that had formerly occupied the site, as well as from classical buildings in the region, which had been a wealthy Roman province. The mosque's interior incorporates *spolia* (reused) columns of slightly varying heights. Two tiers of arches, one over the other, surmount these columns; the upper tier springs from rectangular posts that rise from the columns. This double-tiered design dramatically increases the height of the interior space, inspiring a sense of

monumentality and awe. The distinctively shaped **horseshoe arches**—a form known from Roman times and favored by the Visigoths—came to be closely associated with Islamic architecture in the West (see "Arches," page 271). Another distinctive feature of these arches, adopted from Roman and Byzantine precedents, is the alternation of white stone and red brick voussoirs forming the curved arch. This mixture of materials may have helped the building withstand earthquakes.

In the final century of Umayyad rule, Cordoba emerged as a major commercial and intellectual hub and a flourishing center for the arts, surpassing Christian European cities in science, literature, and philosophy. As a sign of this new wealth, prestige, and power, Abd al-Rahman III (r. 912–961) boldly reclaimed the title of caliph in 929. He and his son al-Hakam II (r. 961–976) made the Great Mosque a focus of patronage, commissioning costly and luxurious renovations such as a new *mihrab* with three bays in front of it. These capped the **maqsura**, an enclosure in front of the *mihrab* reserved for the ruler and other dignitaries, which became a feature of congregational

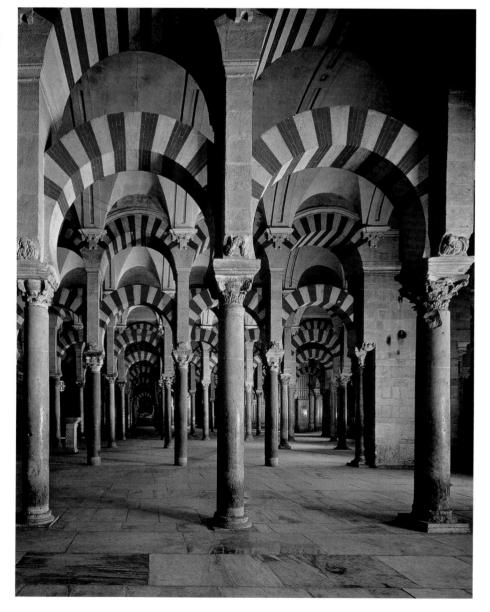

PRAYER HALL, GREAT MOSQUE, CORDOBA, SPAIN
Begun 785/786.

mosques after an assassination attempt on one of the Umayyad rulers. A *minbar* formerly stood by the *mihrab* as the place for the prayer leader and as a symbol of authority. The melon-shaped, ribbed dome over the central bay may be a metaphor for the celestial canopy. It seems to float upon a web of crisscrossing arches, the complexity of the design reflecting the Islamic interest in mathematics and geometry, not purely as abstract concepts but as sources for artistic inspiration. Lushly patterned mosaics with inscriptions, geometric motifs, and stylized vegetation clothe both this dome and the *mihrab* below in brilliant color and gold. These were installed by a Byzantine master who was sent by the emperor in Constantinople, bearing boxes of small glazed ceramic and glass pieces (*tesserae*). Such artistic exchange is emblematic of the interconnectedness of the medieval Mediterranean—through trade, diplomacy, and competition.

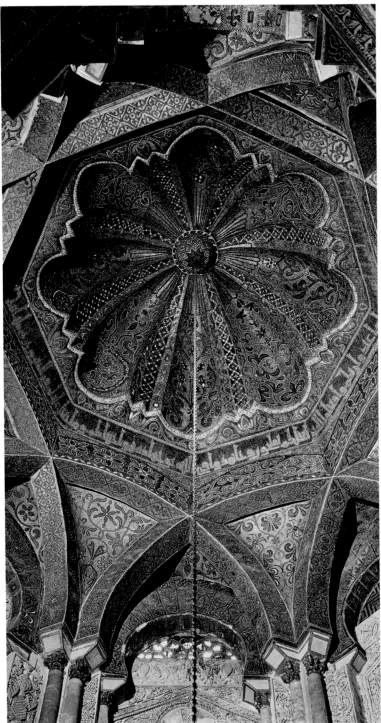

DOME IN FRONT OF THE MIHRAB, GREAT MOSQUE, CORDOBA
965.

mihrab

al-Hakam II addition (961–976 CE)

al-Mansur addition (987 CE)

Abd al-Rahman II addition (822–852 CE)

original mosque (786 CE)

Abd al-Rahman III addition (912–961 CE)

minaret

0   50 meters
0   150 feet

PLAN, GREAT MOSQUE, CORDOBA

EXPLORE MORE: Click the Google Earth link for the Great Mosque at Cordoba **www.myartslab.com**

THE KUTUBIYA MOSQUE.   In the Kutubiya Mosque, the principal mosque of Marrakesh, Morocco, an exceptionally exquisite wooden *minbar* survives from the twelfth century **(FIG. 8–7)**. It consists of a staircase from which the weekly sermon was delivered to the congregation (for example, SEE FIG. 8–1). The sides are paneled in wooden marquetry with strapwork in a geometric pattern of eight-pointed stars and elongated hexagons inlaid with ivory (see "Orna-ment," page 264). The body of each figure is filled with wood carved in swirling vines. The risers of the stairs represent **horseshoe arches** resting on columns with ivory capitals and bases: Thus the pulpit (which had been made originally for the Booksellers' Mosque in Marrakesh) reflected the arcades of its surrounding architectural context. This *minbar* resembled others across the Islamic world, but those at the Kutubiya Mosque and the Great Mosque of Cordoba were the finest, according to Ibn Marzuq (1311–1379), a distin-guished preacher who had given sermons from 48 such *minbars*.

THE LATER PERIOD

The Abbasid caliphate began a slow disintegration in the ninth century, and thereafter power in the Islamic world became fragmented among more or less independent regional rulers. During the eleventh century, the Saljuqs, a Turkic people, swept from north of the Caspian Sea into Khurasan and took Baghdad in

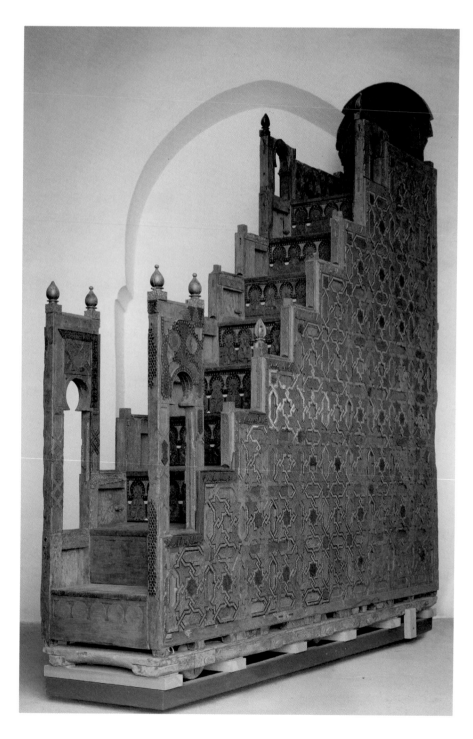

8-7 • *MINBAR*
From the Kutubiya Mosque, Marrakesh, Morocco. 1125–1130. Wood and ivory, 12′8″ × 11′4″ × 2′10″ (3.86 × 3.46 × 0.87 m). Badi Palace Museum, Marrakesh.

Islamic builders explored structure in innovative ways, using a variety of different arch types. The earliest is the simple semicircular arch, inherited from the Romans and Byzantines. It has a single center point that is level with the points from which the arch springs.

The horseshoe arch is a second type, which predates Islam but became the prevalent arch form in the Maghreb (see "The Great Mosque of Cordoba," page 268). The center point of this kind of arch is above the level of the arch's springing point, so that it pinches inward above the capital.

The pointed arch, introduced after the beginning of Islam, has two (sometimes four) center points, the points generating different circles that overlap (for a very slightly pointed arch, SEE FIG. 8–24).

A keel arch has flat sides, and slopes where other arches are curved. It culminates at a pointed apex (see "Ornament," cut tile, page 264).

round arch   horseshoe arch   pointed arch   keel arch

SEE MORE: View a simulation about arches **www.myartslab.com**

1055, becoming the virtual rulers of the Abbasid Empire. The Saljuqs united most of Iran and Iraq, establishing a dynasty that endured from 1037/38 to 1194. A branch of the dynasty, the Saljuqs of Rum, ruled much of Anatolia (Turkey) from the late eleventh to the beginning of the fourteenth century. The central and eastern Islamic world suffered a dramatic rift in the early thirteenth century when the nomadic Mongols—non-Muslims led by Genghiz Khan (r. 1206–1227) and his successors—attacked northern China, Central Asia, and ultimately Iran. The Mongols captured Baghdad in 1258, encountering weak resistance until they reached Egypt, where they were firmly defeated by the new **Mamluk** ruler. The Maghreb (Morocco, Spain, and Portugal) was ruled by various Arab and Berber dynasties. In Spain the borders of Islamic territory were gradually pushed southward by Christian forces until the rule of the last Muslim dynasty, the Nasrids (1230–1492), was ended. Morocco was ruled by the Berber Marinids (from the mid thirteenth century until 1465).

Although the religion of Islam remained a dominant and unifying force throughout these developments, the history of later Islamic society and culture reflects largely regional phenomena. Only a few works have been selected here and in Chapter 23 to characterize the art of Islam, and they by no means provide a comprehensive history of Islamic art.

ARCHITECTURE OF THE MEDITERRANEAN

The new dynasties built on a grand scale, expanding their patronage from mosques and palaces to include new functional buildings, such as tombs, **madrasas** (colleges for religious and legal studies), public fountains, urban hostels, and remote caravanserais (inns) for traveling merchants in order to encourage long-distance trade. A distinguishing characteristic of architecture in the later period is its complexity. Multiple building types were now combined in large and diverse complexes, supported by perpetual endowments (called *waqf*) that funded not only the building, but its administration and maintenance. Increasingly, these complexes included the patron's own tomb, thus giving visual prominence to the act of individual patronage and the expression of personal identity through commemoration. A new plan emerged, organized around a central courtyard framed by four large **iwans** (large vaulted halls with rectangular plans and monumental arched openings); this **four-iwan** plan was used for schools, palaces, and especially mosques.

THE *MADRASA*-MAUSOLEUM-MOSQUE IN CAIRO. Beginning in the eleventh century, Muslim rulers and wealthy individuals endowed hundreds of charitable complexes that displayed piety as well as personal wealth and status. The combined *madrasa*-mausoleum-mosque complex established in mid-fourteenth-century Cairo by

8-8 • *QIBLA* WALL WITH *MIHRAB* AND *MINBAR*, SULTAN HASAN *MADRASA*-MAUSOLEUM-MOSQUE COMPLEX
Main *iwan* (vaulted chamber) in the mosque, Cairo. 1356–1363.

EXPLORE MORE: Click the Google Earth link for the *Qibla* wall with *mihrab* and *minbar*, Sultan Hasan *Madrasa*-Mausoleum-Mosque **www.myartslab.com**

the Mamluk Sultan Hasan (**FIGS. 8–8 and 8–9**) is such an example. A dark corridor—a deflected entrance that is askew from the building's orientation—leads from the street into a central, well-lit courtyard of majestic proportions. The complex has a classic four-*iwan* plan, each *iwan* serving as a classroom for a different branch of study, the students housed in a multi-storied cluster of tiny rooms around each one. The sumptuous *qibla iwan* served as the prayer hall for the complex. Its walls are ornamented with typically Mamluk panels of sharply contrasting marbles (*ablaq* masonry, see "Ornament," page 264) that culminate in a doubly recessed *mihrab* framed by slightly pointed arches on columns. The marble blocks of the arches are ingeniously joined in interlocking pieces called **joggled voussoirs**. The paneling is surmounted by a wide band of **Kufic** (an angular Arabic script) inscription in stucco set against a background of scrolling vines, both the text and the ornament

8-9 • THE SULTAN HASAN *MADRASA*-MAUSOLEUM-MOSQUE COMPLEX
The *qibla iwan* is visible in the top left face of the courtyard, and the domed tomb looms behind it.

A Mamluk Glass Oil Lamp › from Cairo, Egypt. c. 1350–1355. Glass, polychrome enamel, and gold. Diameter of the top 10⅜″ (26 cm), height 13⅝″ (35 cm). British Museum, London.

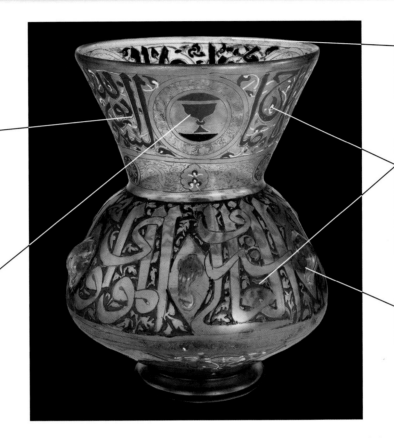

During the thirteenth and fourteenth centuries, glassmakers derived a new elegant thinness through blowing and molding techniques.

The inscription on the vessel's flared neck is a Qur'anic quotation (Surah 24:35): "God is the light of the heavens and the earth. His light is as a niche wherein is a lamp, the lamp in a glass, the glass as a glittering star."

Blue, red, and white enamel and gilding cover the surface of the lamp in vertical bands that include vegetal designs and inscriptions interrupted by roundels containing emblems. Mamluk glassmakers excelled in the application of enameled surface decoration in gold and various colors.

The roundel's emblem, called a blazon, identifies the patron; on this cup, it is the sign of Sayf al-Din Shaykhu al-Umari, who built a mosque in Cairo in 1349. The blazon passed to Western Europe during the crusades, where it evolved into the system we know as heraldry.

This mosque lamp was suspended from chains attached to its handles, although it could also stand on its footed base.

SEE MORE: View the Closer Look feature for the Mamluk Glass Oil Lamp **www.myartslab.com**

---

referring to the paradise that is promised to the faithful. Next to the *mihrab* stands an elaborate, thronelike *minbar*. A platform for reading the Qur'an is in the foreground. Standing just beyond the *qibla iwan*, the patron's monumental domed tomb attached his identity ostentatiously to the architectural complex. The Sultan Hasan complex is excessive in its vast scale and opulent decoration, but money was not an object: The project was financed by the estates of victims of the bubonic plague that had raged in Cairo from 1348 to 1350.

The mosque in the Sultan Hasan complex—and many smaller establishments—required hundreds of lamps, and glassmaking was a booming industry in Egypt and Syria. Made of ordinary sand and ash, glass is the most ethereal of materials. The Egyptians produced the first glassware during the second millennium BCE, yet the tools and techniques for making it have changed little since then.

Exquisite glass was also used for beakers and vases, but lamps, lit from within by oil and wick, glowed with special brilliance (see "A Closer Look," above).

THE ALHAMBRA. Muslim patrons also spent lavishly on luxurious palaces set in gardens. The Alhambra in Granada, in southeastern Spain, is an outstanding example of beautiful and refined Islamic palace architecture. Built on the hilltop site of an early Islamic fortress, this palace complex was the seat of the Nasrids (1232–1492), the last Spanish Muslim dynasty, by which time Islamic territory had shrunk from covering most of the Iberian Peninsula to the region around Granada. To the conquering Christians at the end of the fifteenth century, the Alhambra represented the epitome of luxury. Thereafter, they preserved the complex as much to commemorate the defeat of Islam as for its beauty. Essentially a

8-10 • COURT OF THE LIONS, ALHAMBRA, GRANADA, SPAIN
1354–1391.

EXPLORE MORE: Click the Google Earth link for the Court of the Lions, Alhambra **www.myartslab.com**

small town extending for about half a mile along the crest of a high hill overlooking Granada, it included government buildings, royal residences, gates, mosques, baths, servants' quarters, barracks, stables, a mint, workshops, and gardens. Much of what one sees at the site today was built in the fourteenth century or by Christian patrons in later centuries.

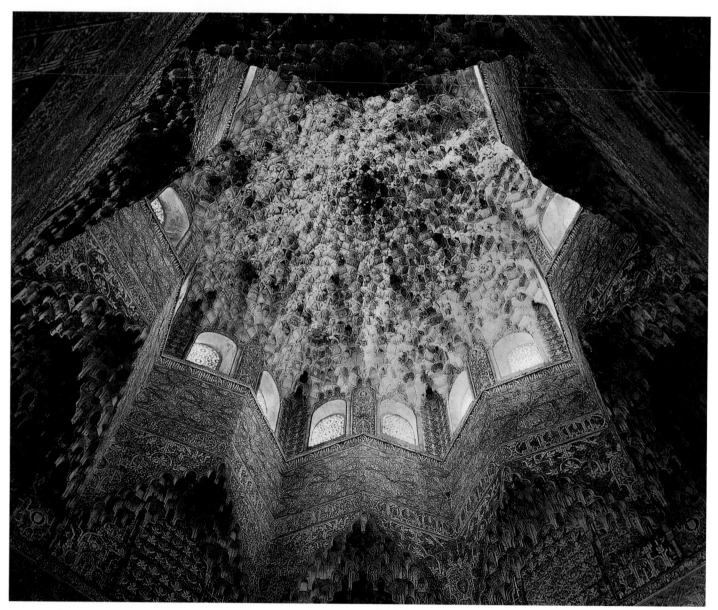

8-11 • *MUQARNAS* DOME, HALL OF THE ABENCERRAJES, PALACE OF THE LIONS, ALHAMBRA
1354–1391.

The stucco *muqarnas* (stalactite) ornament does not support the dome but is actually suspended from it, composed of some 5,000 individual plaster pieces. Of mesmerizing complexity, the vault's effect can be perceived but its structure cannot be fully comprehended.

SEE MORE: View a video about the Alhambra **www.myartslab.com**

The Alhambra offered dramatic views to the settled valley and snow-capped mountains around it, while enclosing gardens within its courtyards. One of these is the Court of the Lions which stood at the heart of the so-called Palace of the Lions, the private retreat of Sultan Muhammad V (r. 1354–1359 and 1362–1391). The Court of the Lions is divided into quadrants by cross-axial walkways—a garden form called a *chahar bagh*. The walkways carry channels that meet at a central marble fountain held aloft on the backs of 12 stone lions (FIG. 8–10). Water animates the fountain, filling the courtyard with the sound of its life-giving abundance. In an adjacent courtyard, the Court of the Myrtles, a basin's round shape responds to the naturally concentric ripples of the water that spouts from a central jet (see "Ornament," page 264). Water has a practical role in the irrigation of gardens, but here it is raised to the level of an art form.

The Court of the Lions is encircled by an arcade of stucco arches embellished with **muqarnas** (see "Ornament," page 264) and supported on single columns or clusters of two and three. Second-floor **miradors**—windows that frame specifically intentioned views—look over the courtyard, which was originally either gardened or more likely paved, with aromatic citrus confined to corner plantings. From these windows, protected by latticework screens, the women of the court, who did not appear in public, would watch the activities of the men below. At one end of the Palace of the Lions, a particularly magnificent *mirador* looks out onto a large, lower garden and the plain below. From here, the sultan literally oversaw the fertile valley that was his kingdom.

On the south side of the Court of the Lions, the lofty Hall of the Abencerrajes was designed as a winter reception hall and music room. In addition to having excellent acoustics, its ceiling exhibits dazzling geometrical complexity and exquisitely carved stucco (FIG. 8–11). The star-shaped vault is formed by a honeycomb of clustered *muqarnas* arches that alternate with corner **squinches** that are filled with more *muqarnas*. The square room thus rises to an eight-pointed star, pierced by 16 windows, that culminates in a burst of *muqarnas* floating high overhead, perceived and yet ultimately unknowable, like the heavens themselves.

ARCHITECTURE OF THE EAST

The Mongol invasions brought devastation and political instability but also renewal and artistic exchange that provided the foundation for successor dynasties with a decidedly eastern identity. One of the empires to emerge after the Mongols was the vast Timurid Empire (1370–1506), which conquered Iran, Central Asia, and the northern part of South Asia. Its founder, Timur (known in the West as Tamerlane), was a Mongol descendant, a lineage strengthened through marriage to a descendant of Genghiz Khan. Timur made his capital at Samarkand, which he embellished by means of the forcible relocation of expert artisans from the areas he subdued. Because the empire's compass was vast, Timurid art could integrate Chinese, Persian, Turkic, and Mediterranean artistic ideas into a Mongol base. Its architecture is characterized by axial symmetry, tall double-shelled domes (an inner dome capped by an outer shell

of much larger proportions), modular planning with rhythmically repeated elements, and brilliant cobalt blue, turquoise, and white glazed ceramics. Although the empire itself lasted only 100 years after the death of Timur, its legacy endured in the art of the later Safavid dynasty in Iran and the Mughals of South Asia.

A TILE MIHRAB. Made during a period of uncertainty as Iran shifted from Mongol to Timurid rule, this *mihrab* (1354), originally from a *madrasa* in Isfahan, is one of the finest examples of architectural ceramic decoration from this era (FIG. 8–12). More than 11 feet tall, it was made by painstakingly cutting each individual piece of tile, including the pieces making up the letters on the curving

8-12 • TILE MOSAIC *MIHRAB*
From the Madrasa Imami, Isfahan, Iran. Founded 1354. Glazed and cut tiles, 11′3″ × 7′6″ (3.43 × 2.29 m). Metropolitan Museum of Art, New York. Harris Brisbane Dick Fund (39.20)

This *mihrab* has three inscriptions: the outer inscription, in cursive, contains Qur'anic verses (Surah 9) that describe the duties of believers and the Five Pillars of Islam. Framing the niche's pointed arch, a Kufic inscription contains sayings of the Prophet. In the center, a panel with a line in Kufic and another in cursive states: "The mosque is the house of every pious person."

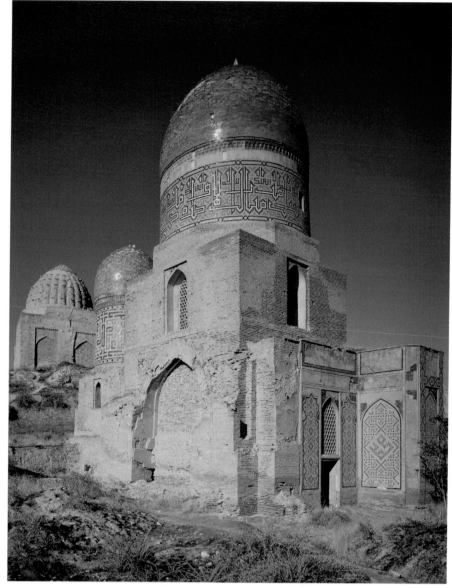

8-13 • SHAH-I ZINDA FUNERARY COMPLEX, SAMARKAND
Late 14th–15th century.

Timurid princesses were buried here and built many of the tombs. The lively experimentation in varied artistic motifs indicates that women were well versed in the arts and empowered to exercise personal taste.

(a cousin of the Prophet and a saint). The women sought burial in the vicinity of the holy man in order to gain *baraka* (blessing) from his presence. Like all Timurid architecture, the tombs reflect modular planning—noticeable in the repeated dome-on-square unit—and a preference for blue glazed tiles. The domes of the individual structures were double-shelled and, for exaggerated effect, stood on high drums inscribed with Qur'anic verses. The ornament adorning the exterior façades consists of an unusually exuberant array of patterns and techniques, from geometry to chinoiserie, and both painted and cut tiles (see "Ornament," page 264). The tombs reflect a range of individual taste and artistic experimentation that was possible precisely because they were private commissions that served the patrons themselves, rather than the city or state (as in a congregational mosque).

PORTABLE ARTS

Islamic society was cosmopolitan, with pilgrimage, trade, and a well-defined road network fostering the circulation of marketable goods. In addition to the import and export of basic foodstuffs and goods, luxury arts brought particular pleasure and status to their owners and were visible signs of cultural refinement. On objects made of ceramics, ivory, and metal, as well as textiles, calligraphy was prominently displayed. These art objects were eagerly exchanged and collected from one end of the Islamic world to the other, and despite their Arabic lettering—or perhaps precisely because of its artistic cachet—they were sought by European patrons as well.

surface of the keel-profiled niche. The color scheme—white against turquoise and cobalt blue with accents of dark yellow and green—was typical of this type of decoration, as were the harmonious, dense, contrasting patterns of organic and geometric forms. The cursive inscription of the outer frame is rendered in elegant white lettering on a blue ground, while the Kufic inscription bordering the pointed arch reverses these colors for a pleasing contrast.

THE SHAH-I ZINDA. Near Samarkand, the preexisting Shah-i Zinda (Living King) funerary complex was adopted for the tombs of Timurid family members, especially princesses, in the late fourteenth and fifteenth centuries (FIG. 8–13). The mausolea are arrayed along a central avenue that descends from the tomb of Qutham b. Abbas

CERAMICS.   Script was the sole decoration on a type of white pottery made from the tenth century onward in and around the region of Nishapur (in Khurasan, in present-day Iran) and Samarkand (in present-day Uzbekistan). These elegant pieces are characterized by the use of a clear lead glaze applied over a black inscription on a white slip-painted ground. In FIGURE 8–14 the script's horizontals and verticals have been elongated to fill the bowl's rim. The fine quality of the lettering indicates that a calligrapher furnished the model. The inscription translates: "Knowledge [or magnanimity]: the beginning of it is bitter to taste, but the end is sweeter than honey," an apt choice for tableware and appealing to an educated patron. The inscriptions on Islamic ceramics provide a storehouse of such popular sayings.

8-14 • BOWL WITH KUFIC BORDER
Khurasan, 11th–12th century. Earthenware with slip, pigment, and lead glaze, diameter 14½″ (33.8 cm). Musée du Louvre, Paris.

The white ground of this piece imitated prized Chinese porcelains made of fine white kaolin clay. Khurasan was connected to the Silk Road, the great caravan route to China (Chapter 10), and was influenced by Chinese culture.

8-15 • THE MACY JUG
Iran. 1215/1216. Composite body glazed, painted fritware and incised (glaze partially stained with cobalt), with pierced outer shell, 6⅝ × 7¾″ (16.8 × 19.7 cm). Metropolitan Museum of Art, New York. Fletcher Fund, 1932 (32.52.1)

Fritware was used to make beads in ancient Egypt and may have been rediscovered there by Islamic potters searching for a substitute for Chinese porcelain. Its components were one part white clay, ten parts quartz, and one part quartz fused with soda, which produced a brittle white ware when fired. The colors on this double-walled ewer and others like it were produced by applying mineral glazes over black painted detailing. The deep blue comes from cobalt and the turquoise from copper. Luster—a thin, transparent glaze with a metallic sheen—was applied over the colored glazes.

In the ninth century, potters developed a technique to produce a lustrous metallic surface on their ceramics. They may have learned the technique from Islamic glassmakers who had produced luster-painted vessels a century earlier. First the potters applied a paint laced with silver, copper, or gold oxides to the surface of already fired and glazed tiles or vessels. In a second firing with relatively low heat and less oxygen, these oxides burned away to produce a reflective sheen. The finished **lusterware** resembled precious metal. At first the potters covered the entire surface with luster, but soon they began to use luster to paint dense, elaborate patterns using geometric design, foliage, and animals in golden brown, red, purple, and green. Lusterware tiles, dated 862/863, decorated the *mihrab* of the Great Mosque at Kairouan.

The most spectacular lusterware pieces are the double-shell fritware, in which an inner solid body is hidden beneath a densely decorated and perforated outer shell. A jar in the Metropolitan Museum known as the *Macy Jug* (after a previous owner) exemplifies this style **(FIG. 8–15)**. The black underglaze-painted decoration represents animals and pairs of harpies and sphinxes set into an elaborate "water-weed" pattern. The outer shell is covered with a turquoise glaze, enhanced by a deep cobalt-blue glaze on parts of the floral decoration and finally an overglaze that gives the entire surface its metallic luster. An inscription includes the date AH 612 (1215/1216 CE).

METAL. Islamic metalsmiths enlivened the surface of vessels with scrolls, interlacing designs, human and animal figures, and calligraphic inscriptions. A shortage of silver in the mid twelfth century prompted the development of inlaid brasswork that used the more precious metal sparingly, as in **FIGURE 8–16**. This basin, made in Mamluk Egypt in the late thirteenth or early fourteenth century, may be the finest work of metal produced by a Muslim artisan. Its dynamic surface is adorned with three bands, the upper and lower depicting running animals, and the center showing chivalric scenes of horsemen flanked by attendants, soldiers, and falcons. The surface is crowded with overlapping figures, in vigorous poses, that nevertheless remain distinct by means of hatching, modeling, and the framing device of the four roundels. The piece was made and signed (six times) by Muhammad Ibn al-Zain. The narrative band displays scenes of the princely art of horsemanship and hunting, but in later metalwork such pictorial cycles were replaced by large-scale inscriptions.

TEXTILES.   A Kufic inscription appears on a tenth-century piece of silk from Khurasan (**FIG. 8–17**): "Glory and happiness to the Commander Abu Mansur Bukhtakin. May God prolong his prosperity." Such good wishes were common in Islamic art, appearing as generic blessings on ordinary goods sold in the marketplace or, as here, personalized for the patron. The woven bands of script are known as *tiraz* ("embroidered"), and they appear in textiles as well as illustrated manuscripts, such as the *Maqamat*, where the robes of figures have *tiraz* on their sleeves (SEE FIG. 8.1). Texts can sometimes help determine where and when a work was made, but they can be frustratingly uninformative when little is known about the patron, and they are not always truthful. Stylistic comparisons—in this case with other textiles, with the way similar subjects appear in other media, and with other inscriptions—sometimes reveal more than the inscription alone.

This silk must have been brought from the Near East to France by knights at the time of the First Crusade. Known as the Shroud of St. Josse, it was preserved in the church of Saint-Josse-sur-Mer, near Caen in Normandy. Rich Islamic textiles of brilliantly hued silk, gold thread, brocade, and especially *tiraz* were prized by Christians and were often preserved in Christian burial chambers and church treasuries. Textiles were one of the most actively traded commodities in the medieval Mediterranean region and formed a significant portion of dowries and inheritances. For these reasons, they were an important means of disseminating

8–17 • TEXTILE WITH ELEPHANTS AND CAMELS
Known today as the Shroud of St. Josse. From Khurasan or Central Asia. Before 961. Dyed silk, largest fragment 20½ × 37″ (52 × 94 cm). Musée du Louvre, Paris.

Silk textiles were both sought-after luxury items and a medium of economic exchange. Government-controlled factories, known as *dar al-tiraz*, produced cloth for the court as well as for official gifts and payments. A number of Islamic fabrics have been preserved in the treasuries of medieval European churches, where they were used for priests' ceremonial robes and as altar cloths, and to wrap the relics of Christian saints.

artistic styles and techniques. This fragment shows two elephants, themselves bearing highly ornamental coverings with Sasanian straps, facing each other on a dark red ground, each with a mythical griffin (a Chinese motif) between its feet. A caravan of two-humped Bactrian camels linked with rope moves up the elaborately patterned border along the left side. The inscription at the bottom is upside down, suggesting that the missing portion of the textile was a fragment from a larger and more complex composition. The technique and design derive from the sumptuous pattern-woven silks of Sasanian Iran (Persia). The Persian weavers had, in turn, adapted Chinese silk technology to the Sasanian taste for paired heraldic beasts and other Near Eastern imagery. The eclecticism of Islamic culture is demonstrated by the blending of Sasanian and Chinese sources in a textile made for a Turkic patron.

THE ARTS OF THE BOOK

The art of book production flourished from the first century of Islam because Islam's emphasis on the study of the Qur'an promoted a high level of literacy among both men and women. With the availability of paper, books on a wide range of religious as well as secular subjects were available, although hand-copied books always remained fairly costly. (Muslims did not adopt the printing press until the eighteenth and nineteenth centuries.) Libraries, often associated with *madrasas*, were endowed by members of the educated elite. Books made for royal patrons had luxurious bindings and highly embellished pages, the result of workshop collaboration between noted calligraphers and illustrators.

CALLIGRAPHY. Muslim society holds **calligraphy** (the art of fine hand lettering) in the highest esteem. Since the Qur'an is believed to reveal the word of God, its words must be written accurately, with devotion and embellishment. Writing was not limited to books and documents but—as we have seen—was displayed on the walls of buildings and on artwork. Since pictorial imagery developed relatively late in Islamic art (and there was no figural imagery at all in the religious context), text became a principal vehicle for visual communication. The written word thus played two roles: It could convey information about a building or object, describing its beauty or naming its patron, and it could delight the eye in an entirely aesthetic sense. Arabic script is written from right to left, and a letter's form varies depending on its position in a word. With its rhythmic interplay between verticals and horizontals, Arabic lends itself to many variations. Formal Kufic script (after Kufa, a city in Iraq) is blocky and angular, with strong upright strokes and long horizontals. It may have developed first for carved or woven inscriptions where clarity and practicality of execution were important.

Most early Qur'ans had large Kufic letters and only three to five lines per page, which had a horizontal orientation. The visual clarity was necessary because one book was often shared by multiple readers simultaneously. A page from a ninth-century Syrian Qur'an exemplifies the style common from the eighth to the tenth century (**FIG. 8–18**). Red diacritical marks (pronunciation guides) accent the dark brown ink; the *surah* ("chapter") title is embedded in the burnished ornament at the bottom of the sheet. Instead of

8-18 • PAGE FROM THE QUR'AN
Surah 2:286 and title of Surah 3 in Kufic script. Syria. 9th century. Black ink pigments, and gold on vellum, 8⅜ × 11⅛″ (21.8 × 29.2 cm). Metropolitan Museum of Art, New York. Rogers Fund, 1937 (37.99.2)

EXPLORE MORE: Gain insight from a primary source, the Qur'an
www.myartslab.com

8-19 • Attributed to Galinus ARABIC MANUSCRIPT PAGE
Iraq. 1199. Bibliothèque Nationale, Paris.

Headings are in ornamental Kufic script with a background of scrolling vines, while the text—a medical treatise—is written horizontally and vertically in *naskhi* script.

skin) and **vellum** (calfskin or a fine parchment). Paper was first manufactured in Central Asia during the mid eighth century, having been introduced earlier by Buddhist monks. Muslims learned how to make high-quality, rag-based paper, and eventually established their own paper mills. By about 1000, paper had largely replaced the more costly parchment for everything but Qur'an manuscripts, which adopted the new medium much later. It was a change as momentous as that brought about by movable type or the internet, affecting not only the appearance of manuscripts but also their content. The inexpensive new medium sparked a surge in book production and the proliferation of increasingly elaborate and decorative cursive scripts which generally superseded Kufic by the thirteenth century. Of the major styles, one extraordinarily beautiful form, known as *naskhi*, was said to have been revealed and taught to scribes in a vision. In **FIGURE 8–19**, its beautifully flowing lines alternate with an eastern variety of Kufic set against a field of swirling vine scrolls.

MANUSCRIPT PAINTING

The manuscript illustrators of Mamluk Egypt (1250–1517) executed intricate nonfigural geometric designs for the Qur'ans they

8-20 • QUR'AN FRONTISPIECE (RIGHT HALF OF TWO-PAGE SPREAD)
Cairo. c. 1368. Ink, pigments, and gold on paper, 24 × 18″ (61 × 45.7 cm). National Library, Cairo. MS. 7

The Qur'an to which this page belonged was donated in 1369 by Sultan Shaban to the *madrasa* established by his mother. A close collaboration between illuminator and scribe can be seen here and throughout the manuscript.

page numbers, the brilliant gold of the framed words and the knoblike projection in the left-hand margin are a distinctive means of marking chapter breaks.

Calligraphers enjoyed the highest status of all artists in Islamic society. Included in their number were princes and women. Apprentice scribes had to learn secret formulas for inks and paints; become skilled in the proper ways to sit, breathe, and manipulate their tools; and develop their individual specialties. They also had to absorb the complex literary traditions and number symbolism that had developed in Islamic culture. Their training was long and arduous, but unlike other artisans who were generally anonymous in the early centuries of Islam, outstanding calligraphers received public recognition.

By the tenth century, more than 20 cursive scripts had come into use. They were standardized by Ibn Muqla (d. 940), an Abbasid official who fixed the proportions of the letters in each script and devised a method for teaching calligraphy that is still in use today. The Qur'an was usually written on **parchment** (treated animal produced. Geometric and botanical ornamentation contributed to unprecedented sumptuousness and complexity. As in architectural decoration, the exuberant ornament was underlaid by strict geometric organization. In an impressive frontispiece originally paired with its mirror image on the facing left page, the design radiates from a 16-pointed starburst, filling the central square (**FIG. 8–20**). The surrounding frames are filled with interlacing foliage and stylized flowers that embellish the holy scripture. The page's resemblance to court carpets was not coincidental. Designers worked in more than one medium, leaving the execution of their efforts to specialized artisans. In addition to religious works, scribes copied and recopied famous secular texts—scientific treatises, manuals of all kinds, stories, and especially poetry. Painters supplied illustrations for these books and also created individual small-scale paintings—miniatures—that were collected by the wealthy and placed in albums.

THE HERAT SCHOOL. One of the great royal centers of miniature painting was at Herat in western Afghanistan. A **school** of painting and calligraphy was founded there in the early fifteenth century under the highly cultured patronage of the Timurid dynasty (1370–1507). In the second half of the fifteenth century, the leader of the Herat School was Kamal al-Din Bihzad (c. 1450–1514). When the Safavids supplanted the Timurids in 1506/07 and established their capital at Tabriz in northwestern Iran, Bihzad moved to Tabriz and briefly resumed his career there. Bihzad's paintings, done around 1494 to illustrate the *Khamsa* (*Five Poems*), written by Nizami, demonstrate his ability to render human activity convincingly. He set his scenes within complex, stagelike architectural spaces that are stylized according to Timurid conventions, creating a visual balance between activity and architecture. In a scene depicting the caliph Harun al-Rashid's visit to a bath (**FIG. 8–21**), the bathhouse, its tiled entrance leading to a high-ceiling dressing room with brick walls, provides the structuring element. Attendants wash long, blue towels and hang them to dry on overhead clotheslines. A worker reaches for one of the towels with a long pole, and a client prepares to wrap himself discreetly in a towel before removing his outer garments. The blue door on the left leads to a room where a barber grooms the caliph while attendants bring water for his bath. The asymmetrical composition depends on a balanced placement of colors and architectural ornaments within each section.

8-21 • Attributed to Kamal al-Din Bihzad THE CALIPH HARUN AL-RASHID VISITS THE TURKISH BATH

From a copy of the 12th-century *Khamsa* (*Five Poems*) of Nizami. From Herat, Afghanistan. c. 1494. Ink and pigments on paper, approx. 7 × 6″ (17.8 × 15.3 cm). The British Library, London. Oriental and India Office Collections MS. Or. 6810, fol. 27v

Despite early warnings against it as a place for the dangerous indulgence of the pleasures of the flesh, the bathhouse (*hammam*), adapted from Roman and Hellenistic predecessors, became an important social center in much of the Islamic world. The remains of an eighth-century *hammam* still stand in Jordan, and a twelfth-century *hammam* is still in use in Damascus. *Hammams* had a small entrance to keep in the heat, which was supplied by steam ducts running under the floors. The main room had pipes in the wall with steam vents. Unlike the Romans, who bathed and swam in pools of water, Muslims preferred to splash themselves from basins, and the floors were slanted for drainage. A *hammam* was frequently located near a mosque, part of the commercial complex provided by the patron to generate income for the mosque's upkeep.

ART AND ARCHITECTURE OF THE THREE EMPIRES

In the pre-modern era, three great powers emerged in the Islamic world. The introduction of gunpowder for use in cannons and guns caused a shift in military strategy because isolated lords in lone castles could not withstand gunpowder sieges. Power lay not in thick walls but in strong centralized governments that had the wherewithal to invest in fire power and train armies in its use. To the west was the Ottoman Empire (1342–1918), which grew from a small principality in Asia Minor. In spite of setbacks inflicted by the Mongols, the Ottomans ultimately created an empire that extended over Anatolia, western Iran, Iraq, Syria, Palestine, western Arabia (including Mecca and Medina), northern Africa (excepting Morocco), and part of eastern Europe. In 1453, their stunning capture of Constantinople (ultimately renamed Istanbul) brought the Byzantine Empire to an end. To the east of the Ottomans, Iran was ruled by the Safavid dynasty (1501–1732), distinguished for their Shi'ite branch of Islam. Their patronage of art and architecture favored the refinement of artistic ideas and techniques drawn from the Timurid period. The other heirs to the Timurids were the Mughals of South Asia (1526–1858). The first Mughal emperor, Babur, invaded Hindustan (India and Pakistan) from Afghanistan, bringing with him a taste for Timurid gardens, architectural symmetry, and modular planning.

THE OTTOMAN EMPIRE

Imperial Ottoman mosques were strongly influenced by Byzantine church plans and reflect a drive toward ever larger domes. The prayer hall interiors are dominated by a large domed space uninterrupted by structural supports. Worship is directed, as in other mosques, toward a *qibla* wall and *mihrab* opposite the entrance.

Upon conquering Constantinople, the rulers of the Ottoman Empire converted the great Byzantine church of Hagia Sophia into a mosque, framing it with two graceful Turkish-style minarets in the fifteenth century and two more in the sixteenth century (SEE FIG. 7–17). In conformance with Islamic aniconism, the church's mosaics were destroyed or whitewashed. Huge calligraphic disks with the names of God (Allah), Muhammad, and the early caliphs were added to the interior in the mid nineteenth century (SEE FIG. 7–19). At present, Hagia Sophia is neither a church nor a mosque but a state museum.

THE ARCHITECT SINAN.   Ottoman architects had already developed the domed, centrally planned mosque, but the vast open interior and structural clarity of Hagia Sophia inspired them to strive for a more ambitious scale. For the architect Sinan (c. 1489–1588) the development of a monumental centrally planned mosque was a personal quest. Sinan began his career in the army and served as engineer in the Ottoman campaigns at Belgrade, Vienna, and Baghdad. He rose through the ranks to become, in 1528, chief architect for Suleyman "the Magnificent," the tenth Ottoman sultan (r. 1520–1566). Suleyman's reign marked the height of Ottoman power, and the sultan sponsored an ambitious building program on a scale not seen since the days of the Roman Empire. Serving Suleyman and his successor, Sinan is credited with more than 300 imperial commissions, including palaces, *madrasas* and Qur'an schools, tombs, public kitchens, hospitals, caravanserais, treasure houses, baths, bridges, viaducts, and 124 large and small mosques.

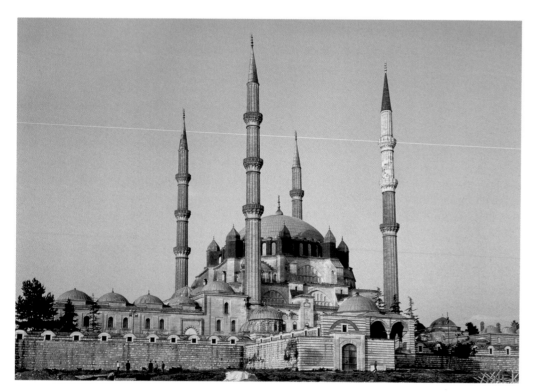

8-22 • Sinan MOSQUE OF SULTAN SELIM
Edirne, Turkey. 1568–1575.

The minarets that pierce the sky around the prayer hall of this mosque, their sleek, fluted walls and needle-nosed spires soaring to more than 295 feet, are only 12½ feet in diameter at the base, an impressive feat of engineering. Only royal Ottoman mosques were permitted multiple minarets, and having more than two was unusual.

EXPLORE MORE: Click the Google Earth link for the Mosque of Sultan Selim www.myartslab.com

8-23 • PLAN OF MOSQUE OF SULTAN SELIM

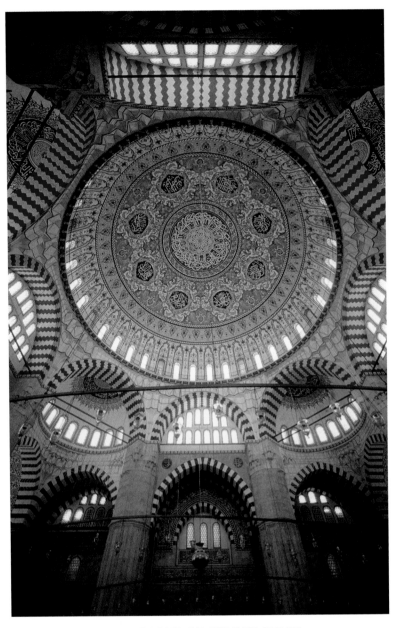

8-24 • INTERIOR, MOSQUE OF SULTAN SELIM

Sinan's crowning accomplishment, completed about 1579, when he was over 80, was a mosque he designed in the provincial capital of Edirne for Suleyman's son Selim II (r. 1566–1574) **(FIGS. 8–22, 8–23)**. The gigantic hemispheric dome that tops this structure is more than 102 feet in diameter, larger than the dome of Hagia Sophia, as Sinan proudly pointed out. It crowns a building of extraordinary architectural coherence. The transition from square base to the central dome is accomplished by corner half-domes that enhance the spatial plasticity and openness of the prayer hall's airy interior **(FIG. 8–24)**. The eight massive piers that bear the dome's weight are visible both within and without—on the exterior they resolve in pointed towers that encircle the main dome—revealing the structural logic of the building and clarifying its form. In the arches that support the dome and span from one pier to the next—and indeed at every level—light pours from windows into the interior, a space at once soaring and serene.

The interior was clearly influenced by Hagia Sophia—an open expanse under a vast dome floating on a ring of light—but it rejects Hagia Sophia's longitudinal pull from entrance to sanctuary. The Selimiye Mosque is truly a centrally planned structure. In addition to the mosque, the complex housed a *madrasa* and other educational buildings, a cemetery, a hospital, and charity kitchens, as well as the income-producing covered market and baths. Framed by the vertical lines of four minarets and raised on a platform at the city's edge, the Selimiye Mosque dominates the skyline.

The Topkapi, the Ottomans' enormous palace in Istanbul, was a city unto itself. Built and inhabited from 1473 to 1853, it consisted of enclosures within walled enclosures that mirrored the immense political bureaucracy of the state. Inside, the sultan was removed from virtually all contact with the public. At the end of the inner palace, a free-standing pavilion, the Baghdad Kiosk (1638), provided him with a sumptuous retreat **(FIG. 8–25)**. The kiosk consists of a low dome set above a cruciform hall with four alcoves. Each recess contains a low sofa (a Turkish word) laid with cushions and flanked by cabinets of wood inlaid with ivory and shell. Alternating with the cabinets are niches with ornate profiles: When stacked in profusion such niches—called *chini khana*— form decorative panels. On the walls, the blue and turquoise glazed tiles contain an inscription of the Throne Verse (2:255) which proclaims God's dominion "over the heavens and the earth," a reference to divine power that appears in many throne rooms and places associated with Muslim sovereigns. Light sparkles through the stained glass above.

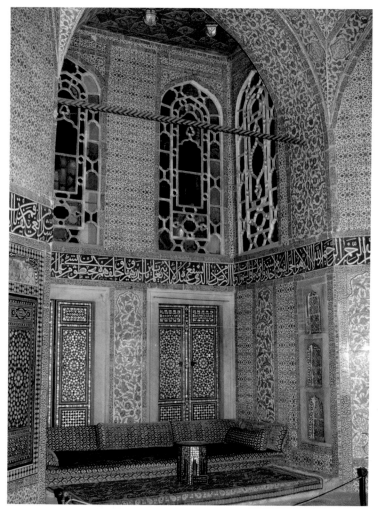

8-25 • BAGHDAD KIOSK
Topkapi Palace, Istanbul. 1638.

ILLUMINATED MANUSCRIPTS AND *TUGRAS*. A combination of abstract setting with realism in figures and details characterizes Ottoman painting. Ottoman painters adopted the style of the Herat School (influenced by Timurid conventions) for their miniatures, enhancing its decorative aspects with an intensity of religious feeling. At the Ottoman court of Sultan Suleyman in Istanbul, the imperial workshops produced remarkable illuminated manuscripts.

Following a practice begun by the Saljuqs and Mamluks, the Ottomans put calligraphy to political use, developing the design of imperial ciphers—**tugras**—into a specialized art form. Ottoman *tugras* combined the ruler's name and title with the motto "Eternally Victorious" into a monogram denoting the authority of the sultan and of those select officials who were also granted an emblem. *Tugras* appeared on seals, coins, and buildings, as well as on official documents called *firmans*, imperial edicts supplementing Muslim law. Suleyman issued hundreds of edicts, and a high court official supervised specialist calligraphers and illuminators who produced the documents with fancy *tugras* (**FIG. 8–26**).

Tugras were drawn in black or blue with three long, vertical strokes to the right of two concentric horizontal teardrops. Decorative foliage patterns fill the space. Fill decoration became more naturalistic by the 1550s and in later centuries spilled outside the emblems' boundary lines. The rare, oversized *tugra* below has a sweeping, fluid line drawn with perfect control according to set proportions. The color scheme of delicate floral interlace enclosed in the body of the *tugra* may have been inspired by Chinese blue-and-white ceramics; similar designs appear on Ottoman ceramics and textiles.

8-26 • ILLUMINATED *TUGRA* OF SULTAN SULEYMAN
From Istanbul, Turkey. c. 1555–1560. Ink, paint, and gold on paper, removed from a *firman* and trimmed to 20½ × 25⅜″ (52 × 64.5 cm). Metropolitan Museum of Art, New York. Rogers Fund, 1938 (38.149.1)

The *tugra* shown here is from a document endowing an institution in Jerusalem that had been established by Suleyman's powerful wife, Hurrem.

THE SAFAVID DYNASTY

Whereas the Ottomans took their inspiration from regional cultures such as that of the Byzantine Empire, the Safavids looked to the Timurid architecture of tall, double-shell domes, sheathed in blue tiles. In the Safavid capital of Isfahan, the typically Timurid taste for modular construction re-emerged on a grand scale that extended well beyond works of architecture to include avenues, bridges, public spaces, and gardens. To the preexisting city of Isfahan, the Safavid Shah Abbas I (1588–1629) added an entirely new extension, planned around an immense central plaza (*maydan*) and a broad avenue, called the Chahar Bagh, that ran through a zone of imperial palace pavilions and gardens down to the river. The city's prosperity and beauty so amazed visitors who flocked from around the world to conduct trade and diplomacy that it led to the popular saying, "Isfahan is half the world."

With the Masjid-i Shah (1611–1638) in Isfahan, the four-*iwan* plan mosque reached its apogee **(FIGS. 8–27, 8–28)**. Stately and huge, it anchors the south end of the city's *maydan*. Its 90-foot portal is aligned with the *maydan*, which is oriented astrologically,

8-27 • PLAN OF THE MASJID-I SHAH

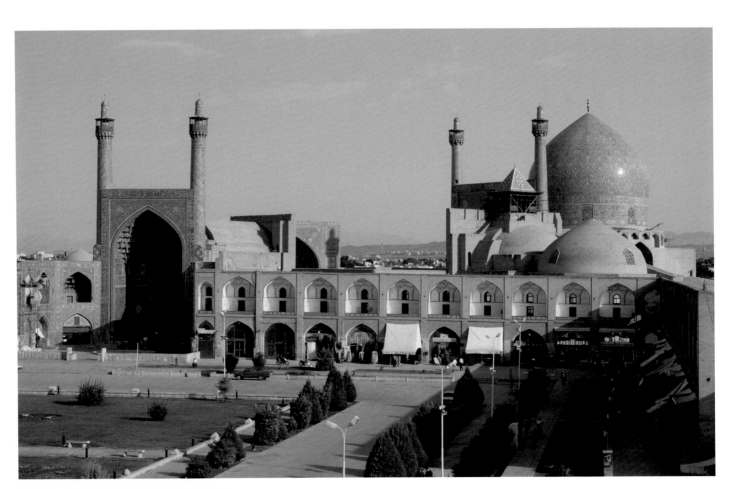

8-28 • MASJID-I SHAH, ISFAHAN
1611–1638.

Four *iwan*s with *pishtaq* frames face onto the courtyard, and a fifth faces the *maydan*. The tall bulbous dome behind the *qibla iwan* and the large *pishtaq*s are pronounced vertical elements that made royal patronage visible not only from the far end of the *maydan* but throughout the city and beyond.

SEE MORE: View a video about Masjid-i Shah www.myartslab.com

Because textiles are made of organic materials that are destroyed through use, very few carpets from before the sixteenth century have survived. There are two basic types of carpet: flat-weave carpets and pile, or knotted, carpets. Both can be made on either vertical or horizontal looms.

The best-known flat-weaves today are kilims, which are typically woven in wool with bold, geometric patterns and sometimes with brocaded details. Kilim weaving is done with a **tapestry** technique called slit tapestry (see a).

Knotted carpets are an ancient invention. The oldest known example, excavated in Siberia and dating to the fourth or fifth century BCE, has designs evocative of Achaemenid art, suggesting that the technique may have originated in Central Asia. In knotted carpets, the pile—the plush, thickly tufted surface—is made by tying colored strands of yarn, usually wool but occasionally silk for deluxe carpets, onto the vertical elements (the **warp**) of a yarn grid (see b and c).

These knotted loops are later trimmed and sheared to form the plush pile surface of the carpet. The **weft** strands (crosswise threads) are shot horizontally, usually twice, after each row of knots is tied, to hold the knots in place and to form the horizontal element common to all woven structures. The weft is usually an undyed yarn and is hidden by the colored knots of the warp. Two common knot tying techniques are the asymmetrical knot, used in many carpets from Iran, Egypt, and Central Asia (formerly termed the Sehna knot), and the symmetrical knot (formerly called the Gördes knot) more commonly used in Anatolian Turkish carpet weaving. The greater the number of knots, the shorter the pile. The finest carpets can have as many as 2,400 knots per square inch, each one tied separately by hand.

Although royal workshops produced luxurious carpets (SEE FIG. 8–29), most knotted rugs have traditionally been made in tents and homes. Depending on local custom, either women or men wove carpets.

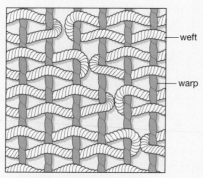

a. Kilim weaving pattern used in flat-weaving

b. Symmetrical knot, used extensively in Turkey

c. Asymmetrical knot, used extensively in Iran

but then turns to conform to the prayer hall, which is oriented to Mecca. The portal's great *iwan* is framed by a *pishtaq* (a rectangular panel framing an *iwan*) that rises above the surrounding walls, slender minarets enhancing its soaring verticality. The hood is filled with *muqarnas* and covered with glazed tiles with vine and flower motifs. The *iwan*'s profile is imitated and repeated by the double-tiered *iwan*s that parade across the façade of the mosque courtyard and the *maydan* as a whole. Achieving unity through the regular replication of a single element—the arch—is a hallmark of Safavid architecture. The Masjid-i Shah represents the culmination of Timurid aesthetics, but achieved on an unprecedented scale and integrated within a well-planned urban setting.

The Safavid period was also a golden age of carpet making (see "Carpet Making," above). Shah Abbas built workshops in Isfahan and Kashan that produced large, costly carpets that were often signed—indicating the weaver's growing prestige. Among the types produced were the medallion, centered around a sun or star, and the garden carpet, which represents Paradise as a shady garden with four rivers. Laid out on the floor of an open-air hall, and per-

haps set with bowls of ripe fruit and other delicacies, such carpets brought the beauty of nature indoors. Written accounts indicate that elaborate patterns appeared on Persian carpets as early as the seventh century. In one fabled royal carpet, garden paths were rendered in real gold, leaves were modeled with emeralds, and highlights on flowers, fruits, and birds were created from pearls and jewels. There were close parallels between carpet making and other arts: Many works of Islamic art represent flowers to evoke both garden and paradisiac associations.

The seventeenth-century *Wagner Carpet* is an extraordinarily sumptuous garden carpet made of wool pile (**FIG. 8–29**). It represents a dense field of trees (including cypresses) and flowers, populated with birds, animals, and even fish, and traversed by three large water channels that form an H with a central pool at the center. The carpet fascinates not only for the fact that so simple a technique as a knotted yarn can produce such complex, layered designs, but also for the combination of perspectives: From above, the carpet resembles a plan, but the trees are shown in profile, as if from ground level.

8-29 • WAGNER CARPET

From Iran. 17th century. Wool pile, cotton warp, cotton and wool weft, 17'5″ × 13'11″ (5.31 × 4.25 m). Burrell Collection, Glasgow.

When this extraordinarily detailed large carpet was laid on the floor of a palace or wealthy home, it gave the illusion of a garden underfoot. Natural motifs in carpets, textiles, and tiled walls, together with large windows and porches offering delightful vistas, invited the outdoors inside and blurred any distinction between them.

Rugs have long been used for Muslim prayer, which involves repeatedly kneeling and touching the forehead to the floor before God. While individuals often had their own small prayer rugs, with representations of niches to orient the faithful in prayer, many mosques were furnished with wool-pile rugs received as pious donations (the floor of the Selimiye Mosque would have had such rugs). In Islamic houses, people sat and slept on cushions, carpets, and thick mats laid directly on the floor, so cushions took the place of the fixed furnishings of Western domestic environments. From the late Middle Ages to today, carpets and textiles are one of the predominant Islamic arts and the Islamic art form best known in the West. Historically, rugs from Iran, Turkey, and elsewhere were highly valued by Westerners, who often displayed them on tables rather than floors.

MUGHAL DYNASTY

Like the Safavids in Iran, the Mughals brought Timurid models with them from Central Asia into Hindustan. Although Islam had flourished in the Delhi region from the early thirteenth century onward, the Mughals unified the Muslim- and Hindu-ruled states of north India into an empire (see Chapter 23). The illustrations of the emperor Babur's memoirs, the *Baburnama*, show his active patronage of forms such as the *chahar bagh* four-part garden plan. In **FIGURE 8–30**, Babur—in an orange robe and turban—oversees the construction of a walled garden in Kabul, teeming with fruit trees and flowers. Babur had been raised in an environment thoroughly saturated with the Timurid artistic legacy of *iwan*s with *pishtaq* frames, tall bulbous domes, modular planning, axial symmetry, and the *chahar bagh*. His introduction of such forms into South Asia culminated several generations later in the Taj Mahal (SEE FIG. 23–1).

8-30 • Bishnadas **"BABUR BUILDS THE BAGH-I WAFA," FROM THE *BABURNAMA***
India. c. 1590. Gouache and gold on paper, 8⅝ × 5⅝" (21.9 × 14.4 cm). Victoria & Albert Museum, London. IM.276-1913, f. 276

The Mughal emperor Babur, on the right, gestures to his architect who holds a red board with grid lines—reflecting the legacy of Timurid modular planning—while workmen measure and shovel, their leggings rolled up to their knees.

8-31 • Paolo Portoghesi, Vittorio Gigliotti, and Sami Mousawi **ISLAMIC MOSQUE AND CULTURAL CENTRE, ROME** 1984–1992.

The prayer hall (197 × 13 feet/ 60 × 40 meters), which has an ablution area on the floor below, can accommodate a congregation of 2,500 on its main floor and balconies. The large central dome (65½ feet/ 20 meters in diameter) is surrounded by 16 smaller domes, all similarly articulated with concrete ribs.

THE MODERN ERA

The twentieth century saw the dissolution of the great Islamic empires and the formation of smaller nation-states in their place. The question of identity and its expression in art changed significantly as Muslim artists and architects sought training abroad and participated in an international movement that swept away many of the visible signs that formerly expressed their cultural character and difference. The abstract work of the architect Zaha Hadid (SEE FIG. 32–55), who was born in Baghdad and studied and practiced in London, is exemplary of the new internationalism. Other architects sought to reconcile modernity with an Islamic cultural identity that was distinct from the West. Thus the Iraqi architect Sami Mousawi and the Italian firm of Portoghesi-Gigliotti designed the Islamic Centre in Rome (completed 1992) with clean modern lines, exposing the structure while at the same time taking full advantage of opportunities for ornament (**FIG. 8–31**). The structural logic appears in the prayer hall's columns, made of concrete with an aggregate of crushed Carrara marble. These rise to meet abstract capitals in the form of plain rings, then spring upward to make a geometrically dazzling eight-pointed star supporting a dome of concentric circles. There are references here to the interlacing ribs of the *mihrab* dome in the Great Mosque of Cordoba, to the great domed spans of Sinan's prayer halls, and to the simple palm-tree trunks that supported the roof of the Mosque of the Prophet in Medina.

THINK ABOUT IT

8.1 The Islamic Empire rapidly spread east to India and west to Spain. Explain how the form of the mosque varies among the far-flung lands of the empire with reference to three examples. Despite the contrasts, what features do mosques typically have in common?

8.2 Select an Islamic structure discussed in this chapter that is influenced by Rome and/or Byzantium, and note which forms are borrowed and how, in their new Islamic context, they are transformed.

8.3 What is a *tugra*? Although it is a secular art form, how is it linked to Islamic religious art traditions?

8.4 Islamic art has no images of people in religious contexts. Instead, what decorative motifs and techniques are used?

8.5 Discuss the spread of carpet making within the rapidly growing Islamic Empire. Can you discern any geographical features that would have expedited the sharing of carpet-making techniques and specific styles? Use the map on page 263.

PRACTICE MORE: Compose answers to these questions, get flashcards for images and terms, and review chapter material with quizzes www.myartslab.com

9-1 • ASHOKAN PILLAR
Lauriya Nandangarh, Bihar, India. Maurya period, c. 246 BCE.

ART OF SOUTH AND SOUTHEAST ASIA BEFORE 1200

According to legend, the ruler Ashoka (r. 273–232 BCE) was stunned by grief and remorse as he looked across the battlefield. As was the custom of his dynasty, he had gone to war, expanding his empire until he had conquered many of the kingdoms that had comprised the Indian subcontinent. Now, about 265 BCE, after the final battle in his conquest of the northern kingdoms, he was suddenly—unexpectedly—shocked by the horror of the suffering he had caused. In the traditional account, it is said that only one form on the battlefield moved: The stooped figure of a Buddhist monk slowly making his way through the carnage. Watching this spectral figure, Ashoka abruptly turned the moment of triumph into one of renunciation. Decrying violence and warfare, he vowed to become a *chakravartin* ("world-conquering ruler"), not through the force of arms but through spreading the teachings of the Buddha and establishing Buddhism as the major religion of his realm.

Although there is no proof that Ashoka himself converted to Buddhism, he erected and dedicated monuments to the Buddha throughout his empire—shrines, monasteries, and the columns commonly called **Ashokan pillars** (FIG. 9–1). With missionary ardor, he dispatched delegates throughout the Indian subcontinent and to countries as distant as Syria, Egypt, and Greece. In his impassioned propagation of Buddhism, perhaps as a means of securing his enormous empire, Ashoka stimulated an intensely rich period of art.

Despite the emissaries he sent and his widespread placement of inscriptions on the face of large rocks, his pillars are few in number and quite concentrated in location. Only eight can be attributed to Ashoka's time by the inscriptions they bear, although several other pillars are commonly assigned to this period. Most were placed at the site of Buddhist monasteries along a route leading from Punjab in the northwest to Ashoka's capital, Pataliputra, in the northeast. One pillar some distance from this route, at Sanchi, suggests that others, perhaps not yet discovered, may have been placed along a more southerly path.

Not only are the pillars the first sculptural remains in India after a hiatus of some 1,600 years, but their inscriptions are the first preserved Indian writing that we can read and interpret. The script, known as Brahmi, was deciphered in 1837 by James Prinsep, a brilliant amateur scholar who served the East India Company as assay master of the Calcutta mint. He discovered that the inscriptions were written in Prakrit, a language closely related to classical Sanskrit, and that they set down laws of righteous behavior for the monks and nuns resident in the monasteries where the pillars were erected, as well as for passing travelers. Like so many aspects of Indian art, these pillars raise intriguing questions that have yet to be answered, most notably: How could such pillars be made in the absence of any known precedent?

LEARN ABOUT IT

9.1 Recognize the characteristic differences between a Hindu temple and a Buddhist stupa.

9.2 Appreciate the diffusion of religion in Southeast Asia.

9.3 Understand the correlation between religious worldviews and architectural form.

9.4 Assess the variety of ways in which storytelling can be accomplished in pictorial art.

9.5 Identify the distinguishing features of a Buddha image.

HEAR MORE: Listen to an audio file of your chapter **www.myartslab.com**

THE INDIAN SUBCONTINENT

The South Asian subcontinent, or Indian subcontinent, as it is commonly called, is a peninsular region that includes the present-day countries of India, Afghanistan, Pakistan, Nepal, Bhutan, Bangladesh, and Sri Lanka (MAP 9–1). From the beginning, these areas have been home to societies whose cultures are closely linked and which have maintained remarkable continuity over time. (South Asia is distinct from Southeast Asia, which includes Brunei, Myanmar, Cambodia, East Timor, Indonesia, Laos, Malaysia, the Philippines, Singapore, Thailand, and Vietnam.) Although the modern Republic of India is about a third the size of the United States, South Asia as a whole is about two-thirds its size. A low mountain range, the Vindhya Hills, acts as a natural division that separates north India from south India. On the northern border rises the protective barrier of the Himalayas, the world's highest mountains. To the northwest are other mountains through whose passes came invasions and immigrations that profoundly affected the civilization of the subcontinent. Over these passes, too, wound the major trade routes that linked the Indian subcontinent by land to the rest of Asia and to Europe. Surrounded on its remaining sides by oceans since ancient times, the subcontinent has also been connected to the world by maritime trade, and during much of the period under discussion here it formed part of a coastal trading network that extended from eastern Africa to China.

Differences in language, climate, and terrain within India have fostered distinct regional and cultural characteristics and artistic traditions. However, despite such diversity, several overarching traits tend to unite Indian art. Most evident is a distinctive sense of beauty, with voluptuous forms and a profusion of ornament, texture, and color. Visual abundance is considered auspicious, and it reflects a belief in the generosity and favor of the gods. Another characteristic is the pervasive symbolism that enriches all Indian arts with intellectual and emotional layers. Third, and perhaps most important, is an emphasis on capturing the vibrant quality of a world seen as infused with the dynamics of the divine. Gods and humans, ideas and abstractions, are given tactile, sensuous forms, radiant with inner spirit.

INDUS CIVILIZATION

The earliest civilization of South Asia was nurtured in the lower reaches of the Indus River, in present-day Pakistan and in northwestern India. Known as the Indus or Harappan civilization (after Harappa, the first-discovered site), it flourished from approximately 2600 to 1900 BCE, or during roughly the same time as the Old Kingdom period of Egypt, the Minoan civilization of the Aegean, and the dynasties of Ur and Babylon in Mesopotamia. Indeed, it is considered, along with Egypt and Mesopotamia, to be one of the world's earliest urban river-valley civilizations.

It was the chance discovery in the late nineteenth century of some small seals, such as those in FIGURE 9–2, that provided the

9-2 • SEAL IMPRESSIONS
a., d. horned animal; b. buffalo; c. sacrificial rite to a goddess (?); e. yogi; f. three-headed animal. Indus Valley civilization, c. 2500–1500 BCE. Steatite, each seal approx. 1¼ × 1¼″ (3.2 × 3.2 cm).

The more than 2,000 small seals and impressions that have been found offer an intriguing window on the Indus Valley civilization. Usually carved from steatite stone, the seals were coated with alkali and then fired to produce a lustrous, white surface. A perforated knob on the back of each may have been for suspending them. The most popular subjects are animals, most commonly a one-horned bovine standing before an altarlike object (a, d). Animals on Indus Valley seals are often portrayed with remarkable naturalism, their taut, well-modeled surfaces implying their underlying skeletons. The function of the seals remains enigmatic, and the script that is so prominent in the impressions has yet to be deciphered.

first clue that an ancient civilization had existed in this region. The seals appeared to be related to, but not the same as, seals known from ancient Mesopotamia (SEE FIG. 2–5). Excavations begun in the 1920s and continuing into the present subsequently uncovered a number of major urban areas at points along the lower Indus River, including Harappa, Mohenjo-Daro, and Chanhu-Daro.

MOHENJO-DARO. The ancient cities of the Indus Valley resemble each other in design and construction, suggesting a coherent culture. At Mohenjo-Daro, the best preserved of the sites, archaeologists discovered an elevated citadel area about 50 feet high, presumably containing important government structures, surrounded by a wall. Among the buildings is a remarkable water tank, a large watertight pool that may have been a public bath but could also have had a ritual use (FIG. 9–3). Stretching out below the elevated area was the city, arranged in a gridlike plan with wide avenues and narrow side streets. Its houses, often two stories high, were generally built

MAP 9–1 • SOUTH AND SOUTHEAST ASIA

The borders of India are created by natural features, with the Himalayas to the north and the Indian Ocean on the remaining borders. Nearly all the rivers in the region flow east–west and are an important conduit for trade and new ideas.

9-3 • LARGE WATER TANK, MOHENJO-DARO
Indus Valley civilization (Harappan), c. 2600–1900 BCE.

Possibly a public or ritual bathing area.

around a central courtyard. Like other Indus Valley cities, Mohenjo-Daro was constructed of fired brick, in contrast to the less durable sun-dried brick used in other cultures of the time. The city included a network of covered drainage systems that channeled away waste and rainwater. Clearly the technical and engineering skills of this civilization were highly advanced. At its peak, about 2500 to 2000 BCE, Mohenjo-Daro was approximately 6–7 square miles in size and had a population of about 20,000–50,000.

INDUS VALLEY SEALS. Although our knowledge of the Indus civilization is limited by the fact that we cannot read its writing, motifs on seals as well as the few artworks that have been discovered strongly suggest continuities with later South Asian cultures. The seal in FIGURE 9–2e, for example, depicts a man in the meditative posture associated in Indian culture with a yogi, one who seeks mental and physical purification and self-control, usually for spiritual purposes. In FIGURE 9–2c, the persons with elaborate headgear in a row or procession observe a figure standing in a tree—possibly a goddess—and a kneeling worshiper. This scene may offer some insight into the religious or ritual customs of Indus people, whose deities may have been ancient prototypes of later Indian gods and goddesses.

Numerous terra-cotta figurines and a few stone and bronze statuettes have been found at Indus sites. They reveal a confident maturity of artistic conception and technique. The terra cottas resemble Mesopotamian art in their motifs and rather abstract rendering. On the other hand, the stone figures foreshadow the later Indian artistic tradition in their sensuous naturalism.

"PRIEST-KING" FROM MOHENJO-DARO. The identity of the male torso in FIGURE 9–4, sometimes called the "priest-king," is uncertain, suggesting a structure of society—where priests functioned as kings—for which we have no evidence at all. Several features of this figure, including a low forehead, a broad nose, thick lips, and long slit eyes, are seen on other works from Mohenjo-Daro. The man's garment is patterned with a **trefoil** (three-lobed) motif. The depressions of the trefoil pattern were originally filled with red paint, and the eyes were inlaid with colored shell or stone. A narrow band with a circular ornament encircles the upper arm and the head. It falls in back into two long strands and may be an indication of rank. Certainly, with its formal pose and simplified, geometric form, the statue conveys a commanding human presence.

NUDE TORSO FROM HARAPPA. Although its date is disputed by some, a nude male torso found at Harappa is an example of a contrasting naturalistic style (FIG. 9–5) of ancient Indus origins. Less than 4 inches tall, it is one of the most extraordinary portrayals of the human form to survive from any early civilization. In contrast to the more athletic male ideal developed much later in ancient Greece, this sculpture emphasizes the soft texture of the human body and the subtle nuances of muscular form. The abdomen is relaxed in the manner of a yogi able to control his breath. With these characteristics the Harappa torso forecasts the essential aesthetic attributes of later Indian sculpture.

The reasons for the demise of this flourishing civilization are not yet understood. All we know is

9-4 • TORSO OF A "PRIEST-KING"
From Mohenjo-Daro. Indus Valley civilization, c. 2600–1900 BCE. Steatite, height 6⅞″ (17.5 cm). National Museum of Pakistan, Karachi.

9-5 • TORSO
From Harappa. Indus Valley civilization, c. 2600–1900 BCE. Red sandstone, height 3¾″ (9.5 cm). National Museum, New Delhi.

that between 2000 and 1750—possibly because of climate change, a series of natural disasters, and invasions—the cities of the Indus civilization declined, and predominantly rural societies evolved.

THE VEDIC PERIOD

About 2000 BCE nomadic shepherds, the Aryans, entered India from central Asia and the Russian steppes. Gradually they supplanted the indigenous populations and introduced the horse and chariot, the Sanskrit language, a hierarchical social order, and religious practices that centered on the propitiation of gods through fire sacrifice. Their sacred writings known as the Vedas, gave the period its name. The earliest Veda consists of hymns to various Aryan gods including the divine king Indra. The importance of the fire sacrifice, overseen by a powerful priesthood—the Brahmins—and religiously sanctioned social classes, persisted through the Vedic period. At some point, the class structure became hereditary and immutable, with lasting consequences for Indian society.

During the latter part of this period, from about 800 BCE, the Upanishads were composed. These metaphysical texts examine the meanings of the earlier, more cryptic Vedic hymns. They focus on the relationship between the individual soul, or *atman*, and the universal soul, or Brahman, as well as on other concepts central to subsequent Indian philosophy. One is the assertion that the material world is illusory and that only Brahman is real and eternal. Another holds that our existence is cyclical and that beings are caught in *samsara*, a relentless cycle of birth, life, death, and rebirth. Believers aspire to attain liberation from *samsara* and to unite the individual *atman* with the eternal, universal Brahman.

The latter portion of the Vedic period also saw the flowering of India's epic literature, written in the melodious and complex Sanskrit language. By around 400 BCE, the 18-volume *Mahabharata*, the longest epic in world literature, and the *Ramayana*, the most popular and enduring religious epic in India and Southeast Asia, were taking shape. These texts, the cornerstones of Indian literature, relate histories of gods and humans that bring the philosophical ideas of the Vedas to a more accessible and popular level.

In this stimulating religious, philosophical, and literary climate numerous religious communities arose. The most influential teachers of these times were Shakyamuni Buddha and Mahavira. The Buddha, or "enlightened one," lived and taught in India around 500 BCE; his teachings form the basis of the Buddhist religion (see "Buddhism," page 297). Mahavira (c. 599–527 BCE), regarded as the last of 24 highly purified superbeings called pathfinders *(tirthankaras)*, was the founder of the Jain religion. Both Shakyamuni Buddha and Mahavira espoused some basic Upanishadic tenets, such as the cyclical nature of existence and the need for liberation from the material world. However, they rejected the authority of the Vedas, and with it the legitimacy of the fire sacrifice and the hereditary class structure of Vedic society, with its powerful, exclusive priesthood. In contrast, Buddhism and Jainism were open to all, regardless of social position.

Buddhism became a vigorous force in South Asia and provided the impetus for much of the major surviving art created between the third century BCE and the fifth century CE. The Vedic tradition, meanwhile, continued to evolve, emerging later as Hinduism, a loose term that encompasses the many religious forms that resulted from the mingling of Vedic culture with indigenous beliefs (see "Hinduism," page 298).

THE MAURYA PERIOD

After about 700 BCE, cities again began to reappear on the subcontinent, especially in the north, where numerous kingdoms arose. For most of its subsequent history, India was a shifting mosaic of regional kingdoms. From time to time, however, a particularly powerful dynasty formed an empire. The first of these was the Maurya dynasty (c. 322–185 BCE), which extended its rule over all but the southernmost portion of the subcontinent.

9-6 • FEMALE FIGURE HOLDING A FLY-WHISK
From Didarganj, Patna, Bihar, India. Probably Maurya period, c. 250 BCE. Polished sandstone, height 5′4¼″ (1.63 m). Patna Museum, Patna.

Commonly identified as a *yakshi*, this sculpture has become one of the most famous works of Indian art. Holding a fly-whisk in her raised right hand, the figure wears only a long shawl and a skirtlike cloth. The cloth rests low on her hips, held in place by a girdle. Subtly sculpted parallel creases indicate that it is gathered closely about her legs. The ends, drawn back up over the girdle, cascade down to her feet in a broad, central loop of flowing folds ending in a zigzag of hems. Draped low over her back, the shawl passes through the crook of her arm and then flows to the ground. (The missing left side of the shawl probably mirrored this motion.) The figure's jewelry is prominent. A double strand of pearls hangs between her breasts, its shape echoing and emphasizing the voluptuous curves of her body. Another strand of pearls encircles her neck. She wears a simple tiara, plug earrings, and rows of bangles. The nubbled tubes about her ankles probably represent anklets made of beaten gold. Her hair is bound behind in a large bun, and a small bun sits on her forehead. This hairstyle appears again in Indian sculpture of the later Kushan period (c. second century CE).

FEMALE FIGURE FROM DIDARGANJ. The art of the Maurya period reflects an age of heroes. At this time emerged the ideal of upholding *dharma*, the divinely ordained moral law believed to keep the universe from falling into chaos. This heroic ideal seems fully embodied in a life-size statue found at Didarganj, near the Maurya capital of Pataliputra (**FIG. 9–6**). The statue, dated by most scholars to the Maurya period, probably represents a **yakshi**, a spirit associated with the productive forces of nature. With its large breasts and pelvis, the figure embodies the association of female beauty with procreative abundance, bounty, and auspiciousness—qualities that in turn reflect the generosity of the gods and the workings of *dharma* in the world.

Sculpted from fine-grained sandstone, the statue conveys the *yakshi's* authority through the frontal rigor of her pose, the massive volumes of her form, and the strong, linear patterning of her

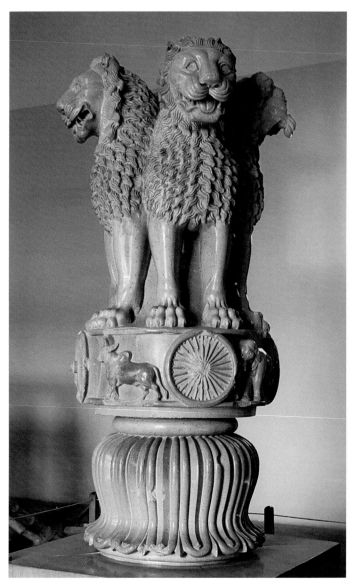

9-7 • LION CAPITAL
From Ashokan pillar at Sarnath, Uttar Pradesh, India. Maurya period, c. 250 BCE. Polished sandstone, height 7′ (2.13 m). Archaeological Museum, Sarnath.

Buddhism

The Buddhist religion developed from the teachings of Shakyamuni Buddha, who lived from about 563 to 483 BCE in the present-day regions of Nepal and northern India. At his birth, it is believed, seers foretold that the infant prince, named Siddhartha Gautama, would become either a *chakravartin* ("world-conquering ruler") or a *buddha* ("fully enlightened being"). Hoping for a ruler like himself, Siddhartha's father tried to surround his son with pleasure and shield him from pain. Yet the prince was eventually exposed to the sufferings of old age, sickness, and death—the inevitable fate of all mortal beings. Deeply troubled by the human condition, Siddhartha at age 29 left the palace, his family, and his inheritance to live as an ascetic in the wilderness. After six years of meditation, he attained complete enlightenment at a site in India now called Bodh Gaya.

Following his enlightenment, the Buddha ("Enlightened One") gave his first teaching in the Deer Park at Sarnath. Here he expounded the Four Noble Truths that are the foundation of Buddhism: (1) life is suffering; (2) this suffering has a cause, which is ignorance; (3) this ignorance can be overcome and extinguished; (4) the way to overcome this ignorance is by following the eightfold path of right view, right resolve, right speech, right action, right livelihood, right effort, right mindfulness, and right concentration. After the Buddha's death at age 80, his many disciples developed his teachings and established the world's oldest monastic institutions.

A buddha is not a god but rather one who sees the ultimate nature of the world and is therefore no longer subject to *samsara*, the cycle of birth, death, and rebirth that otherwise holds us in its grip, whether we are born into the world of the gods, humans, animals, demons, tortured spirits, or hellish beings.

The early form of Buddhism, known as Theravada or Hinayana, stresses self-cultivation for the purpose of attaining *nirvana*, which is the extinction of *samsara* for oneself. Theravada Buddhism has continued mainly in Sri Lanka and Southeast Asia. Within 500 years of the Buddha's death, another form of Buddhism, known as Mahayana, became popular mainly in northern India; it eventually flourished in China, Korea, Japan, and in Tibet (as Vajrayana). Compassion for all beings is the foundation of Mahayana Buddhism, whose goal is not *nirvana* for oneself but buddhahood (enlightenment) for every being throughout the universe. Mahayana Buddhism recognizes buddhas other than Shakyamuni from the past, present, and future. One such is Maitreya, the next buddha to appear on earth. Another is Amitabha Buddha, the Buddha of Infinite Light and Infinite Life (that is, incorporating all space and time), who dwells in a paradise known as the Western Pure Land. Amitabha Buddha became particularly popular in east Asia. Mahayana Buddhism also developed the category of **bodhisattvas** ("those whose essence is wisdom"), saintly beings who are on the brink of achieving buddhahood but have vowed to help others achieve buddhahood before crossing over themselves. In art, bodhisattvas and buddhas are most clearly distinguished by their clothing and adornments: bodhisattvas wear the princely garb of India, while buddhas wear monks' robes.

EXPLORE MORE: Gain insight from a primary source of words spoken by the Buddha www.myartslab.com

---

ornaments and dress. Alleviating and counterbalancing this hierarchical formality are her soft, youthful face, the precise definition of prominent features such as the stomach muscles, and the polished sheen of her exposed flesh. This lustrous polish is a special feature of Maurya sculpture.

THE RISE OF BUDDHISM. During the reign of the third Maurya emperor Ashoka (ruled c. 273–232 BCE), Buddhism was expanded from a religion largely localized in the Maurya heartland, a region known as Magadha, to one extending across the entire empire. Among the monuments he erected were monolithic pillars set up primarily at the sites of Buddhist monasteries.

Pillars may have been used as flag-bearing standards in India since earliest times. Thus the creators of the pillars erected during Ashoka's reign may have adapted this already ancient form to the symbolism of Indian creation myths and the new religion of Buddhism. The fully developed Ashokan pillar—a slightly tapered sandstone shaft that usually rested on a stone foundation slab sunk more than 10 feet into the ground—rose to a height of around 50 feet (SEE FIG. 9–1). On it were carved inscriptions relating to rules of *dharma* that ideal kings were enjoined to uphold, and that many later Buddhists interpreted as also referring to Buddhist teachings or exhorting the Buddhist community to unity. At the top, carved from a separate block of sandstone, an elaborate capital bore animal sculpture. Both shaft and capital were given the characteristic Maurya polish. Scholars believe that the pillars symbolized the **axis mundi** ("axis of the world"), joining earth with the cosmos. It represented the vital link between the human and celestial realms, and through it the cosmic order was impressed onto the terrestrial.

LION CAPITAL FROM SARNATH. The capital in **FIGURE 9–7** originally crowned the pillar erected at Sarnath in north central India, the site of the Buddha's first sermon. The lowest portion represents the down-turned petals of a lotus blossom. Because the lotus flower emerges from murky waters without any mud sticking to its petals, it symbolizes the presence of divine purity in the imperfect world. Above the lotus is an **abacus** (the slab forming the top of a capital) embellished with low-relief carvings

Hinduism

Hinduism is not one religion but many related beliefs and innumerable sects. It results from the mingling of Vedic beliefs with indigenous, local beliefs and practices. All three major Hindu sects draw upon the texts of the Vedas, which are believed to be sacred revelations set down about 1200–800 BCE. The gods lie outside the finite world, but they can appear in visible form to believers. Each Hindu sect takes its particular deity as supreme. By worshiping gods with rituals, meditation, and intense love, individuals may be reborn into increasingly higher positions until they escape the cycle of life, death, and rebirth, which is called *samsara*. The most popular deities are Vishnu, Shiva, and the Great Goddess, Devi. Deities are revealed and depicted in multiple aspects.

Vishnu: Vishnu is a benevolent god who works for the order and well-being of the world. He is often represented lying in a trance or asleep on the Cosmic Waters, where he dreams the world into existence. His symbols are the wheel and a conch shell, the mace and lotus. He usually has four arms and wears a crown and lavish jewelry. He rides a man-bird, Garuda. Vishnu appears in ten different incarnations, including Rama and Krishna, who have their own sects. Rama embodies virtue, and, assisted by the monkey king, he fights the demon Ravana. As Krishna, Vishnu is a supremely beautiful, blue-skinned youth who lives with the cowherds, loves the maiden Radha, and battles the demon Kansa.

Shiva: Shiva is both creative and destructive, light and dark, male and female. His symbol is the *linga*, an upright phallus, which is represented as a low pillar. As an expression of his power and creative energy, he is often represented as Lord of the Dance, dancing the Cosmic Dance, the endless cycle of death and rebirth,

destruction and creation (see "Shiva Nataraja of the Chola Dynasty," page 314). He dances within a ring of fire, his four hands holding fire, a drum, and gesturing to the worshipers. Shiva's animal vehicle is the bull. His consort is Parvati; their sons are the elephant-headed Ganesha, the overcomer of obstacles, and Karttikeya, often associated with war.

Devi: Devi, the Great Goddess, controls material riches and fertility. She has forms indicative of beauty, wealth, and auspiciousness, but also forms of wrath, pestilence, and power. As the embodiment of cosmic energy, she provides the vital force to all the male gods. Her symbol is an abstract depiction of female genitals, often associated with the *linga* of Shiva. When armed and riding a lion (as the goddess Durga), she personifies righteous fury. As the goddess Lakshmi, she is the goddess of wealth and beauty. She is often represented by the basic geometric forms: squares, circles, triangles.

Brahma: Brahma, who once had his own cult, embodies spiritual wisdom. His four heads symbolize the four cosmic cycles, four earthly directions, and four classes of society: priests (brahmins), warriors, merchants, and laborers.

There are countless other deities, but central to Hindu practice are *puja* (forms of worship) and *darshan* (beholding a deity), generally performed to obtain a deity's favor and in the hope that this favor will lead to liberation from *samsara*. Because desire for the fruits of our actions traps us, the ideal is to consider all earthly endeavors as sacrificial offerings to a god. Pleased with our devotion, he or she may grant us an eternal state of pure being, pure consciousness, and pure bliss.

---

of wheels, called in Sanskrit *chakra*s, alternating with four different animals: lion, horse, bull, and elephant. The animals may symbolize the four great rivers of the world, which are mentioned in Indian creation myths. Standing on this abacus are four back-to-back lions. Facing the four cardinal directions, the lions may be emblematic of the universal nature of Buddhism and the universal currency of Ashoka's law inscribed on the pillar. Their roar might be compared with the speech of the Buddha that spreads far and wide. The lions may also refer to the Buddha himself, who is known as "the lion of the Shakya clan" (the clan into which the Buddha was born as prince). The lions originally supported a great wheel, now lost. A universal Buddhist symbol, the wheel refers to Buddhist teaching, for with his sermon at Sarnath the Buddha "set the wheel of the law [*dharma*] in motion." The wheel is also a symbol of the *chakravartin*, the ideal universal monarch, and so refers to Ashoka as well as the Buddha.

Their formal, heraldic pose imbues the lions with something of the monumental quality evident in the statue of the *yakshi* of the same period. We also find the same strong patterning of realistic

elements: Veins and tendons stand out on the legs; the claws are large and powerful; the mane is richly textured; and the jaws have a loose and fluttering edge.

THE PERIOD OF THE SHUNGAS AND EARLY ANDHRAS

With the demise of the Maurya Empire, India returned to rule by regional dynasties. Between the second century BCE and the early first century CE, two of the most important of these dynasties were the Shunga dynasty (185–72 BCE) in central India and the Andhra dynasty (72 BCE–third century CE) who initially ruled in central India and after the first century in the south. During this period, some of the most magnificent early Buddhist structures were created.

STUPAS

Religious monuments called **stupas**, solid mounds enclosing a reliquary, are fundamental to Buddhism (see "Stupas and Temples," page 301). A stupa may be small and plain or large and elaborate. Its

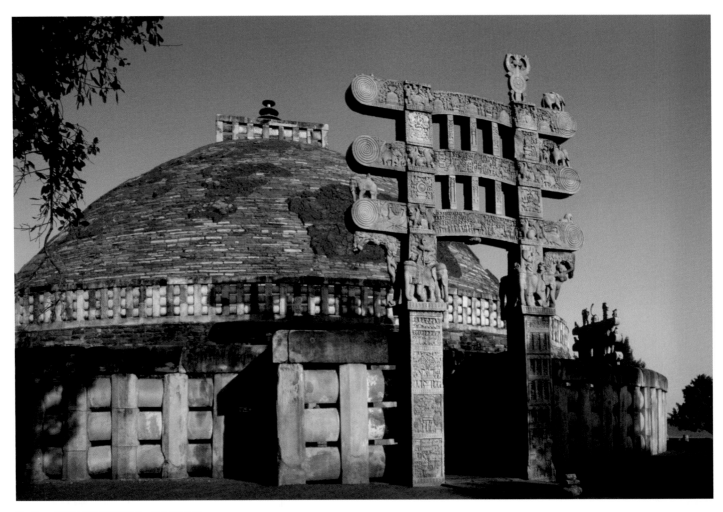

9-8 • GREAT STUPA, SANCHI
Madhya Pradesh, India. Founded 3rd century BCE, enlarged c. 150–50 BCE.

SEE MORE: View a video about the Great Stupa, Sanchi **www.myartslab.com**

form may vary from region to region, but its symbolic meaning remains virtually the same, and its plan is a carefully calculated **mandala**, or diagram of the cosmos as it is envisioned in Buddhism. Stupas are open to all for private worship.

The first stupas were constructed to house the Buddha's remains after his cremation. According to tradition, the relics were divided into eight portions and placed in eight **reliquaries**. Each reliquary was then encased in its own burial mound, called a stupa. Since the early stupas held actual remains of the Buddha, they were venerated as his body and, by extension, his enlightenment and attainment of *nirvana* (liberation from rebirth). The method of veneration was, and still is, to circumambulate, or walk around, the stupa in a clockwise direction. In the mid third century BCE, King Ashoka is said to have opened the original eight stupas and divided their relics among many more stupas, probably including the Great Stupa at Sanchi.

THE GREAT STUPA AT SANCHI. Probably no early Buddhist structure is more famous than the **GREAT STUPA** at Sanchi in central India (FIG. 9–8). In its original form probably dating to the

time of Ashoka, the Great Stupa was part of a large monastery complex crowning a hill. During the mid second century BCE, it was enlarged to its present size, and the surrounding stone railing was constructed. About 100 years later, elaborately carved stone gateways were added to the railing.

The Great Stupa at Sanchi is a representative of the early central Indian type. Its solid, hemispherical dome was built up from rubble and dirt, faced with dressed stone, then covered with a shining white plaster made from lime and powdered seashells. The dome—echoing the arc of the sky—sits on a raised base. Around the perimeter is a walkway enclosed by a railing; an elevated walkway is approached by a staircase on the south side. As is often true in religious architecture, the railing provides a physical and symbolic boundary between an inner, sacred area and the outer, profane world. On top of the dome, another stone railing, square in shape, defines the abode of the gods atop the cosmic mountain. It encloses the top of a mast bearing three stone disks, or "umbrellas," of decreasing size. These disks have been interpreted in various ways. They may correspond to the "Three Jewels of Buddhism"—the Buddha, the Law, and the Monastic

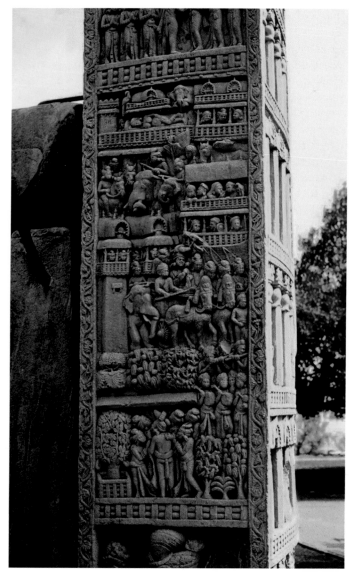

inscription, also on the south gateway, specifies a gift during the reign of King Satakarni of the Andhra dynasty, providing the first-century BCE date for the gateways. The only elements of the Great Stupa at Sanchi to be ornamented with sculpture, the gateways rise to a height of 35 feet. Their square posts and horizontal members are carved with symbols and scenes drawn mostly from the Buddha's life and the **jataka tales**, stories of the Buddha's past lives. A relief from the east gateway is illustrated in **FIGURE 9–9**. Typical of Indian narrative relief of the second and first centuries BCE, the scenes are organized not in a time sequence, but according to where they take place. Thus, at the top of this relief is a scene of Queen Maya's dream anticipating the birth of the Buddha, while below is a scene showing the Buddha's father in a chariot, riding out to greet his return, and at the bottom the Buddha, symbolized by a plank, levitates above the crowd gathered to witness the gift of a garden for the Buddha and his followers. All three of these scenes take place at Kapilavastu, the city of his birth.

9-9 • RELIEF FROM EAST GATEWAY OF THE GREAT STUPA, SANCHI
Early Andhra period, mid 1st century BCE. Stone.

This relief illustrates the birth of the Buddha at the top and the return of the Buddha to the city of his birth in the panels below.

Order—and they may also refer to the Buddhist concept of the three realms of existence: desire, form, and formlessness. The mast itself symbolizes an *axis mundi*, connecting the Cosmic Waters below the earth with the celestial realm above it and anchoring everything in its proper place.

A 10-foot-tall stone railing demarcates a circumambulatory path at ground level. Carved with octagonal uprights and lens-shaped crossbars, it probably simulates the wooden railings of the time. This design pervaded early Indian art, appearing in relief sculpture and as architectural ornament. Four stone gateways, or **toranas**, punctuate the railing. Aligned with the four cardinal directions, the gateways symbolize the Buddhist cosmos. An inscription on the south gateway indicates that it was provided by ivory carvers from the nearby town of Vidisha, while another

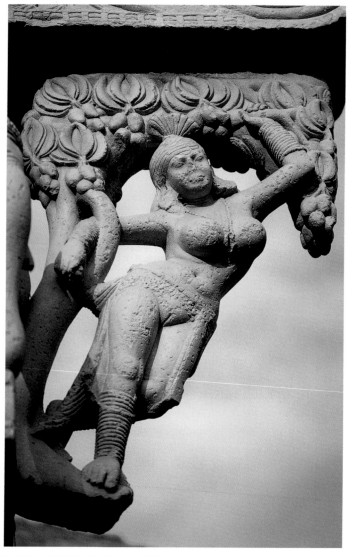

9-10 • *YAKSHI* BRACKET FIGURE
East *torana* of the Great Stupa at Sanchi. Stone, height approx. 60″ (152.4 cm).

Buddhist architecture in South Asia consists mainly of stupas and temples, often at monastic complexes containing **viharas** (monks' cells and common areas). These monuments may be either structural—built up from the ground—or rock-cut—hewn out of a mountainside. Stupas derive from burial mounds and contain relics beneath a solid, dome-shaped core. A major stupa is surrounded by a railing that creates a sacred path for ritual circumambulation at ground level. This railing is punctuated by gateways, called **toranas** in Sanskrit, aligned with the cardinal points. The stupa sits on a round or square terrace; stairs lead to an upper circumambulatory path around the platform's edge. On top of the stupa's dome a railing defines a square, from the center of which rises a mast supporting tiers of disk-shaped "umbrellas."

Hindu architecture in South Asia consists mainly of temples, either structural or rock-cut, executed in a number of styles and dedicated to diverse deities. The two general Hindu temple types are the northern and southern styles prevalent in northern India and southern India respectively. Within these broad categories is great stylistic diversity, though all are raised on plinths and dominated by their superstructures. In north India, the term **shikhara** is used to refer to the entire superstructure, while in the south it refers only to the finial, that is, the uppermost member of the superstructure. North Indian *shikhara*s are crowned by **amalakas**. Inside, a series of **mandapas** (halls) leads to an inner sanctuary, the **garbhagriha**, which contains a sacred image. An *axis mundi* is imagined to run vertically up from the Cosmic Waters below the earth, through the *garbhagriha*'s image, and out through the top of the tower.

Jain architecture consists mainly of structural and rock-cut monasteries and temples that have much in common with their Buddhist and Hindu counterparts. Buddhist, Hindu, and Jain temples may share a site, as may the structures of still other religions.

stupa

northern-style temple

southern-style temple

SEE MORE: View a simulation of stupas and temples www.myartslab.com

The capitals above the posts consist of four back-to-back elephants on the north and east gates, dwarfs on the west gate, and lions on the south gate. The capitals in turn support a three-tiered superstructure in which posts and crossbars are elaborately carved with still more symbols and scenes, and studded with free-standing sculptures depicting such subjects as *yakshi*s and *yaksha*s, riders on real and mythical animals, and the Buddhist wheel. As in other early Buddhist art before the late first century BCE, the Buddha himself is not shown in human form. Instead, he is represented by symbols such as his footprints, an empty "enlightenment" seat, or a plank.

Forming a bracket between each capital and the lowest cross-bar is a sculpture of a *yakshi* (**FIG. 9–10**). These *yakshi*s are some of the finest female figures in Indian art, and they make an instructive comparison with the *yakshi* of the Maurya period (SEE FIG. 9–6).

The earlier figure was distinguished by a formal, somewhat rigid pose, an emphasis on realistic details, and a clear distinction between clothed and nude parts of the body. In contrast, the Sanchi *yakshi* leans daringly into space with casual abandon, supported by one leg as the other charmingly crosses behind. Her thin, diaphanous garment is noticeable only by its hems, and so she appears almost nude, which emphasizes her form. The band pulling gently at her abdomen accentuates the suppleness of her flesh. The swelling, arching curves of her body evoke this deity's procreative and bountiful essence. As the personification of the waters, she is the source of life. Here she symbolizes the sap of the tree, which flowers at her touch.

The profusion of designs, symbols, scenes, and figures carved on all sides of the gateways to the Great Stupa not only relates the history and lore of Buddhism, but also represents the teeming life of the world and the gods.

BUDDHIST ROCK-CUT HALLS

From ancient times, caves have been considered hallowed places in India, for they were frequently the abode of holy men and ascetics. Around the second century BCE, cavelike sanctuaries were hewn out of the stone plateaus in the region of south central India known as the Deccan. Made for the use of Buddhist monks, the sanctuaries were carved from top to bottom like great pieces of sculpture, with all details completely finished in stone. To enter one of these remarkable halls is to feel transported to an otherworldly, sacred space. The atmosphere created by the dark recess and the echo that magnifies the smallest sound combine to promote a state of heightened awareness.

THE CHAITYA HALL AT KARLE. The monastic community made two types of rock-cut halls. One was the **vihara**, used for the monks' living quarters, and the other was the **chaitya** ("sanctuary"), which usually enshrined a stupa. A *chaitya* hall at Karle, dating from the first century BCE to the first century CE, is one of the largest and most fully developed examples of these early Buddhist works **(FIG. 9–11)**. At the entrance, columns once supported a balcony, in front of which a pair of Ashokan-type

9-11 • CHAITYA HALL, KARLE
Maharashtra, India. 1st century BCE–1st century CE.

pillars stood. The walls of the vestibule are carved in relief with rows of small balcony railings and arched windows, simulating the façade of a great multi-storied palace. At the base of the side walls, enormous statues of elephants seem to be supporting the entire structure on their backs. Dominating the upper portion of the main façade is a large horseshoe-shaped opening, which provides the hall's main source of light. The window was originally fitted with a carved wood screen, some of which remains, that filtered the light streaming inside.

Three entrances pierce the main façade. Flanking the entrances are sculpted panels of **mithuna** couples, amorous male and female figures that evoke the harmony and fertility of life and suggest the devotion with which the worshiper should confront the Buddha represented by the stupa inside. The interior hall, 123 feet long, has a 46-foot-high ceiling carved in the form of a barrel vault ornamented with arching wooden ribs. Both the interior and exterior of the hall were once brightly painted. Pillars demarcate a pathway for circumambulation around the stupa in the apse at the far end.

The side aisles are separated from the main aisle by closely spaced columns whose bases resemble a large pot set on a stepped pyramid of planks. From this potlike form rises a massive octagonal shaft. Crowning the shaft, a bell-shaped lotus capital supports an inverted pyramid of planks, which serves in turn as a platform for sculpture. The statues depict pairs of kneeling elephants, each bearing a *mithuna* couple. These figures, the only sculpture within this austere hall, may represent the nobility coming to pay homage at the temple. The pillars around the apse are plain, and the stupa is simple. A railing motif ornaments the base; the dome was once topped with wooden "umbrella" disks, only one of which remains. As with nearly everything in the cave, the stupa is carved from the cliff's rock. Like the stupa at Sanchi, the sculptural decoration is restricted to the entranceway. This stupa, however, could not contain the Buddha's relics because it is solid rock; likely it was worshiped as if it did.

THE KUSHAN AND LATER ANDHRA PERIODS

Around the first century CE, the regions of present-day Afghanistan, Pakistan, and north India came under the control of the Kushans, originally a nomadic people forced out of northwest China by the Han. Exact dates are uncertain, but they ruled from the first to the third century CE. The beginning of the long reign of their most illustrious king, Kanishka, is variously dated from 78 to 143 CE.

Buddhism during this period underwent a profound evolution that resulted in the form known as Mahayana, or Great Vehicle (see "Buddhism," page 297). This vital new movement, which was to sweep most of northern India and eastern Asia, probably inspired the first depictions of the Buddha himself in art. (Previously, as in the Great Stupa at Sanchi, the Buddha had been indicated solely by symbols.) Distinctive styles arose in the Gandhara region in the northwest (present-day Pakistan and Afghanistan) and in the famous religious center of Mathura in central India. Both of these areas were ruled by the Kushans. About the same time, a third style evolved in southeast India under the Andhra dynasty, whose rule continued in this region through the third century CE.

9-12 • STANDING BUDDHA
From Gandhara, Pakistan. Kushan period, c. 2nd–3rd century CE. Schist, height 7'6" (2.28 m). Lahore Museum, Lahore.

While all three styles are quite distinct, they shared a basic visual language, or iconography, in which the Buddha is readily recognized by certain characteristics. He wears a monk's robe, a long length of cloth draped over the left shoulder and around the body. The Buddha is said to have had 32 major distinguishing marks, called **lakshanas**, some of which are reflected in the iconography (see "Buddhist Symbols," page 362). These include a golden-colored body, long arms that reached to his knees, the impression of a wheel *(chakra)* on the palms of his hands and the soles of his feet, and the **urna**—a tuft of white hair between his eyebrows. Because he had been a prince in his youth and had worn the customary heavy earrings, his earlobes are usually shown elongated. The top of his head is said to have had a protuberance called an **ushnisha**, which in images often resembles a bun or top-knot and symbolizes his enlightenment.

THE GANDHARA STYLE

Gandhara art combines elements of Hellenistic, Persian, and Indian styles. A typical image from Gandhara portrays the Buddha as a superhuman figure, more powerful and heroic than an ordinary human (**FIG. 9–12**). Although it is difficult to determine the dates of Gandhara images, this over-life-size Buddha may date to the fully developed stage of the Gandhara style, possibly around the third century CE. It is carved from schist, a fine-grained dark stone. The Buddha's body, revealed through the folds of the garment, is broad and massive, with heavy shoulders and limbs and a well-defined torso. His left knee bends gently, suggesting a slightly relaxed posture.

The treatment of the robe is especially characteristic of the Gandhara manner. Tight, riblike folds alternate with delicate creases, setting up a clear, rhythmic pattern of heavy and shallow lines. On the upper part of the figure, the folds break asymmetrically along the left arm; on the lower part, they drape in a symmetric U shape. The strong tension of the folds suggests life and power within the image. This complex fold pattern resembles the treatment of togas on certain Roman statues (SEE PAGE 177, FIG. A), and it exerted a strong influence on portrayals of the Buddha in central and east Asia. The Gandhara region's relations with the Hellenistic world may have led to this strongly Western style in its art. Pockets of Hellenistic culture had thrived in neighboring Bactria (present-day northern Afghanistan and southern Uzbekistan) since the fourth century BCE, when the Greeks under Alexander the Great reached the borders of India. Also, Gandhara's position near the east–west trade routes appears to have stimulated contact with Roman culture in the Near East during the early centuries of the first millennium CE.

THE MATHURA STYLE

The second major style of Buddhist art in the Kushan period—that found at Mathura—was not allied with the Hellenistic-Roman tradition. Instead, the Mathura style evolved from representations of *yakshas*, the indigenous male nature deities. Images produced at

Mudras

*Mudra*s (the Sanskrit word for "signs") are ancient symbolic hand gestures that are regarded as physical expressions of different states of being. In Buddhist art, they function iconographically. *Mudra*s are also used during meditation to release these energies. The following are the most common *mudra*s in Asian art.

Dharmachakra Mudra

The gesture of teaching, setting the *chakra* (wheel) of the *dharma* (law or doctrine) in motion. Hands are at chest level.

Dhyana Mudra

A gesture of meditation and balance, symbolizing the path toward enlightenment. Hands are in the lap, the lower representing *maya*, the physical world of illusion, the upper representing *nirvana*, enlightenment and release from the world.

Vitarka Mudra

This variant of *dharmachakra mudra* stands for intellectual debate. The right and/or left hand is held at shoulder level with thumb and forefinger touching.

Abhaya Mudra

The gesture of reassurance, blessing, and protection, this *mudra* means "have no fear." The right hand is at shoulder level, palm outward.

Bhumisparsha Mudra

This gesture calls upon the earth to witness Shakyamuni Buddha's enlightenment at Bodh Gaya. A seated figure's right hand reaches toward the ground, palm inward.

Varada Mudra

The gesture of charity, symbolizing the fulfillment of all wishes. Alone, this *mudra* is made with the right hand; but when combined with *abhaya mudra* in standing Buddha figures (as is most common), the left hand is shown in *varada mudra*.

Mudras

Mathura during the early days of the Kushan period may be the first representations of the Buddha to appear in art.

The stele in **FIGURE 9–13** is one of the finest of the early Mathura images. The sculptors worked in a distinctive red sandstone flecked with cream-colored spots. Carved in **high relief** (forms projecting strongly from the background), it depicts a seated Buddha with two attendants. The Buddha sits in a yogic posture on a pedestal supported by lions. His right hand is raised in a symbolic gesture meaning "have no fear." Images of the Buddha rely on a repertoire of such gestures, called **mudras**, to communicate certain ideas, such as teaching, meditation, or the attaining of enlightenment (see "Mudras," above). The Buddha's *urna*, his *ushnisha*, and the impressions of wheels on his palms and soles are

all clearly visible in this figure. Behind his head is a large, circular halo; the scallop points of its border represent radiating light. Behind the halo are branches of the pipal tree, the tree under which the Buddha was seated when he achieved enlightenment. Two celestial beings hover above.

As in Gandhara sculptures, the Mathura work gives a powerful impression of the Buddha. Yet this Buddha's riveting outward gaze and alert posture impart a more intense, concentrated energy. The robe is pulled tightly over the body, allowing the fleshy form to be seen as almost nude. Where the pleats of the robe appear, such as over the left arm and fanning out between the legs, they are depicted abstractly through compact parallel formations of ridges with an incised line in the center of each ridge. This characteristic

9-13 • BUDDHA AND ATTENDANTS
From Katra Keshavdev, Mathura, Madhya Pradesh, India. Kushan period, c. late 1st–early 2nd century CE. Red sandstone, height 27¼" (69.2 cm). Government Museum, Mathura.

Mathura tendency to abstraction also appears in the face, whose features take on geometric shapes, as in the rounded forms of the widely opened eyes. Nevertheless, the torso with its subtle and soft modeling is strongly naturalistic.

THE SOUTHEAST INDIAN STYLE

Events from the Buddha's life were popular subjects in the reliefs decorating stupas and Buddhist temples. One example from Nagarjunakonda depicts a scene when he was Prince Siddhartha, before his renunciation of his princely status and his subsequent quest for enlightenment **(FIG. 9–14)**. Carved in low relief, the panel reveals a scene of pleasure around a pool of water. Gathered around Siddhartha, the largest figure and the only male, are some of the palace women. One holds his foot, entreating him to come into the water; another sits with legs drawn up on the nearby rock; others lean over his shoulder or fix their hair; one comes into the scene with a box of jewels on her head. The panel is framed by decorated columns, crouching lions, and amorous *mithuna* couples. (One of these couples is visible at the right of the illustration.) The scene is skillfully orchestrated to revolve around the prince as the main focus of all eyes. Typical of the southeast Indian style, the figures are slighter than those of Gandhara and Mathura. They are sinuous and mobile, even while at rest. The rhythmic nuances of the limbs and varied postures not only create interest in the activity of each individual but also engender a light and joyous effect.

During the first to third century CE, each of the three major styles of Buddhist art developed its own distinct idiom for expressing the complex imagery of Buddhism and depicting the image of the Buddha. The production of art in Gandhara and the region around Nagarjunakonda declined over the ensuing centuries. However, the artists of central India continued to work productively, and from them came the next major development in Indian Buddhist art.

9-14 • SIDDHARTHA IN THE PALACE
Detail of a relief from Nagarjunakonda, Andhra Pradesh, India. Later Andhra period, c. 3rd century CE. Limestone. National Museum, New Delhi.

EXPLORE MORE: Gain insight from a primary source about the life of the Buddha
www.myartslab.com

THE FOURTH THROUGH SEVENTH CENTURIES

The Guptas, who founded a dynasty in the eastern region of central India known as Magadha, expanded their territories during the fourth century CE to form an empire that encompassed northern and much of central India. Although Gupta power ended in 550, the influence of Gupta culture was felt long after that.

The period of the Guptas and their contemporaries is renowned for the flourishing artistic and literary culture that brought forth some of India's most widely admired sculpture and painting. While Buddhism continued to be a major religion, the earliest surviving Hindu temples also date from this time.

BUDDHIST SCULPTURE

Two distinctive styles of Gupta Buddhist sculpture prevailed during the second and third quarters of the fifth century and dominated in northern India: one was based at Mathura, the major center of north Indian sculpture during the Kushan period, and the other at Sarnath, whose style is reflected in Buddhist sculpture over much of northern India.

The **STANDING BUDDHA** in **FIGURE 9–15** embodies the fully developed Sarnath Gupta style. Carved from fine-grained sandstone, the figure stands in a mildly relaxed pose, the body clearly visible through a clinging robe. This plain robe, portrayed with none of the creases and folds so prominent in the Kushan period images, is distinctive of the Sarnath style. Its effect is to concentrate attention on the form of the body, which emerges in high relief. The body is graceful and slight, with broad shoulders and a well-proportioned torso. Only a few lines of the garment at the neck, waist, and hems interrupt the purity of its subtly shaped surfaces; the face, smooth and ovoid, has the same refined elegance. The downcast eyes suggest otherworldly introspection, yet the gentle, open posture maintains a human link. Behind the head are the remains of a large, circular halo. Carved in concentric circles of pearls and foliage, the ornate halo contrasted with the plain surfaces of the figure. Details also may have been indicated by paint.

At the site of Bamiyan, about 155 miles northwest of Kabul, Afghanistan, were two enormous Buddhas carved from the rock of a cliff, one some 115 feet in height **(FIG. 9–16)**, the other about 165 feet. They were seen by a Chinese pilgrim who came to Bamiyan in the fifth century, so they clearly date before his visit, probably to the early fifth century. Pilgrims could walk within the cliff up a staircase on the right side of the smaller figure that ended at the Buddha's shoulder. There they could look into the vault of the niche and see a painted image of the sun god, suggesting a metaphoric pilgrimage to the heavens. They then could circumambulate the figure at the level of the head and return to ground level on a staircase on the figure's left side. These huge figures likely served as the model for those at rock-cut sanctuaries in China, for example, at Yungang. Despite the historical and religious importance of these figures, and

9-15 • STANDING BUDDHA
From Sarnath, Uttar Pradesh, India. Gupta period, 474 CE. Chunar sandstone, height 6′4″ (1.93 m). Archaeological Museum, Sarnath.

ignoring the pleas of world leaders, the Taliban demolished the Bamiyan Buddhas in 2001.

PAINTING

The Gupta aesthetic also found expression in painting, though in a region of India just beyond the Gupta realm. Some of the finest surviving works are murals from the Buddhist rock-cut halls of Ajanta, in the western Deccan region of India **(FIG. 9–17)**. Under a ruling house known as the Vakataka dynasty, many caves were carved around 475 CE, including Cave I, a large *vihara* hall with monks' chambers around the sides and a Buddha shrine chamber in the back. The walls of the central court were covered with murals painted in mineral pigments on a prepared plaster surface. Some of these paintings depict episodes from the Buddha's past lives. Flanking the entrance to the shrine chamber are two large **bodhisattvas**, one of which is seen in FIGURE 9–17.

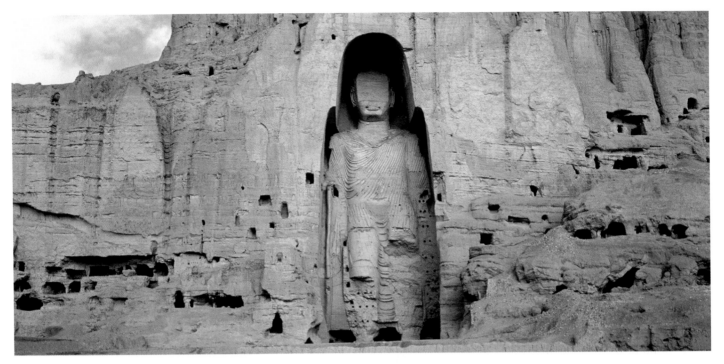

9-16 • STANDING BUDDHA
Bamiyan, Afghanistan. c. 5th century CE.

Bodhisattvas are enlightened beings who postpone *nirvana* and buddhahood to help others achieve enlightenment. They are distinguished from Buddhas in art by their princely garments. The bodhisattva here is lavishly adorned with delicate ornaments. He wears a bejeweled crown, large earrings, a pearl necklace, armbands, and bracelets. A striped cloth covers his lower body. The graceful bending posture and serene gaze impart a sympathetic attitude. His spiritual power is suggested by his large size in comparison to the surrounding figures, and his identity as the compassionate bodhisattva Avalokiteshvara is indicated by the lotus flower he holds in his right hand.

The naturalistic style balances outline and softly graded color tones. Outline drawing, always a major ingredient of Indian painting, clearly defines shapes; tonal gradations impart the illusion of three-dimensional form, with lighter tones used for protruding parts such as the nose, brows, shoulders, and chest muscles. Together with the details of the jewels, these highlighted areas resonate against the subdued tonality of the figure. Sophisticated, realistic detail is balanced by the languorous human form. In no other known examples of Indian painting do bodhisattvas appear so graciously divine yet, so palpably human. This particular synthesis is evident also in the Sarnath statue (SEE FIG. 9–15), which shares much in common as well with the sculpture of Ajanta.

Although Buddhism had flourished in India during the fifth century, some of the most important Buddhist monasteries, attracting pilgrims from as far away as China, prospered especially after the Gupta period. Hindu temples, generally small and relatively simple structures during the fifth century, subsequently became increasingly complex and elaborately adorned with sculptured images.

9-17 • BODHISATTVA
Detail of a wall painting in Cave I, Ajanta, Maharashtra, India. Vakataka dynasty, c. 475 CE.

9-18 • VISHNU TEMPLE, DEOGARH
Uttar Pradesh, India. Gupta dynasty, c. 530 CE.

THE EARLY NORTHERN TEMPLE

The Hindu temple developed many different forms throughout India, but it can be classified broadly into two types: northern and southern. The northern type is chiefly distinguished by a superstructure called a **shikhara** (see "Stupas and Temples," page 301). The *shikhara* rises as a solid mass above the flat stone ceiling and windowless walls of the sanctum, or **garbhagriha**, which houses an image of the temple's deity. As it rises, it curves inward in a mathematically determined ratio. (In geometric terms, the *shikhara* is a paraboloid.) Crowning the top is a circular, cushion-like element called an **amalaka**, a fruit. From the *amalaka*, a **finial** (a knoblike decoration at the top point of a spire) takes the eye to a point where the earthly world is thought to join the cosmic world. An imaginary *axis mundi* penetrates the entire temple, running from the point of the finial, through the exact center of the *amalaka* and *shikhara*, down through the center of the *garbhagriha* and its image, finally passing through the base of the temple and into the earth below. In this way the temple becomes a conduit between the celestial realms and the earth. This theme, familiar from Ashokan pillars and Buddhist stupas, is carried out with elaborate exactitude in Hindu temples, and it is one of the most important elements underlying their form and function (see "Meaning and Ritual in Hindu Temples and Images," page 310).

TEMPLE OF VISHNU AT DEOGARH.   One of the earliest northern-style temples is the temple of Vishnu at Deogarh in north central India, which dates from around 530 CE **(FIG. 9–18)**. Much of the *shikhara* has crumbled away, so we cannot determine its original shape with precision. Nevertheless, it was clearly a massive, solid structure built of large cut stones. It would have given the impression of a mountain, which is one of several metaphoric meanings of a Hindu temple. This early temple has only one chamber, the *garbhagriha*, which corresponds to the center of a sacred diagram called a *mandala* on which the entire temple site is patterned. As the deity's residence, the *garbhagriha* is likened to a sacred cavern within the "cosmic mountain" of the temple.

Large panels sculpted in relief with images of Vishnu appear as "windows" on the temple's exterior. These elaborately framed panels do not function literally to let light *into* the temple; they function symbolically to let the light of the deity *out* of the temple to be seen by those outside.

One panel depicts Vishnu lying on the Cosmic Waters at the beginning of creation **(FIG. 9–19)**. He sleeps on the serpent of infinity, Ananta, whose body coils endlessly into space. Stirred by his female aspect (*shakti*, or female energy), personified here by the goddess Lakshmi, seen holding his foot, Vishnu dreams the universe into existence. From his navel springs a lotus (shown in this relief behind Vishnu), and the unfolding of space-time begins.

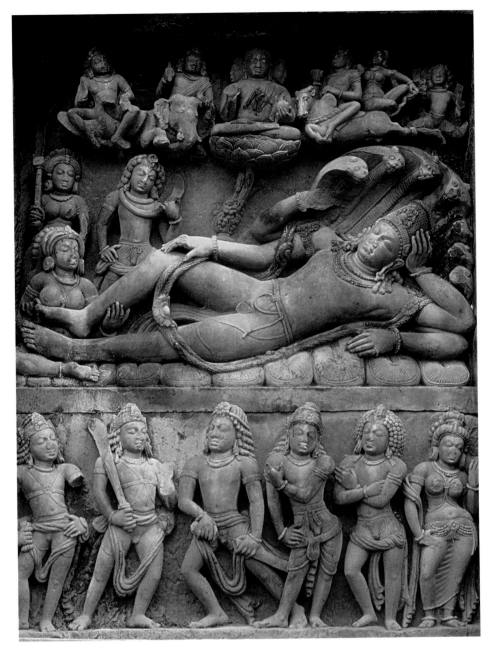

9-19 • VISHNU ON THE COSMIC WATERS
Relief panel in the Vishnu Temple, Deogarh. c. 530 CE. Stone, height approx. 5' (1.5 m).

SEE MORE: View a video about the process of sculpting in relief
www.myartslab.com

frieze below personify Vishnu's four attributes. They stand ready to fight the appearance of evil, represented at the left of the frieze by two demons who threaten to kill Brahma and jeopardize all creation.

The birth of the universe and the appearance of evil are thus portrayed here in three clearly organized registers. Typical of Indian religious and artistic expression, these momentous events are set before our eyes not in terms of abstract symbols, but as a drama acted out by gods in super-human form.

MONUMENTAL NARRATIVE RELIEFS

The Hindu god Shiva exhibits a wide range of aspects or forms, both gentle and wild: He is the Great Yogi who dwells for vast periods of time in meditation in the Himalayas; he is also the husband par excellence who makes love to the goddess Parvati for eons at a time; he is the Slayer of Demons; and he is the Cosmic Dancer who dances the destruction and re-creation of the world.

TEMPLE OF SHIVA AT ELEPHANTA. Many of these forms of Shiva appear in the monumental relief panels adorning the cave-temple of Shiva carved in the mid sixth century on the island of Elephanta off the coast of Mumbai in western India. The cave-temple is complex in layout and conception, perhaps to reflect the nature of Shiva. While most temples have one entrance, this temple offers three—one facing north, one east, and one west. The interior, impressive in its size and grandeur, is designed along two main axes, one running north–south, the other east–west. The three entrances provide the only source of light, and the resulting cross and backlighting effects add to the sense of the cave as a place of mysterious, almost confusing complexity.

Along the east–west axis, large pillars cut from the rock appear to support the low ceiling and its beams, although, as with all architectural elements in a cave-temple, they are not structural (FIG. 9–20). The pillars form orderly rows, but the rows are hard to discern within the framework of the cave shape, which is neither square nor longitudinal, but formed of overlapping *mandalas* that create a symmetric yet irregular space. The pillars are an important aesthetic component of the cave. Each has an

The first being to be created is Brahma (not to be confused with Brahman), who appears here as the central, four-headed figure in the row of gods portrayed above the reclining Vishnu. Brahma turns himself into the universe of space and time by thinking, "May I become Many."

The sculptor has depicted Vishnu as a large, resplendent figure with four arms. His size and his multiple arms denote his omnipotence. He is lightly garbed but richly ornamented. The ideal of the Gupta style is evident in the smooth, perfected shape of the body and in the lavishly detailed jewelry, including Vishnu's characteristic cylindrical crown. The four figures on the right in the

Meaning and Ritual in Hindu Temples and Images

The Hindu temple is one of the most complex and meaningful architectural forms in Asian art. Age-old symbols and ritual functions are embedded not only in a structure's many parts, but also in the process of construction itself. Patron, priest, and architect worked as a team to ensure the sanctity of the structure from start to finish. No artist or artisan was more highly revered in ancient Indian society than the architect, who could oversee the construction of an abode in which a deity would dwell.

For a god to take up residence, however, everything had to be done properly in exacting detail. By the end of the first millennium, the necessary procedures had been recorded in texts called the *Silpa Shastra*. First, an auspicious site was chosen; a site near water was especially favored, for water makes the earth fruitful. Next, the ground was prepared in an elaborate process that took several years: Spirits already inhabiting the site were invited to leave; the ground was planted and harvested through two seasons; then cows—sacred beasts since the Indus civilization—were pastured there to lend their potency to the site. When construction began, each phase was accompanied by ritual to ensure its purity and sanctity.

All Hindu temples are built on a plan known as a **mandala**, a schematic design of a sacred realm or space—specifically, Vastupurusha *mandala*, the *mandala* of the Cosmic Man, the primordial progenitor of the human species. His body, fallen on earth, is imagined as superimposed on the *mandala* design; together, they form the base on which the temple rises. The Vastupurusha *mandala* always takes the form of a square subdivided into a number of equal squares (usually 64) surrounding a central square. The central square represents Brahman, the primordial, unmanifest Formless One. This square corresponds to the temple's sanctum, the windowless *garbhagriha* ("womb chamber"). The nature of Brahman is clear, pure light; that we perceive the *garbhagriha* as dark is considered a testament to our deluded nature. The surrounding squares belong to lesser deities, while the outermost compartments hold protector gods. These compartments are usually represented by the enclosing wall of a temple compound.

The *garbhagriha* houses the temple's main image—most commonly a stone, bronze, or wood statue of Vishnu, Shiva, or Devi. In the case of Shiva, the image is often symbolic rather than anthropomorphic. To ensure perfection, the proportions of the image follow a set canon, and rituals surround its making. When the image is completed, a priest recites *mantras* (mystic syllables), that bring the deity into the image. The belief that a deity is literally present is not taken lightly. Even in India today, any image "under worship"—whether it be in a temple or a field, an ancient work or a modern piece—will be respected and not taken from the people who worship it.

A Hindu temple is a place for individual devotion, not congregational worship. It is the place where a devotee can make offerings to one or more deities and be in the presence of the god who is embodied in the image in the *garbhagriha*. Worship generally consists of prayers and offerings such as food and flowers or water and oil for the image, but it can also be much more elaborate, including dancing and ritual sacrifices.

---

unadorned, square base rising to nearly half its total height. Above is a circular column, which has a curved contour and a billowing "cushion" capital. Both column and capital are delicately fluted, adding a surprising refinement to these otherwise sturdy forms. The focus of the east–west axis is a square **linga shrine**, shown here at the center of illustration 9–20. Each of its four entrances is flanked by a pair of colossal standing guardian figures. In the center of the shrine is the *linga*, the phallic symbol of Shiva. The *linga* represents the presence of Shiva as the unmanifest Formless One, or Brahman. It symbolizes both his erotic nature and his aspect as the Great Yogi who controls his seed. The *linga* is synonymous with Shiva and is seen in nearly every Shiva temple and shrine.

The focus of the north–south axis, in contrast, is a relief on the south wall with a huge bust of Shiva representing his Sadashiva, or **ETERNAL SHIVA**, aspect (**FIG. 9–21**). Three heads are shown resting upon the broad shoulders of the upper body, but five heads are implied: the fourth behind and the fifth, never depicted, on top. The heads summarize Shiva's fivefold nature as creator (back),

protector (left), destroyer (right), obscurer (front), and releaser (top). The head in the front depicts Shiva deep in introspection. The massiveness of the broad head, the large eyes barely delineated, and the mouth with its heavy lower lip suggest the god's serious depths. Lordly and majestic, he easily supports his huge crown, intricately carved with designs and jewels, and the matted, piled-up hair of a yogi. On his left shoulder, his protector nature is depicted as female, with curled hair and a pearl-festooned crown. On his right shoulder, his wrathful, destroyer nature wears a fierce expression, and snakes encircle his neck.

Like the relief panels at the temple to Vishnu in Deogarh (SEE FIG. 9–19), the reliefs at Elephanta are early examples of the Hindu monumental narrative tradition. Measuring 11 feet in height, they are set in recessed niches. The panels portray the range of Shiva's powers and some of his different aspects, presented in the context of narratives that help devotees understand his nature. Taken as a whole, the reliefs represent the manifestation of Shiva in our world. Indian artists often convey the many aspects or essential nature of a deity through multiple heads or arms—which they

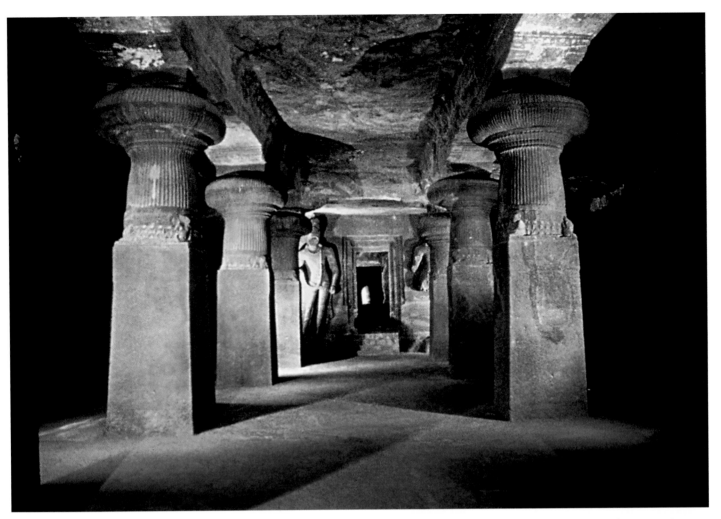

9-20 • CAVE-TEMPLE OF SHIVA, ELEPHANTA
Maharashtra, India. Post-Gupta period, mid 6th century CE. View along
the east–west axis to the *linga* shrine.

do with such convincing naturalism that we readily accept the
additions. Here, for example, the artist has united three heads onto
a single body so skillfully that we still relate to the statue as an
essentially human presence.

"DESCENT OF THE GANGES" RELIEF AT MAMALLAPURAM. An
enormous relief at Mamallapuram, near Chennai, in southeastern
India, depicts the penance of a king, Bhagiratha, who sought to
save his people from drought by subjecting himself to terrible
austerities. In response, the god Shiva sent the Ganges River,
represented by the natural cleft in the rock, to earth, thereby
ending the drought (see "A Closer Look," page 313). Bhagiratha is
shown standing in frigid waters while staring directly at the sun
through his parted fingers, standing for interminable periods on

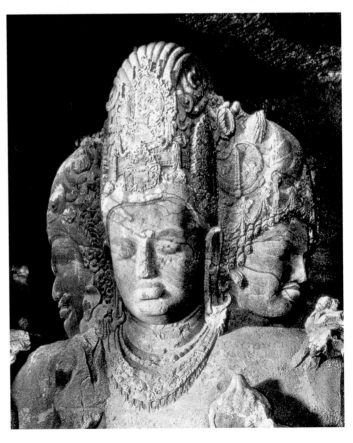

9-21 • ETERNAL SHIVA
Rock-cut relief in the cave-temple of Shiva, Elephanta.
Mid 6th century CE. Height approx. 11′ (3.4 m).

one foot, and in deep prayer before a temple. In the upper left part of the relief, Shiva, shown four-armed, appears before Bhagiratha to grant his wish. Elsewhere in the relief, animal families are depicted, generally in mutually protective roles.

This richly carved relief was executed under the Pallava dynasty, which flourished in southeastern India from the seventh to ninth century CE. It very likely serves as a visual allegory for the benevolent king, who protects his people, perhaps specifically by providing canals to control water, a notion reinforced by the relief carved in a cave-temple on the same boulder, to the left of the Descent relief. It shows the god Krishna protecting his people from a deluge by raising a mountain to serve as a sort of natural umbrella. Themes relating to water are particularly appropriate to Mamallapuram, situated on the Bay of Bengal and possibly serving as a port for the Pallavas.

THE EARLY SOUTHERN TEMPLE

The coastal city of Mamallapuram was also a major temple site under the Pallavas. Along the shore are many large granite boulders and cliffs, and from these the Pallava-period stonecutters carved entire temples as well as reliefs such as the one discussed in "A Closer Look," opposite. Among the most interesting of these rock-cut temples is a group known as the Five Rathas, which preserve diverse early architectural styles that probably reflect the forms of contemporary wood or brick structures that have long since disappeared.

DHARMARAJA RATHA AT MAMALLAPURAM. One of this group, called today the Dharmaraja Ratha, epitomizes the early southern-style temple (FIG. 9–22). Although strikingly different in appearance from the northern style, it uses the same symbolism to link the heavens and earth and it, too, is based on a *mandala*. The temple, square in plan, remains unfinished, and the *garbhagriha* usually found inside was never hollowed out, suggesting that, like cave-temples, Dharmaraja Ratha was executed from the top downward. On the lower portion, only the columns and niches have been carved. The use of a single deity in each niche forecasts the main trend in temple sculpture in the centuries ahead: The tradition of narrative reliefs declined, and the stories they told became concentrated in statues of individual deities, which conjure up entire mythological episodes through characteristic poses and a few symbolic objects.

Southern- and northern-style temples are most clearly distinguished by their superstructures. The Dharmaraja Ratha does not culminate in the paraboloid of the northern *shikhara* but in a pyramidal tower. Each story of the superstructure is articulated by a cornice and carries a row of miniature shrines. Both shrines and cornices are decorated with a window motif from which faces peer. The shrines not only demarcate each story, but also provide loftiness for this palace intended to enshrine a god. Crowning the superstructure is a dome-shaped octagonal capstone quite different from the *amalaka* of the northern style.

During the centuries that followed, both northern- and southern-style temples developed into complex, monumental forms, but their basic structure and symbolism remained the same as those we have seen in these simple, early examples at Deogarh and Mamallapuram.

THE EIGHTH THROUGH THE FOURTEENTH CENTURIES

During the eighth through the fourteenth centuries, regional styles developed in the realms of the dynasties ruling kingdoms that were generally smaller than the Maurya and Kushan empires. Some dynasties were relatively long-lived, such as the Pallavas and Cholas in the south and the Palas in the northeast. Although Buddhism remained strong in a few areas—notably under the Palas—it generally declined, while the Hindu gods Vishnu, Shiva, and the Great Goddess (mainly Durga) grew increasingly popular. Monarchs rivaled each other in the building of temples to their favored deity, and many complicated and subtle variations of the Hindu temple emerged with astounding rapidity in different regions. By around 1000 the Hindu temple reached unparalleled heights of grandeur and engineering.

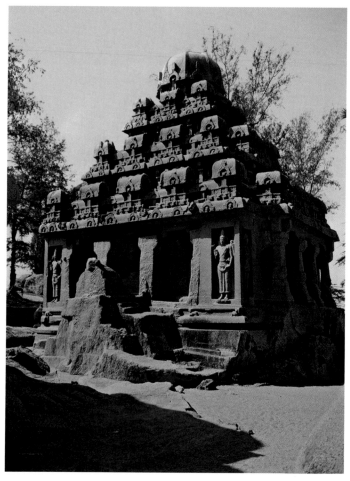

9-22 • DHARMARAJA RATHA, MAMALLAPURAM
Tamil Nadu, India. Pallava period, c. mid 7th century CE.

"Descent of the Ganges" Relief

Rock-cut relief, Mamallapuram, Tamil Nadu, India.
Pallava period, c. mid 7th century CE. Granite, height approx. 20' (6 m).

Unfinished cave. Beyond it, on the same rock formation, is the Krishna Cave.

Unfinished portion of the relief suggesting work from the top downward, as at other Mamallapuram monuments.

Shiva offering boon to Bhagiratha.

Bhagiratha meditating in front of a temple.

Bhagiratha gazing directly at the sun.

A cat imitating the penance of Bhagiratha, a whimsical touch by the artist.

A family of elephants, the bull elephant in front protecting his young elephant, probably a metaphor for the king's protection of his people.

SEE MORE: View the Closer Look feature for the "Descent of the Ganges" relief at Mamallapuram
www.myartslab.com

THE MONUMENTAL NORTHERN TEMPLE

The Kandariya Mahadeva, a temple dedicated to Shiva at Khajuraho, in central India, was probably built by a ruler of the Chandella dynasty in the late tenth or early eleventh century **(FIG. 9–23)**. Khajuraho was the capital and main temple site for the Chandellas, who constructed more than 80 temples there, about 25 of which are well preserved. The Kandariya Mahadeva

Temple is in the northern style, with a curvilinear *shikhara* rising over its *garbhagriha*. Larger, more extensively ornamented, and expanded through the addition of halls on the front and porches to the sides and back, the temple seems at first glance to have little in common with its precursor at Deogarh (SEE FIG. 9–18). Actually, however, the basic elements and their symbolism remain unchanged.

Shiva Nataraja of the Chola Dynasty

Perhaps no sculpture is more representative of Hinduism than the statues of Shiva Nataraja, or Dancing Shiva, a form perfected by sculptors under the royal patronage of the south Indian Chola dynasty in the late tenth to eleventh century. (For the architecture and painting of the period, SEE FIGS. 9–25, 9–26.) The dance of Shiva is a dance of cosmic proportions, signifying the universe's cycle of death and rebirth; it is also a dance for each individual, signifying the liberation of the believer through Shiva's compassion. In the iconography of the Nataraja, this sculpture shows Shiva with four arms dancing on the prostrate body of Apasmara, a dwarf figure who symbolizes "becoming" and whom Shiva controls. Shiva's extended left hand holds a ball of fire; a circle of fire rings the god. The fire is emblematic of the destruction of *samsara* and the physical universe as well as the destruction of *maya* (illusion) and our ego-centered perceptions. Shiva's back right hand holds a drum; its beat represents the irrevocable rhythms of creation and destruction, birth and death. His front right arm gestures the "have no fear" *mudra* (see "Mudras," page 304). The front left arm, gracefully stretched across his body with the hand pointing to his raised foot, signifies the promise of liberation.

The artist has rendered the complex pose with great clarity. The central axis, which aligns the nose, navel, and insole of the weight-bearing foot, maintains the figure's equilibrium while the remaining limbs asymmetrically extend far to each side. Shiva wears a short loincloth, a ribbon tied above his waist, and delicately tooled ornaments. The scant clothing reveals his perfected form with its broad shoulders tapering to a supple waist. The jewelry is restrained and the detail does not detract from the beauty of the body.

The deity does not appear self-absorbed and introspective as he did in the Eternal Shiva relief at Elephanta (SEE FIG. 9–21). He turns to face the viewer, appearing lordly and aloof yet fully aware of his benevolent role as he generously displays himself for the devotee. Like the Sarnath Gupta Buddha (SEE FIG. 9–15), the Chola Shiva Nataraja presents a characteristically Indian synthesis

of the godly and the human, this time expressing the *bhakti* belief in the importance of an intimate relationship with a lordly god through whose compassion one is saved. The earlier Hindu emphasis on ritual and the depiction of the heroic feats of the gods is subsumed into the all-encompassing, humanizing factor of grace.

The fervent religious devotion of the *bhakti* movement was fueled by the sublime writings of a series of poet-saints who lived in the south of India. One of them, Appar, who lived from the late sixth to mid seventh century CE, wrote this vision of the Shiva Nataraja. The ash the poem refers to is one of many symbols associated with the deity.

In penance for having lopped off one of the five heads of Brahma, the first created being, Shiva smeared his body with ashes and went about as a beggar.

> If you could see
> the arch of his brow,
> the budding smile
> on lips red as the kovvai fruit,
> cool matted hair,
> the milk-white ash on coral skin,
> and the sweet golden foot
> raised up in dance,
> then even human birth on this wide earth
> would become a thing worth having.

(Translated by Indira Vishvanathan Peterson)

SHIVA NATARAJA
From Thanjavur, Tamil Nadu. Chola dynasty, 12th century CE. Bronze, height 32″ (81.25 cm). National Museum of India, New Delhi.

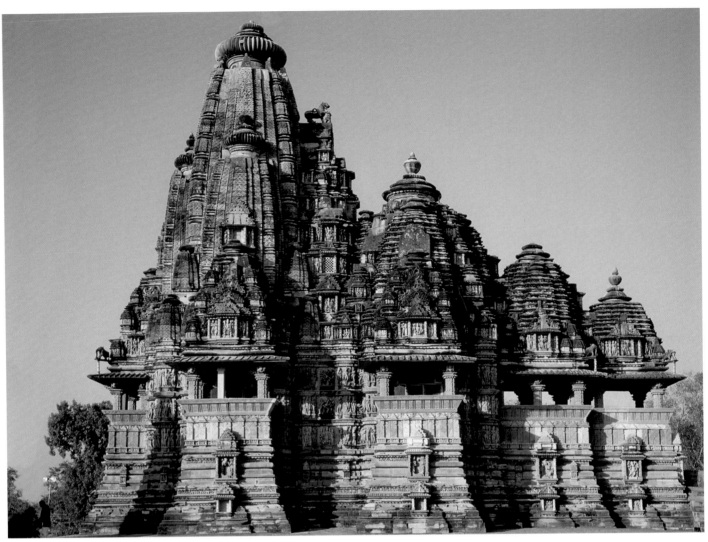

9-23 • KANDARIYA MAHADEVA TEMPLE, KHAJURAHO
Madhya Pradesh, India. Chandella dynasty, c. 1000 CE.

As at Deogarh, the temple rests on a stone terrace that sets off a sacred space from the mundane world. A steep flight of stairs at the front (to the right in the illustration) leads to a series of three halls, called **mandapas** (distinguished on the outside by pyramidal roofs), preceding the *garbhagriha*. The *mandapas* serve as spaces for ritual, such as dances performed for the deity, and for the presentation of offerings. The temple is built of stone blocks using only post-and-lintel construction. Because vault and arch techniques are not used, the interior spaces are not large.

The exterior has a strong sculptural presence, its massiveness suggesting a "cosmic mountain" composed of ornately carved stone. The *shikhara* rises more than 100 feet over the *garbhagriha* and is crowned by a small *amalaka*. The *shikhara* is bolstered by the many smaller *shikhara* motifs bundled around it. This decorative scheme adds a complex richness to the surface, but it also obscures the shape of the main *shikhara*, which is slender, with a swift and impetuous upward movement. The roofs of the *mandapas* contribute to the impression of rapid ascent by growing progressively taller as they near the *shikhara*.

Despite its apparent complexity, the temple has a clear structure and unified composition. The towers of the superstructure are separated from the lower portion by strong horizontal moldings and by the open spaces over the *mandapas* and porches. The **moldings** (shaped or sculpted strips) and rows of sculpture adorning the lower part of the temple create a horizontal emphasis that stabilizes the vertical thrust of the superstructure. Three rows of sculpture—some 600 figures—are integrated into the exterior walls. Approximately 3 feet tall and carved in high relief, the sculptures depict gods and goddesses, as well as figures in erotic postures. They are thought to express Shiva's divine bliss, the manifestation of his presence within, and the transformation of one into many.

In addition to its horizontal emphasis, the lower portion of the temple is characterized by a verticality that is created by protruding and receding elements. Their visual impact is similar to that of engaged columns and buttresses, and they account for much of the rich texture of the exterior. The porches, two on each side and one in the back, contribute to the complexity by outwardly expanding the ground plan, yet their bases also

9-24 • EROTIC COUPLES ON WALL OF KANDARIYA MAHADEVA TEMPLE, KHAJURAHO
Height of sculptures approx. 3'3" (1 m).

reinforce the sweeping vertical movements that unify the entire structure.

The Khajuraho temples are especially well known for their numerous erotic sculptures such as those illustrated in **FIGURE 9–24**. These carvings are not placed haphazardly, but rather in a single vertical line at the juncture of the walls enclosing the *garbhagriha* and the last *mandapa*. Their significance is uncertain; perhaps they derive from the amorous couples that adorn temple doorways leading to the *garbhagriha*. Such couples are found on some early temples such as the Deogarh temple as well as on Buddhist rock-cut sanctuaries such as the one at Karle, serving as reminders that devotion to god resembles the passion of love.

THE MONUMENTAL SOUTHERN TEMPLE

The Cholas, who succeeded the Pallavas in the mid ninth century, founded a dynasty that governed most of the far south well into the late thirteenth century. The Chola dynasty reached its peak during the reign of Rajaraja I (r. 985–1014). As an expression of gratitude for his many victories in battle, Rajaraja built the Rajarajeshvara Temple to Shiva in his capital, Thanjavur (formerly known as Tanjore). The name Rajarajeshvara means the temple of Rajaraja's Lord, that is, Shiva. Commonly called the Brihadeshvara (the temple of the Great Lord), this temple is a remarkable achievement of the southern style of Hindu architecture **(FIG. 9–25)**. It stands within a huge, walled compound near the banks of the Kaveri River. Although smaller shrines dot the compound, the Rajarajeshvara dominates the area.

Clarity of design, a formal balance of parts, and refined décor contribute to the Rajarajeshvara's majesty. Rising to an astonishing height of 216 feet, this temple was probably the tallest structure in India in its time. Like the contemporaneous Kandariya Mahadeva Temple at Khajuraho, the Rajarajeshvara has a longitudinal axis and greatly expanded dimensions, especially with regard to its superstructure. Typical of the southern style, the *mandapa* at the front of the Rajarajeshvara has a flat roof, as opposed to the pyramidal roofs of the northern style. The walls of the sanctum rise for two

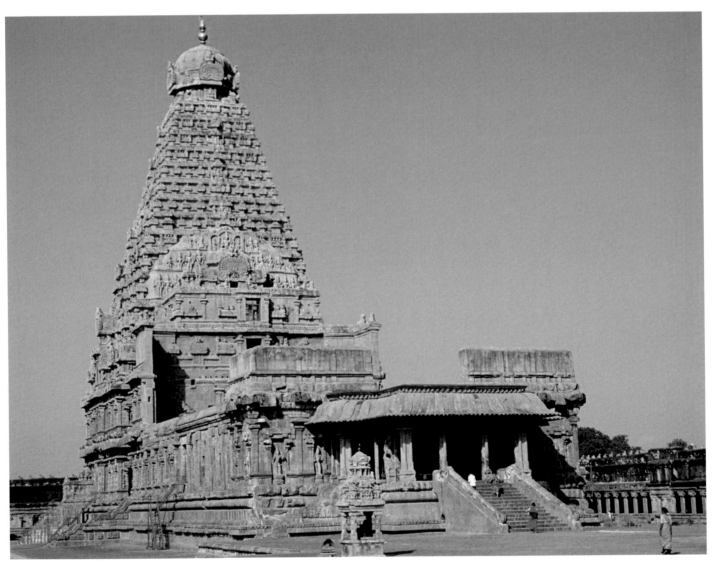

9-25 • RAJARAJESHVARA TEMPLE OF SHIVA, THANJAVUR
Tamil Nadu, India. Chola Dynasty, 1003–1010 CE.

stories, with each story emphatically articulated by a large cornice. The exterior walls are ornamented with niches, each of which holds a single statue, usually depicting a form of Shiva. The clear, regular, and wide spacing of the niches imparts a calm balance and formality to the lower portion of the temple, in marked contrast to the irregular, concave-convex rhythms of the northern style.

The superstructure of the Rajarajeshvara is a four-sided, hollow pyramid that rises for 13 stories. Each story is decorated with miniature shrines, window motifs, and robust dwarf figures who seem to be holding up the next story. Because these sculptural elements are not large in the overall scale of the superstructure, they appear well integrated into the surface and do not obscure the thrusting shape. This is quite different from the effect of the small shikhara motifs on the superstructure of the Kandariya Mahadeva Temple (SEE FIG. 9–23). Notice also that in the earlier southern style, as embodied in the Dharmaraja Ratha (SEE FIG. 9–22), the shrines on the temple superstructure were much larger in proportion to the whole and thus each appeared to be nearly as prominent as the superstructure's overall shape.

Because the Rajarajeshvara superstructure is not obscured by its decorative motifs, it forcefully ascends skyward. At the top is an octagonal dome-shaped capstone similar to the one that crowned the earlier southern-style temple. This huge capstone is exactly the same size as the garbhagriha housed 13 stories directly below. It thus evokes the shrine a final time before the eye ascends to the point separating the worldly from the cosmic sphere above.

9-26 • RAJARAJA I AND HIS TEACHER
Detail of a wall painting in the Rajarajeshvara Temple to Shiva. Chola dynasty, c. 1010 CE.

THE BHAKTI MOVEMENT IN ART

Throughout this period, two major religious movements were developing that affected Hindu practice and its art: the Tantric, or Esoteric, and the *bhakti*, or devotional. Although both movements evolved throughout India, the influence of Tantric sects appeared during this period primarily in the art of the north (see Chapter 23 for a discussion of their continued development), while the *bhakti* movements found artistic expression in the south as well as the north.

The *bhakti* devotional movement was based on ideas expressed in ancient texts, especially the *Bhagavad-Gita*. *Bhakti* revolves around the ideal relationship between humans and deities. According to *bhakti*, it is the gods who create *maya* (illusion), in which we are all trapped. They also reveal truth to those who truly love them and whose minds are open to them. Rather than focusing on ritual and the performance of *dharma* according to the Vedas, *bhakti* stresses an intimate, personal, and loving relation with the god, and complete devotion and surrender to the deity. Inspired and influenced by *bhakti*, Indian artists produced some of South Asia's most interesting works, among them the few remaining mural paintings and the famous bronze works of sculpture (see "Shiva Nataraja of the Chola Dynasty," page 314).

WALLPAINTING AT RAJARAJESHVARA TEMPLE. Rajaraja's building of the Rajarajeshvara was in part a reflection of the fervent Shiva *bhakti* movement which had reached its peak by that time. The corridors of the circumambulatory passages around the *garbhagriha* were originally adorned with wall paintings. Overpainted later, they were only recently rediscovered. One painting apparently depicts the ruler Rajaraja himself, not as a warrior or majestic king on his throne, but as a simple mendicant humbly standing behind his religious teacher (**FIG. 9–26**). With his white beard and dark skin, the aged teacher contrasts with the youthful, bronze-skinned king. The position of the two suggests that the king treats the saintly teacher, who in the devotee's or *bhakta*'s view is equated with god, with intimacy and respect. Both figures allude to their devotion to Shiva by holding a small flower as an offering, and both emulate Shiva in their appearance by wearing their hair in the "ascetic locks" of Shiva in his Great Yogi aspect.

The portrayal does not represent individuals so much as a contrast of types: the old and the youthful, the teacher and the devotee, the saint and the king—the highest religious and worldly models, respectively—united as followers of Shiva. Line is the essence of the painting. With strength and grace, the even, skillfully executed line defines the boldly simple forms and features. With less shading and fewer details, these figures are flattened, more linear versions of those in the earlier paintings at Ajanta (SEE FIG. 9–17). A cool, sedate calm infuses the monumental figures, but the power of line also invigorates them with a sense of strength and inner life.

The *bhakti* movement spread during the ensuing centuries into northern India. However, during this period a new religious culture penetrated the subcontinent: Turkic peoples, Persians, and Afghans had been crossing the northwest passes into India since the tenth century, bringing with them Islam and its artistic tradition. New religious forms eventually evolved from Islam's long and complex interaction with the peoples of the subcontinent, and so too arose uniquely Indian forms of Islamic art, adding yet another dimension to India's artistic heritage.

ART OF SOUTHEAST ASIA

Trade and cultural exchange, notably by the sea routes linking China and India, brought Buddhism, Hinduism, and other aspects of India's civilization to the various regions of Southeast Asia and the Asian archipelago. Although Theravada Buddhism (see "Buddhism," page 297) had the most lasting impact in the region, other trends in Buddhism, including Mahayana and esoteric (tantric) traditions, also played a role. Elements of Hinduism, including its epic literature, were also adopted.

THAILAND—PRAKHON CHAI STYLE. Even the earliest major flowering of Buddhist art in eighth- and ninth-century Southeast Asia was characterized by distinctly local interpretations of the inheritance from India. For example, a strikingly beautiful style of Buddhist sculpture in Thailand, one with distinct iconographic elements, has been identified based on the 1964 discovery of a hoard of images in an underground burial chamber in the vicinity of Prakhon Chai, Buriram Province, near the present-day border with Cambodia. Distinguished by exquisite craftsmanship and a charming naturalism, enhanced by inlaid materials for the eyes, a standing figure of the bodhisattva Maitreya (FIG. 9–27) exemplifies the lithe and youthful proportions typical of the Prakhon Chai style. The iconography departs from the princely interpretation of

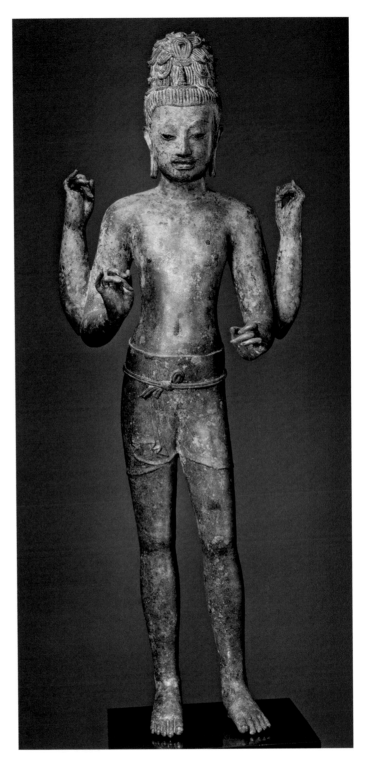

9-27 • BUDDHA MAITREYA
From Buriram Province, Thailand. 8th century CE. Copper alloy with inlaid black glass eyes, 38″ (96.5 cm). Asia Society, New York. Mr. and Mrs. John D. Rockefeller 3rd Collection, 1979.063

the Buddha, presenting instead ascetic elements—abbreviated clothing and a loose arrangement of long hair. The esoteric (tantric) associations of these features are further emphasized by the multiple forearms, an element that was highly developed in Hindu sculpture and which came to be common in Esoteric Buddhist art.

9-29 • PLAN OF BOROBUDUR

9-28 • BUDDHA SHAKYAMUNI
From Thailand. Mon Dvaravati period, 9th century CE. Sandstone. Norton Simon Museum, Los Angeles.

THAILAND—DVARAVATI STYLE. The Dvaravati kingdom, of Mon people, flourished in central Thailand from at least the sixth to the eleventh century. This kingdom embraced Theravada Buddhism and produced some of the earliest Buddhist images in Southeast Asia, perhaps based on Gupta-period Indian models. During the later centuries, Dvaravati sculptors restated elements of the Gupta style (SEE FIG. 9–15), and introduced Mon characteristics into classical forms inherited from India (FIG. 9–28).

JAVA—BOROBUDUR. The most monumental of Buddhist sites in Southeast Asia is **BOROBUDUR (FIGS. 9–29, 9–30)** in central Java, an island of Indonesia. Built about 800 CE and rising more than 100 feet from ground level, this stepped pyramid of volcanic-stone blocks is surmounted by a large stupa, itself ringed by 72 smaller openwork stupas. Probably commissioned to celebrate the Buddhist merit of the Shailendra dynasty rulers, the monument expresses a complex range of Mahayana symbolism, incorporating earthly and cosmic realms. Jataka tales and scenes from the Buddha's life are elaborately narrated in the reliefs of the lower galleries (FIG. 9–31), and more than 500 sculptures of transcendental buddhas on the balustrades and upper terraces complete the monument, conceived as a *mandala* in three dimensions.

CAMBODIA—ANGKOR VAT. In Cambodia, Khmer kings ruled at Angkor for more than 400 years, from the ninth to the thirteenth century. Among the state temples, Buddhist as well as Hindu, they built **ANGKOR VAT (FIG. 9–32)**, the crowning achievement of Khmer architecture. Angkor had already been the site of royal capitals of the Khmer, who had for centuries vested temporal as well as spiritual authority in their kings, long before King Suryavarman II (r. 1113–1150) began to build the royal complex known today as Angkor Vat. Dedicated to the worship of Vishnu, the vast array of structures is both a temple and a symbolic cosmic mountain. The complex incorporates a stepped pyramid with five towers set within four enclosures of increasing perimeter. Suryavarman's predecessors had associated themselves with Hindu and Buddhist deities at Angkor by building sacred structures. His

9-30 • BOROBUDUR
Central Java, Indonesia. c. 800 CE.

SEE MORE: View a video about Borobudur **www.myartslab.com**

9-31 • MAYA RIDING TO LUMBINI
Detail of a narrative relief sculpture, Borobudur.

9–32 • ANGKOR VAT
Angkor, Cambodia. 12th century CE.

SEE MORE: View a video about Angkor Vat **www.myartslab.com**

9–33 • VISHNU CHURNING THE OCEAN OF MILK
Detail of relief sculpture, Angkor Vat.

9-34 • PARINIRVANA OF THE BUDDHA
Gal Vihara, near Polonnaruwa, Sri Lanka. 11th–12th century CE. Stone.

construction pairs him with Vishnu to affirm his royal status as well as his ultimate destiny of union with the Hindu god. Low-relief sculptures illustrate scenes from the *Ramayana*, the *Mahabharata*, and other Hindu texts (**FIG. 9–33**), and also depict Suryavarman with his armies.

SRI LANKA. Often considered a link to Southeast Asia, the island of Sri Lanka is so close to India's southeastern coast that Ashoka's son is said to have brought Buddhism there within his father's lifetime. Sri Lanka played a major role in the strengthening of Theravada traditions, especially by preserving scriptures and relics, and it became a focal point for the Theravada Buddhist world. Sri Lankan sculptors further refined Indian styles and iconography in colossal Buddhist sculptures. The rock-cut Parinirvana of the Buddha at Gal Vihara (**FIG. 9–34**) is one of three colossal Buddhas at the site. This serene and dignified image restates one of the early themes of Buddhist art, that of the Buddha's final transcendence, with a sophistication of modeling and proportion that updates and localizes the classical Buddhist tradition.

THINK ABOUT IT

9.1 Describe the typical form of Indian temples. Contrast the stupa and the temple directly, paying attention to specific building features, such as the superstructure.

9.2 Angkor Vat in Cambodia draws both religious and architectural influence from the Indian subcontinent. Explain what the Khmer architects in Cambodia took from India, with reference to specific religious architectural forms borrowed.

9.3 How does architecture in India and Southeast Asia express a view of the world, even the cosmos?

9.4 Select one architectural work from the chapter, and explain how either Buddhist or Hindu stories are told through its decoration.

9.5 What are some distinguishing features of representations of Buddha?

PRACTICE MORE: Compose answers to these questions, get flashcards for images and terms, and review chapter material with quizzes
www.myartslab.com

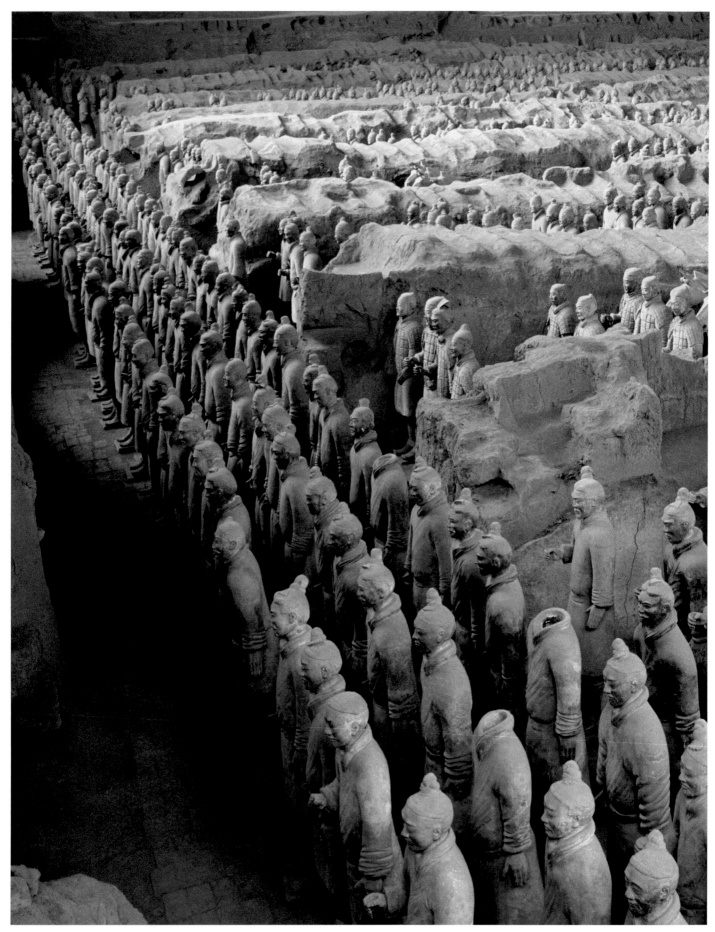

10-1 • SOLDIERS From the mausoleum of Emperor Shihuangdi, Lintong, Shaanxi. Qin dynasty, c. 210 BCE. Earthenware, life-size.

CHINESE AND KOREAN ART BEFORE 1279

As long as anyone could remember, the huge mound in China's Shaanxi Province in northern China had been part of the landscape. No one dreamed that an astonishing treasure lay beneath the surface until one day in 1974 peasants digging a well accidentally brought to light the first hint of riches. When archaeologists began to excavate, they were stunned by what they found: a vast underground army of some 8,000 life-size terra-cotta soldiers with 100 life-size ceramic horses standing in military formation, facing east, supplied with weapons, and ready for battle (FIG. 10–1). For more than 2,000 years, while the tumultuous history of China unfolded overhead, they had guarded the tomb of Emperor Shihuangdi, the ruthless ruler who first united the states of China into an empire, the Qin.

In ongoing excavations at the site, additional bronze carriages and horses were found, further evidence of the technology and naturalism achieved by artisans during Qin Shihuangdi's reign. The tomb mound itself has not been excavated.

China has had a long-standing fascination with antiquity, but archaeology is a relatively young discipline there. Only since the 1920s have scholars methodically dug into the layers of history at thousands of sites across the country, yet so much has been unearthed that ancient Chinese history has been rewritten many times.

The archaeological record shows that Chinese civilization arose several millennia ago, and was distinctive for its early advances in ceramics and metalwork, as well as for the elaborate working of jade. Early use of the potter's wheel, mastery of reduction firing, and the early invention of high-fired stoneware and porcelain distinguish the technological advancement of Chinese ceramics. Highly imaginative bronze castings and proficient techniques of mold making characterize early Chinese metalworking. Early attainments in jade reflect a technological competence with rotary tools and abrasive techniques, and a passion for the subtleties of shape, proportion, and surface texture.

Archaeology has supplemented our understanding of historically appreciated Chinese art forms. These explored human relationships and heroic ideals, exemplifying Confucian values and teaching the standards of conduct that underlie social order. Later, China also came to embrace the Buddhist tradition from India. In princely representations of Buddhist divinities and in sublime and powerful, but often meditative, figures of the Buddha, China's artists presented the divine potential of the human condition. Perhaps the most distinguished Chinese tradition is the presentation of philosophical ideals through the theme of landscape. Paintings simply in black ink, depictions of mountains and water, became the ultimate artistic medium for expressing the vastness, abundance, and endurance of the universe.

Chinese civilization radiated its influence throughout east Asia. Chinese learning repeatedly stimulated the growth of culture in Korea, which in turn transmitted influence to Japan.

LEARN ABOUT IT

10.1 Examine the interaction of art and ritual in early periods of Chinese and Korean history.

10.2 Discuss the development of Confucian philosophy and its impact on the pictorial art of China.

10.3 Analyze the Daoist elements in early landscape motifs of China.

10.4 Assess the introduction and spread of Buddhism, and its adherents as patrons (including the court) in both China and Korea.

10.5 Discuss the development of naturalistic depiction and the achievement of verisimilitude in both landscapes and figures in the painting and sculpture of China before 1279.

HEAR MORE: Listen to an audio file of your chapter **www.myartslab.com**

THE MIDDLE KINGDOM

Among the cultures of the world, China is distinguished by its long, uninterrupted development, now traced back some 8,000 years. From Qin, pronounced "chin," comes our name for the country that the Chinese call the Middle Kingdom, the country in the center of the world. Present-day China occupies a large landmass in the center of Asia, covering an area slightly larger than the continental United States. Within its borders lives one-fifth of the human race.

The historical and cultural heart of China is the land watered by its three great rivers, the Yellow, the Yangzi, and the Xi (MAP 10–1). The Qinling Mountains divide Inner China into north and south, regions with strikingly different climates, cultures, and historical fates. In the south, the Yangzi River flows through lush green hills to the fertile plains of the delta. Along the southern coastline, rich with natural harbors, arose China's port cities, the focus of a vast maritime trading network. The Yellow River, nicknamed "China's Sorrow" because of its disastrous floods, winds through the north. The north country is a dry land of steppe and desert, hot in the summer and lashed by cold winds in the winter. Over its vast and vulnerable frontier have come the nomadic invaders that are a recurring theme in Chinese history, but caravans and emissaries from Central Asia, India, Persia, and, eventually, Europe also crossed this border.

10-2 • BOWL
From Banpo, near Xi'an, Shaanxi. Neolithic period, Yangshao culture, 5000–4000 BCE. Painted pottery, height 7″ (17.8 cm). Banpo Museum.

NEOLITHIC CULTURES

Early archaeological evidence had led scholars to believe that agriculture, the cornerstone technology of the Neolithic period, made its way to China from the ancient Near East. More recent findings, however, suggest that agriculture based on rice and millet arose independently in east Asia before 5000 BCE and that knowledge of Near Eastern grains followed some 2,000 years later. One of the clearest archaeological signs of Neolithic culture in China is evidence of the vigorous emergence of towns and cities. At Jiangzhai, near modern Xi'an, for example, the foundations of more than 100 dwellings have been discovered surrounding the remains of a community center, a cemetery, and a kiln. Dated to about 4000 BCE, the ruins point to the existence of a highly developed early society. Elsewhere in China, the foundations of the earliest known palace have been uncovered and dated to about 2000 BCE.

PAINTED POTTERY CULTURES

In China, as in other places, distinctive forms of Neolithic pottery identify different cultures. One of the most interesting objects thus far recovered is a shallow red bowl with a turned-out rim (FIG. 10–2). Found in the village of Banpo near the Yellow River, it was crafted sometime between 5000 and 4000 BCE. The bowl is an artifact of the Yangshao culture, one of the most important of the so-called Painted Pottery cultures of Neolithic China. Although the potter's wheel had not yet been developed, the bowl is perfectly round and its surfaces are highly polished, bearing witness to a distinctly advanced technology. The decorations are especially intriguing. The marks on the rim may be evidence of the beginnings of writing in China, which was fully developed by the time the first definitive examples appear during the second millennium BCE, in the later Bronze Age.

Inside the bowl, a pair of stylized fish suggests that fishing was an important activity for the villagers. The image between the two fish represents a human face with four more fish, one on each side. Although there is no certain interpretation of the image, it may be a depiction of an ancestral figure who could assure an abundant catch, for the worship of ancestors and nature spirits was a fundamental element of later Chinese beliefs.

LIANGZHU CULTURE

Banpo lies near the great bend in the Yellow River, in the area traditionally regarded as the cradle of Chinese civilization, but archaeological finds have revealed that Neolithic cultures arose over a far broader area. Recent excavations in sites more than 800 miles away, near Hangzhou Bay, in the southeastern coastal region, have turned up human and animal images—often masks or faces—more than 5,000 years old (FIG. 10–3). Large, round eyes, a flat nose, and a rectangular mouth protrude slightly from the background pattern of wirelike lines. Above the forehead, a second, smaller face grimaces from under a huge headdress. The upper face may be human, perhaps riding the animal figure below. The image is one of eight that were carved in low relief on the outside of a large jade **cong**, an object resembling a cylindrical tube encased in

MAP 10-1 • CHINA AND KOREA

The map shows the borders of contemporary China and Korea. Bright-colored areas indicate the extent of China's Han dynasty (206 BCE–221 CE).

**10-3 • DETAIL OF MASK DECORATION
ON A JADE *CONG***

Neolithic period, Liangzhu culture, 3200–2200 BCE.

10-4 • CONG

Neolithic period, Liangzhu culture, 3200–2200 BCE. Jade, height 1⅞ × width 2⅝″ (5 × 6.6 cm). Shanghai Museum.

The *cong* is one of the most prevalent and mysterious of early Chinese jade shapes. Originating in the Neolithic period, it continued to play a prominent role in burials through the Shang and Zhou dynasties. Many experts believe the *cong* was connected with the practice of contacting the spirit world. They suggest that the circle symbolized heaven; the square, earth; and the hollow, the axis connecting these two realms.

a rectangular block. Another *cong* **(FIG. 10–4)** also from Liangzhu bears a beautiful finish and similar delineated mask motifs. These were found near the remains of persons buried with what appear to be sets of numerous jade objects.

The intricacy of the carving shows the technical sophistication of this jade-working culture, named the Liangzhu, which seems to have emerged around 3300 BCE. Jade, a stone cherished by the Chinese throughout their history, is extremely hard and is difficult to carve. Liangzhu artists must have used sand as an abrasive to slowly grind the stone down; modern artisans marvel at how they produced such fine work.

The meaning of the masklike image in FIGURE 10–3 is open to interpretation. Its combination of human and animal features seems to show how the ancient Chinese imagined supernatural beings, either deities or dead ancestors. Similar masks later formed the primary decorative motif of Bronze Age ritual objects. Still later, Chinese historians began referring to the ancient mask motif as **taotie**, but the motif's original meaning had already been lost. The jade carving here seems to be a forerunner of this most central and mysterious image.

BRONZE AGE CHINA

China entered its Bronze Age in the second millennium BCE. As with agriculture, scholars at first theorized that the technology had been imported from the Near East. Archaeological evidence now makes clear, however, that bronze casting using the **piece-mold casting** technique arose independently in China, where it attained an un-paralleled level of excellence (see "Piece-Mold Casting," opposite).

SHANG DYNASTY

Traditional Chinese histories tell of three Bronze Age dynasties: the Xia, the Shang, and the Zhou. Experts at one time tended to dismiss the Xia and Shang as legendary, but twentieth-century archaeological discoveries fully established the historical existence of the Shang (c. 1700–1100 BCE) and point strongly to the historical existence of the Xia as well.

Shang kings ruled from a succession of capitals in the Yellow River Valley, where archaeologists have found walled cities, palaces, and vast royal tombs. Their state was surrounded by numerous other states—some rivals, others clients—and their culture spread widely. Society seems to have been highly stratified, with a ruling group that had the bronze technology needed to make weapons. They maintained their authority in part by claiming power as intermediaries between the supernatural and human realms. The chief Shang deity, Shangdi, may have been a sort of "Great Ancestor." It is thought that nature and fertility spirits were also honored, and that regular sacrifices were thought necessary to keep the spirits of dead ancestors vital so that they might help the living.

Shang priests communicated with the supernatural world through oracle bones. An animal bone or piece of tortoiseshell was inscribed with a question and heated until it cracked, then the crack was interpreted as an answer. Oracle bones, many of which have been recovered and deciphered, contain the earliest known form of Chinese writing, a script fully recognizable as the ancestor of the system still in use today (see "Chinese Characters," page 331).

RITUAL BRONZES.   Shang tombs reveal a warrior culture of great splendor and violence. Many humans and animals were sacrificed to accompany the deceased. In one tomb, for example, chariots were found with the skeletons of their horses and drivers; in another, dozens of human skeletons lined the approaches to the central burial chamber. The tombs contain hundreds of jade, ivory, and lacquer objects, gold and silver ornaments, and bronze vessels. The enormous scale of Shang burials illustrates the great wealth of the civilization and the power of a ruling class able to consign such great quantities of treasure to the earth, and also suggests this culture's reverence for the dead.

Bronze vessels are the most admired and studied of Shang artifacts. Like oracle bones and jade objects, they were connected with ritual practices, serving as containers for offerings of food and wine. A basic repertoire of about 30 shapes evolved. Some shapes derive from earlier pottery forms, while others seem to reproduce wooden containers. Still others are highly sculptural and take the form of fantastic composite animals.

One functional shape, the **fang ding**, a rectangular vessel with four legs, was used for food offerings. Early examples (see "Piece-Mold Casting," oppposite) featured decoration of raised bosses and mask-like (*taotie*) motifs in horizontal registers on the sides and the legs. A late Shang example, one of hundreds of veresels recovered from the royal tombs near the last of the Shang capitals, Yin

TECHNIQUE | Piece-mold Casting

The early piece-mold technique for bronze casting is different from the lost-wax process developed in the ancient Mediterranean and Near East. Although we do not know the exact steps ancient Chinese artists followed, we can deduce the general procedure for casting a vessel.

First, a model of the bronze-to-be was made of clay and dried. Then, to create a mold, damp clay was pressed onto the model; after the clay mold dried, it was cut away in pieces, which were keyed for later reassembly and then fired. The original model itself was shaved down to serve as the core for the mold. After this, the pieces of the mold were reassembled around the core and held in place by bronze spacers, which locked the core in position and ensured an even casting space around the core. The reassembled mold was then covered with another layer of clay, and a sprue, or pouring duct, was cut into the clay to receive the molten metal. A riser duct may also have been cut to allow the hot gases to escape. Molten bronze was then poured into the mold. When the metal cooled, the mold was broken apart to reveal a bronze copy of the original clay model. Finely cast relief decoration could be worked into the model or carved into the sectional molds, or both. Finally, the vessel could be burnished—a long process that involved scouring the surface with increasingly fine abrasives.

The vessel shown here is a *fang ding*. A *ding* is a ceremonial cooking vessel used in Shang rituals and buried in Shang tombs. The Zhou people also made, used, and buried *ding* vessels.

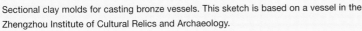

Sectional clay molds for casting bronze vessels. This sketch is based on a vessel in the Zhengzhou Institute of Cultural Relics and Archaeology.

(present-day Anyang), is extraordinary for its size. Weighing nearly 2,000 pounds, it is the largest Shang *ding* vessel thus far recovered. In typical Shang style, its surface is decorated with a complex array of images based on animal forms, including *taotie* masks, confronting horned animals (dragons?) and composite beaked animals (birds?). A ritual pouring vessel, called a *guang* (FIG. 10–5), shows a highly sculptural rendition of animal forms. The pouring spout and cover are modeled as the head and body of a tiger, while the rear portion of the vessel and cover is conceived as an owl. Overall geometric decoration combines with suggestive zoomorphic forms. Such images seem to be related to the hunting life of the Shang, but their deeper significance is unknown. Sometimes strange, sometimes fearsome, Shang creatures seem always to have a sense of mystery, evoking the Shang attitude toward the supernatural world.

ZHOU DYNASTY

Around 1100 BCE, the Shang were conquered by the Zhou from western China. During the Zhou dynasty (1100–221 BCE) a feudal society developed, with nobles related to the king ruling over numerous small states. (Zhou nobility are customarily ranked in English by such titles as duke and marquis.) The supreme deity became known as Tian, or Heaven, and the king ruled as the Son of Heaven. Later Chinese ruling dynasties continued to follow the belief that imperial rule emanated from a mandate from Heaven.

The first 300 years of this longest-lasting Chinese dynasty were generally stable and peaceful. In 771 BCE, however, the Zhou suffered defeat in the west at the hands of a nomadic tribe. Although they quickly established a new capital to the east, their authority had been crippled, and the later Eastern Zhou period was a troubled one. States grew increasingly independent, giving

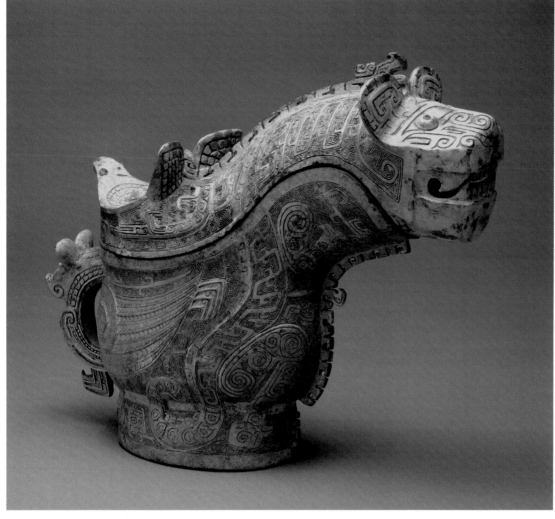

10-5 • COVERED RITUAL WINE-POURING VESSEL (*GUANG*) WITH TIGER AND OWL DÉCOR

Shang dynasty, 13th century BCE. Cast bronze, height with cover 9¾" (25 cm), width including handle 12⅜" (31.5 cm). Arthur M. Sackler Museum, Harvard Art Museum, Cambridge, Massachusetts. Bequest of Grenville L. Winthrop 1943.52.103

the Zhou kings merely nominal allegiance. Smaller states were swallowed up by their larger neighbors. During the time historians call the Spring and Autumn period (722–481 BCE), 10 or 12 states, later reduced to seven, emerged as powers. During the ensuing Warring States period (481–221 BCE) intrigue, treachery, and increasingly ruthless warfare became routine.

Against this background of social turmoil, China's great philosophers arose—such thinkers as Confucius, Laozi, and Mozi. Traditional histories speak of China's "one hundred schools" of philosophy, indicating a shift of focus from the supernatural to the human world. Nevertheless, elaborate burials on an even larger scale than before reflected the continuation of traditional beliefs.

BRONZE BELLS. Ritual bronze objects continued to play an important role during the Zhou dynasty, and new forms developed. One of the most spectacular recent discoveries is a carillon of 65 bronze components, mostly bells arranged in a formation 25 feet long (FIG. 10–6), found in the tomb of Marquis Yi of the state of Zeng. Each bell is precisely calibrated to sound two tones—one when struck at the center, another when struck at a corner. The bells are arranged in scale patterns in a variety of registers, and several musicians would have moved around the carillon, striking the bells in the appointed order.

Music may well have played a part in rituals for communicating with the supernatural, for the *taotie* typically appears on the front and back of each bell. The image is now much more intricate and stylized, partly in response to the refinement available with the lost-wax casting process (see "Lost-Wax Casting," page 413), which had replaced the older piece-mold technique. On the coffin of the marquis are painted guardian warriors with half-human, half-animal attributes. The marquis, who died in 433 BCE, must have considered music important, for among the more than 15,000 objects recovered from his tomb were many musical instruments. Zeng was one of the smallest and shortest-lived states of the Eastern Zhou, but the contents of this tomb, in quantity and quality, attest to the high level of its culture.

Chinese Characters

Each word in Chinese is represented by its own unique symbol, called a character. Some characters originated as **pictographs**, images that mean what they depict. Writing reforms over the centuries have often disguised the resemblance, but if we place modern characters next to their ancestors, the picture comes back into focus:

	water	horse	moon	child	tree	mountain
Ancient	川	馬	月	子	米	山
Modern	水	馬	月	子	木	山

Other characters are **ideographs**, pictures that represent abstract concepts or ideas:

sun	+	moon	=	bright
日		月		明

woman	+	child	=	good
女		子		好

Most characters were formed by combining a radical, which gives the field of meaning, with a phonetic, which originally hinted at pronunciation. For example, words that have to do with water have the character for "water" 水 abbreviated to three strokes 氵 as their radical. Thus "to bathe," 沐 pronounced *mu*, consists of the water radical and the phonetic 木, which by itself means "tree" and is also pronounced *mu*. Here are other "water" characters. Notice that the connection to water is not always literal.

river	sea	weep	pure, clear	extinguish, destroy
河	海	泣	清	滅

These phonetic borrowings took place centuries ago. Many words have shifted in pronunciation, and for this and other reasons there is no way to tell how a character is pronounced or what it means just by looking at it. While at first this may seem like a disadvantage, in the case of Chinese it is advantageous. Spoken Chinese has many dialects. Some are so far apart in sound as to be virtually different languages. But while speakers of different dialects cannot understand each other, they can still communicate through writing, for no matter how they say a word, they write it with the same character. Writing has thus played an important role in maintaining the unity of Chinese civilization through the centuries.

10-6 • SET OF BELLS
From the tomb of Marquis Yi of Zeng, Suixian, Hubei. Zhou dynasty, 433 BCE. Bronze, with bronze and timber frame, frame height 9′ (2.74 m), length 25′ (7.62 m). Hubei Provincial Museum, Wuhan.

THE CHINESE EMPIRE: QIN DYNASTY

Toward the middle of the third century BCE, the state of Qin launched military campaigns that led to its triumph over the other states by 221 BCE. For the first time in its history, China was united under a single ruler. This first emperor of Qin, Shihuangdi, a man of exceptional ability, power, and ruthlessness, was fearful of both assassination and rebellion. Throughout his life, he sought ways to attain immortality. Even before uniting China, he began his own mausoleum at Lintong, in Shaanxi Province. This project continued throughout his life and after his death, until rebellion abruptly ended the dynasty in 206 BCE. Since that time, the mound over the mausoleum has always been visible, but not until an accidental discovery in 1974 was its army of terra-cotta soldiers and horses even imagined (SEE FIG. 10–1). Modeled from clay and then fired, the figures claim a prominent place in the great tradition of Chinese ceramic art. Individualized faces and meticulously rendered uniforms and armor demonstrate the sculptors' skill. Literary sources suggest that the tomb itself, which has not yet been opened, reproduces the world as it was known to the Qin, with stars overhead and rivers and mountains below. Thus did the tomb's architects try literally to ensure that the underworld—the world of souls and spirits—would match the human world.

Qin rule was harsh and repressive. Laws were based on a totalitarian philosophy called legalism, and all other philosophies were banned, their scholars executed, and their books burned. Yet the Qin also established the mechanisms of centralized bureaucracy that molded China both politically and culturally into a single entity. Under the Qin, the country was divided into provinces and prefectures, the writing system and coinage were standardized, roads were built to link different parts of the country with the capital, and battlements on the northern frontier were connected to form the Great Wall. To the present day, China's rulers have followed the administrative framework first laid down by the Qin.

HAN DYNASTY

The commander who overthrew the Qin became the next emperor and founded the Han dynasty (206 BCE–220 CE). During this period the Chinese enjoyed peace, prosperity, and stability. Borders were extended and secured, and Chinese control over strategic stretches of Central Asia led to the opening of the Silk Road, a land route that linked China by trade all the way to Rome. One of the precious goods traded, along with spices, was silk, which had been cultivated and woven in China since at least the third millennium BCE. From as early as the third century BCE, Chinese silk cloth was treasured in Greece and Rome (for more on this topic, see "The Silk Road during the Tang Period," page 342).

PAINTED BANNER FROM CHANGSHA. The early Han dynasty marks the twilight of China's so-called mythocentric age, when people believed in a close relationship between the human and supernatural

10–7 • PAINTED BANNER
From the tomb of the Marquess of Dai, Mawangdui, Changsha, Hunan. Han dynasty, c. 160 BCE. Colors on silk, height 6′8½″ (2.05 m). Hunan Provincial Museum.

worlds. The most elaborate and most intact painting that survives from this time is a T-shaped silk banner, which summarizes this early worldview **(FIG. 10–7)**. Found in the tomb of a noblewoman on the outskirts of present-day Changsha, the banner dates from the second century BCE and is painted with scenes representing three levels of the universe: heaven, earth, and underworld. The pictorial motifs include a portrait of the deceased.

The heavenly realm is shown at the top, in the crossbar of the T. In the upper-right corner is the sun, inhabited by a mythical crow; in the upper left, a mythical toad stands on a crescent moon. Between them is a primordial deity shown as a man with a long serpent's tail—a Han image of the Great Ancestor. Dragons and other celestial creatures swarm below.

A gate guarded by two seated figures stands where the horizontal of heaven meets the banner's long, vertical stem. Two intertwined dragons loop through a circular jade piece known as a **bi**, itself usually a symbol of heaven, dividing this vertical segment into two areas. The portion above the *bi* represents the earthly realm. Here, the deceased woman and three attendants stand on a platform while two kneeling figures offer gifts. The portion beneath the *bi* represents the underworld. Silk draperies and a stone chime hanging from the *bi* form a canopy for the platform below. Like the bronze bells we saw earlier, stone chimes were ceremonial instruments dating from Zhou times. On the platform, ritual bronze vessels contain food and wine for the deceased, just as they did in Shang tombs. The squat, muscular man holding up the platform stands in turn on a pair of fish whose bodies form another *bi*. The fish and the other strange creatures in this section are inhabitants of the underworld.

PHILOSOPHY AND ART

The Han dynasty marked the beginning of a new age. During this dynasty, the philosophical ideals of Daoism and Confucianism, formulated during the troubled times of the Eastern Zhou, became central to Chinese thought. Their influence since then has been continuous and fundamental.

DAOISM AND NATURE.   Daoism emphasizes the close relationship between humans and nature. It is concerned with bringing the individual life into harmony with the Dao, or the Way, of the universe (see "Daoism," page 334). For some a secular, philosophical path, Daoism on a popular level developed into an organized religion, absorbing many traditional folk practices and the search for immortality.

Immortality was as intriguing to Han rulers as it had been to the first emperor of Qin. Daoist adepts experimented with diet, physical exercise, and other techniques in the belief that immortal life could be achieved on earth. Popular Daoist legend told of the Land of Immortals in the Eastern Sea, depicted on a bronze **INCENSE BURNER** from the tomb of Prince Liu Sheng, who died in 113 BCE **(FIG. 10–8)**. Around the bowl, gold inlay outlines the stylized waves of the sea. Above them rises the mountainous island, busy with birds, animals, and the immortals themselves, all cast in bronze with highlights of inlaid gold. Technically, this exquisite piece represents the ultimate development of the long tradition of bronze casting in China.

10–8 • INCENSE BURNER
From the tomb of Prince Liu Sheng, Mancheng, Hebei. Han dynasty, 113 BCE. Bronze with gold inlay, height 10½″ (26 cm). Hebei Provincial Museum, Shijiazhuang.

CONFUCIANISM AND THE STATE.   In contrast to the metaphysical focus of Daoism, Confucianism is concerned with the human world, and its goal is the attainment of equity. To this end, it proposes a system of ethics based on reverence for ancestors and the correct relationships among people. Beginning with self-discipline in the individual, Confucianism teaches how to rectify relationships within the family, and then, in ever-widening circles, with friends and others, all the way up to the level of the emperor and the state (see "Confucius and Confucianism," page 337).

Emphasis on social order and respect for authority made Confucianism especially attractive to Han rulers, who were eager to distance themselves from the disastrous legalism of the Qin. The Han emperor Wudi (r. 141–87 BCE) made Confucianism the official imperial philosophy, and it remained the state ideology of China for more than 2,000 years, until the end of imperial rule in the twentieth century. Once institutionalized, Confucianism took on so many rituals that it too eventually assumed the form and force of a religion. Han philosophers contributed to this process by

Daoism

Daoism is an outlook on life that brings together many ancient ideas regarding humankind and the universe. Its primary text, a slim volume called the *Daodejing* (*The Way and Its Power*), is ascribed to the Chinese philosopher Laozi, who is said to have been a contemporary of Confucius (551–479 BCE). Later, a philosopher named Zhuangzi (369–286 BCE) took up many of the same ideas in a book that is known simply by his name: *Zhuangzi*. Together the two texts formed a body of ideas that crystallized into a school of thought during the Han period.

A *dao* is a way or path. The Dao is the Ultimate Way, the Way of the universe. The Way cannot be named or described, but it can be hinted at. It is like water. Nothing is more flexible and yielding, yet water can wear down the hardest stone. Water flows downward, seeking the lowest ground. Similarly, a Daoist sage seeks a quiet life, humble and hidden, unconcerned with worldly success. The Way is great precisely because it is small. The Way may be nothing, yet nothing turns out to be essential.

To recover the Way, we must unlearn. We must return to a state of nature. To follow the Way, we must practice *wu wei* (nondoing). "Strive for nonstriving," advises the *Daodejing*.

All our attempts at asserting ourselves, at making things happen, are like swimming against a current and are thus ultimately futile, even harmful. If we let the current carry us, however, we will travel far. Similarly, a life that follows the Way will be a life of pure effectiveness, accomplishing much with little effort.

It is often said that the Chinese are Confucians in public and Daoists in private, and the two approaches do seem to balance each other. Confucianism is a rational political philosophy that emphasizes propriety, deference, duty, and self-discipline. Daoism is an intuitive philosophy that emphasizes individualism, nonconformity, and a return to nature. If a Confucian education molded scholars outwardly into responsible, ethical officials, Daoism provided some breathing room for the artist and poet inside.

infusing Confucianism with traditional Chinese cosmology. They emphasized the Zhou idea, taken up by Confucius, that the emperor ruled by the mandate of Heaven. Heaven itself was reconceived more abstractly as the moral force underlying the universe. Thus the moral system of Confucian society became a reflection of universal order (see "Confucius and Confucianism," page 337).

Confucian subjects turn up frequently in Han art. Among the most famous examples are the reliefs from the Wu family shrines built in 151 CE in Jiaxiang. Carved and engraved in low relief on stone slabs, the scenes were meant to teach Confucian themes such as respect for the emperor, filial piety, and wifely devotion. Daoist motifs also appear, as do figures from traditional myths and legends. Such mixed iconography is characteristic of Han art (see "A Closer Look," opposite).

When compared with the Han-dynasty banner (SEE FIG. 10–7), this late Han relief clearly shows the change that took place in the Chinese worldview in the span of 300 years. The banner places equal emphasis on heaven, earth, and the underworld; human beings are dwarfed by a great swarming of supernatural creatures and divine beings. In the relief in the Wu shrine, the focus is clearly on the human realm. The composition conveys the importance of the emperor as the holder of the

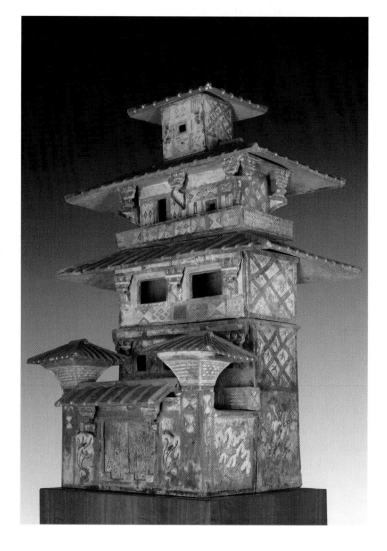

10-9 • TOMB MODEL OF A HOUSE
Eastern Han dynasty, 1st–mid 2nd century CE. Painted earthenware, 52 × 33½ × 27" (132.1 × 85.1 × 68.6 cm). The Nelson-Atkins Museum of Art, Kansas City, Missouri. Purchase, Nelson Trust (33-521)

Rubbing of a Stone Relief

Detail from a rubbing of a stone relief in the Wu family shrine (Wuliangci). Jiaxiang, Shandong. Han dynasty, 151 CE. 27½ × 66½" (70 × 169 cm).

Birds and small figures, possibly alluding to mythical creatures or immortals.

Women—and an empress?—receiving visitors on the upper floor.

The archer Yi saves the world by shooting the extra sun-crows that were threatening it.

More visitors arriving in horse-drawn chariots.

Men—and the emperor?—receiving visitors on the lower floor.

SEE MORE: View the Closer Look feature for the Rubbing of a Stone Relief in the Wu Family Shrine (Wuliangci) www.myartslab.com

mandate of Heaven and illustrates fundamental Confucian themes of social order and decorum.

ARCHITECTURE

Contemporary literary sources are eloquent on the wonders of the Han capital. Unfortunately, nothing of Han architecture remains except ceramic models. One model of a house found in a tomb, where it was provided for the dead to use in the afterlife, represents a Han dwelling (FIG. 10–9). Its four stories are crowned with a watchtower and face a small walled courtyard. Pigs and oxen probably occupied the ground floor, while the family lived in the upper stories.

Aside from the multi-level construction, the most interesting feature of the house is the **bracketing** system (architectural elements projecting from the wall) that supports the rather broad eaves of its tiled roofs. Bracketing became a standard element of east Asian architecture, not only in private homes but more typically in palaces and temples (SEE, FOR EXAMPLE, FIG. 10–15). Another interesting aspect of the model is the elaborate painting on the exterior walls. Much of the painting is purely decorative, though some of it illustrates structural features such as posts and lintels. Still other images evoke the world outdoors, for example, the trees flanking the gateway with crows perched in their branches. Literary sources describe the walls of Han palaces as decorated with paint and lacquer, and also inlaid with precious metals and stones.

SIX DYNASTIES

With the fall of the Han in 220 CE, China splintered into three warring kingdoms. In 280 CE the empire was briefly reunited, but invasions by nomadic peoples from central Asia, a source of disruption throughout Chinese history, soon forced the court to flee south. For the next three centuries, northern and southern China developed separately. In the north, 16 kingdoms carved out by invaders rose and fell before giving way to a succession of largely foreign dynasties. Warfare was commonplace. Tens of thousands of Chinese fled south, where six short-lived dynasties succeeded each other in an age of almost constant turmoil broadly known as the Six Dynasties period or the period of the Southern and Northern dynasties (265–589 CE).

In such chaos, the Confucian system lost influence. In the south especially, many intellectuals—the creators and custodians of China's high culture—turned to Daoism, which contained a strong escapist element. Educated to serve the government, they increasingly withdrew from public life. They wandered the landscape, drank, wrote poems, practiced calligraphy, and expressed their disdain for the world through willfully eccentric behavior.

The rarefied intellectual escape route of Daoism was available only to the educated elite. Far more people sought answers in the magic and superstitions of Daoism in its religious form. Though weak and disorganized, the southern courts continued to patronize traditional Chinese culture, and Confucianism remained the official doctrine. Yet ultimately it was a newly arrived religion, Buddhism, that flourished in the troubled China of the Six Dynasties.

PAINTING

Although few paintings survive from the Six Dynasties, abundant descriptions in literary sources make clear that the period was an important one for painting. Landscape, later a major theme of Chinese art, first appeared as a subject during this era. For Daoists, wandering through China's countryside was a source of spiritual refreshment. Painters and scholars of the Six Dynasties found that wandering in the mind's eye through a painted landscape could serve the same purpose. This new emphasis on the spiritual value of painting contrasted with the Confucian view, which had emphasized art's moral and didactic uses.

Reflections on the tradition of painting also inspired the first works on theory and aesthetics. Some of the earliest and most succinct formulations of the ideals of Chinese painting are the six principles set out by the scholar Xie He (fl. c. 500–535 CE). The first two principles in particular offer valuable insight into the spirit in which China's painters worked.

The first principle announces that "spirit consonance" imbues a painting with "life's movement." This "spirit" is the Daoist *qi*, the breath that animates all creation, the energy that flows through all things. When a painting has *qi*, it will be alive with inner essence, not merely outward resemblance. Artists must cultivate their own spirit so that this universal energy flows through them and infuses their work. The second principle recognizes that brushstrokes are the "bones" of a picture, its primary structural element. Traditional Chinese judge a painting above all by the quality of its brushwork. Each brushstroke is a vehicle of expression; it is through the vitality of a painter's brushwork that "spirit consonance" makes itself felt. We can sense this attitude already in the rapid, confident brushstrokes that outline the figures of the Han banner (SEE FIG. 10–7) and again in the more controlled, rhythmical lines of one of the most important works associated with this period, a painted scroll known as *Admonitions of the Imperial Instructress to Court Ladies*. Attributed to the painter Gu Kaizhi (344–407 CE), it alternates illustrations and text to relate seven Confucian stories of wifely virtue from Chinese history.

The first illustration depicts the courage of Lady Feng (**FIG. 10–10**). An escaped circus bear rushes toward her husband, a Han emperor, who is filled with fear. Behind his throne, two female servants have turned to run away. Before him, two male attendants, themselves on the verge of panic, try to fend off the bear with

10–10 • After Gu Kaizhi **DETAIL OF *ADMONITIONS OF THE IMPERIAL INSTRUCTRESS TO COURT LADIES***
Six Dynasties period. Handscroll, ink and colors on silk, 9¾″ × 11′6″ (24.8 × 348.2 cm). British Museum, London.

Confucius and Confucianism

Confucius was born in 551 BCE in the state of Lu, roughly present-day Shandong Province, into a declining aristocratic family. While still in his teens he set his heart on becoming a scholar; by his early twenties he had begun to teach.

By this time, wars for supremacy had begun among the various states of China, and the traditional social fabric seemed to be breaking down. Looking back to the early Zhou dynasty as a sort of golden age, Confucius thought about how a just and harmonious society could again emerge. For many years he sought a ruler who would put his ideas into effect, but to no avail. Frustrated, he spent his final years teaching. After his death in 479 BCE, his conversations with his students were collected by his disciples and their followers into a book known in English as the *Analects*, which is the only record of his words.

At the heart of Confucian thought is the concept of *ren* (human-heartedness). *Ren* emphasizes morality and empathy as the basic standards for all human interaction. The virtue of *ren* is most fully realized in the Confucian ideal of the *junzi* (gentleman). Originally indicating noble birth, the term was redefined to mean one who through education and self-cultivation had become a superior person, right-thinking and right-acting in all situations. A *junzi* is the opposite of a petty or small-minded person. His characteristics include moderation, integrity, self-control, loyalty, reciprocity, and altruism. His primary concern is justice.

Together with human-heartedness and justice, Confucius emphasized *li* (etiquette). *Li* includes everyday manners as well as ritual, ceremony, and protocol—the formalities of all social conduct and interaction. Such forms, Confucius felt, choreographed life so that an entire society moved in harmony. *Ren* and *li* operate in the realm of the Five Constant Relationships that define Confucian society: parent and child, husband and wife, elder sibling and younger sibling, elder friend and younger friend, ruler and subject. Deference to age is clearly built into this view, as is the deference to authority that made Confucianism attractive to emperors. Yet responsibilities flow the other way as well: The duty of a ruler is to earn the loyalty of subjects, of a husband to earn the respect of his wife, of age to guide youth wisely.

During the early years of the People's Republic of China, and especially during the Great Proletarian Cultural Revolution (1966–1976), Confucius and Confucian thought were denigrated. Recently, however, Confucian temples in Beijing and elsewhere have been restored. Notably, the Chinese government has used the philosopher's name officially in establishing hundreds of Confucius Institutes in more than 80 countries, to promote the learning of the Chinese language abroad.

---

spears. Only Lady Feng is calm as she rushes forward to place herself between the beast and the emperor.

The figures are drawn with a brush in a thin, even-width line, and a few outlined areas are filled with color. Facial features, especially those of the men, are quite well depicted. Movement and emotion are shown through conventions such as the scarves flowing from Lady Feng's dress, indicating that she is rushing forward, and the upturned strings on both sides of the emperor's head, suggesting his fear. There is no hint of a setting; instead, the artist relies on careful placement of the figures to create a sense of depth.

The painting is on silk, which was typically woven in bands about 12 inches wide and up to 20 or 30 feet long. Early Chinese painters thus developed the format used here, the **handscroll**—a long, narrow, horizontal composition, compact enough to be held in the hand when rolled up. Handscrolls are intimate works, meant to be viewed by only two or three people at a time. They were not displayed completely unrolled as we commonly see them today in museums. Rather, viewers would open a scroll and savor it slowly from right to left, displaying only an arm's length at a time.

CALLIGRAPHY

The emphasis on the expressive quality and structural importance of brushstrokes finds its purest embodiment in calligraphy. The same brushes are used for both painting and calligraphy, and a relationship between them was recognized as early as Han times. In his teachings, Confucius had extolled the importance of the pursuit of knowledge and the arts. Among the visual arts, painting was felt to reflect moral concerns, while calligraphy was believed to reveal the character of the writer.

Calligraphy is regarded as one of the highest forms of expression in China. For more than 2,000 years, China's **literati**, Confucian scholars and literary men who also served the government as officials, have enjoyed being connoisseurs and practitioners of this abstract art. During the fourth century CE, calligraphy came to full maturity. The most important practitioner of the day was Wang Xizhi (c. 307–365), whose works have served as models of excellence for all subsequent generations. The example here comes from a letter, now somewhat damaged and mounted as part of an album, known as *Feng Ju* (FIG. 10–11).

Feng Ju is an example of "walking" or semicursive style, which is neither too formal nor too free but is done in a relaxed, easy-going manner. Brushstrokes vary in width and length, creating rhythmic vitality. Individual characters remain distinct, yet within each character the strokes are run together and simplified as the brush moves from one to the other without lifting off the page. The effect is fluid and graceful, yet still strong and dynamic. The

**10–11 • Wang Xizhi PORTION OF A LETTER FROM THE
FENG JU ALBUM**

Six Dynasties period, mid-4th century CE. Ink on paper, 9¾ × 18½"
(24.7 × 46.8 cm). National Palace Museum, Taibei, Taiwan, Republic
of China.

The stamped characters that appear on Chinese artworks are **seals**—
personal emblems. The use of seals dates from the Zhou dynasty, and
to this day seals traditionally employ the archaic characters, known
appropriately as "seal script," of the Zhou or Qin. Cut in stone, a seal may
state a formal, given name, or it may state any of the numerous personal
names that China's painters and writers adopted throughout their lives.
A treasured work of art often bears not only the seal of its maker, but also
those of collectors and admirers through the centuries. In the Chinese view,
these do not disfigure the work but add another layer of interest. This
sample of Wang Xizhi's calligraphy, for example, bears the seals of two
Song-dynasty emperors, a Song official, a famous collector of the sixteenth
century, and two Qing-dynasty emperors of the eighteenth and nineteenth
centuries.

walking style as developed by Wang Xizhi came to be officially
accepted and learned along with other script styles.

BUDDHIST ART AND ARCHITECTURE

Buddhism originated in India during the fifth century BCE (see
Chapter 9), then gradually spread north into central Asia. With the
opening of the Silk Road during the Han dynasty, its influence
reached China. To the Chinese of the Six Dynasties, beset by constant
warfare and social devastation, Buddhism offered consolation in
life and the promise of salvation after death. The faith spread
throughout the country to all social levels, first in the north, where
many of the invaders promoted it as the official religion, then

slightly later in the south, where it found its first great patron
in the emperor Liang Wu Di (r. 502–549 CE). Thousands of
temples and monasteries were built, and many people became
monks and nuns.

Almost nothing remains in China of the Buddhist
architecture of the Six Dynasties, but we can see what it must
have looked like in the Japanese temple Horyuji (SEE FIG.
11–4), which was based on Chinese models of this period. The
slender forms and linear grace of Horyuji might be compared
to the figures in Gu Kaizhi's handscroll (SEE FIG. 10–10), and
they indicate the delicate, almost weightless style cultivated in
southern China.

ROCK-CUT CAVES OF THE SILK ROAD.   The most impressive
works of Buddhist art surviving from the Six Dynasties are the
hundreds of northern rock-cut caves along the trade routes
between Xinjiang in central Asia and the Yellow River Valley.
Both the caves and the sculptures that fill them were carved
from the solid rock of the cliffs. Small caves high above the
ground were retreats for monks and pilgrims, while larger
caves at the base of the cliffs were wayside shrines and temples.

The caves at Yungang, in Shanxi Province in central
China, contain many examples of the earliest phase of
Buddhist sculpture in China, including the monumental
seated Buddha in Cave 20 (FIG. 10–12). The figure was carved
in the latter part of the fifth century by the imperial decree of
a ruler of the Northern Wei dynasty (386–534 CE), the
longest-lived and most stable of the northern kingdoms. Most
Wei rulers were avid patrons of Buddhism, and under their
rule the religion made its greatest advances in the north.

The front part of the cave has crumbled away, and the
45-foot statue, now exposed to the open air, is clearly visible
from a distance. The elongated ears, protuberance on the head
(*ushnisha*), and monk's robe are traditional attributes of the
Buddha. The masklike face, full torso, massive shoulders, and
shallow, stylized drapery indicate strong central Asian
influence. The overall effect of this colossus is remote and
austere, less human than the more sensuous expression of the
early Buddhist traditions in India.

SUI AND TANG DYNASTIES

In 581 CE, a general from the last of the northern dynasties
replaced a child emperor and established a dynasty of his own, the
Sui. Defeating all opposition, he molded China into a centralized
empire as it had been in Han times. The short-lived Sui dynasty fell
in 618, but, in reunifying the empire, paved the way for one of the
greatest dynasties in Chinese history: the Tang (618–907). Even
today many Chinese living abroad still call themselves "Tang
people." To them, Tang implies that part of the Chinese character
that is strong and vigorous (especially in military power), noble and
idealistic, but also realistic and pragmatic.

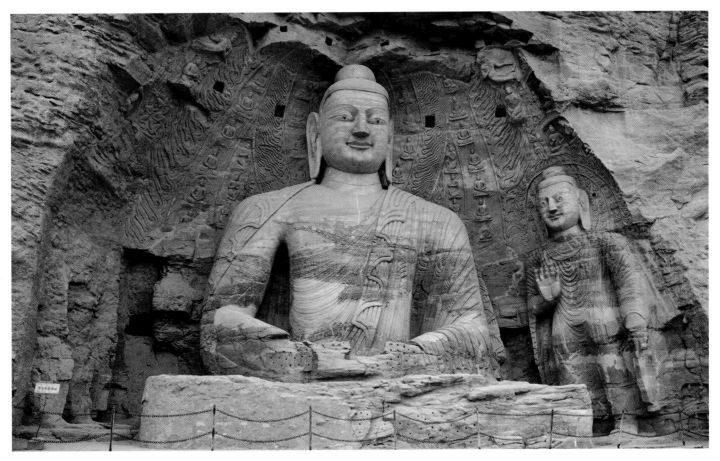

10-12 • SEATED BUDDHA, CAVE 20, YUNGANG
Datong, Shanxi. Northern Wei dynasty, c. 460. Stone, height 45′ (13.7 m).

BUDDHIST ART AND ARCHITECTURE

The new Sui emperor was a devout Buddhist, and his reunification of China coincided with a fusion of the several styles of Buddhist sculpture that had developed. This new style is seen in a bronze altar to Amitabha Buddha (FIG. 10–13), one of the many Buddhas of Mahayana Buddhism. Amitabha dwelled in the Western Pure Land, a paradise into which his faithful followers were promised rebirth. With its comparatively simple message of salvation, the Pure Land sect eventually became the most popular form of Buddhism in China and one of the most popular in Japan (see Chapter 11).

The altar depicts Amitabha in his paradise, seated on a lotus throne beneath a canopy of trees. Each leaf cluster is set with jewels. Seven celestial figures sit on the topmost clusters, and ropes of "pearls" hang from the tree trunks. Behind Amitabha's head is a halo of flames. To his left, the bodhisattva Guanyin holds a pomegranate; to his right, another bodhisattva clasps his hands in prayer. Behind are four disciples who first preached the teachings of the Buddha. On the lower level, an incense burner is flanked by

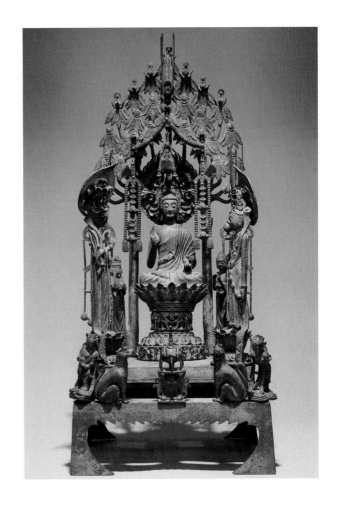

10-13 • ALTAR TO AMITABHA BUDDHA
Sui dynasty, 593. Bronze, height 30⅛″ (76.5 cm). Museum of Fine Arts, Boston. Gift of Mrs. W. Scott Fitz (22.407) and Gift of Edward Holmes Jackson in memory of his mother, Mrs. W. Scott Fitz (47.1407–1412)

10-14 • THE WESTERN PARADISE OF AMITABHA BUDDHA
Detail of a wall painting in Cave 217, Dunhuang, Gansu. Tang dynasty, c. 750. 10′2″ × 16′ (3.1 × 4.86 m).

seated lions and two smaller bodhisattvas. Focusing on Amitabha's benign expression and filled with objects symbolizing his power, the altar combines the sensuality of Indian styles, the schematic abstraction of central Asian art, and the Chinese emphasis on linear grace and rhythm into a harmonious new style.

Buddhism reached its greatest development in China during the subsequent Tang Dynasty, which for nearly three centuries ruled China and controlled much of Central Asia. From emperors and empresses to common peasants, virtually the entire country adopted the Buddhist faith. A Tang vision of the most popular sect, Pure Land, was expressed in a wall painting from a cave in Dunhuang **(FIG. 10–14)**. A major stop along the Silk Road, Dunhuang has nearly 500 caves carved out of its sandy cliffs, all filled with painted clay sculpture and decorated with wall paintings from floor to ceiling. The site was worked on continuously from the fourth to the fourteenth century, a period of almost 1,000 years. In the detail shown here, Amitabha Buddha is seated in the center, surrounded by four bodhisattvas, who serve as his messengers to the

world. Two other groups of bodhisattvas are clustered at the right and left. In the foreground, musicians and dancers create a heavenly atmosphere. In the background, great halls and towers rise. The artist has imagined the Western Paradise in terms of the grandeur of Tang palaces. Indeed, the lavish entertainment depicted could just as easily be taking place at the imperial court. This worldly vision of paradise, recorded with great attention to naturalism in the architectural setting, gives us our best visualization of the splendor of Tang civilization at a time when Chang'an (present-day Xi'an) was probably the greatest city in the world.

The early Tang emperors proclaimed a policy of religious tolerance, but during the ninth century a conservative reaction set in. Confucianism was reasserted and Buddhism was briefly persecuted as a "foreign" religion. Thousands of temples, shrines, and monasteries were destroyed and innumerable bronze statues melted down. Nevertheless, several Buddhist structures survive from the Tang dynasty. One of them, the Nanchan Temple, is the earliest important example of surviving Chinese architecture.

NANCHAN TEMPLE. Of the few structures earlier than 1400 CE to have survived, the Nanchan Temple is the most significant, for it shows characteristics of both temples and palaces of the Tang Dynasty **(FIG. 10–15)**. Located on Mount Wutai (Wutaishan) in the eastern part of Shanxi Province, this small hall was constructed in 782. The tiled roof, seen earlier in the Han tomb model (SEE FIG. 10–9), has taken on a curved silhouette. Quite subtle here, this curve became increasingly pronounced in later centuries. The very broad overhanging eaves are supported by a correspondingly elaborate bracketing system.

Also typical is the bay system of construction, in which a cubic unit of space, a bay, is formed by four posts and their lintels. The bay functioned in Chinese architecture as a **module**, a basic unit of construction. To create larger structures, an architect multiplied the number of bays. Thus the Nanchan Temple—modest in scope with three bays—gives an idea of the vast, multi-storied palaces of the Tang depicted in such paintings as FIGURE 10–14.

GREAT WILD GOOSE PAGODA. Another important monument of Tang architecture is the Great Wild Goose Pagoda at the Ci'en Temple in Chang'an, the Tang capital **(FIG. 10–16)**. The temple was constructed in 645 for the famous monk Xuanzang (600–664) on his return from a 16-year pilgrimage to India. At the Ci'en Temple, Xuanzang taught and translated the materials he had brought back with him.

The **pagoda**, a typical east Asian Buddhist structure, originated in the Indian Buddhist stupa, the elaborate burial mound that housed relics of the Buddha (see "Pagodas," page 345). In India the stupa had developed a multi-storied form in the Gandhara region under the Kushan dynasty (c. 50–250 CE). In China this form blended with a traditional Han watchtower to produce the pagoda. Built entirely in masonry, the Great Wild Goose Pagoda nevertheless imitates the wooden architecture of the time. The walls are decorated in low relief to resemble bays,

and bracket systems are reproduced under the projecting roofs of each story. Although modified and repaired in later times (its seven stories were originally five, and a new finial has been added), the pagoda still preserves the essence of Tang architecture in its simplicity, symmetry, proportions, and grace.

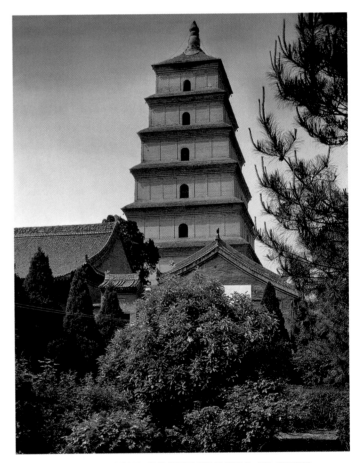

10-16 • GREAT WILD GOOSE PAGODA AT CI'EN TEMPLE, CHANG'AN
Shanxi. Tang dynasty, first erected 645; rebuilt mid 8th century CE.

The Silk Road during the Tang Period

Under a series of ambitious and forceful Tang emperors, Chinese control once again extended over central Asia. Goods, ideas, and influence flowed along the Silk Road. In the South China Sea, Arab and Persian ships carried on a lively trade with coastal cities. Chinese cultural influence in east Asia was so important that Japan and Korea sent thousands of students to study Chinese civilization.

Cosmopolitan and tolerant, Tang China was confident and curious about the world. Many foreigners came to the splendid new capital Chang'an (present-day Xi'an), and they are often depicted in the art of the period. A ceramic statue of a camel carrying a troupe of musicians reflects the Tang fascination with the "exotic" Turkic cultures of central Asia. The three bearded musicians (one with his back to us) are central Asian, while the two smooth-shaven ones are Han Chinese. Bactrian, or two-humped, camels, themselves exotic central Asian "visitors," were beasts of burden in the caravans that traversed the Silk Road. The stringed lute (which the Chinese called the *pipa*) came from central Asia to become a lasting part of Chinese music.

Stylistically, the statue reveals a new interest in naturalism, an important trend in both painting and sculpture. Compared with the rigid, staring ceramic soldiers of the first emperor of Qin, this Tang band is alive with gesture and expression. The majestic camel throws its head back; the musicians are vividly captured in mid-performance. Ceramic figurines such as this, produced by the thousands for Tang tombs, offer glimpses into the gorgeous variety of Tang life. The statue's three-color glaze technique was a specialty of Tang ceramicists. The glazes—usually chosen from a restricted palette of amber-yellow, green, and blue—were splashed freely and allowed to run over the surface during firing to convey a feeling of spontaneity. The technique is emblematic of Tang culture itself in its robust, colorful, and cosmopolitan expressiveness.

The Silk Road had first flourished in the second century CE. A 5,000-mile network of caravan routes from the Han capital (near present-day Luoyang, Henan, on the Yellow River) to Rome, it brought Chinese luxury goods to Western markets.

The journey began at the Jade Gate (Yumen) at the westernmost end of the Great Wall, where Chinese merchants turned their goods over to central Asian traders. Goods would change hands many more times before reaching the Mediterranean. Caravans headed first for the nearby desert oasis of Dunhuang. Here northern and southern routes diverged to skirt the vast Taklamakan Desert. At Khotan, in western China, farther west than the area shown in MAP 10–1, travelers on the southern route could turn off toward a mountain pass into Kashmir, in northern India. Or they could continue on, meeting up with the northern route at Kashgar, on the western border of the Taklamakan, before proceeding over the Pamir Mountains into present-day Afghanistan. There, travelers could turn off into present-day Pakistan and India, or travel west through present-day Uzbekistan, Iran, and Iraq, arriving finally at Antioch, in Syria, on the coast of the Mediterranean. From there, land and sea routes led to Rome.

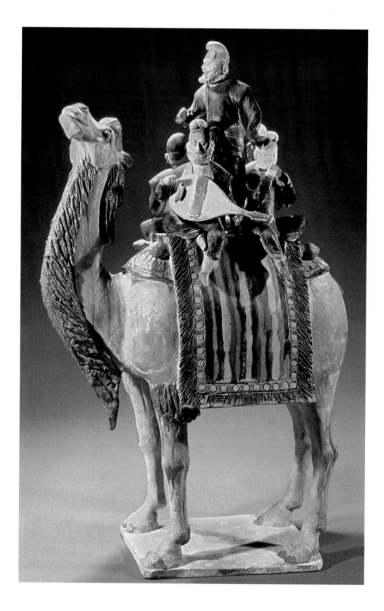

CAMEL CARRYING A GROUP OF MUSICIANS
From a tomb near Xi'an, Shanxi. Tang dynasty, c. mid 8th century CE. Earthenware with three-color glazes, height 26⅛" (66.5 cm). National Museum, Beijing.

10-17 • Attributed to Emperor Huizong DETAIL OF LADIES PREPARING NEWLY WOVEN SILK
Copy after a lost Tang dynasty painting by Zhang Xuan. Northern Song dynasty, early 12th century CE. Handscroll, ink and colors on silk, 14½ × 57½″ (36 × 145.3 cm). Museum of Fine Arts, Boston. Chinese and Japanese Special Fund (12.886)

Confucius said of himself, "I merely transmit, I do not create; I love and revere the ancients." In this spirit, Chinese painters regularly copied paintings of earlier masters. Painters made copies both to absorb the lessons of their great predecessors and to perpetuate the achievements of the past. In later centuries, they took up the practice of regularly executing a work "in the manner of" some particularly revered ancient master. This was at once an act of homage, a declaration of artistic allegiance, and a way of reinforcing a personal connection with the past.

FIGURE PAINTING

Later artists looking back on their heritage recognized the Tang dynasty as China's great age of figure painting. Unfortunately, very few scroll paintings that can be definitely identified as Tang still exist. We can get some idea of the character of Tang figure painting from the wall paintings of Dunhuang (SEE FIG. 10–14). Another way to savor the particular flavor of Tang painting is to look at copies made by later, Song-dynasty artists. An outstanding example can be seen in *Ladies Preparing Newly Woven Silk*, attributed to Huizong (r. 1101–1126 CE), the last emperor of the Northern Song dynasty **(FIG. 10–17)**. A long handscroll, it depicts the activities of court women as they weave and iron silk. An inscription on the scroll informs us that the painting is a copy of a famous work by Zhang Xuan, an eighth-century painter known for his depictions of women at the Tang court. The original no longer exists, so we cannot know how faithful the copy is. Still, its refined lines and bright colors seem to share the grace and dignity of Tang sculpture and architecture. Two horses and riders **(FIG. 10–18)**, a man and a woman, made for use as tomb furnishings, reveal more of the robust naturalism and exuberance achieved during the Tang period. Accurate in proportion and lively in demeanor, the figures are not glazed (as is the tomb figure in "The Silk Road during the Tang Period," opposite) but are "cold-painted" using pigments after firing to render details of costume and facial features. The pair are indicative of the lively participation of women as well as men in sport and riding.

10-18 • TWO EQUESTRIAN FIGURES
Tang dynasty, first half 8th century CE. Molded, reddish-buff earthenware with cold-painted pigments over white ground, height (male figure) 14½″ (37 cm). Arthur M. Sackler Museum, Harvard Art Museum, Cambridge, Massachusetts. Gift of Anthony M. Solomon (2003.207.1-2)

The figures, one male, one female, each have pointed boots and are mounted on a standing, saddled and bridled horse; their hands are positioned to hold the reins. The male figure wears a tall, elaborately embellished hat, and the female figure has her hair arranged in a topknot.

SONG DYNASTY

A brief period of disintegration followed the fall of the Tang before China was again united, this time under the Song dynasty (960–1279), which established a new capital at Bianjing (present-day Kaifeng), near the Yellow River. In contrast to the outgoing confidence of the Tang, the mood during the Song was more introspective, a reflection of China's weakened military situation. In 1126 the Jurchen tribes of Manchuria invaded China, sacked the capital, and took possession of much of the northern part of the country. Song forces withdrew south and established a new capital at Hangzhou. From this point on, the dynasty is known as the Southern Song (1127–1179), with the first portion called in retrospect the Northern Song (960–1126).

Although China's territory had diminished, its wealth had increased because of advances in agriculture, commerce, and technology begun under the Tang. Patronage was plentiful, and the arts flourished.

SEATED GUANYIN BODHISATTVA.   In spite of changing political fortunes in the eleventh and twelfth centuries, artists continued to create splendid works. No hint of political disruption or religious questioning intrudes on the sublime grace and beauty of this seated Guanyin bodhisattva (FIG. 10–19). Bodhisattvas, beings who are close to enlightenment but who voluntarily remain on earth to help others achieve enlightenment, are represented as young princes wearing royal garments and jewelry, their finery indicative of their worldly but virtuous lives. Guanyin is the Bodhisattva of Infinite Compassion, who appears in many guises, in this case as the Water and Moon Guanyin. He sits on rocks by the sea, in the position known as royal ease. His right arm rests on his raised and

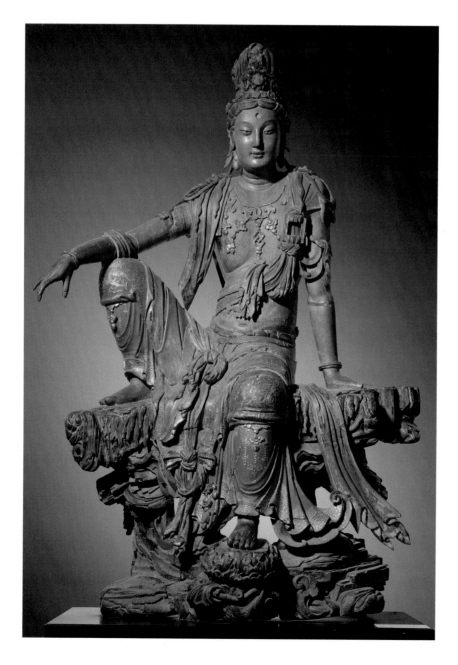

10-19 • SEATED GUANYIN BODHISATTVA
Liao dynasty, 10th–12th century CE. Wood with paint and gold, 95 × 65″ (241.3 × 165.1 cm). The Nelson-Atkins Museum of Art, Kansas City, Missouri. Purchase, Nelson Trust (34–10)

Pagodas developed from Indian stupas as Buddhism spread northeast along the Silk Road. Stupas merged with the watchtowers of Han-dynasty China in multi-storied stone or wood structures with projecting tiled roofs. This transformation culminated in wooden pagodas with upward-curving roofs supported by elaborate bracketing in China, Korea, and Japan. Buddhist pagodas retain the *axis mundi* masts of stupas. Like their south Asian prototypes, early east Asian pagodas were symbolic rather than enclosing structures. Later examples often provided access to the ground floor and sometimes to upper levels.

early stupa
India, 2nd century BCE

later stupa
Central Asia,
5th–6th century CE

watchtower
China, Han dynasty,
c. 206 BCE–220 CE

stone pagoda
northwestern China,
c. 5th century CE

wooden pagoda
Japan, 7th century CE

SEE MORE: View a simulation about pagodas www.myartslab.com

bent right knee and his left arm and foot hang down, the foot touching a lotus blossom. The wooden figure was carved in the eleventh or twelfth century in a territory on the northern border of Song China, a region ruled by the Liao dynasty (907–1125); the painting and gilding were restored in the sixteenth century.

Song culture is noted for its refined taste and intellectual grandeur. Where the Tang had reveled in exoticism, eagerly absorbing influences from Persia, India, and Central Asia, Song culture was more self-consciously Chinese. Philosophy experienced its most creative era since the "one hundred schools" of the Zhou. Song scholarship was brilliant, especially in history, and its poetry is noted for its depth. Perhaps the finest expressions of the Song are in art, especially painting and ceramics.

PHILOSOPHY: NEO-CONFUCIANISM

Song philosophers continued the process, begun during the Tang, of restoring Confucianism to dominance. In strengthening Confucian thought, they drew on Daoist and especially Buddhist ideas, even as they openly rejected Buddhism itself as foreign. These innovations provided Confucianism with a metaphysical aspect it had previously lacked, allowing it to propose a more satisfying, all-embracing explanation of the universe. This new synthesis of China's three main paths of thought is called Neo-Confucianism.

Neo-Confucianism teaches that the universe consists of two interacting forces known as *li* (principle or idea) and *qi* (matter). All pine trees, for example, consist of an underlying *li* we might call "Pine Tree Idea" brought into the material world through *qi*. All the *li* of the universe, including humans, are but aspects of an eternal first principle known as the Great Ultimate (*taiji*), which is completely present in every object. Our task as human beings is to rid our *qi* of impurities through education and self-cultivation so that our *li* may realize its oneness with the Great Ultimate. This lifelong process resembles the striving to attain buddhahood, and if we persist in our attempts, one day we will be enlightened—the term itself comes directly from Buddhism.

NORTHERN SONG PAINTING

The Neo-Confucian ideas found visual expression in art, especially in landscape, which became the most highly esteemed subject for painting. Northern Song artists studied nature closely to master its many appearances—the way each species of tree grew, the distinctive character of each rock formation, the changes of the seasons, the myriad birds, blossoms, and insects. This passion for realistic detail was the artist's form of self-cultivation: Mastering outward forms showed an understanding of the principles behind them.

Yet despite the convincing accumulation of detail, the paintings

10-20 • Fan Kuan TRAVELERS AMONG MOUNTAINS AND STREAMS
Northern Song dynasty, early 11th century CE. Hanging scroll, ink and colors on silk, height 6'9½" (2.06 m). National Palace Museum, Taibei, Taiwan, Republic of China.

do not record a specific site. The artist's goal was to paint the eternal essence of "mountain-ness," for example, not to reproduce the appearance of a particular mountain. Painting a landscape required an artist to orchestrate his cumulative understanding of *li* in all its aspects—mountains and rocks, streams and waterfalls, trees and grasses, clouds and mist. A landscape painting thus expressed

the desire for the spiritual communion with nature that was the key to enlightenment. As the tradition progressed, landscape also became a vehicle for conveying human emotions, even for speaking indirectly of one's own deepest feelings.

In the earliest times, art reflected the mythocentric worldview of the ancient Chinese. Later, as religion came to dominate people's lives, the focus of art shifted, and religious images and human actions became important subjects. Subsequently, during the Song dynasty, artists developed landscape as the chief means of expression, preferring to avoid direct depiction of the human condition and to show ideals in a symbolic manner. The major form of Chinese artistic expression thus moved from the mythical, through the religious and ethical, and finally to the philosophical and aesthetic.

FAN KUAN.   One of the first great masters of Song landscape was the eleventh-century painter Fan Kuan (active c. 990–1030 CE), whose surviving major work, **TRAVELERS AMONG MOUNTAINS AND STREAMS**, is regarded as one of the great monuments of Chinese art **(FIG. 10–20)**. The work is physically large—almost 7 feet high—but the sense of monumentality also radiates from the composition itself, which makes its impression even when much reduced.

The composition unfolds in three stages, comparable to three acts of a drama. At the bottom a large, low-lying group of rocks, taking up about one-eighth of the picture surface, establishes the extreme foreground. The rest of the landscape pushes back from this point. In anticipating the shape and substance of the mountains to come, the rocks introduce the main theme of the work, much as the first act of a drama introduces the principal characters. In the middle ground, travelers and their mules are coming from the right. Their size confirms our human scale—how small we are, how vast is nature. This middle ground takes up twice as much picture surface as the foreground, and, like the second act of a play, shows variation and development. Instead of a solid mass, the rocks here are separated into two groups by a waterfall that is spanned by a bridge. In the hills to the right, the rooftops of a temple stand out above the trees.

Mist veils the transition to the background, with the result that the mountain looms suddenly. This background area, almost twice as large as the foreground and middle ground combined, is the climactic third act of the drama. As our eyes begin their ascent, the mountain solidifies. Its ponderous weight increases as it billows upward, finally bursting into the sprays of energetic brushstrokes that describe the scrubby growth on top. To the right, a slender waterfall plummets, not to balance the powerful upward thrust of the mountain but simply to enhance it by contrast. The whole painting, then, conveys the feeling of climbing a high mountain, leaving the human world behind to come face to face with the Great Ultimate in a spiritual communion.

All the elements are depicted with precise detail and in proper scale. Jagged brushstrokes describe the contours of rocks and trees and express their rugged character. Layers of short, staccato strokes

10-21 • Xu Daoning **SECTION OF FISHING IN A MOUNTAIN STREAM**
Northern Song dynasty, mid 11th century CE. Handscroll, ink on silk, 19″ × 6′10″ (48.9 cm × 2.09 m).
The Nelson-Atkins Museum of Art, Kansas City, Missouri. Purchase, Nelson Trust (33–1559)

(translated as "raindrop texture" from the Chinese) accurately mimic the texture of the rock surface. Spatial recession from foreground through middle ground to background is logically and convincingly handled, if not quite continuous.

Although it contains realistic details, the landscape represents no specific place. In its forms, the artist expresses the ideal forms behind appearances; in the rational, ordered composition, he expresses the intelligence of the universe. The arrangement of the mountains, with the central peak flanked by lesser peaks on each side, seems to reflect both the ancient Confucian notion of social hierarchy, with the emperor flanked by his ministers, and the Buddhist motif of the Buddha with bodhisattvas at his side. The landscape, a view of nature uncorrupted by human habitation, expresses a kind of Daoist ideal. Thus we find the three strains of Chinese thought united, much as they are in Neo-Confucianism itself.

The ability of Chinese landscape painters to take us out of ourselves and to let us wander freely through their sites is closely linked to the avoidance of perspective as it is understood in the West. Fifteenth-century European painters, searching for fidelity to appearances, developed a scientific system for recording exactly the view that could be seen from a single, fixed vantage point. The goal of Chinese painting is precisely to avoid such limits and show a totality beyond what we are normally given to see. If the ideal for centuries of Western painters was to render what can be seen from a fixed viewpoint, that of Chinese artists was to reveal nature through a distant, all-seeing, and mobile viewpoint.

XU DAONING. The sense of shifting perspective is clearest in the handscroll, where our vantage point changes constantly as we move through the painting. One of the finest handscrolls to survive from the Northern Song is **FISHING IN A MOUNTAIN STREAM (FIG. 10–21)**, a painting executed in the middle of the eleventh century by Xu Daoning (c. 970–c. 1052). Starting from a thatched hut in the right foreground, we follow a path that leads to a broad, open view of a deep vista dissolving into distant mists and mountain peaks. (Remember that viewers observed only a small section of the scroll at a time. To mimic this effect, use two pieces of paper to frame a small viewing area, then move them slowly leftward.) Crossing over

a small footbridge, we are brought back to the foreground with the beginning of a central group of high mountains that show extraordinary shapes. Again our path winds back along the bank, and we have a spectacular view of the highest peaks from another small footbridge the artist has placed for us. At the far side of the bridge, we find ourselves looking up into a deep valley, where a stream lures our eyes far into the distance. We can imagine ourselves resting for a moment in the small pavilion halfway up the valley on the right. Or perhaps we may spend some time with the fishers in their boats as the valley gives way to a second, smaller group of mountains, serving both as an echo of the spectacular central group and as a transition to the painting's finale, a broad, open vista. As we cross the bridge here, we meet travelers coming toward us who will have our experience in reverse. Gazing out into the distance and reflecting on our journey, we again feel that sense of communion with nature that is the goal of Chinese artistic expression.

Such handscrolls have no counterpart in the Western visual arts and are often compared instead to the tradition of Western music, especially symphonic compositions. Both are generated from opening motifs that are developed and varied, both are revealed over time, and in both our sense of the overall structure relies on memory, for we do not see the scroll or hear the composition all at once.

ZHANG ZEDUAN. The Northern Song fascination with precision extended to details within landscape. The emperor Huizong, whose copy of *Ladies Preparing Newly Woven Silk* was seen in FIGURE 10–17, gathered around himself a group of court painters who shared his passion for quiet, exquisitely detailed, delicately colored paintings of birds and flowers. Other painters specialized in domestic and wild animals, still others in palaces and buildings. One of the most spectacular products of this passion for observation is **SPRING FESTIVAL ON THE RIVER**, a long handscroll painted in the late eleventh or early twelfth century by Zhang Zeduan, an artist connected to the court **(FIG. 10–22)**. Beyond its considerable visual delights, the painting is also a valuable record of daily life in the Song capital.

The painting depicts a festival day when local inhabitants and visitors from the countryside thronged the streets. One high

10-22 • Zhang Zeduan SECTION OF SPRING FESTIVAL ON THE RIVER
Northern Song dynasty, late 11th–early 12th century CE. Handscroll, ink and colors on silk, 9½″ ×
7′4″ (24.8 × 2.28 m). The Palace Museum, Beijing.

point is the scene reproduced here, which takes place at the
Rainbow Bridge. The large boat to the right is probably bringing
goods from the southern part of China up the Grand Canal that
ran through the city at that time. The sailors are preparing to pass
beneath the bridge by lowering the sail and taking down the
mast. Excited figures on ship and shore gesture wildly, shouting
orders and advice, while a noisy crowd gathers at the bridge
railing to watch. Stalls on the bridge are selling food and other
merchandise; wine shops and eating places line the banks of the
canal. Everyone is on the move. Some people are busy carrying
goods, some are shopping, some are simply enjoying themselves.
Each figure is splendidly animated and full of purpose; the
depiction of buildings and boats is highly detailed, almost
encyclopedic.

Little is known about the painter Zhang Zeduan other than
that he was a member of the scholar-official class, the highly
educated elite of imperial China. His painting demonstrates skill in
the fine-line architectural drawing called *jiehua* ("ruled-line")
painting. Interestingly, some of Zhang Zeduan's peers were already
beginning to cultivate quite a different attitude toward painting as
a form of artistic expression, one that placed overt display of
technical skill at the lowest end of the scale of values. This
emerging scholarly aesthetic, developed by China's literati, later
came to dominate Chinese thinking about art.

SOUTHERN SONG PAINTING AND CERAMICS

Landscape painting took a very different course after the fall of the
north to the Jurchen in 1127, and the removal of the court to its
new capital in the south, Hangzhou.

XIA GUI. A new sensibility is reflected in the extant portion of
TWELVE VIEWS OF LANDSCAPE (FIG. 10–23) by Xia Gui (fl. c.
1195–1235), a member of the newly established Academy of
Painters. In general, academy members continued to favor such
subjects as birds and flowers in the highly refined, elegantly colored
court style patronized earlier by Huizong (SEE FIG. 10–17). Xia
Gui, however, was interested in landscape and cultivated his own
style. Only the last four of the 12 views that originally made up

10-23 • Xia Gui SECTION OF TWELVE VIEWS OF LANDSCAPE
Southern Song dynasty, early 13th century CE. Handscroll, ink on silk, height 11″ (28 cm); length of extant portion 7′7½″
(2.31 m). The Nelson-Atkins Museum of Art, Kansas City, Missouri. Purchase, Nelson Trust (32-159/2)

this long handscroll have survived, but they are enough to illustrate the unique quality of his approach.

In contrast to the majestic, austere landscapes of the Northern Song painters, Xia Gui presents an intimate and lyrical view of nature. Subtly modulated, perfectly controlled ink washes evoke a landscape veiled in mist, while a few deft brushstrokes suffice to indicate the details showing through the mist—the grasses growing by the bank, the fishers at their work, the trees laden with moisture, the two bent-backed figures carrying their heavy loads along the path that skirts the hill. Simplified forms, stark contrasts of light and dark, asymmetrical composition, and great expanses of blank space suggest a fleeting world that can be captured only in glimpses. The intangible has more presence than the tangible. By limiting himself to a few essential details, the painter evokes a deep feeling for what lies beyond.

This development in Song painting from the rational and intellectual to the emotional and intuitive, from the tangible to the intangible, had a parallel in philosophy. During the late twelfth century a new school of Neo-Confucianism called School of the Mind insisted that self-cultivation could be achieved through contemplation, which might lead to sudden enlightenment. The idea of sudden enlightenment may have come from Chan Buddhism, better known in the West by its Japanese name, Zen. Chan Buddhists rejected formal paths to enlightenment such as scripture, knowledge, and ritual, in favor of meditation and techniques designed to "short-circuit" the rational mind. Xia Gui's painting seems also to suggest this intuitive approach.

The subtle and sophisticated paintings of the Song were created for a highly cultivated audience who were equally discerning in other arts such as ceramics. Building on the considerable accomplishments of the Tang, Song potters achieved a technical and aesthetic perfection that has made their wares models of excellence throughout the world. Like their painter contemporaries, Song potters turned away from the exuberance of Tang styles to create more quietly beautiful pieces.

GUAN WARE. Among the most prized of the many types of Song ceramics is Guan ware, made mainly for imperial use **(FIG. 10–24)**. The everted lip, high neck, and rounded body of this simple vase show a strong sense of harmony. Enhanced by a

10-24 • GUAN WARE VASE
Southern Song dynasty, 13th century CE. Gray stoneware with crackled grayish-blue glaze, height 6⅝" (16.8 cm). Percival David Foundation of Chinese Art, British Museum, London.

SEE MORE: View a video about the process of ceramic making **www.myartslab.com**

lustrous grayish-blue glaze, the form flows without break from base to lip. The piece has an introspective quality as eloquent as the blank spaces in Xia Gui's painting. The aesthetic of the Song is most evident in the crackle pattern on the glazed surface. The crackle technique was probably discovered accidentally, but came to be used deliberately in some of the most refined Song wares. In the play of irregular, spontaneous crackles over a perfectly regular, perfectly planned form we can sense the same spirit that hovers behind the self-effacing virtuosity and freely intuitive insights of Xia Gui's landscape.

In 1279 the Southern Song dynasty fell to the conquering forces of the Mongol leader Kublai Khan (1215–1294). China was subsumed into the vast Mongol Empire. Mongol rulers founded the Yuan dynasty (1279–1368), setting up their capital in the northeast in what is now Beijing. Yet the cultural center of China remained in the south, in the cities that rose to prominence during the Song, especially Hangzhou. This separation of political and cultural centers, coupled with a lasting resentment toward "barbarian" rule, created the climate for later developments in the arts.

THE ARTS OF KOREA

Set between China and Japan, Korea occupies a peninsula in northeast Asia. Inhabited for millennia, the peninsula gave rise to a distinctively Korean culture during the Three Kingdoms period.

THE THREE KINGDOMS PERIOD

Traditionally dated 57 BCE to 668 CE, the Three Kingdoms period saw the establishment of three independent nation-states: Silla in the southeast, Baekje in the southwest, and Goguryeo in the north. Large tomb mounds built during the fifth and sixth centuries are enduring monuments of this period.

A GOLD HEADDRESS.	The most spectacular items recovered from these tombs are trappings of royal authority (FIG. 10–25). Made expressly for burial, this elaborate crown was assembled from cut pieces of thin gold sheet, held together by gold wire. Spangles of gold embellish the crown, as do comma-shaped ornaments of green and white jadeite—a form of jade mineralogically distinct from the nephrite prized by the early Chinese. The tall, branching forms rising from the crown's periphery resemble trees and antlers. Within the crown is a conical cap woven of narrow strips of sheet gold and ornamented with appendages that suggest wings or feathers.

HIGH-FIRED CERAMICS.	The tombs have also yielded ceramics in abundance. Most are containers for offerings of food placed in the tomb to nourish the spirit of the deceased. These items generally are of unglazed **stoneware**, a high-fired ceramic ware that is impervious to liquids, even without glaze.

The most imposing ceramic shapes are the tall stands that were used to support round-bottomed jars (FIG. 10–26). Such stands typically have a long, cylindrical shaft set on a bulbous base. Cut into the moist clay before firing, their openwork apertures lighten what otherwise would be rather ponderous forms. Although few examples of Three Kingdoms ceramics exhibit surface ornamentation, other than an occasional combed wave pattern or an incised configuration of circles and **chevrons** (v-shapes), here snakes inch their way up the shaft of the stand.

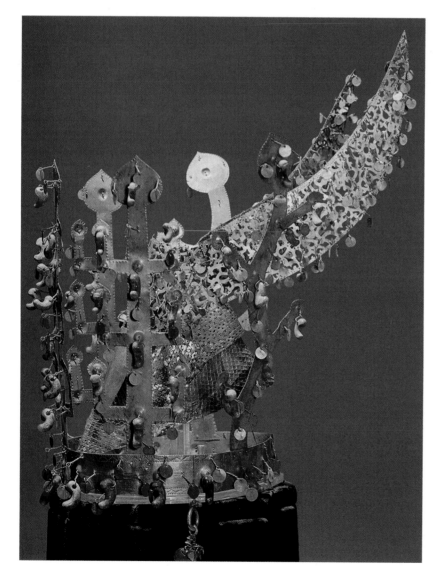

10-25 • CROWN
Korea. Three Kingdoms period, Silla kingdom, probably 6th century CE. From the Gold Crown Tomb, Gyeongju, North Gyeongsang Province. Gold with jadeite ornaments, height 17½″ (44.5 cm). National Museum of Korea, Seoul, Republic of Korea.

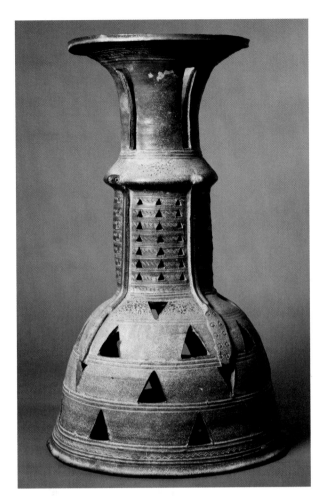

10-26 • CEREMONIAL STAND WITH SNAKE, ABSTRACT, AND OPENWORK DECORATION

Korean. Three Kingdoms period, Silla kingdom, 5th–6th century CE. Gray stoneware with combed, stamped, applied, and openwork decoration and with traces of natural ash glaze, height 23⅛″ (58.7 cm). Reportedly recovered in Andong, North Gyeongsang Province. Arthur M. Sackler Museum, Harvard University, Cambridge, Massachusetts. Partial gift of Maria C. Henderson and partial purchase through the Ernest B. and Helen Pratt Dane Fund for the Acquisition of Oriental Art (1991.501)

A BODHISATTVA SEATED IN MEDITATION. Buddhism was introduced into the Goguryeo kingdom from China in 372 CE and into Baekje by 384. Although it probably reached Silla in the second half of the fifth century, Buddhism gained recognition as the official religion of the Silla state only in 527.

At first, Buddhist art in Korea was a mere imitation of Chinese art. However, by the late sixth century, Korean sculptors had created a style of their own, as illustrated by a magnificent gilt bronze image of a bodhisattva (probably the bodhisattva Maitreya) seated in meditation that likely dates to the early seventh century (FIG. 10–27). Although the pose links it to Chinese sculpture of the late sixth century, the slender body, elliptical face, elegant drapery folds, and trilobed crown distinguish it as Korean.

Buddhism was introduced to Japan from Korea—from the Baekje kingdom, according to literary accounts. In fact, historical sources indicate that numerous Korean sculptors were active in

10-27 • BODHISATTVA SEATED IN MEDITATION

Korean. Three Kingdoms period, probably Silla kingdom, early 7th century CE. Gilt bronze, height 35⅞″ (91 cm). National Museum of Korea, Seoul, Republic of Korea (formerly in the collection of the Toksu Palace Museum of Fine Arts, Seoul).

Japan in the sixth and seventh centuries; several early masterpieces of Buddhist art in Japan show pronounced Korean influence (SEE FIG. 11–6).

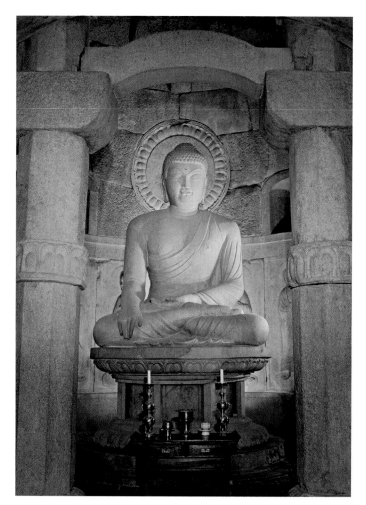

10-28 • SEATED SHAKYAMUNI BUDDHA
Seokguram Grotto, near Gyeongju, North Gyeongsang Province, Korea. Unified Silla period, c. 751 CE. Granite, height of Buddha 11′2½″ (342 cm).

The Buddha's hands are in the *bhumisparsha mudra*, the earth-touching gesture symbolizing his enlightenment.

THE UNIFIED SILLA PERIOD

In 660, the Silla kingdom conquered Baekje, and, in 668, through an alliance with Tang-dynasty China, it vanquished Goguryeo, uniting the peninsula under the rule of the Unified Silla dynasty, which lasted until 935. Buddhism prospered under Unified Silla, and many large, important temples were erected in and around Gyeongju, the Silla capital.

SEOKGURAM.   The greatest monument of the Unified Silla period is Seokguram, an artificial cave-temple constructed under royal patronage atop Mount Toham, near Gyeongju. The temple is modeled after Chinese cave-temples of the fifth, sixth, and seventh centuries, which were in turn inspired by the Buddhist cave-temples of India.

Built in the mid eighth century of cut blocks of granite, Seokguram consists of a small rectangular antechamber joined by a narrow vestibule to a circular main hall with a domed ceiling. More than 11 feet in height, a huge seated Buddha dominates the

main hall **(FIG. 10–28)**. Seated on a lotus pedestal, the image represents the historical Buddha Shakyamuni at the moment of his enlightenment, as indicated by his earth-touching gesture, or *bhumisparsha mudra*. The full, taut forms, diaphanous drapery, and anatomical details of his chest relate this image to eighth-century Chinese sculptures. Exquisitely carved low-relief images of bodhisattvas and lesser deities grace the walls of the antechamber, vestibule, and main hall.

GORYEO DYNASTY

Established in 918, the Goryeo dynasty eliminated the last vestiges of Unified Silla rule in 935; it would continue until 1392, ruling from its capital at Gaeseong—to the northwest of present-day Seoul and now in North Korea. A period of courtly refinement, the Goryeo dynasty is best known for its celadon-glazed ceramics.

CELADON-GLAZED CERAMICS.   The term **celadon** refers to a high-fired, transparent glaze of pale bluish-green hue, typically applied over a pale gray stoneware body. Chinese potters invented celadon glazes

10-29 • MAEBYEONG BOTTLE WITH DECORATION OF BAMBOO AND BLOSSOMING PLUM TREE
Korea. Goryeo dynasty, late 12th–early 13th century CE. Inlaid celadon ware: light gray stoneware with decoration inlaid with black and white slips under celadon glaze, height 13¼″ (33.7 cm). Tokyo National Museum, Tokyo, Japan. (TG-2171)

10-30 • SEATED WILLOW-BRANCH GWANSE'EUM BOSAL (THE BODHISATTVA AVALOKITESHVARA)
Korea. Goryeo dynasty, late 14th century CE. Hanging scroll, ink, colors, and gold pigment on silk, height 62½" (159.6 cm). Arthur M. Sackler Museum, Harvard University, Cambridge, Massachusetts. Bequest of Grenville L. Winthrop (1943.57.12)

techniques of decoration. Most notable among their inventions was inlaid decoration, in which black and white slips, or finely ground clays, were inlaid into the intaglio lines of decorative elements incised or stamped in the body, creating underglaze designs in contrasting colors. The bottle in **FIGURE 10–29** displays three different pictorial scenes inlaid in black and white slips. The scene featured here depicts a clump of bamboo growing at the edge of a lake, the stalks intertwined with the branches of a blossoming plum tree (which flowers in late winter, before donning its leaves). Geese swim in the lake and butterflies flutter above, linking the several scenes around the bottle. Called *maebyeong* ("plum bottle"), such broad-shouldered vessels were used as storage jars for wine, vinegar, and other liquids. A small, bell-shaped cover originally capped the bottle, protecting its contents and complementing its curves.

BUDDHIST PAINTING.   Buddhism, the state religion of Goryeo, enjoyed royal patronage; many temples were thus able to commission the very finest architects, sculptors, and painters. The most sumptuous Buddhist works produced during the Goryeo period were paintings. Wrought in ink and colors on silk, the fourteenth-century hanging scroll illustrated in **FIGURE 10–30** depicts Gwanse'eum Bosal (whom the Chinese called Guanyin), the bodhisattva of compassion. The flesh tones used for the bodhisattva's face and hands, along with the rich colors and gold pigment used for the deity's clothing, reflect the luxurious taste of the period. Numerous paintings of this type were exported to Japan, where they influenced the course of Buddhist painting.

THINK ABOUT IT

10.1 Examine the *guang* (fig. 10–5) and consider how its iconography may have related to a ritual-oriented culture in Bronze Age China.

10.2 Summarize the main tenets of Confucianism. Then select a work from the chapter that gives visual form to Confucian philosophy and explain how it does so.

10.3 Select one of the Song-era Chinese landscape paintings included in the chapter and explain how it may embody Daoist ideals.

10.4 Compare and contrast the Chinese seated Guanyin bodhisattva (FIG. 10–19) and the Korean bodhisattva seated in meditation (FIG. 10–27). Define the meaning of bodhisattva, and examine how the artists gave visual expression to the deity's attributes.

10.5 Based on examples illustrated in the chapter, identify parallel developments in painting and sculpture from the Han through the Song dynasty.

PRACTICE MORE: Compose answers to these questions, get flashcards for images and terms, and review chapter material with quizzes
www.myartslab.com

and had initiated the continuous production of celadon-glazed wares as early as the first century CE. Korean potters began to experiment with such glazes in the eighth and ninth centuries; their earliest celadons reflect the strong imprint of Chinese ware. Soon, the finest Goryeo celadons rivaled the best Chinese court ceramics. These wares were used by people of various socioeconomic classes during the Goryeo dynasty, with the finest examples going to the palace, nobles, or the powerful Buddhist clergy.

Prized for their classic simplicity, Korean celadons of the eleventh century often have little decoration, while those of the twelfth century frequently sport incised, carved, or molded decoration, thus generally mimicking the style and ornamentation of contemporaneous Chinese ceramics. By the mid twelfth century, Korean potters began to explore new styles and

11–1 • KASUGA SHRINE MANDALA Kamakura period, early 14th century CE. Hanging scroll, ink, color, and gold on silk, 39½ × 15⅝″ (100.3 × 39.8 cm). Mary and Jackson Burke Collection.

JAPANESE ART BEFORE 1333

A group of Buddhist deities hovers in the sky across the top of this painting (FIG. 11–1), above verdant hills and meadows filled with blossoming cherry and plum trees, and a diagrammatic, bird's-eye view of a religious compound. The sacred site depicted in recognizable, but partially idealized, form is the Kasuga Shrine in Nara, dedicated to deities, known as *kami*, of Japan's native Shinto religion. It served as the family shrine for the most powerful aristocratic clan in ancient Japan, the Fujiwara, who chose the site because of its proximity to their home as well as for its natural beauty. As life in Japan revolved around natural seasonal rhythms, so too did conceptions of *kami*, who give and protect life and embody the life-sustaining forces of nature. The Japanese believe that *kami* descend from mysterious heavens at supremely beautiful places such as majestic mountains, towering waterfalls, old and gnarled trees, or unusual rock formations, thus rendering such locations holy. They consider them as places where they can go to commune with *kami*. The deer glimpsed scampering about the grounds are sacred messengers of *kami*, and freely roam the area even today.

That foreign deities associated with Buddhism preside over a native Shinto shrine presents no anomaly to the Japanese. By the Heian period (794–1185 CE), the interaction of Buddhist and Shinto doctrines resulted in the belief that *kami* were emanations of Buddhist deities who were their original forms. When Buddhism first entered Japan in the sixth century, efforts began to integrate that new faith with the indigenous Japanese religious belief system centered around *kami*, which only later came to be called Shinto. Until the government forcibly separated the two religions in the latter part of the nineteenth century, and elevated Shinto to bolster worship of the emperor, the two religions were intimately intertwined and evolved in a co-mingled manner. The two faiths could exist side by side because of their complementary values. Shinto explains the origins of the Japanese people and its deities protect them, while Buddhism offers salvation after death.

This painting encapsulates various aspects of the essential character of Japanese art and culture in the ancient and early medieval eras. Like all religious art from early Japan, it was created to aid religious teachings and beliefs. In its own time it was not considered a work of art. It testifies to the importance of nature in the Japanese worldview and how reverence for the natural world informed religious practice and visual vocabulary. Additionally, it shows how the Japanese integrated the foreign religion of Buddhism with indigenous belief systems without sacrificing either one. Finally, it reveals the existence at this early date of a sophisticated and uniquely Japanese courtly style aesthetic.

LEARN ABOUT IT

11.1 Recognize the native elements in early Japanese art.

11.2 Understand Japan's cultural relationship with China and Korea.

11.3 Summarize the transformation of Japanese Buddhist sculpture.

11.4 Discuss the ways Shinto influences Japanese aesthetic perceptions.

11.5 Distinguish different uses of Buddhist paintings in connection with the different sects of Buddhism for which they were made.

HEAR MORE: Listen to an audio file of your chapter **www.myartslab.com**

PREHISTORIC JAPAN

Human habitation in Japan dates to around 30,000 years ago (**MAP 11–1**). Sometime after 15,000 years ago Paleolithic peoples gave way to Neolithic hunter-gatherers, who gradually developed the ability to make and use ceramics. Recent scientific dating methods have shown that some works of Japanese pottery date to earlier than 10,000 BCE, making them the oldest now known.

JOMON PERIOD

The early potters lived during the Jomon period (c. 11,000–400 BCE), named for the patterns on much of the pottery they produced. They made functional earthenware vessels, probably originally imitating reed baskets, by building them up with coils of clay, then firing them in bonfires at relatively low temperatures. They also created small humanoid figures known as **dogu**, which were probably effigies that manifested a kind of sympathetic magic. Around 5000 BCE agriculture emerged with the planting and harvesting of beans and gourds.

YAYOI PERIOD

During the succeeding Yayoi era (c. 400 BCE–300 CE), the introduction of rice cultivation by immigrants from Korea helped transform Japan into an agricultural nation. As it did elsewhere in the world, this shift to agriculture brought larger permanent settlements, class structure with the division of labor into agricultural and nonagricultural tasks, more hierarchical forms of social organization, and a more centralized government. Korean settlers also brought metal technology. Bronze was used to create weapons as well as ceremonial objects such as bells. Iron metallurgy developed later in this period, eventually replacing stone tools in everyday life.

KOFUN PERIOD

Centralized government developed further during the ensuing Kofun ("old tombs") period (c. 300–552 CE), named for the large royal tombs that were built then. With the emergence of a more complex social order, the veneration of leaders grew into the beginnings of an imperial system. Still in existence today in Japan, this system eventually explained that the emperor (or, very rarely, empress) descended directly from Shinto deities. When an emperor died, chamber tombs were constructed following Korean examples. Various grave goods were placed inside the tomb chambers, including large amounts of pottery, presumably to pacify the spirits of the dead and to serve them in their next life. As part of a general cultural transfer from China through Korea, fifth-century potters in Japan gained knowledge of finishing techniques and improved kilns, and began to produce high-fired ceramic ware.

The Japanese government has never allowed the major sacred tombs to be excavated, but much is known about the mortuary practices of Kofun-era Japan. Some of the huge tombs of the fifth and sixth centuries were constructed in a shape resembling a large

MAP 11–1 • JAPAN

Melting glaciers at the end of the Ice Age in Japan 15,000 years ago raised the sea level and formed the four main islands of Japan: Hokkaido, Honshu, Shikoku, and Kyushu.

keyhole and surrounded by moats dug to protect the sacred precincts. Tomb sites might extend over more than 400 acres, with artificial hills built over the tombs themselves. On the top of the hills were placed ceramic works of sculpture called **haniwa**.

HANIWA. The first *haniwa* were simple cylinders that may have held jars with ceremonial offerings. By the fifth century, these cylinders came to be made in the shapes of ceremonial objects, houses, and boats. Gradually, living creatures were added to the repertoire of *haniwa* subjects, including birds, deer, dogs, monkeys, cows, and horses. By the sixth century, **HANIWA** in human shapes were crafted, including males and females of various types, professions, and classes (**FIG. 11–2**).

Haniwa illustrate several enduring characteristics of Japanese aesthetic taste. Unlike Chinese tomb ceramics, which were often

ART AND ITS CONTEXTS

Writing, Language, and Culture

Chinese culture enjoyed great prestige in east Asia. Written Chinese served as an international language of scholarship and cultivation, much as Latin did in medieval Europe. Educated Koreans, for example, wrote almost exclusively in Chinese until the fifteenth century. In Japan, Chinese continued to be used for certain kinds of writing, such as Buddhist *sutra*s, philosophical and legal texts, and Chinese poetry (by Japanese writers), into the nineteenth century.

When it came to writing their own language, the Japanese initially borrowed Chinese characters, or *kanji*. Differences between the Chinese and Japanese languages made this system extremely unwieldy, so during the ninth century they developed two syllabaries, or *kana*, from simplified Chinese characters. (A syllabary is a system of lettering in which each symbol stands for a syllable.) *Katakana*, consisting of angular symbols, was developed to aid pronunciation of Chinese Buddhist texts and now is generally used for foreign words. *Hiragana*, comprised of graceful, cursive symbols, was the written language the Japanese first used to write native poetry and prose. Eventually it came to be used to represent only the grammatical portions of the written Japanese language in conjunction with Chinese characters that convey meaning. Japanese written in *hiragana* was once called "women's hand" because its rounded forms looked feminine. During the Heian period *hiragana* were used to create a large body of literature, written either by women or sometimes for women by men.

A charming poem originated in Heian times to teach the new writing system. In two stanzas of four lines each, it uses almost all of the syllable sounds of spoken Japanese and thus almost every *kana* symbol. It was memorized as we would recite our ABCs. The first stanza translates as:

Although flowers glow with color
They are quickly fallen,
And who in this world of ours
Is free from change?
(Translation by Earl Miner)

Like Chinese, Japanese is written in columns from top to bottom and across the page from right to left. (Following this logic, Chinese and Japanese narrative paintings also read from right to left.) Below is the stanza written three ways. At the right, it appears in *katakana* glossed with the original phonetic value of each symbol. (Modern pronunciation has shifted slightly.) In the center, the stanza appears in flowing *hiragana*. To the left is the mixture of *kanji* and *hiragana* that eventually became standard.

kanji hiragana mixed

常ならむ
我世誰ぞ
散りぬるを
色は匂へど

hiragana

つねならむ
わかよたれそ
ちりぬるを
いろはにほへと

katakana

ツネナラム — Tsu-ne-na-ra-mu
ワカヨタレソ — Wa-ka-yo-ta-re-so
チリヌルヲ — Chi-ri-nu-ru-wo
イロハニホヘト — I-ro-ha-ni-he-to

11-2 • HANIWA
Kyoto. Kofun period, 6th century CE. Earthenware, height 27″ (68.5 cm). Collection of the Tokyo National Museum. Important Cultural Property.

There have been many theories as to the function of *haniwa*. The figures seem to have served as some kind of link between the world of the dead, over which they were placed, and the world of the living, from which they could be viewed. This figure has been identified as a seated female shaman, wearing a robe, belt, and necklace and carrying a mirror at her waist. In early Japan, shamans acted as agents between the natural and the supernatural worlds, just as *haniwa* figures were links between the living and the dead.

glazed, *haniwa* were left with their clay bodies unglazed. Nor do *haniwa* show a preoccupation with technical skill seen in Chinese ceramics. Instead, their makers explored the expressive potentials of simple and bold form. *Haniwa* are never perfectly symmetrical; their slightly off-center eye slits, irregular cylindrical bodies, and unequal arms impart the idiosyncrasy of life and individuality.

SHINTO. As described at the outset of this chapter, Shinto is Japan's indigenous religious belief system. It encompasses a variety of ritual practices that center around family, village, and national devotion to *kami* (Shinto deities). The term Shinto was not coined until after the arrival of Buddhism in the sixth century CE, and as *kami* worship was influenced by and incorporated into Buddhism it became more systematized, with shrines, a hierarchy of deities, and more strictly regulated ceremonies.

THE ISE SHRINE. One of the great Shinto monuments is the Grand Shrine of Ise, on the coast southwest of Tokyo **(FIG. 11–3)**, where the main deity worshiped is the sun goddess Amaterasu-o-mi-*kami*, the legendary progenitor of Japan's imperial family. Japan's earliest written historical texts recorded by the imperial

court in the eighth century state that the Ise Shrine dates to the first century CE. Although we do not know for certain if this is true, it is known that it has been ritually rebuilt, alternately on two adjoining sites at 20-year intervals with few breaks since the year 690, a time when the imperial family was solidifying its hegemony. Its most recent rebuilding took place in 1993, by carpenters who train for the task from childhood. After the *kami* is ceremonially escorted to the freshly copied shrine, the old shrine is dismantled. Thus—like Japanese culture itself—this exquisite shrine is both ancient and constantly renewed. In this sense it embodies one of the most important characteristics of Shinto faith—ritual purification—derived from respect for the cycle of the seasons in which pure new life emerges in springtime and gives way to death in winter, yet is reborn again in the following year.

Although Ise is visited by millions of pilgrims each year, only members of the imperial family and a few Shinto priests are allowed within the enclosure that surrounds its inner shrine. Although detailed documents on its appearance date back to the tenth century, shrine authorities never allowed photographers access to its inner compound until 1953, when the iconic photograph of it reproduced in FIGURE 11–3 was taken by a photographer officially

11-3 • **MAIN HALL, INNER SHRINE, ISE**
Mie Prefecture. Last rebuilt 1993. Photograph by Watanabe Yoshio (1907–2000), 1953. National Treasure.

SEE MORE: View a video about the re-building of the Ise Shrine
www.myartslab.com

engaged by a quasi-governmental cultural relations agency. The reluctance of shrine officials to permit photography even then may stem from beliefs that such intimate pictures would violate the privacy of the shrine's most sacred spaces.

The Ise Shrine has many aspects that are typical of Shinto architecture, including wooden piles raising the building off the ground, a thatched roof held in place by horizontal logs, the use of unpainted cypress wood, and the overall feeling of natural simplicity rather than overwhelming size or elaborate decoration. The building's shape is indebted to raised granaries used by the Yayoi people, which are known from drawings on bronze artifacts of the Yayoi period. The sensitive use of wood and thatch in the Ise Shrine suggests an early origin for the Japanese appreciation of natural materials that persists to the present day.

ASUKA PERIOD

During the Asuka period's single century (552–645 CE), new forms of philosophy, medicine, music, food, clothing, agriculture, city planning, religion, visual art, and architecture entered Japan from Korea and China at an astonishing pace. Most significant among these were the Buddhist religion, a centralized governmental structure, and a system of writing. Each was adopted and gradually modified to suit Japanese conditions, and each has had an enduring legacy.

Buddhism reached Japan in Mahayana form, with its many buddhas and bodhisattvas (see "Buddhism," page 297). After being accepted by the imperial family, it was soon adopted as a state religion. Buddhism represented not only different gods from Shinto but an entirely new concept of religion. Worship of Buddhist deities took place inside worship halls of temples situated in close proximity to imperial cities. The temples looked like nothing constructed in Japan before, with Chinese-influenced buildings housing anthropomorphic Buddhist icons possessing an elaborate iconography (see "Buddhist Symbols," page 362). At that time, *kami* were not portrayed in human form. Yet Buddhism attracted followers because it offered a rich cosmology with profound teachings of meditation and enlightenment, and the protective powers of its deities enabled the ruling elites to justify their own power, through association with Buddhism. They called upon Buddhist deities to nurture and protect the populace over whom they ruled. Many highly developed aspects of continental Asian art accompanied the new religion, including new methods of painting and sculpture.

HORYUJI

The most significant surviving early Japanese temple is Horyuji, located on Japan's central plains not far from Nara. The temple was founded in 607 by Prince Shotoku (574–622), who ruled Japan as a regent and became the most influential early proponent of Buddhism. Rebuilt after a fire in 670, Horyuji is the oldest wooden temple in the world. It is so famous that visitors are often surprised at its modest size. Yet its just proportions and human scale, together with the artistic treasures it contains, make Horyuji an enduringly beautiful monument to Buddhist faith in early Japan.

The main compound of Horyuji consists of a rectangular courtyard surrounded by covered corridors, one of which contains a gateway. Within the compound are only two buildings, the **kondo** (golden hall), and a five-story pagoda. Within a simple asymmetrical layout, the large *kondo* perfectly balances the tall, slender pagoda **(FIG. 11–4)**. The *kondo* is filled with Buddhist images and is used for worship and ceremonies. The pagoda serves as a reliquary and is not entered. Other monastery buildings lie outside the main compound, including an outer gate, a lecture hall, a repository for sacred texts, a belfry, and dormitories for monks.

Among the many treasures still preserved in Horyuji is a shrine decorated with paintings in lacquer. It is known as the Tamamushi Shrine after the *tamamushi* beetle, whose iridescent wings were originally affixed to the shrine to make it glitter, much

11–5 • HUNGRY TIGRESS JATAKA
Panel of the Tamamushi Shrine, Horyuji. Asuka period, c. 650 CE. Lacquer on wood, height of shrine 7'7½" (2.33 m). Horyuji Treasure House, Nara. National Treasure.

transmitted to Japan via China and Korea. These illustrations of Jataka tales helped popularize Buddhism in Japan.

SHAKA TRIAD. Another example of the international style of early Buddhist art at Horyuji is the sculpture called the Shaka Triad, traditionally identified as being made by Tori Busshi (FIG. 11–6). (Shaka is the Japanese name for Shakyamuni, the historical Buddha.) Tori Busshi (Busshi means Buddhist image-maker) may have been a descendant of Korean craftsmen who emigrated to Japan as part of an influx of Buddhists and artisans from Korea. The Shaka Triad reflects the strong influence of Chinese art of the Northern Wei dynasty (SEE FIG. 10–12). The frontal pose, the outsized face and hands, and the linear treatment of the drapery all suggest that the maker of this statue was well aware of earlier continental models, while the fine bronze casting of the figures shows his advanced technical skill. The Shaka Triad and the Tamamushi Shrine reveal the importance of Buddhist imagery to the transmission of the faith.

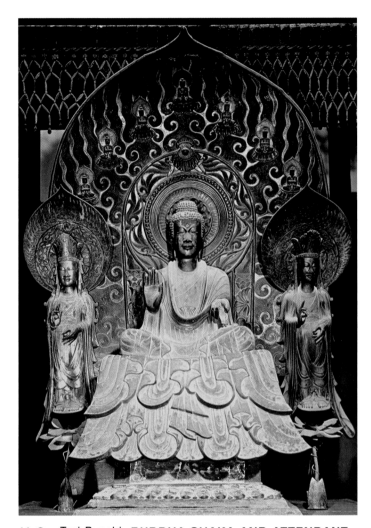

11-6 • Tori Busshi **BUDDHA SHAKA AND ATTENDANT BODHISATTVAS IN THE HORYUJI** *KONDO*
Asuka period, c. 623 CE. Gilt bronze, height of seated figure 34½" (87.5 cm). Horyuji, Nara. National Treasure.

like mother-of-pearl. Its architectural form replicates an ancient palace-form building type that predates Horyuji itself.

HUNGRY TIGRESS JATAKA. Paintings on the sides of the Tamamushi Shrine are among the few two-dimensional works of art to survive from the Asuka period. Most celebrated among them are two that illustrate Jataka tales, stories about former lives of the Buddha. One depicts the future Buddha nobly sacrificing his life in order to feed his body to a starving tigress and her cubs (FIG. 11–5). The tigers are at first too weak to eat him, so he must jump off a cliff to break open his flesh. The anonymous artist has created a full narrative within a single frame. The graceful form of the Buddha appears three times, harmonized by the curves of the rocky cliff and tall sprigs of bamboo. First, he hangs his shirt on a tree, then he dives downward onto the rocks, and finally starving animals devour his body. The elegantly slender renditions of the figure and the somewhat abstract treatment of the cliff, trees, and bamboo represent an international Buddhist style that was

NARA PERIOD

The Nara period (645–794) is named for Japan's first permanent imperial capital, founded in 710. Previously, an emperor's death was thought to taint his entire capital city, so for reasons of purification (and perhaps also of politics), his successor usually selected a new site. As the government adopted ever more complex aspects of the Chinese political system, necessitating construction of huge administrative complexes, it abandoned this custom in the eighth century when Nara was founded. During this period, divisions of the imperial bureaucracy grew exponentially and hastened the swelling of the city's population to perhaps 200,000 people.

One result of the strong central authority was the construction in Nara of magnificent Buddhist temples and Shinto shrines that dwarfed those built previously. The expansive park in the center of Nara today is the site of the largest and most important of these, including the Shinto Kasuga Shrine illustrated in FIGURE 11–1. The grandest of the Buddhist temples in Nara Park is Todaiji, which Emperor Shomu (r. 724–749) conceived as the headquarters of a vast network of branch temples throughout the nation. He had it constructed because of his deep faith in Buddhism. Todaiji served as both a state-supported central monastic training center and as the setting for public religious ceremonies. The most spectacular of these took place in 752 and celebrated the consecration of the main Buddhist statue of the temple in a traditional "eye-opening" ceremony, in its newly constructed Great Buddha Hall (*Daibutsuden*; see "The Great Buddha Hall," page 364). The statue, a giant gilt bronze image of the Buddha Birushana (Vairochana in Sanskrit), was inspired by the Chinese tradition of erecting monumental stone Buddhist statues in cave-temples (SEE, FOR EXAMPLE, FIG. 10–12).

The ceremony, which took place in the vast courtyard in front of the Great Buddha Hall, was presided over by an illustrious

Buddhist Symbols

A few of the most important Buddhist symbols, which have myriad variations, are described here in their most generalized forms.

Lotus flower: Usually shown as a white waterlily, the lotus (Sanskrit, *padma*) symbolizes spiritual purity, the wholeness of creation, and cosmic harmony. The flower's stem is an *axis mundi* ("axis of the world").

Lotus throne: Buddhas are frequently shown seated on an open lotus, either single or double, a representation of *nirvana* (SEE FIG. 11–10).

Chakra: An ancient sun symbol, the *chakra* (wheel) symbolizes both the various states of existence (the Wheel of Life) and the Buddhist doctrine (the Wheel of the Law). A *chakra*'s exact meaning depends on how many spokes it has (SEE FIG. 9–7).

Marks of a buddha: A buddha is distinguished by 32 physical attributes (*lakshana*s). Among them are a bulge on top of the head (*ushnisha*), a tuft of hair between the eyebrows (*urna*), elongated earlobes, and 1,000-spoked *chakra*s on the soles of the feet.

Mandala: *Mandala*s are diagrams of cosmic realms, representing order and meaning within the spiritual universe. They may be simple or complex, three- or two-dimensional, and in a wide array of forms— such as an Indian stupa (SEE FIG. 9–8) or a Womb World *mandala* (SEE FIG. 11–8), an early Japanese type.

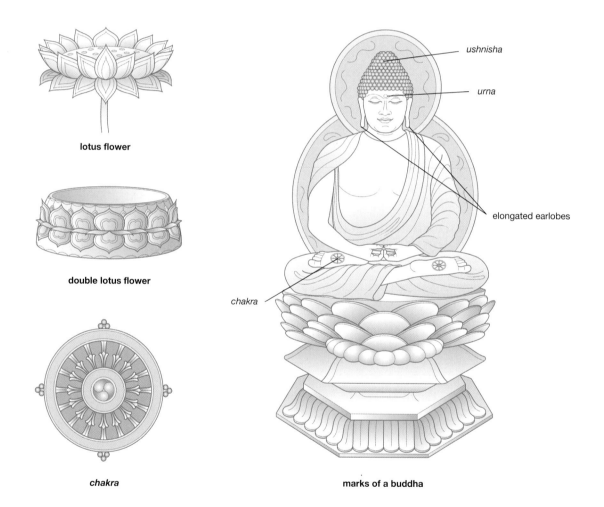

lotus flower

double lotus flower

chakra

ushnisha

urna

elongated earlobes

chakra

marks of a buddha

Indian monk and included *sutra* chanting by over 10,000 Japanese Buddhist monks and sacred performances by 4,000 court musicians and dancers. Vast numbers of Japanese courtiers and emissaries from the Asian continent comprised the audience. Numerous ritual objects used in the ceremony came from exotic Asian and Near Eastern lands. The resulting cosmopolitan atmosphere reflected the position Nara then held as the eastern terminus of the Central Asian Silk Road.

Many of these treasures have been preserved in the Shosoin Imperial Repository at Todaiji, which today contains some 9,000

11–7 • FIVE-STRINGED LUTE (*BIWA*) WITH DESIGN OF A CENTRAL ASIAN MAN PLAYING A *BIWA* ATOP A CAMEL
Chinese. Tang dynasty, 8th century CE. Red sandalwood and chestnut inlaid with mother-of-pearl, amber, and tortoiseshell. Length 42½″ (108.1 cm), width 12″ (30.9 cm), depth 3½″ (9 cm). Shosoin, Todaiji, Nara.

objects. The Shosoin came into being in the year 756, when Emperor Shomu died and his widow donated some 600 of his possessions to the temple, including a number of objects used during the Great Buddha's consecration ceremony. Many years later, objects used in Buddhist rituals and previously stored elsewhere at Todaiji were added to these. The objects formerly owned by Emperor Shomu consisted mainly of his personal possessions, such as documents, furniture, musical instruments, games, clothing, medicine, weapons, food and beverage vessels of metal, glass, and lacquer, and some Buddhist ritual objects. Some of these were made in Japan while others were clearly not and came from as far away as China, India, Iran, Greece, Rome, and Egypt. They reflect the vast international trade network that existed at this early date.

One of the items Emperor Shomu's widow donated in 756 is a magnificently crafted five-stringed lute (*biwa*) made of lacquered red sandalwood and chestnut, and inlaid with mother-of-pearl, amber, and tortoiseshell. Its plectrum guard features a design of a man of central Asian origin (apparent from his clothing and physical features) sitting atop a camel and playing a lute **(FIG. 11–7)**. This instrument is the only existing example of an ancient five-stringed lute. Its form was invented in India and transmitted to China and Japan via the Silk Road. The Shosoin piece is generally identified as Chinese. However, as with many of the objects preserved in the Shosoin, the location of its manufacture is not absolutely certain. While it was most likely crafted in China and imported to Japan for use in the consecration ceremony (researchers have recently conclusively determined that it was indeed played), it is also plausible that Chinese (or Japanese) craftsmen made it in Japan using imported materials. Its meticulous workmanship reveals the high level of crafts production that artists of this era achieved. Such consummate skill has been a hallmark of Japanese crafts since then.

Influenced by Emperor Shomu, the Buddhist faith permeated all aspects of court society of the Nara period. Indeed, in 749 Shomu abdicated the throne to retire as a monk. His daughter, who succeeded him as empress, was also a devout Buddhist and wanted to cede her throne to a Buddhist monk. This dismayed her advisors and prompted them to move the capital city away from Nara, where they felt Buddhist influence had become overpowering, and establish a new one, Kyoto, within whose bounds, at first, only a few Buddhist temples would be allowed. The move of the capital to Kyoto marked the end of the Nara period.

HEIAN PERIOD

The Japanese fully absorbed and transformed their cultural borrowings from China and Korea during the Heian period (794–1185). Generally peaceful conditions contributed to a new air of self-reliance. The imperial government severed ties to China in the ninth century, a time when the power of related aristocratic families increased. An efficient method of writing the Japanese language was developed, and the rise of vernacular literature generated such prose masterpieces as Lady Murasaki's *The Tale of Genji*. During these four centuries of splendor and refinement, two major streams of Buddhism emerged—first, esoteric sects and, later, those espousing salvation in the Pure Land Western Paradise of the Buddha Amida.

ESOTERIC BUDDHIST ART

With the removal of the capital to Kyoto, the older Nara temples lost their influence. Soon two new Esoteric sects of Buddhism, Tendai and Shingon, grew to dominate Japanese religious life. Strongly influenced by polytheistic religions such as Hinduism,

The Great Buddha Hall (*Daibutsuden*) is distinguished today as the largest wooden structure in the world. To give a sense of its unprecedented scale, it was so large that the area surrounding only one of the two pagodas that flanked it, within its own cloistered compound, could accommodate the entire main compound of Horyuji. Yet the present Great Buddha Hall, dating to a reconstruction of 1707, is 30 percent smaller than the original, which towered nearly 90 feet in height. Since it was first erected in 752 CE natural disasters and intentional destruction by foes of the imperial family necessitated its reconstruction four times. It was first destroyed during civil wars in the twelfth century and rebuilt in 1203, then destroyed in yet another civil war in 1567. Reconstruction did not occur until the late seventeenth century under the direction of a charismatic monk who solicited funds not from the government, which was then impoverished, but through popular subscription. This building, completed in 1707, is essentially the structure that stands on the site today. However, by the late nineteenth century its condition had deteriorated so profoundly that restoration finally undertaken between 1906 and 1913 entailed completely dismantling it and putting it back together, this time utilizing steel (imported from England) and concrete to provide invisible support to the roof, which had nearly collapsed. Architects adapted this nontraditional solution mainly because no trees of sufficiently large dimensions could be found, and no traditional carpenters then living possessed knowledge of ancient construction techniques. This project occurred only after laws were enacted in 1897 to preserve ancient architecture. Since then, another major restoration on the building took place between 1973 and 1980.

Like the building, the Great Buddha Daibutsu statue has not survived intact. Its head was completely destroyed in the late sixteenth century and replaced as part of the hall's reconstruction in the late seventeenth century, when its torso and lotus petal throne also required extensive restoration. The present statue, though impressive in scale, appears stiff and rigid. Its more lyrical original appearance can be approximated from that of engraved images of

seated Buddhist deities found on a massive cast-bronze lotus petal from the original statue that has survived in fragmentary form. The petal features a buddha with a narrow waist, broad shoulders, and elegantly flowing robes that characterize the style of contemporaneous buddha images of the Tang dynasty (see, for example, the central buddha in FIG. 10–14).

THE BUDDHA SHAKA, DETAIL OF A PARADISE SCENE
Engraved bronze lotus petal from the original Great Buddha (Daibutsu) statue of the Buddha Birushana. 8th century CE. Height of petal 79″ (200 cm). *Daibutsuden*, Todaiji. National Treasure.

GREAT BUDDHA HALL (*DAIBUTSUDEN*), TODAIJI, NARA
Original structure completed in 752 CE. Destroyed and rebuilt in 1707. Extensively restored 1906–13. UNESCO World Heritage Site, National Treasure.

11–8 • WOMB WORLD *MANDALA*
Heian period, late 9th century CE. Hanging scroll, colors on silk, 6′ × 5′1½″ (1.83 × 1.54 m). Toji, Kyoto. National Treasure.

*Mandala*s are used not only in teaching, but also as vehicles for practice. A monk, initiated into secret teachings, may meditate upon and assume the gestures of each deity depicted in the *mandala*, gradually working out from the center, so that he absorbs some of each deity's powers. The monk may also recite magical phrases, called *mantra*s, as an aid to meditation. The goal is to achieve enlightenment through the powers of the different forms of the Buddha. *Mandala*s are created in sculptural and architectural forms as well as in paintings (SEE FIG. 9–29). Their integration of the two most basic shapes, the circle and the square, is an expression of the principles of ancient geomancy (divining by means of lines and figures) as well as Buddhist cosmology.

Esoteric Buddhism (known as Tantric Buddhism in Nepal and Tibet) included a daunting number of deities, each with magical powers. The historical Buddha was no longer very important. Instead, most revered was the universal Buddha, called Dainichi ("Great Sun") in Japanese, who was believed to preside over the universe. He was accompanied by buddhas and bodhisattvas, as well as guardian deities who formed fierce counterparts to the more benign gods.

Esoteric Buddhism is hierarchical, and its deities have complex relationships to one another. Learning all the different gods and their interrelationships was assisted greatly by works of art, especially *mandalas*, cosmic diagrams of the universe that portray the deities in schematic order. The Womb World *mandala* from Toji, for example, is entirely filled with depictions of gods. Dainichi is at the center, surrounded by buddhas of the four directions (**FIG. 11–8**). Other deities, including some with multiple heads and limbs, branch out in diagrammatical order, each with a specific symbol of power. To believers, the *mandala* represents an ultimate reality beyond the visible world.

Perhaps the most striking attribute of many Esoteric Buddhist images is their sense of spiritual force and potency, especially in depictions of the wrathful deities, which are often surrounded by flames, like those visible in the Womb World *mandala* just below the main circle of Buddhas. Esoteric Buddhism, with its intricate theology and complex doctrines, was a religion for the educated aristocracy, not for the masses. Its intricate network of deities, hierarchy, and ritual found a parallel in the elaborate social divisions of the Heian court.

PURE LAND BUDDHIST ART

Rising militarism, political turbulence, and the excesses of the imperial court marked the beginning of the eleventh century in Japan. To many Japanese of this century, the unsettled times seemed to confirm the coming of *Mappo*, a long-prophesied dark age of spiritual degeneration. Japanese of all classes reacted by increasingly turning to the promise of salvation after death through simple faith in the existence of a Buddhist realm known as the Western Paradise of the Pure Land, a resplendent place filled with divine flowers and music. Amida (Amithaba in Sanskrit) and his attendant bodhisattvas preside there as divine protectors who compassionately accept into their land of bliss all who submit wholeheartedly to their benevolent powers. Pure Land beliefs had spread to Japan from China by way of Korea, where they also enjoyed great popularity. They offered a more immediate and easy means to achieve salvation than the elaborate rituals of the Esoteric sects. The religion held that merely by chanting *Namu Amida Butsu* ("Hail to Amida Buddha"), the faithful would be reborn into the Western Paradise.

Wood is a temperamental material because fluctuations in moisture content cause it to swell and shrink. Cut from a living, sap-filled tree, it takes many years to dry to a state of stability. While the outside of a piece of wood dries fairly rapidly, the inside yields its moisture only gradually, causing a difference in the rates of shrinkage between the inside and the outside, which induces the wood to crack. Consequently, a large statue carved from a single log must inevitably crack as it ages. Natural irregularities in wood, such as knots, further accentuate this problem. Thus, wood with a thinner cross section and fewer irregularities is less susceptible to cracking because it can dry more evenly. (This is the logic behind sawing logs into boards before drying.)

Japanese sculptors developed an ingenious and unique method, the joined-block technique, to reduce cracking in heavy wooden statues. This allowed them to create larger statues in wood than ever before, enabled standardization of body proportions, and encouraged division of labor among teams of carvers, some of whom became specialists in certain parts, such as hands or crossed legs or lotus thrones. To create large statues seated in the lotus pose, sculptors first put four blocks together vertically two by two in front and back, to form the main body, then added several blocks horizontally at what would become the front of the statue for the lap and knees. After carving each part, they assembled the figure and hollowed out the interior. This cooperative approach also had the added benefit of enabling workshops to produce large statues more quickly to meet a growing demand. Jocho is credited as the master sculptor who perfected this technique. The diagram shows how he assembled the Amida Buddha at the Byodoin (SEE FIG. 11–10).

Diagram of the joined-block wood sculpture technique used on the Amida statue by Jocho (SEE FIG. 11–10).

SEE MORE: View a simulation about the joined-block technique **www.myartslab.com**

11-9 • PHOENIX HALL, BYODOIN, UJI
Kyoto Prefecture. Heian period, c. 1053 CE. Unesco World Heritage Site, National Treasure.

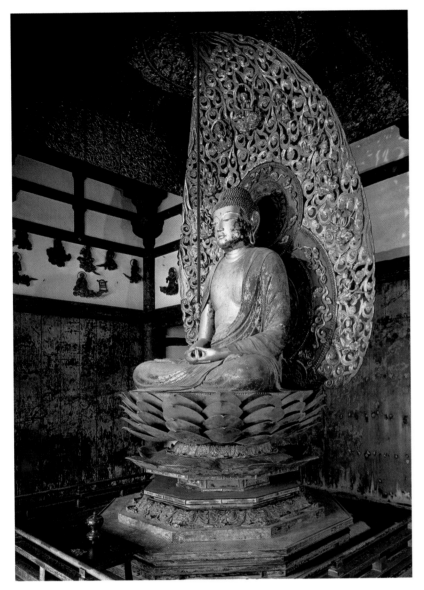

11-10 • Jocho AMIDA BUDDHA
Phoenix Hall, Byodoin. Heian period, c. 1053 CE. Gold leaf and lacquer on wood, height 9′8″ (2.95 m). National Treasure.

BYODOIN. One of the most beautiful temples of Pure Land Buddhism is the Byodoin, located in the Uji Mountains not far from Kyoto (FIG. 11–9). The temple itself was originally a secular palace whose form was intended to suggest the appearance of the palatial residence of Amida in his Western Paradise (SEE FIG. 10–14). It was built for a member of the powerful Fujiwara family who served as the leading counselor to the emperor. After the counselor's death in the year 1052, his descendants converted the palace into a memorial temple to honor his spirit. The Byodoin is often called the Phoenix Hall, not only for the pair of phoenix images on its roof, but also because the shape of the building itself suggests the mythical bird. Its thin columns give the Byodoin a sense of airiness, as though the entire temple could easily rise up through the sky to Amida's Western Paradise. The hall rests gently in front of an artificial pond created in the shape of the Sanskrit letter A, the sacred symbol for Amida.

The Byodoin's central image of Amida, carved by the master sculptor Jocho (d. 1057), exemplifies the serenity and compassion of this Buddha (FIG. 11–10). When reflected in the water of the pond before it, the Amida image seems to shimmer in its private mountain retreat. The figure was not carved from a single block of wood like earlier sculpture, but from several blocks in Jocho's new **joined-block** method of construction (see "Joined-Block Wood Sculpture," opposite). This technique allowed sculptors to create larger and lighter statuary. It also reflects the growing importance of wood as the medium of choice for Buddhist sculpture, reflecting the Japanese love for this natural material.

Surrounding the Amida on the walls of the Byodoin are smaller wooden figures of bodhisattvas and angels, some playing musical instruments. Everything about the Byodoin was designed to simulate the appearance of the paradise that awaits the believer after death. Its remarkable state of preservation after more than 900 years allows visitors to experience the late Heian religious ideal at its most splendid.

SECULAR PAINTING AND CALLIGRAPHY

Alongside the permeation of Buddhism during the Heian era (794–1185), a refined secular culture also arose at court. Gradually, over the course of these four centuries, the pervasive influence of Chinese culture in aristocratic society gave rise to new, uniquely Japanese developments. Above all, Heian court culture greatly valued refinement: Pity any man or woman at court who was not accomplished in several forms of art. A woman would be admired merely for the way she arranged the 12 layers of her robes by color, or a man for knowing which kind of incense was being burned. Concurrently, court life became preoccupied by the poetical expression of human love. In this climate, women became a vital force in Heian society. Although the status of women was to decline in later periods, they contributed greatly to art at the Heian court and became famous for their prose and poetry.

Although male couriers continued to be required to read and write Chinese, both men and women of court society wrote prose and poetry in their native Japanese language using the newly devised *kana* script (see "Writing, Language, and Culture," page 357). They also used *kana* on text portions of new types of small-scale secular paintings—handscrolls or folding albums designed to be appreciated in private settings.

At the beginning of the eleventh century, the lady-in-waiting Lady Murasaki transposed the lifestyle of Heian aristocrats into fiction for the amusement of her fellow court ladies, in *The Tale of Genji*, which some experts consider the world's first novel. The Japanese today admire this book as the pinnacle of their culture's

The Tale of Genji ▶

Scene from *The Tale of Genji*, Kashiwagi chapter.
Heian period, 12th century CE. Handscroll, ink and colors on paper, 8⅝ × 18⅞″ (21.9 × 47.9 cm). Tokugawa Art Museum, Nagoya. National Treasure.

Only 19 illustrated scenes from this earliest known example of an illustrated handscroll of *The Tale of Genji*, created about 100 years after the novel was written, have been preserved. Scholars assume that it once contained illustrations from the entire novel of 54 chapters, approximately 100 pictures in all. Each scroll seems to have been produced by a team of artists. One was the calligrapher, most likely a member of the nobility. Another was the master painter, who outlined two or three illustrations per chapter in fine brushstrokes and indicated the color scheme. Next, colorists went to work, applying layer after layer of color to build up patterns and textures. After they had finished, the master painter returned to reinforce outlines and apply the finishing touches, among them the details of the faces.

Thickly applied mineral colors are now cracking and flaking.

A "line for an eye, hook for a nose" style is used for facial features.

The building interior is seen from a bird's-eye perspective via a "blown-away roof".

A court lady beneath 12 layers of robes holds a fan to shield her face.

Court ladies have long, flowing hair.

A free-standing curtain screen creates privacy.

Wooden verandas surround Japanese houses, merging interior and exterior.

SEE MORE: View the Closer Look feature for the Scene from *The Tale of Genji* www.myartslab.com

literary achievements (in 2009, the official 1,000-year anniversary of its completion, numerous exhibitions and celebrations took place throughout Japan). Underlying the story of the love affairs of Prince Genji and his companions is the Japanese conception of fleeting pleasures and ultimate sadness in life, an echo of the Buddhist view of the vanity of earthly pleasures.

YAMATO-E HANDSCROLLS—*THE TALE OF GENJI*. One of the earliest extant secular paintings from Japan in a new native style is a series of scenes from an illustrated handscroll that depicts *The Tale of Genji*, which unknown artists painted in the twelfth century. The painting of Japanese native subjects in Japanese rather than Chinese styles is known as *yamato-e* (native Japanese-style pictures; Yamato is the old Japanese word for Japan). The type of *yamato-e* painting in the handscroll alternated sections of text with illustrations of scenes from the story and featured delicate lines, strong (but sometimes muted) mineral colors, and asymmetrical compositions. The *Genji* paintings have a refined, subtle emotional impact. They generally show court figures in architectural settings, with the frequent addition of natural elements, such as sections of gardens, that help to convey the mood of the scene. Thus a blossoming cherry tree appears in a scene of happiness, while unkempt weeds appear in a depiction of loneliness. Such correspondence between nature and human emotion is an enduring feature of Japanese poetry and art. The figures in *The Tale of Genji* paintings do not show their emotions directly on their faces, which are rendered with a few simple lines. Instead, their feelings are conveyed by colors, poses, and the total composition of the scenes.

One scene evokes the seemingly happy Prince Genji holding a baby boy borne by his wife, Nyosan. In fact, the baby was fathered by another court noble. Since Genji himself has not been faithful to Nyosan, who appears in profile below him, he cannot complain; meanwhile the true father of the child has died, unable to acknowledge his only son (see "A Closer Look," opposite). Thus, what should be a joyful scene has undercurrents of irony and sorrow. The irony is even greater because Genji himself is the illegitimate son of an emperor.

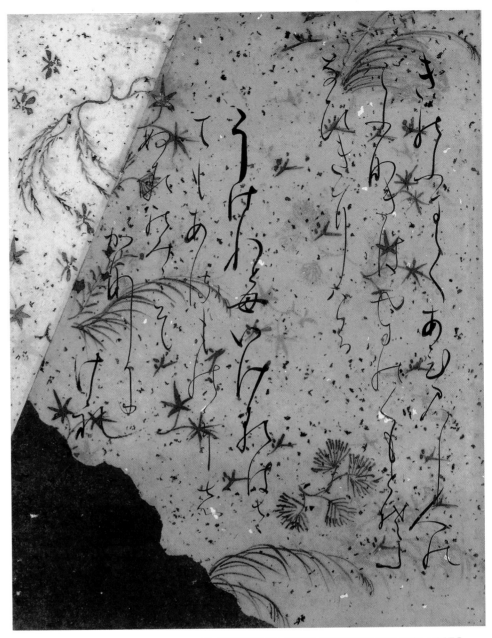

11–11 • ALBUM LEAF FROM THE *ISHIYAMA-GIRE* (DISPERSED VOLUMES, ONCE OWNED BY THE ISHIYAMA TEMPLE, OF THE ANTHOLOGY OF THE THIRTY-SIX IMMORTAL POETS)

Heian period, early 12th century CE. Ink with gold and silver on decorated and collaged paper, 52 × 17⅓″ (131.8 × 44 cm). Freer Gallery of Art, Smithsonian Institution, Washington, D.C. (F1969.4)

One might expect a painting of such an emotional scene to focus on the people involved. Instead, they are rendered in rather small size, and the scene is dominated by a screen that effectively squeezes Genji and his wife into a corner. This composition deliberately represents how their positions in courtly society have forced them into this unfortunate situation.

CALLIGRAPHY IN JAPANESE. The text portions of the *The Tale of Genji* handscroll were written in *kana* script, which was also used to write poetry in Japanese. In the Heian period, the most popular form of native poetry was a 31-syllable format known as *waka*, which had first been composed in the eighth century. During the Heian era, the finest *waka* by various writers were collected together and hand-copied in albums, the most popular of which, compiled in the eleventh century, featured writers collectively known as the Thirty-Six Immortal Poets, which is still appreciated by educated Japanese today. The earliest of many surviving examples of this iconic collection originally contained 39 volumes of poems. Two volumes were taken apart and sold in 1929, and now survive in single page sections **(FIG. 11–11)**. Collectively these separated volumes are known as the *Ishiyama-gire* (Ishiyama fragments, named after Ishiyamadera, the temple that originally owned the volumes).

11-12 • Attributed to Toba Sojo DETAIL OF *FROLICKING ANIMALS*
Heian period, 12th century CE. Handscroll, ink on paper, height 12″ (30.5 cm). Kozanji, Kyoto. National Treasure.

With its simple, flowing symbols interspersed occasionally with more complex Chinese characters, this style of writing created a distinctive asymmetrical balance to the appearance of the written words, entirely different from the formal symmetry of Chinese calligraphy. In these album leaves, the poems seem to float elegantly on fine colored papers decorated with painting, block printing, scattered gold and silver, and sometimes paper collage. Often, as in FIGURE 11–11, the irregular pattern of torn paper edges adds a serendipitous element. The page shown here reproduces two verses by the eighth-century courtier Ki no Tsurayuki that express melancholy emotions. One reads:

> Until yesterday
> I could meet her,
> But today she is gone—
> Like clouds over the mountain
> She has been wafted away.

The spiky, flowing calligraphy and the patterning of the papers, the rich use of gold, and the suggestions of natural imagery match the elegance of the poetry, epitomizing courtly Japanese taste.

YAMATO-E HANDSCROLLS—*FROLICKING ANIMALS*. In its sedate portrayal of courtly life, *The Tale of Genji* scroll represents one side of *yamato-e*. But another style of native painting emerged contemporaneously. Characterized by bold, rapid strokes of the brush, and little or no use of color, it most often depicted subjects outside the court, in playful and irreverent activities. One of the early masterpieces of this style is *Frolicking Animals*, a set of handscrolls satirizing the life of many different levels of society. Painted entirely in ink,

the scrolls are attributed to Toba Sojo, the abbot of a Buddhist temple, and they represent the humor of Japanese art to the full.

In one scene, a frog buddha sits upon an altar while a monkey dressed as a monk prays proudly to him; in other scenes frogs, donkeys, foxes, and rabbits play, swim, and wrestle, with one frog boasting of his prowess when he flings a rabbit to the ground **(FIG. 11–12)**. Unlike the *Genji* scroll, there is no text to *Frolicking Animals*, so it is hard to know exactly what was being satirized. Nevertheless, the universality of the humorous antics portrayed in this scroll highlights an important aspect of Japanese art that makes it instantly engaging to viewers everywhere.

KAMAKURA PERIOD

The courtiers of the Heian era became so engrossed in their own refinement that they neglected their responsibilities for governing the country. Clans of warriors—samurai—from outside the capital grew increasingly strong. Two of these, the Taira and Minamoto, wielded the most power and took opposing sides in the factional conflicts of the imperial court, in order to control the weakened emperor and take charge of running the country.

The Kamakura era (1185–1333) began when the head of the Minamoto clan, Yoritomo (1147–1199), defeated the Taira family and ordered the emperor to appoint him as shogun (general-in-chief). To resist the softening effects of courtly life in Kyoto, he established his military capital in Kamakura, while the emperor continued to reside in Kyoto. Although Yoritomo's newly invented title of shogun nominally respected the authority of the emperor, at the same time it assured him of supreme military and political

Arms and Armor

Battles such as the one depicted in *Night Attack on the Sanjo Palace* (SEE FIG. 11–13) were fought largely by archers on horseback. Samurai archers charged the enemy at full gallop and loosed their arrows just before they wheeled away. The scroll clearly shows their distinctive bow, with its asymmetrically placed handgrip. The lower portion of the bow is shorter than the upper so it can clear the horse's neck. The samurai wear a long, curved sword at the waist.

By the tenth century, Japanese swordsmiths had perfected techniques for crafting their legendarily sharp swords. Sword-makers face a fundamental difficulty: steel hard enough to hold a razor-sharp edge is brittle and breaks easily, but steel resilient enough to withstand rough use is too soft to hold a keen edge. The Japanese ingeniously forged a blade which laminated a hard cutting edge within less brittle support layers.

The earliest form of samurai armor, illustrated here, known as *yoroi*, was intended for use by warriors on horseback, as seen in FIGURE 11–13. It was made of overlapping iron and lacquered leather scales, punched with holes and laced together with leather thongs and brightly colored silk braids. The principal piece wrapped around the chest, left side, and back. Padded shoulder straps hooked it together back to front. A separate piece of armor was tied to the body to protect the right side. The upper legs were protected by a four-sided skirt that attached to the body armor, while two large rectangular panels tied on with cords guarded the arms. The helmet was made of iron plates riveted together. From it hung a neckguard flared sharply outward to protect the face from arrows shot at close range as the samurai wheeled away from an attack.

helmet

detail of scales

body armor

power. This tradition of rule by shogun that Yoritomo initiated lasted in various forms until 1868.

A BATTLE HANDSCROLL. The battles for domination between the Minamoto and the Taira became famous not only in medieval Japanese history but also in literature and art. One of the great painted handscrolls depicting these battles is **NIGHT ATTACK ON THE SANJO PALACE (FIG. 11–13)**. Painted perhaps 100 years after the actual event, the scroll conveys a sense of eye-witness reporting even though the anonymous artist had to imagine the scene from verbal (and at best semifactual) descriptions. The style of the painting includes some of the brisk and lively linework of *Frolicking Animals* and also traces of the more refined brushwork, use of color, and bird's-eye viewpoint of *The Tale of Genji* scroll. The main element, however, is the savage depiction of warfare (see "Arms and Armor," above). Unlike the *Genji* scroll, *Night Attack* is full of action: flames engulf the palace, horses charge, warriors behead their enemies, court ladies try to hide, and a sense of

energy and violence is conveyed with great sweep and power. The era of poetic refinement was now over in Japan, and the new world of the samurai began to dominate the secular arts.

PURE LAND BUDDHIST ART

By the beginning of the Kamakura period, Pure Land Buddhist beliefs had swept throughout Japan, and several charismatic priests founded new sects to preach this ideology. They traveled all around the country spreading the new gospel, which appealed to people of all levels of education and sophistication. They were so successful that since the Kamakura period, Pure Land Buddhist sects have remained the most popular form of Buddhism in Japan.

A PORTRAIT SCULPTURE. The itinerant monk Kuya (903–972), famous for urging country folk to join him in singing chants in praise of the Buddha Amida, was one of the early proponents of Pure Land practices. Kamakura-period Pure Land Buddhist followers regarded him as a founder of their religious tradition.

11-13 • SECTION OF *NIGHT ATTACK ON THE SANJO PALACE*

Kamakura period, late 13th century CE. Handscroll, ink and colors on paper, 16¼ × 275½″ (41.3 × 699.7 cm). Museum of Fine Arts, Boston. Fenollosa-Weld Collection (11.4000)

The battles between the Minamoto and Taira clans were fought primarily by mounted and armored warriors, who used both bows and arrows, and the finest swords. In the year 1160, some 500 Minamoto rebels opposed to the retired emperor Go-Shirakawa carried out a daring raid on the Sanjo Palace. In a surprise attack in the middle of the night, they abducted the emperor. The scene was one of great carnage, much of it caused by the burning of the wooden palace. Despite the drama of the scene, this was not the decisive moment in the war. The Minamoto rebels would eventually lose more important battles to their Taira enemies. Yet Minamoto forces, heirs to those who carried out this raid, would eventually prove victorious, destroying the Taira clan in 1185.

Believers would have immediately recognized Kuya in this thirteenth-century portrait statue by Kosho (**FIG. 11–14**): The traveling clothes, the small gong, the staff topped by deer horns (symbolic of his slaying a deer, whose death converted him to Buddhism), clearly identify the monk, whose sweetly intense expression gives this sculpture a radiant sense of faith. As for Kuya's chant, Kosho's solution to the challenge of putting words into sculptural form was simple but brilliant: He carved six small buddhas emerging from Kuya's mouth, one for each of the six syllables of *Na-mu-A-mi-da-Buts(u)* (the final u is not articulated). Believers would have understood that these six small buddhas embodied the Pure Land chant.

RAIGO PAINTINGS.   Pure Land Buddhism taught that even one sincere invocation of the sacred chant could lead the most wicked sinner to the Western Paradise. Paintings called **raigo** ("welcoming approach") were created depicting the Amida Buddha, accompanied by bodhisattvas, coming down to earth to welcome the soul of the dying believer. Golden cords were often attached to these paintings, which were taken to the homes of the dying. A person near death held onto these cords, hoping that Amida would escort the soul directly to paradise.

Raigo paintings differ significantly in style from the complex *mandala*s and fierce guardian deities of esoteric Buddhism. The

11-14 • Kosho KUYA PREACHING

Kamakura period, before 1207 CE. Painted wood with inlaid eyes, height 46½″ (117.5 cm). Rokuhara Mitsuji, Kyoto. Important Cultural Property.

11–15 • DESCENT OF AMIDA AND THE TWENTY-FIVE BODHISATTVAS
Kamakura period, 13th century CE. Hanging scroll, colors and gold on silk, 57¼ × 61½" (145 × 155.5 cm). Chionin, Kyoto. National Treasure.

earliest known example of this subject is found on the walls and doors of the Phoenix Hall, surrounding Jocho's sculpture of Amida (SEE FIG. 11–10). Like that statue, they radiate warmth and compassion. In the Kamakura period, *raigo* paintings were made in great numbers, reflecting the popularity of Pure Land Buddhism at that time. One magnificent example portrays Amida Buddha and 25 bodhisattvas swiftly descending over mountains. The artist used gold paint and thin slivers of gold leaf cut in elaborate patterning to suggest the divine radiance of the deities **(FIG. 11–15)**. This painstaking cut-gold leaf technique, known as *kirikane*, is one of the great achievements of early Japanese Buddhist artists. It originated in China, but Japanese artists refined and perfected it. In this painting, the darkened silk behind the figures heightens the sparkle of their golden aura. In the flickering light of oil lamps and torches, *raigo* paintings would have appeared magical in a temple or a dying person's home.

One of the most remarkable aspects of this painting is its sensitive rendering of the landscape, full of rugged peaks and

Daruma, Founder of Zen

Zen monks modeled their behavior on that of the patriarch or founder of their lineage, the mythical Indian Buddhist sage Daruma (Bodhidharma in Sanskrit), who emigrated to China in the sixth century CE, and famously transmitted his teachings to a Chinese disciple, who became the second Chan patriarch. This portrait of *Daruma* (FIG. A) is one of the earliest surviving examples of a Japanese Zen painting. Using fine ink outlines and a touch of color for the robe and the figure's sandals, the artist portrays the Zen master seated meditating atop a rock, with an unwavering focused gaze that is intended to convey his inner strength and serenity. At the top of the scroll is an inscription in Chinese by Yishan Yining (1247–1317), one of several influential early Chinese Chan masters to emigrate to Japan. He had actually planned only to visit in his role as head of an official diplomatic delegation from China in 1299, but he wound up staying for the duration of his life. Although wary of him at first, his sincere intentions to teach Zen and his erudite abilities quickly attracted influential supporters, to whom he taught Chinese religious practices and cultural traditions. Thus soon after arrival, Yishan was appointed as the tenth head abbot of the

large Zen temple of Kenchoji in Kamakura, a post he held briefly, before moving on to head several other Zen temples.

Kenchoji had been founded in 1253 by another emigrant Chan master, Lanxi Daolong (1213–1278). Lanxi had been the first Chan master to travel to Japan. There, he was warmly received by the fifth Minamoto shogun who helped him plan construction of Kenchoji where, for the first time, authentic Chinese Chan Buddhism was to be taught in Japan. Kenchoji remains one of the most important Zen monasteries in Japan today. The temple owns many formal portraits of its founder, including this one (FIG. B), considered by many to be the best, in that it seems to capture Daolong's inner spirit as well as his outer form. This type of painting is peculiar to Chan and Zen sects and is known as *chinso*. These paintings were often gifts given by a master to disciples when they completed their formal training and departed his presence to officiate at their

own temples. They served as personal reminders of their master's teachings and tangible evidence of their right to transmit Zen teachings to their own pupils (like a diploma). Lanxi Daolong dedicated the inscription of this painting to an important regent (samurai official), a confidant of the shogun, and not an ordained Zen monk. This shows that Zen, from its early days in Japan, also strove to attract followers from among those in power who could not abandon their secular life for the rigorous, cloistered existence required of Zen monks who lived in temples.

A. DARUMA
Artist unknown, inscription by Chinese Chan (Zen) master Yishan Yining (1247–1317). Kamakura period, early 14th century CE. Hanging scroll, ink and colors on silk, 39⅝ × 20″ (100.8 × 50.8 cm). Tokyo National Museum. Important Cultural Property.

B. PORTRAIT OF THE CHINESE ZEN MASTER LANXI DAOLONG
Inscription by Lanxi Daolong. Kamakura period, dated 1271 CE. Hanging scroll, colors on silk, 41⅓ × 18″ (105 × 46.1 cm). Kenchoji, Kamakura. National Treasure.

flowering trees. These natural elements reveal that the Japanese possessed great appreciation for the beautiful land in which they dwelled, an appreciation that stems from Shinto beliefs. Coincidence cannot account for the fact that Shinto pictures portraying the landscape of Japan as divine first appeared in the Kamakura period, just when Pure Land Buddhism grew popular. One of these paintings is the Kasuga Shrine *mandala* of FIGURE 11–1. It illustrates how artists contributed to the merging of the two faiths of Buddhism and Shinto at that time. The artist of this work intentionally made the shrine buildings resemble those of the palatial abode of Amida in his Western Paradise and rendered the landscape details with the radiant charm of Amida's heaven.

ZEN BUDDHIST ART

Toward the latter part of the Kamakura period, Zen Buddhism was introduced to Japan from China where it was already highly developed and known as Chan. Zen had been slow to reach Japan because of the interruption of relations between the two countries during the Heian period. But during the Kamakura era, both emigrant Chinese (see "Daruma, Founder of Zen," opposite) and Japanese monks who went to China to study Buddhism, and returned home enthused about the new teachings they learned there, brought Zen to Japan. The monk Kuya, represented in the statue by Kosho (SEE FIG. 11–14), epitomized the itinerant life of a Pure Land Buddhist monk who wandered the countryside and relied on the generosity of believers to support him. Zen monks lived very differently. They secluded themselves in monasteries, leading an austere life of simplicity and self-responsibility.

In some ways, Zen resembles the original teachings of the historical Buddha in that it emphasizes individual enlightenment through meditation, without the help of deities or magical chants. It especially appealed to the self-disciplined spirit of samurai warriors, who were not satisfied with the older forms of Buddhism connected with the Japanese court. Zen was the last major form of Buddhism to reach Japan from the Asian mainland and it had a profound and lasting impact on Japanese arts and culture.

Just as the *Night Attack* (SEE FIG. 11–13) reveals a propensity for recording the consequences of political turbulence through representation of gruesome battle scenes in vivid colors, Kamakura-era Buddhist sculpture and painting also emphasized realism. Various factors account for this new taste. Society was dominated by samurai warriors, who possessed a more pragmatic outlook on the world than the Heian-period courtiers who lived a dreamlike existence at court. In addition, renewed contacts with China introduced new styles for Buddhist art that also emphasized realism. Finally, forging personal connections with heroic exploits and individuals, both past and present, political and religious, greatly concerned the people of the Kamakura period. Representing these figures in arresting pictorial and sculpted images helped reinforce legends and perpetuate their influence, which accounts for the predominance of these subjects in the period's art.

As the Kamakura era ended, the seeds of the future were planted both politically and culturally: The coming age witnessed the nation's continued dominance by the warrior class and the establishment of Zen as the religion of choice among those warriors who wielded power at the highest levels. As before, the later history of Japanese art continued to be marked by an intriguing interplay between native traditions and imported foreign culture.

THINK ABOUT IT

11.1 Discuss Japan's relationship with China during the Kamakura period with respect to patterns of influence. Include specific examples related to society, as well as art techniques learned, referring to Chapter 10 as necessary.

11.2 Discuss the development of Japanese native-style arts during the Heian period. Define the main characteristics of native traditions of writing and secular painting. Describe how the innovations in new forms of Buddhist sculpture then differed from older forms in appearance, technique, and materials used.

11.3 Discuss the development of Buddhist practice and Buddhist sculpture over the course of time in Japan by selecting an image or object from three of the following four periods: Asuka, Nara, Heian, Kamakura. Explain each work in the context of its respective culture, including its relation to particular practices of Buddhism, for example Zen.

11.4 Summarize the beliefs of the Shinto religion and discuss the integration of Shinto and Buddhist traditions in Japanese culture.

11.5 Distinguish the defining characteristics of esoteric and Pure Land Buddhist painting and explain these differences with reference to one work of each from the chapter.

PRACTICE MORE: Compose answers to these questions, get flashcards for images and terms, and review chapter material with quizzes
www.myartslab.com

12-1 • OFFERING 4, LA VENTA   Mexico. Olmec culture, c. 900–400 BCE. Jade, greenstone, and sandstone, height of figures 6¼–7″ (16–18 cm). Museo Nacional de Antropología, Mexico City.

ART OF THE AMERICAS BEFORE 1300

The scene hints at a story in progress. Fifteen figures of precious greenstone converge on a single figure made of a baser, more porous stone. The tall oblong stones (**celts**) in the background evoke an architectural space, perhaps a location within the Olmec center of La Venta, where this tableau was created sometime between 900 and 400 BCE. The figures have the slouching bodies, elongated heads, almond-shaped eyes, and downturned mouths characteristic of Olmec art. Holes for earrings and the simple lines of the bodies suggest that these sculptures may originally have been dressed and adorned with perishable materials. The poses of the figures, with their knees slightly bent and their arms flexed at their sides, lend a sense of arrested movement to this enigmatic scene. Is it a council? a trial? an initiation? Are the greenstone figures marching in front of the reddish granite figure as he reviews them, or moving to confront him? With no texts to explain the scene, the specific tale it narrates may never be known, but it is clear that this offering commemorates an important event.

And it was remembered. This tableau (**FIG. 12–1**) was set up in the earth and buried underneath a plaza at La Venta, one of a number of offerings of works of art and precious materials beneath the surface of the city. Colored sand and floors covered the offerings, each colored floor signifying a successive renovation of the plaza. Over a century after these sculptures were buried, a hole was dug directly over the offering and it was viewed once more. Pieces of the later floors fell into the hole, but the figures themselves were not disturbed. After this, the scene was buried once again. The precision of this later excavation suggests that the exact location of the tableau was remembered. The archaeological record makes clear that this work of art, although hidden, still exerted tremendous power.

This extraordinary find demonstrates the importance of scientific archaeological excavations for understanding ancient art. Had these objects been torn out of the ground by looters and sold piecemeal on the black market, we would never have known how Olmec sculptures were used to create narrative installations or imagined that buried art could be remembered for so long. Instead, this discovery provides a context for isolated greenstone figures that have been found throughout Mesoamerica (modern Mexico, Guatemala, and Honduras). It provides evidence that these sculptures were made by the Olmec, Mesoamerica's first great civilization, and suggests that these objects, scattered today, might have once been assembled in meaningful ways like the offering at La Venta.

LEARN ABOUT IT

12.1 Recognize how differences in environmental conditions affected the artistic output of Mesoamerica, South America, and North America.

12.2 Explore how the role or function of an object is critical to understanding its meaning in ancient American visual arts.

12.3 Compare and contrast the use of urban planning in ancient American cultures.

12.4 Examine how Maya writing functions, and how it relates to Maya images.

HEAR MORE: Listen to an audio file of your chapter **www.myartslab.com**

THE NEW WORLD

In recent years the question of the original settlement of the Americas has become an area of debate. The traditional view has been that human beings arrived in North and South America from Asia during the last Ice Age, when glaciers trapped enough of the world's water to lower the level of the oceans and expose a land bridge across the Bering Strait. Although most of present-day Alaska and Canada was covered by glaciers at that time, an ice-free corridor along the Pacific coast would have provided access from Asia to the south and east. Thus, this theory holds that sometime before 12,000 years ago, perhaps as early as 20,000 to 30,000 years ago, Paleolithic hunter-gatherers emerged through this corridor and began to spread out into two vast, uninhabited continents. This view is now challenged by the early dates of some new archaeological finds and by evidence suggesting the possibility of early connections with Europe as well, perhaps along the Arctic coast of the North Atlantic. In any event, by between 10,000 and 12,000 years ago, bands of hunters roamed throughout the Americas, and after the ice had retreated, the peoples of the Western Hemisphere were essentially cut off from the rest of the world until they were overrun by European invaders, beginning at the end of the fifteenth century CE.

In this isolation the peoples of the Americas experienced cultural transformations similar to those seen elsewhere around the world following the end of the Paleolithic era. In most regions they developed an agricultural way of life. A trio of native plants—corn, beans, and squash—was especially important, but people also cultivated potatoes, tobacco, cacao, tomatoes, and avocados. New World peoples also domesticated many animals: dogs, turkeys, guinea pigs, llamas, and their camelid cousins—alpacas, guanacos, and vicuñas.

As elsewhere, the shift to agriculture in the Americas was accompanied by population growth and, in some places, the rise of hierarchical societies, the appearance of ceremonial centers and towns with monumental architecture, and the development of sculpture, ceramics, and other arts. The people of Mesoamerica—the region that extends from central Mexico well into Central America—developed writing, astronomy, a complex and accurate calendar, and a sophisticated system of mathematics. Central and South American peoples had advanced metallurgy and produced exquisite gold, silver, and copper objects. The metalworkers of the Andes, the mountain range along the western coast of South America, began to produce metal jewelry, weapons, and agricultural implements in the first millennium CE, and people elsewhere in the Americas made tools, weapons, and art from other materials such as bone, ivory, stone, wood, and, where it was available, obsidian, a volcanic glass capable of a cutting edge 500 times finer than surgical steel. Basketry and weaving became major art forms. In the American Southwest, Native American people built multi-storied, apartmentlike village and cliff dwellings, as well as elaborate irrigation systems with canals. Evidence of weaving in the American Southwest dates to about 7400 BCE.

Extraordinary artistic traditions flourished in many regions in the Americas before 1300 CE. This chapter explores the accomplishments of some of the cultures in five of those areas: Mesoamerica, Central America, the central Andes of South America, the Southeastern Woodlands and great river valleys of North America, and the North American Southwest.

MESOAMERICA

Ancient Mesoamerica encompasses the area from north of the Valley of Mexico (the location of Mexico City) to present-day Belize, Honduras, and western Nicaragua in Central America (MAP 12–1). The region is one of great contrasts, ranging from tropical rainforest to semiarid mountains. The civilizations that arose in Mesoamerica varied, but they were linked by cultural similarities and trade. Among their shared features were a ballgame with religious and political significance (see "The Cosmic Ballgame," page 389), aspects of monumental building construction, and a complex system of multiple calendars including a 260-day divinatory cycle and a 365-day ritual and agricultural cycle. Many Mesoamerican societies were sharply divided into elite and commoner classes.

The transition to farming began in Mesoamerica between 7000 and 6000 BCE, and by 3000 to 2000 BCE settled villages were widespread. Customarily the region's subsequent history is divided into three broad periods: Formative or Preclassic (1500 BCE–250 CE), Classic (250–900 CE), and Postclassic (900–1521 CE). This chronology derives primarily from the archaeology of the Maya—the people of Guatemala, southern Mexico, and the Yucatan Peninsula—with the Classic period bracketing the era during which the Maya erected dated stone monuments. The term reflects the view of early scholars that the Classic period was a kind of golden age. Although this view is no longer current—and the periods are only roughly applicable to other cultures of Mesoamerica—the terminology has endured.

THE OLMEC

The first major Mesoamerican art style, that of the Olmec, emerged during the Formative/Preclassic period, beginning around 1500 BCE. Many of the key elements of Mesoamerican art, including monumental stone sculpture commemorating individual rulers, finely carved jades, elegant ceramics, and architectural elements such as pyramids, plazas, and ballcourts, were first developed by the Olmec. In the fertile, swampy coastal areas of the present-day Mexican states of Veracruz and Tabasco, the Olmec raised massive earth mounds on which they constructed ceremonial centers. These centers probably housed an elite group of rulers and priests supported by a larger population of farmers who lived in villages of pole-and-thatch houses. The presence at Olmec sites of goods such as obsidian, iron ore, and jade that are not found in the Gulf of Mexico region but come from throughout Mesoamerica indicates that the Olmec participated in extensive long-distance trade. They went to especially great lengths

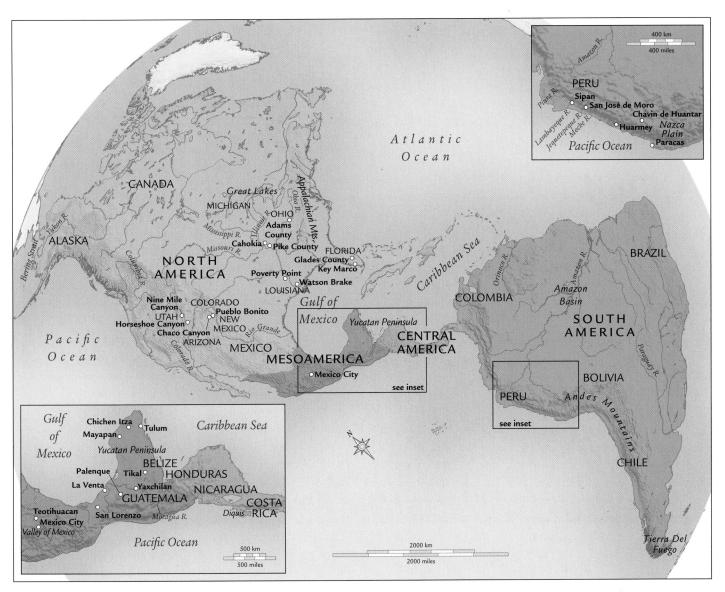

MAP 12–1 • THE AMERICAS BEFORE 1300

People moved across North America, then southward through Central America until they reached the Tierra del Fuego region of South America.

to acquire jade, which was one of the most precious materials in ancient Mesoamerica.

The earliest Olmec ceremonial center (c. 1200–900 BCE), at San Lorenzo, was built atop a giant earthwork, nearly three-quarters of a mile long, with an elaborate stone drainage system running throughout the mound. Other architectural features included a palace with basalt columns, a possible ballcourt, and a stone-carving workshop. Another center, at La Venta, thriving from about 900 to 400 BCE, was built on high ground between rivers. Its most prominent feature, an earth mound known as the Great Pyramid, still rises to a height of over 100 feet (FIG. 12–2). The pyramid stands at the south end of a large, open plaza arranged on a north–south axis and defined by long, low earth mounds. Many of the physical features of La Venta—including the symmetrical arrangement of earth mounds, platforms, and central open spaces along an axis that was probably determined by

astronomical observations—are characteristic of later monumental and ceremonial architecture throughout Mesoamerica. What was buried beneath the surface of La Venta—massive stone mosaics, layers of colored clay, and greenstone figures like those in FIGURE 12–1, discussed at the beginning of the chapter—may have been as important as what was visible on the surface.

The Olmec produced an abundance of monumental basalt sculpture, including **COLOSSAL HEADS** (FIG. 12–3), altars, and seated figures. The huge basalt blocks for the large works of sculpture were quarried at distant sites and transported to San Lorenzo, La Venta, and other centers. Colossal heads ranged in height from 5 to 12 feet and weighed from 5 to more than 20 tons. The heads portray adult males wearing close-fitting caps with chin straps and large, round earspools (cylindrical earrings that pierce the earlobe). The fleshy faces have almond-shaped eyes, flat broad noses, thick protruding lips, and downturned mouths. Each face is different, suggesting that

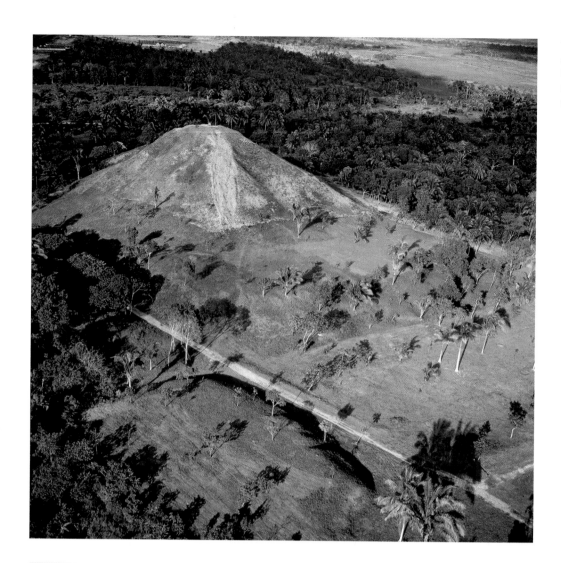

12-2 • GREAT PYRAMID AND PLAZA, LA VENTA
Mexico. Olmec culture, c. 900–400 BCE. Pyramid height approx. 100′ (30 m).

12-3 • COLOSSAL HEAD, SAN LORENZO
Mexico. Olmec culture, c. 1200–900 BCE. Basalt, height 7′5″ (2.26 m).

they may represent specific individuals. Ten colossal heads were found at San Lorenzo. Many had been mutilated and buried by about 900 BCE, when the site went into decline. At La Venta, 102 basalt monuments have been found, including four more colossal heads, massive thrones or altars, tall stone **stelae**, and other kinds of figural sculpture. The colossal heads and the subjects depicted on other monumental sculpture suggest that the Olmec elite were interested in commemorating rulers and historic events.

In addition to these heavy basalt monuments, Olmec artists also made smaller, more portable jade and ceramic objects (SEE FIG. 12–1). Jade, available only from the Motagua River valley in present-day Guatemala, was prized for its brilliant blue-green color and the smooth, shiny surfaces it could achieve with careful polishing. Jade is one of the hardest materials in Mesoamerica, and with only stone tools available, Olmec craftsmen used jade tools and powdered jade dust as an abrasive to carve and polish these sculptures. Other figurines were made out of softer and more malleable greenstones, like serpentine, which occur in many parts of Mesoamerica. Olmec ceramics, including decorated vessels and

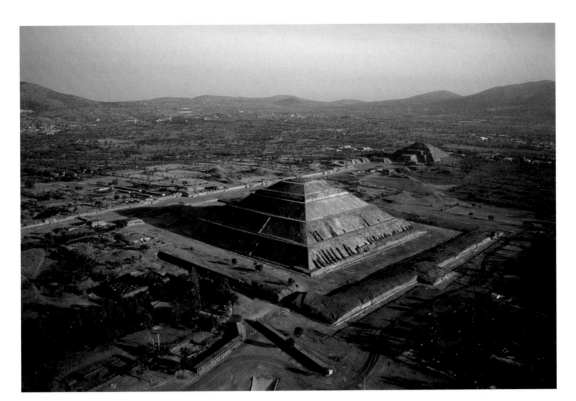

12-4 • CEREMONIAL CENTER OF THE CITY OF TEOTIHUACAN

Mexico. Teotihuacan culture, c. 100–650 CE. View from the southeast. The Pyramid of the Sun is in the foreground, and the Pyramid of the Moon is visible in the distance. The Avenue of the Dead, the north–south axis of the city, which connects the two pyramids, continues for over a mile.

SEE MORE: View a simulation about the Ceremonial Center of Teotihuacan
www.myartslab.com

remarkably lifelike clay babies, also appear to have been prized far beyond the Olmec heartland. Olmec greenstone and ceramic objects have been found throughout Mesoamerica, evidence of the extensive reach and influence of Olmec art and culture.

By 200 CE, forests and swamps had begun to reclaim Olmec sites, but Olmec civilization had spread widely throughout Mesoamerica and was to have an enduring influence on its successors. As the Olmec centers of the Gulf Coast faded, the great Classic period centers in the Maya region and Teotihuacan area in the Valley of Mexico were beginning their ascendancy.

TEOTIHUACAN

Located some 30 miles northeast of present-day Mexico City, the city of Teotihuacan experienced a period of rapid growth early in the first millennium CE. By 200 CE, it had emerged as Mesoamerica's first truly urban settlement, a significant center of commerce and manufacturing. At its height, between 300 and 650, Teotihuacan covered nearly nine square miles and had a population of at least 125,000, making it the largest city in the Americas and one of the largest in the world at that time (FIG. 12–4). Its residents lived in walled "apartment compounds," and the entire city was organized on a grid (FIG. 12–5), its orientation chosen both for its calendrical significance and to respond to the surrounding landscape.

Although Teotihuacan declined in power after 650, it was never forgotten. Centuries later, it remained a legendary pilgrimage center. The much later Aztec people (c. 1300–1525) revered the site, believing it to be the place where the gods created the sun and the moon. In fact, Teotihuacan, a word indicating a place of divinity, is the Aztec name for the city. The names we use for its principal monuments are also Aztec names. We do not know what

12-5 • PLAN OF THE CEREMONIAL CENTER OF TEOTIHUACAN

12-6 • PYRAMID OF THE FEATHERED SERPENT

The Ciudadela, Teotihuacan, Mexico. Teotihuacan culture, c. 200 CE.

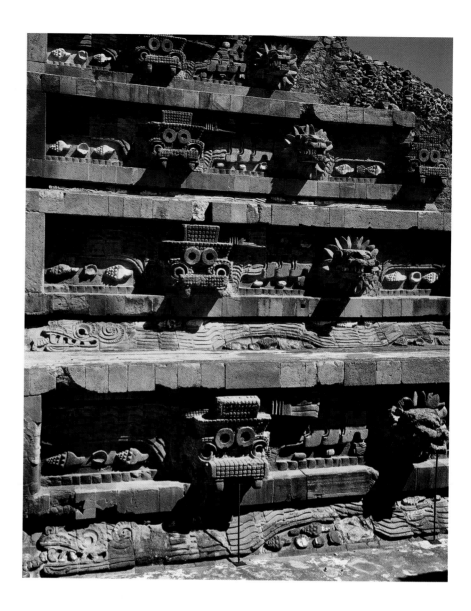

the original inhabitants of Teotihuacan called these buildings or what they called their own city.

The center of the city is bisected by a broad thoroughfare laid out on a north–south axis, extending for more than a mile and in places as much as 150 feet wide, which the Aztecs called the Avenue of the Dead. At the center of the Teotihuacan grid, a series of canals forced the San Juan River to run perpendicular to the avenue. At the north end of this central axis stands the Pyramid of the Moon, facing a large plaza flanked by smaller, symmetrically placed platforms. It seems to echo the shape of the mountain behind it, and as one walks towards the pyramid, it looms above, eclipsing the mountain completely. The Pyramid of the Moon was enlarged several times, as were many Mesoamerican pyramids; each enlargement completely enclosed the previous structure and was accompanied by rich sacrificial offerings.

The largest of Teotihuacan's architectural monuments, the Pyramid of the Sun, located just to the east of the Avenue of the Dead, is slightly over 200 feet high and measures about 720 feet on each side at its base, similar in size to, but not as tall as, the largest Egyptian pyramid at Giza. It is built over a multi-chambered cave

with a spring that may have been the original focus of worship at the site and its source of prestige. The pyramid rises in a series of sloping steps to a flat platform, where a small temple once stood. A monumental stone stairway led from level to level up the side of the pyramid to the temple platform. The exterior was faced with stone, which was then stuccoed and painted.

At the southern end of the ceremonial center, and at the heart of the city, is the Ciudadela (Spanish for a fortified city center), a vast sunken plaza surrounded by temple platforms. One of the city's principal religious and political centers, the plaza could accommodate an assembly of more than 60,000 people. Early in Teotihuacan's history, its focal point was the **PYRAMID OF THE FEATHERED SERPENT (FIG. 12–6)**. This seven-tiered structure exhibits the *talud-tablero* (slope-and-panel) construction that is a hallmark of the Teotihuacan architectural style. The *talud* (sloping base) of each platform supports a *tablero* (entablature), that rises vertically and is surrounded by a frame.

Archaeological excavations of the temple's early phase have revealed undulating feathered serpents floating in a watery space punctuated by reliefs of aquatic shells. Their flat, angular, abstract

12–7 • BLOODLETTING RITUAL
Fragment of a fresco from Teotihuacan, Mexico. Teotihuacan culture, c. 550–650 CE. Pigment on lime plaster, 32¼ × 45¼″ (82 × 116.1 cm). The Cleveland Museum of Art. Purchase from the J. H. Wade Fund (63.252)

The maguey plant supplied the people of Teotihuacan with food, with fiber for making clothing, rope, and paper, and with the precious drink pulque. As this painting indicates, priestly officials used its spikes in rituals to draw their own blood as a sacrifice.

style, typical of Teotihuacan art, is in marked contrast to the curvilinear forms of Olmec art. While the bodies of the feathered serpents are rendered in low relief, three-dimensional fanged serpent heads emerge from aureoles of stylized feathers. In the vertical *tablero* sections, each serpent carries on its body a squarish headdress with a protruding upper jaw, huge, round eyes originally inlaid with obsidian, and a pair of round goggles on its forehead between the eyes. These mosaic headdresses seem to represent an aspect of the Teotihuacan Storm God associated with warfare—other works of art at Teotihuacan and elsewhere in Mesoamerica show armed warriors wearing the same headdress. Inside the pyramid, this militaristic message was reinforced by the burials of dozens of sacrificial victims, some of them wearing necklaces made of human maxillae and jawbones (or shell imitations thereof), their arms tied behind their backs. In the fourth century, the elaborate sculptural façade of the Pyramid of the Feathered Serpent was concealed behind a plainer *talud-tablero* structure tacked onto the front of the pyramid.

The residential sections of Teotihuacan fanned out from the city's center. The large and spacious palaces of the elite, with as many as 45 rooms and seven patios, stood nearest the ceremonial center. Artisans, foreign traders, and peasants lived farther away, in more crowded compounds, all aligned to the Teotihuacan grid. Palaces and more humble homes alike were rectangular one-story structures with high walls and suites of rooms arranged around open courtyards. Walls were plastered and covered with paintings.

Teotihuacan's artists worked in a fresco technique, applying pigments directly on damp lime plaster. Once the paint was applied, the walls were polished to give a smooth, shiny, and durable surface. The style, like that of the sculpture, was flat, angular, and abstract, often featuring processions of similarly dressed figures, rows of mythological animals, or other kinds of repeating images. Teotihuacan painters worked in several different coloristic modes, including a bright polychrome and a more restricted palette emphasizing tones of red. A detached fragment of a wall painting, now in the Cleveland Museum of Art, depicts a **BLOODLETTING RITUAL** in which an elaborately dressed man enriches and revitalizes the earth with his own blood **(FIG. 12–7)**. The man's large animal headdress, decorated with precious feathers from the quetzal bird, indicates his high rank. He stands between rectangular plots of earth or bundles of grass pierced with bloody maguey spines (used in bloodletting), and he scatters seeds or drops of blood from his right hand, as indicated by the stream of conventionalized symbols for blood, seeds, and flowers falling from his hand. The sound scroll emerging from his open mouth symbolizes his ritual chant. The visual weight accorded the headdress and the sound scroll suggests that the man's priestly office and chanted words were essential elements of the ceremony. Such bloodletting rituals were widespread in Mesoamerica.

Teotihuacan was a wealthy and cosmopolitan city, home to people from all over Mesoamerica. One reason for its wealth was its control of a source of high-quality obsidian. Goods made at Teotihuacan, including obsidian tools and pottery, were distributed widely throughout Mesoamerica in exchange for luxury items such as the brilliant green feathers of the quetzal bird. Yet not all interactions between Teotihuacan and other Mesoamerican centers were peaceful—the threat of Teotihuacan military force, so clearly expressed at the Pyramid of the Feathered Serpent, was always present.

Sometime in the early seventh century disaster struck Teotihuacan. The ceremonial center was sacked and burned, and the city went into a permanent decline. Nevertheless, its influence continued as other centers throughout Mesoamerica, as far south as the highlands of Guatemala, borrowed and transformed its imagery over the next several centuries.

THE MAYA

The ancient Maya are noted for a number of achievements. In densely populated cities they built imposing pyramids, temples, palaces, and administrative structures. They developed the most advanced hieroglyphic writing in Mesoamerica and perfected a sophisticated version of the Mesoamerican calendrical system (see "Maya Writing," opposite). Using these, they recorded the accomplishments of their rulers on sculpture, ceramic vessels, wall paintings, and in books. They studied astronomy and the natural cycles of plants and animals, and used sophisticated mathematical concepts such as zero and place value.

An increasingly detailed picture of the Maya has been emerging from recent archaeological research and from advances in deciphering their writing. That picture shows a society divided into competing city-states, each with a hereditary ruler and an elite class of nobles and priests supported by a large group of farmer-commoners. Rulers established their legitimacy, maintained links with their divine ancestors, commemorated important calendrical dates, and sustained the gods through elaborate rituals, including ballgames, bloodletting ceremonies, and human sacrifice. Rulers commemorated such events and their military exploits on carved stelae. A complex pantheon of deities presided over the Maya universe.

12-8 • BASE OF NORTH ACROPOLIS (LEFT) AND TEMPLE I
Tikal, Guatemala. Maya culture. North Acropolis, 4th century BCE–5th century CE; Temple I (Tomb of Ruler A), c. 734 CE.

Maya Writing

Maya writing is **logosyllabic**—it consists of ideographs or logographs that represent entire words as well as a set of symbols that stand for the sound of each syllable in the Maya language. Thus, a word like *balam* (jaguar) could be written in many different ways: with the logograph "BALAM", a picture of the head of a jaguar (top right); with three syllables, "ba-la-ma", for the sounds of the word *balam* (bottom right); or a combination of the two systems—the logograph "BALAM" complemented with one or more phonetic syllables, to make it clear which logograph was represented (to avoid the possibility of confusing this logograph with the symbol for *hix*, another kind of feline, for example) (middle right). The combination of these two systems allowed Maya scribes extraordinary flexibility, and some calligraphers seem to have delighted in finding as many different ways as possible to write the same word. Many Maya logographs remained very pictorial, like the glyph for jaguar illustrated here, which meant that Maya writing was never too distant from other kinds of image making. In fact, the same word, *ts'ib*, signified both writing and painting in the Classic Mayan language.

With major advances in the decipherment of Maya hieroglyphic writing—beginning in the 1950s and continuing to this day—it has become clear that the inscriptions on Maya architecture and stelae appear almost entirely devoted to historical events. They record the dates of royal marriages, births of heirs, alliances between cities, and great military victories, and they tie these events to astronomical events and propitious dates in the Maya calendar. We know that the Maya also wrote books, but only four of these fragile manuscripts—called codices—have survived, all of them from the Postclassic period.

BALAM

ba-BALAM

BALAM-ma

ba-BALAM-ma

ba-la-ma

Maya civilization emerged during the late Preclassic period (400 BCE–250 CE), reached its peak in the southern lowlands of Mexico and Guatemala during the Classic period (250–900 CE), and shifted to the northern Yucatan Peninsula during the Postclassic period (900–1521 CE). Throughout this time, the Maya had strong ties with other regions of Mesoamerica: They inherited many ideas and technologies from the Olmec, had trade and military interactions with Teotihuacan, and, centuries later, were in contact with the Aztec Empire.

TIKAL. The monumental buildings of Maya cities were masterly examples of the use of architecture for public display. Tikal (in present-day Guatemala) was one of the largest Maya cities, with a population of as many as 70,000 at its height. Like other Maya cities—yet unlike Teotihuacan, with its grid plan—Tikal conformed to the uneven terrain of the rainforest. Plazas, pyramid-temples, ballcourts, and other structures stood on high ground connected by wide elevated roads, or causeways.

Tikal was settled in the Late Preclassic period, in the fourth century BCE, and continued to flourish through the Early Classic period. The kings of Tikal were buried in funerary pyramids in the North Acropolis, visible on the left in **FIGURE 12–8**, which was separated by a wide plaza from the royal palace to the south.

Tikal suffered a major upheaval in 378 CE, recorded in texts from the city and surrounding centers, when the arrival of strangers from Teotihuacan precipitated the death of Tikal's king and the installation of a new ruler with ties to Central Mexico. Art from this period shows strong Teotihuacan influence in ceramic and architectural forms, though both were soon adapted to suit local Maya aesthetics. The city enjoyed a period of wealth and regional dominance until a military defeat led to a century of decline.

In the eighth century CE, the city of Tikal again flourished during the reign of Jasaw Chan K'awiil (nicknamed Ruler A before his name could be fully read, r. 682–734), who initiated an ambitious construction program and commissioned many stelae decorated with his own portrait. One of these, Stela 16, was dedicated on the period-ending date of 9.14.0.0.0 in the Maya calendar (December 5, 711; see "A Closer Look," page 387). His portrait fills nearly the entire space of this nearly 6-foot-tall stone. He stands with his head in profile, his body frontal, and his legs splayed out with the heels together. His elaborate costume—embellished with quetzal feathers, jade, and other precious materials—almost completely conceals his body. Ruler A's program culminated in the construction of Temple I (SEE FIG. 12–8), a tall pyramid that faces a companion pyramid, Temple II, across a large central plaza. Containing Ruler A's tomb in the limestone bedrock

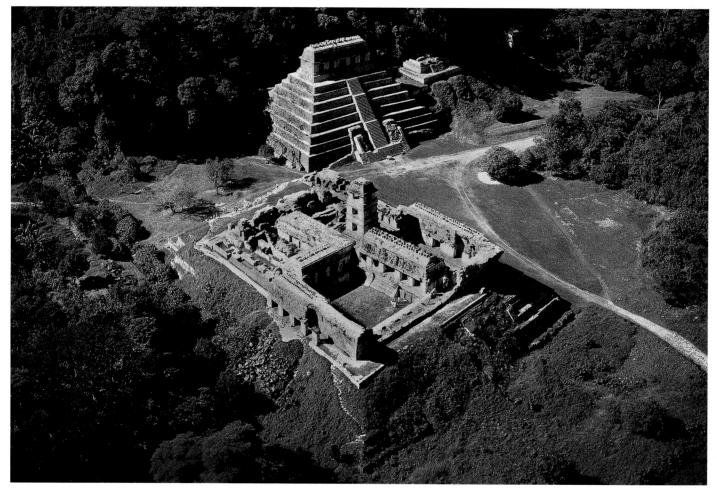

12-9 • PALACE (FOREGROUND) AND TEMPLE OF THE INSCRIPTIONS
Palenque, Mexico. Maya culture. Palace, 5th–8th century CE; Temple of the Inscriptions (Tomb of Pakal the Great), c. 683 CE.

below, Temple I rises above the forest canopy to a height of more than 140 feet. Its base has nine layers, probably reflecting the belief that the underworld had nine levels. Priests climbed the steep stone staircase on the exterior to the temple on top, which consists of two narrow, parallel rooms covered with a steep roof supported by corbel vaults. The crest that rises over the roof of the temple, known as a **roof comb**, was originally covered with brightly painted sculpture. Ritual performances on the narrow platform at the top of the pyramid would have been visible throughout the plaza. Inspired by Ruler A's building program, later kings of Tikal also built tall funerary pyramids that still tower above the rainforest canopy.

PALENQUE.   The small city-state of Palenque (in the present-day Mexican state of Chiapas) rose to prominence later than Tikal, during the Classic period. Hieroglyphic inscriptions record the beginning of its royal dynasty in 431 CE, but the city had only limited regional importance until the ascension of a powerful ruler, K'inich Janahb Pakal (*pakal* is Mayan for "shield"), who ruled from 615 to 683. Known as Pakal the Great, he and his sons, who succeeded him, commissioned most of the structures visible at Palenque today. As at Tikal, urban planning responds to the

landscape. Perched on a ridge over 300 feet above the swampy lowland plains, the buildings of Palenque are terraced into the mountains with a series of aqueducts channeling rivers through the urban core. The center of the city houses the palace, the Temple of the Inscriptions, and other temples **(FIG. 12–9)**. Still other temples, elite palaces, and a ballcourt surround this central group.

The palace was an administrative center as well as a royal residence. At its core was the throne room of Pakal the Great, a spacious structure whose stone roof imitated the thatched roofs of more humble dwellings. Over time, the palace grew into a complex series of buildings organized around four courtyards, where the private business of the court was transacted. From the outside, the palace presented an inviting façade of wide staircases and open colonnades decorated with stucco sculptures, but access to the interior spaces was tightly limited.

Next to the palace stands the Temple of the Inscriptions, Pakal the Great's funerary pyramid. Rising 75 feet above the plaza, it has nine levels like Temple I at Tikal (SEE FIG. 12–8). The shrine on the summit consists of a portico with five entrances and a vaulted inner chamber originally surmounted by a tall roof comb. Its façade still retains much of its stucco sculpture. The inscriptions that give the

A CLOSER LOOK

Maya Stela ➤

Stela 16
Tikal, Guatemala. Maya culture, 711 CE.

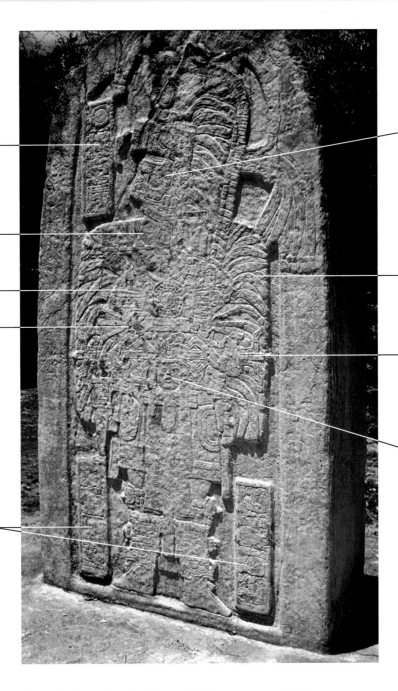

The text in this cartouche records the dedication date for this stela, 6 Ahaw 13 Muwaan (9.14.0.0.0, or December 5, 711 CE), an important period-ending date that was celebrated throughout the Maya region.

Ruler A's face peers out from all his finery. He wears large jade earspools and a long bar or nose ornament reaches out in front of his face.

Pectoral necklaces, made of jade and bone, lie above a collar of round jade beads. Jade and feathers were among the most precious materials in ancient Mesoamerica, so this costume is a stunning display of wealth.

The text in these two cartouches names Jasaw Chan K'awiil (Ruler A) as Holy Lord of Tikal and lists other of his titles.

Elaborate feathered headdress decorated with a skull mask, perhaps representing a deity that Ruler A impersonated in the dedication ceremony for this monument. Note how some of the plumes break the borders of the stela.

This feathered backrack, like the feathered headdress, may have been made out of quetzal feathers or other precious tropical plumes. These brightly colored, iridescent feathers would have shimmered as Ruler A moved.

In his hands Ruler A holds a ceremonial bar of rulership, the traditional emblem of authority of Maya kings.

Ruler A also wears a belt decorated with three jade masks, one shown frontally at the center and two shown in profile at the hips. Jade masks like these have been found at several Maya sites.

SEE MORE: View the Closer Look feature for the Maya Stela **www.myartslab.com**

building its name consist of three large panels of text that line the back wall of the outer chamber at the top of the temple, linking Pakal's accomplishments to the mythical history of the city. A corbel-vaulted stairway beneath the summit shrine zigzags down 80 feet to a small subterranean chamber that contained the undisturbed tomb of Pakal, which was discovered in the 1950s.

Pakal the Great lay in a monolithic carved sarcophagus that represented him balanced between the underworld and the earth.

12-10 • PORTRAIT OF PAKAL THE GREAT
From Pakal's tomb, Temple of the Inscriptions, Palenque, Mexico. Maya culture, mid 7th century CE. Stucco and red paint, height 16⅞″ (43 cm). Museo Nacional de Antropología, Mexico City.

lintel from a temple in the city of Yaxchilan, dedicated in 726 by Lady Xok, the principal wife and queen of the ruler nicknamed "Shield Jaguar the Great." In this retrospective image of a rite conducted when Shield Jaguar became the ruler of Yaxchilan in 681, Lady Xok conjures up a serpent vision that spews forth a warrior in Teotihuacan costume who aims his spear at the kneeling queen **(FIG. 12–11)**. The relief is unusually high, giving the sculptor ample opportunity to display a virtuoso carving technique, for example, in Lady Xok's garments and jewelry. The lintels were originally brightly painted as well. The calm idealized face of the queen recalls the portrait of Pakal the Great. That the queen commissioned her depictions on the lintels of this temple is an indication of her importance at court, and of the power that elite Maya women could attain.

His ancestors, carved on the sides of the sarcophagus, witness his death and apotheosis. The stucco portrait of Pakal found with his sarcophagus shows him as a young man wearing a diadem of jade and flowers **(FIG. 12–10)**. His features—sloping forehead and elongated skull (babies' heads were bound to produce this shape), large curved nose (enhanced by an ornamental bridge), full lips, and open mouth—are characteristic of the Maya ideal of beauty, that of the youthful Maize God whose stepped and upswept hairstyle this portrait adopts. His long, narrow face and jaw are individual characteristics. Traces of pigment indicate that this portrait, like much Maya sculpture, was colorfully painted.

SCULPTURE FOR LADY XOK. Elite men and women, rather than gods, were the usual subjects of Maya sculpture, and most works show rulers performing religious rituals in elaborate costumes and headdresses. Although they excelled at three-dimensional clay and stucco sculpture (SEE FIG. 12–10), the Maya favored low relief for carving stelae and buildings. One outstanding example is a carved

12-11 • LADY XOK'S VISION (ACCESSION CEREMONY)
Lintel 25 of a temple (Structure 23), Yaxchilan, Mexico. Maya culture. Dedicated in 726 CE. Limestone, 46½ × 29⅛″ (118 × 74 cm). British Museum. Acquired by the British Museum in 1883

The Cosmic Ballgame

The ritual ballgame was one of the defining characteristics of Mesoamerican society. It was generally played on a long, rectangular court with a large, solid, heavy rubber ball. Using their elbows, knees, or hips—but not their hands—heavily padded players directed the ball toward a goal or marker. The rules, size and shape of the court, the number of players on a team, and the nature of the goal varied. The largest surviving ballcourt at Chichen Itza was about the size of a modern football field. Large stone rings set in the walls of the court about 25 feet above the field served as goals.

The game was a common subject in Mesoamerican art (SEE FIG. 12–12). Players, complete with equipment, appear as ceramic figurines and on stone sculptures and painted vases. The game may have had religious and political significance: It features in creation stories, and was sometimes associated with warfare. Captive warriors might have been made to play the game, and players might have been sacrificed when the stakes were high.

PAINTING. Artists had high status in Maya society: Vase painters and scribes were sometimes members of the ruling elite, perhaps even members of the royal family. Some of our most vivid impressions of Maya courtly life and painting style come from cylindrical vessels. The example illustrated in **FIGURE 12–12** shows four lords playing the ballgame, the architectural space of the ballcourt suggested by a few horizontal lines (see "The Cosmic Ballgame," above). The men wear elaborate headdresses and padded protective gear to protect them from the heavy rubber ball. The painter has chosen a moment of arrested movement: One player kneels to hit the ball—or has just hit it—while the others gesture and lean toward him. The roll-out photograph here shows the entire scene, but a person holding the vase would have to turn the vessel to see what was happening. The text running around the rim of the vase is a standard dedicatory inscription, naming it as a vessel for drinking chocolate, and tests of residues inside such vases have confirmed this use. Without sugar or milk, Maya chocolate was a very different drink from the one we are used to, a frothy and bitter beverage consumed on courtly and ritual occasions.

12-12 • CYLINDRICAL VESSEL WITH BALLGAME SCENE
(Roll-out photograph) Maya culture, 600–800 CE. Painted ceramic, diameter 6⅜″ (15.9 cm), height 8⅛″ (20.5 cm).
Dallas Museum of Art. 1983.148. Gift of Mr. and Mrs. Raymond Nasher

EXPLORE MORE: Gain insight from a primary source on the Maya civilization **www.myartslab.com**

POSTCLASSIC PERIOD. After warfare and environmental crisis led to the abandonment of the lowland Maya city-states around 800, the focus of Maya civilization shifted north to the Yucatan Peninsula. One of the principal cities of the Postclassic period was Chichen Itza, which means "at the mouth of the well of the Itza," and may refer to the deep *cenote* (sinkhole) at the site that was sacred to the Maya. The city flourished from the ninth to the thirteenth century, and at its height covered about 6 square miles.

One of Chichen Itza's most conspicuous structures is a massive nine-level pyramid in the center of a large plaza, nicknamed El Castillo ("the castle" in Spanish) **(FIG. 12–13)**. A stairway on each side of the radial pyramid leads to a square temple on the summit. At the spring and fall equinoxes, the setting sun casts undulating shadows on the stairway, forming bodies for the serpent heads carved at the base of the north balustrades, pointing towards the Sacred Cenote. Many prominent features of Chichen Itza are markedly different from earlier Maya sites and hint at ties to Central Mexico, including long, colonnaded halls and inventive columns in the form of inverted, descending serpents. Brilliantly colored relief sculpture and painting covered the buildings of Chichen Itza. Many of the surviving works show narrative scenes that emphasize military conquests. Sculpture at Chichen Itza, including the serpent columns and balustrades, and the half-reclining figures known as **chacmools**, has the sturdy forms, proportions, and angularity of architecture, rather than the curving subtlety of Classic Maya sculpture. The *chacmool*s may represent fallen warriors and were used to receive sacrificial offerings.

After Chichen Itza's decline, Mayapan, in the center of the Yucatan Peninsula, became the principal Maya center. But by the time the Spanish arrived in the early sixteenth century, Mayapan, too, had declined (destroyed in the mid fifteenth century), and smaller cities like Tulum, located on the Caribbean coast, were all that remained. The Maya people and much of their culture would survive the devastation of the conquest, adapting to the imposition of Hispanic customs and beliefs. Many Maya continue to speak their own languages, to venerate traditional sacred places, and to follow traditional ways.

CENTRAL AMERICA

Unlike their neighbors in Mesoamerica, who lived in complex hierarchical societies, the people of Central America lived in extended family groups, in towns led by chiefs. A notable example of these small chiefdoms was the Diquis culture (located in present-day Costa Rica), which lasted from about 700 to 1500 CE. The Diquis occupied fortified villages and seem to have engaged in constant warfare with one another. Although they did not produce monumental architecture or sculpture, they created fine featherwork, ceramics, textiles, and objects of gold and jade.

Metallurgy and the use of gold and copper-gold alloys were widespread in Central America. The technique of lost-wax casting probably first appeared in present-day Colombia between 500 and 300 BCE. From there it spread north to the Diquis. A small, exquisite pendant **(FIG. 12–14)** illustrates the style and technique of Diquis goldwork. The pendant depicts a male figure wearing bracelets, anklets, and a belt with a snake-headed penis sheath. He plays a drum while holding the tail of a snake in his teeth and its head in his left hand. The wavy forms with serpent heads emerging from his scalp suggest an elaborate headdress, and the creatures emerging from his legs suggest some kind of reptile costume. The inverted triangles on the headdress probably represent birds' tails.

In Diquis mythology, serpents and crocodiles inhabited a lower world, humans and birds a higher one. Diquis art depicts animals and insects as fierce and dangerous. Perhaps the man in the pendant is a shaman transforming himself into a composite serpent-bird or performing a ritual snake dance surrounded by serpents or crocodiles. The scrolls on the sides of his head may represent the shaman's power to hear and understand the speech of

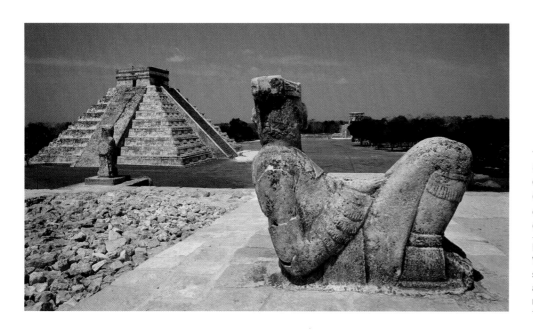

12-13 • PYRAMID ("EL CASTILLO") WITH CHACMOOL IN FOREGROUND
Chichen Itza, Yucatan, Mexico. Maya culture, 9th–12th century CE. Library, Getty Research Institute, Los Angeles.

From the top of the Temple of the Warriors, where a reclining *chacmool* sculpture graces the platform, there is a clear view of the radial pyramid nicknamed "El Castillo."

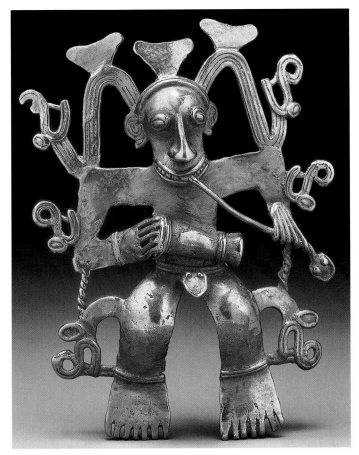

12-14 • SHAMAN WITH DRUM AND SNAKE
Costa Rica. Diquis culture, c. 13–16th century CE. Gold, 4¼ × 3¼"
(10.8 × 8.2 cm). Museos del Banco Central de Costa Rica, San José,
Costa Rica.

animals. Whatever its specific meaning, the pendant evokes a ritual
of mediation between earthly and cosmic powers involving music,
dance, and costume.

Whether gold figures of this kind were protective amulets
or signs of high status, they were certainly more than personal
adornment. Shamans and warriors wore gold to inspire fear,
perhaps because gold was thought to capture the energy and
power of the sun. This energy was also thought to allow shamans to
leave their bodies and travel into cosmic realms.

SOUTH AMERICA: THE CENTRAL ANDES

Like Mesoamerica, the central Andes of South America—
primarily present-day Peru and Bolivia—saw the development of
complex hierarchical societies with rich and varied artistic
traditions. The area is one of dramatic contrasts. The narrow coastal
plain, bordered by the Pacific Ocean on the west and the abruptly
soaring Andes mountains on the east, is one of the driest deserts in
the world. Life here depends on the rich marine resources of the
Pacific Ocean and the rivers that descend from the Andes, forming
a series of valley oases. The Andes themselves are a region of lofty

snowcapped peaks, high grasslands, steep slopes, and deep, fertile
river valleys. The high grasslands are home to the Andean camelids
that have served for thousands of years as beasts of burden and a
source of wool and meat. The lush eastern slopes of the Andes
descend to the tropical rainforest of the Amazon basin.

In contrast to developments in other parts of the world,
Andean peoples developed monumental architecture and textiles
long before ceramics and intensive agriculture, usually the two hallmarks of early civilization. Thus, the earliest period of monumental
architecture, beginning around 3000 BCE, is called the Preceramic
period. On the coast, sites with ceremonial mounds and plazas were
located near the sea, while in the highlands early centers consisted
of multi-roomed stone-walled structures with sunken central fire
pits for burning ritual offerings. In the second millennium BCE (the
Initial Period), as agriculture became more important both in the
highlands and on the coast, the scale and pace of construction
increased dramatically. Communities in the coastal valleys built
massive U-shaped ceremonial complexes, while highland religious
centers focused on sunken circular courtyards. By adding to these
constructions bit by bit over generations, and using older constructions as the nucleus of new buildings, relatively small communities
could generate mountain-size pyramids.

CHAVIN DE HUANTAR

Located on a trade route between the coast and the Amazon basin,
the highland site of Chavin de Huantar was an important religious
center between 900 and 200 BCE, home to an art style that spread
through much of the Andes. In Andean chronology, this era is
known as the Early Horizon, the first of three so-called Horizon
periods. The period was one of artistic and technical innovation in
ceramics, metallurgy, and textiles.

The architecture of Chavin synthesizes coastal and highland
traditions, combining the U-shaped pyramid typical of the coast
with a sunken circular plaza lined with carved reliefs, a form
common in the highlands. The often fantastical animals that adorn
Chavin sculpture have features of jaguars, hawks, caimans, and
other tropical Amazonian beasts.

Within the U-shaped Old Temple at Chavin is a mazelike system of narrow galleries, at the very center of which lies a sculpture
called the Lanzón (**FIG. 12–15**). Wrapped around a 15-foot-tall
blade-shaped stone with a narrow projection at the top—a form
that may echo the shape of traditional Andean planting sticks—
this complex carving depicts a powerful creature with a humanoid
body, clawed hands and feet, and enormous fangs. Its eyebrows and
strands of hair terminate in snakes—a kind of composite and
transformational imagery shared by many Chavin images. The
image is bilaterally symmetrical, except that the creature has one
hand raised and the other lowered. Compact frontality, flat relief,
curvilinear design, and the combination of human, animal, bird,
and reptile parts characterize this early art.

It has been suggested that the Lanzón was an oracle (a chamber
directly above the statue would allow priests' disembodied voices to

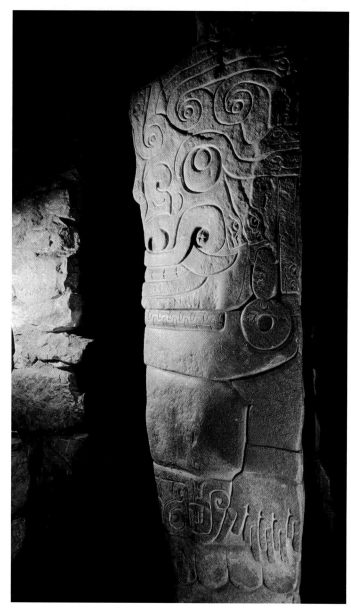

12-15 • LANZÓN, CHAVIN DE HUANTAR
Peru. Chavin culture, c. 900 BCE. Height, 15′ (4.5 m). Granite.

filter into the chamber below), which would explain why people from all over the Andes made pilgrimages to Chavin, bringing exotic goods to the highland site and spreading its art style throughout the Andean region as they returned home.

THE PARACAS AND NAZCA CULTURES

While Chavin de Huantar was flourishing as a highland center whose art was enormously influential throughout the Andes, different valleys on the Pacific coast developed distinctive art styles and cultures.

PARACAS. The Paracas culture of the Peruvian south coast flourished from about 600 BCE to 200 CE, overlapping the Chavin period. It is best known for its stunning textiles, which were found in cemeteries as wrappings, in many layers, around the

bodies of the dead. Some bodies were wrapped in as many as 200 pieces of cloth.

Weaving is of great antiquity in the central Andes and continues to be among the most prized arts in the region (see "Andean Textiles," page 394). Fine textiles were a source of prestige and wealth. The designs on Paracas textiles include repeated embroidered figures of warriors, dancers, and composite creatures such as bird-people (**FIG. 12–16**). Embroiderers used tiny overlapping stitches to create colorful, curvilinear patterns, sometimes using as many as 22 different colors within a single figure, but only one simple stitch. The effect of the clashing and contrasting colors and tumbling figures is dazzling.

NAZCA. The Nazca culture, which dominated portions of the south coast of Peru from about the year 0 to 700 CE, overlapped the Paracas culture to the north. Nazca artisans wove fine fabrics, and also produced multicolored pottery with painted and modeled images reminiscent of those on Paracas textiles.

The Nazca are best known for their colossal earthworks, or **geoglyphs**, which dwarf even the most ambitious twentieth-century environmental sculpture. On great stretches of desert they literally drew in the earth. By removing dark, oxidized stones, they exposed the light underlying stones. In this way they created gigantic images—including a hummingbird with a beak 120 feet long (**FIG. 12–17**), a killer whale, a monkey, a spider, a duck, and other birds—similar to those with which they decorated their pottery. They also made abstract patterns and groups of straight, parallel lines that extend for up to 12 miles. The purpose and meaning of the glyphs remain a mystery, but the "lines" of stone are wide enough to have been ceremonial pathways.

12-16 • MANTLE WITH BIRD IMPERSONATORS
Paracas Peninsula, Peru. Paracas culture, c. 200 BCE–200 CE. Camelid fiber, plain weave with stem-stitch embroidery (detail), approx. 40″ × 7′11″ (1.01 × 2.41 m). Museum of Fine Arts, Boston. Denman Waldo Ross Collection (16.34a)

THE MOCHE CULTURE

The Moche culture dominated the north coast of Peru from the Piura Valley to the Huarmey Valley—a distance of some 370 miles—between about 100 and 700 CE. Moche lords ruled each valley in this region from a ceremonial-administrative center. The largest of these, in the Moche Valley (from which the culture takes its name), contained the so-called Huaca del Sol (Pyramid of the Sun) and Huaca de la Luna (Pyramid of the Moon), both built of **adobe** brick (sun-baked blocks of clay mixed with straw). The Huaca del Sol, one of the largest ancient structures in South America, was originally 1,100 feet long by 500 feet wide, rising in a series of terraces to a height of 59 feet. Much of this pyramid was destroyed in the seventeenth century, when a Spanish mining company diverted a river through it to wash out the gold contained in its many burials. Recent excavations at the Huaca de la Luna have revealed brightly painted reliefs of deities, captives, and warriors, remade during successive renovations of the pyramid. This site had been thought to be the capital of the entire Moche realm, but evidence is accumulating that indicates that the Moche maintained a decentralized social network.

The Moche were exceptional potters and metalsmiths. Vessels were made in the shape of naturalistically modeled human beings, animals, and architectural structures. They developed ceramic molds, which allowed them to mass-produce some forms. They also created realistic **PORTRAIT VESSELS** (FIG. 12–18) and recorded mythological narratives and ritual scenes in intricate fine-line painting. Similar scenes were painted on the walls of

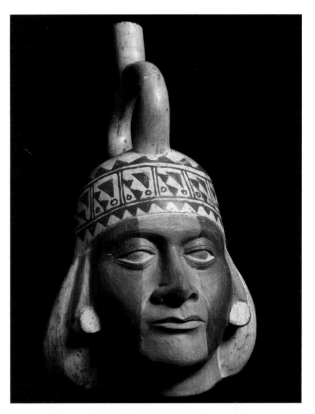

12–18 • MOCHE PORTRAIT VESSEL
Moche culture, Peru. c. 100–700 CE. Clay, height 11" (28 cm). Ethnologisches Museum, Staatliche Museen zu Berlin.

This is one of several portrait vessels, made from the same mold, that seems to show a particular individual.

12–17 • EARTH DRAWING (GEOGLYPH) OF A HUMMINGBIRD, NAZCA PLAIN
Southwest Peru. Nazca culture, c. 0–700 CE. Length approx. 450′ (137 m); wingspan approx. 220′ (60.9 m).

Textiles were one of the most important forms of art and technology in Andean society. Specialized fabrics were developed for everything from ritual burial shrouds and shamans' costumes to rope bridges and knotted cords for record keeping. Clothing indicated ethnic group and social status and was customized for certain functions, the most rarefied being royal ceremonial garments made for specific occasions and worn only once. The creation of textiles, among the most technically complex cloths ever made, consumed a major portion of ancient Andean societies' resources.

Andean textile artists used two principal materials: cotton and camelid fiber. (Camelid fiber—llama, alpaca, guanaco, or vicuña hair—is the Andean equivalent of wool.) Cotton grows on the coast, while llamas, alpacas, and other camelids thrive in the highlands. The presence of cotton fibers in the highlands and camelid fibers on the coast demonstrates trade between the two regions from very early times. The production of textiles was an important factor in the domestication of both plants (cotton) and animals (llamas).

The earliest Peruvian textiles were made by twining, knotting, wrapping, braiding, and looping fibers. Those techniques continued to be used even after the invention of weaving looms in the early second millennium BCE. Most Andean textiles were woven on a simple, portable backstrap loom in which the undyed cotton warp (the lengthwise threads) was looped and stretched between two bars. One bar was tied to a stationary object and the other strapped to the waist of the weaver. The weaver controlled the tension of the warp threads by leaning back and forth while threading a shuttle from side to side to insert the weft (crosswise threads). Changing the arrangement of the warp threads between each passage of the weft created a stable interlace of warp and weft: a textile.

Andean artists used a variety of different techniques to decorate their textiles, creating special effects that were prized for their labor-intensiveness and difficulty of manufacture as well as their beauty. In tapestry weaving, a technique especially suited to representational textiles, the weft does not run the full width of the fabric; each colored section is woven as an independent unit. Embroidery with needle and thread on an already woven textile allows even greater freedom from the rigid warp-and-weft structure of the loom, allowing the artist to create curvilinear forms with thousands of tiny stitches. As even more complex techniques developed, the production of a single textile might involve a dozen processes requiring highly skilled workers. Dyeing technology, too, was an advanced art form in the ancient Andes, with some textiles containing dozens of colors.

Because of their complexity, deciphering how these textiles were made can be a challenge, and scholars rely on contemporary Andean weavers—inheritors of this tradition—for guidance. Now, as then, fiber and textile arts are primarily in the hands of women.

MANTLE WITH BIRD IMPERSONATORS (DETAIL)
From the Paracas Peninsula, Peru. Paracas culture, c. 200 BCE–200 CE. Camelid fiber, plain weave with stem-stitch embroidery. Museum of Fine Arts, Boston. Denman Waldo Ross Collection (16.34a)

---

temples and administrative buildings. Moche metalsmiths, the most sophisticated in the central Andes, developed several innovative metal alloys.

THE TOMB OF THE WARRIOR PRIEST.   A central theme in Moche iconography is the sacrifice ceremony, in which prisoners captured in battle are sacrificed and several elaborately dressed figures then drink their blood. Archaeologists have labeled the principal figure in the ceremony as the Warrior Priest and other important figures as the Bird Priest and the Priestess. The recent discovery of a number of spectacularly rich Moche tombs indicates that the sacrifice ceremony was an actual Moche ritual and that Moche lords and ladies assumed the roles of the principal figures. The occupant of a tomb at Sipán, in the Lambayeque Valley on the northwest coast, was buried with the regalia of the Warrior Priest. In tombs at the site of San José de Moro, just south of Sipán, several women were buried with the regalia of the Priestess.

Among the riches accompanying the Warrior Priest at Sipán was a pair of exquisite gold-and-turquoise **EARSPOOLS**, each of which depicts three Moche warriors (**FIG. 12–19**). The central figure bursts into three dimensions, while his companions are shown in profile, in a flat inlay technique. All three are adorned

12-19 • EARSPOOL
Sipán, Peru. Moche culture, c. 300 CE. Gold, turquoise, quartz, and shell, diameter approx. 3″ (9.4 cm). Bruning Archaeological Museum, Lambayeque, Peru.

with tiny gold-and-turquoise earspools, simpler versions of the object they themselves adorn. They wear gold-and-turquoise headdresses topped with delicate sheets of gold that resemble the crescent-shaped knives used in sacrifices. The central figure has a crescent-shaped nose ornament and carries a removable gold club and shield. A necklace of owl's-head beads strung with gold thread hangs around his shoulders; similar objects have been found in other tombs at Sipán. These earspools illustrate some of the most notable features of Moche art: its capacity for naturalism and its close attention to detail.

NORTH AMERICA

Compared to the densely inhabited agricultural regions of Mesoamerica and South America, most of North America remained sparsely populated. Early people lived primarily by hunting, fishing, and gathering edible plants. Agriculture was developed on a limited scale: People cultivated squash, sunflowers, and other plants to supplement their diet of game, fish, and berries.

THE EAST

The culture of eastern North America is only beginning to be understood. Archaeologists have shown that people lived in communities that included both burial and ceremonial earthworks—mounds of earth-formed platforms that probably supported a chief's house and served as the shrines of ancestors and places for a sacred fire, tended by special guardians. One of the

largest, though not the earliest of the ceremonial centers (this distinction goes to Watson Brake, Louisiana, dating to 3400–3000 BCE), is Poverty Point, Louisiana. Between 1800 and 500 BCE people constructed huge, concentric earthen arcs three-quarters of a mile wide. Scholars have noted that these earthworks are contemporary with Stonehenge in England (SEE FIG. 1–21) and with Olmec constructions in Mexico (SEE FIG. 12–2).

THE WOODLAND PERIOD. The Woodland period (300 BCE–1000 CE) saw the creation of impressive earthworks along the great river valleys of the Ohio and Mississippi. People built monumental mounds and buried individuals with valuable grave goods. Objects discovered in these burials indicate that the people of the Mississippi, Illinois, and Ohio river valleys traded widely with other regions of North and Central America. For example, the burial sites of the Adena (c. 1100 BCE–200 CE) and the Hopewell (c. 100 BCE–550 CE) cultures contained objects made with copper from present-day Michigan's Upper Peninsula, and cut sheets of mica from the Appalachian Mountains, turtle shells and sharks' teeth from Florida, and obsidian from Wyoming and Idaho. The pipes the Hopewell people created from fine-grained pipestone have been found from Lake Superior to the Gulf of Mexico.

The Hopewell carved their pipes with representations of forest animals and birds, sometimes with inlaid eyes and teeth of freshwater pearls and bone. Combining realism and elegant simplification, a beaver crouching on a platform forms the bowl of a pipe found in present-day Illinois (FIG. 12–20). As in a modern pipe, the bowl—a hole in the beaver's back—could be filled with tobacco or other dried leaves, the leaves lighted, and smoke drawn through the hole in the stem. Using the pipe in this way, the

12-20 • BEAVER EFFIGY PLATFORM PIPE
Bedford Mound, Pike County, Illinois. Hopewell culture, c. 100–400 CE. Pipestone, river pearls, and bone, 4⁹⁄₁₆ × 1⅞ × 2″. Gilcrease Museum, Tulsa, Oklahoma.

12-21 • GREAT SERPENT MOUND
Adams County, Ohio.
c. 1070 CE. Length approx.
1,254′ (328.2 m).

smoker would be face to face with the beaver, whose shining pearl eyes may suggest an association with the spirit world.

THE MISSISSIPPIAN PERIOD. The Mississippian period (c. 700–1550 CE) is characterized by the widespread distribution of complex chiefdoms, both large and small, that proliferated throughout the region. The people of the Mississippian culture continued the mound-building tradition begun by the Adena, Hopewell, and others. From 1539 to 1543 Hernando de Soto explored the region and encountered Mississippian societies. However, contact between native North American people and Europeans resulted in catastrophe. The Europeans introduced the germs of diseases, especially smallpox, to which native populations had had no previous exposure and hence no immunity. In short order, 80 percent of the native population perished, an extraordinary disruption of society, far worse than the Black Death in fourteenth-century Europe. By the time other Europeans reached the area, the great earthworks of the Mississippian culture were long abandoned.

One of the most impressive Mississippian period earthworks is the **GREAT SERPENT MOUND** in present-day Adams County, Ohio (**FIG. 12–21**). Researchers using carbon-14 dating have recently proposed dating the mound at about 1070 CE. There have been many interpretations of the twisting snake form, especially the "head" at the highest point, a Y-shape and an oval enclosure that some see as the

12-22 • RECONSTRUCTION OF CENTRAL CAHOKIA, AS IT WOULD HAVE APPEARED ABOUT 1150 CE
East St. Louis, Illinois. Mississippian culture, c. 1000–1300 CE. East–west length approx. 3 miles (4.5 km), north–south length approx. 2¼ miles (3.6 km); base of great mound, 1,037 × 790′ (316 × 241 m), height approx. 100′ (30 m). Monk's Mound is the large platform in the center of the image. Painting by William R. Iseminger. Courtesy of Cahokia Mounds Historic site.

12-23 • PELICAN FIGUREHEAD
Florida Glades culture, Key Marco, Florida. c. 1000 CE. Wood and paint, 4⅜ × 2⅜ × 3⅛″ (11.2 × 6 × 8 cm). The University Museum of Archaeology and Anthropology, Philadelphia. (T4.303)

Pos013holes indicate that woodhenges (circles of wooden columns) were a significant feature of Cahokia. The largest (seen to the extreme left in FIGURE 12–22) had 48 posts forming a circle with a diameter of about 420 feet. Sight lines between a 49th post set east of the center of the enclosure and points on the perimeter enabled native astronomers to determine solstices and equinoxes.

FLORIDA GLADES CULTURE. In 1895, excavators working in submerged mud and shell mounds off Key Marco on the west coast of Florida made a remarkable discovery. Posts carved with birds and animals were found preserved in the swamps. The large mound called Fort Center, in Glades Country, Florida, gives the culture its name: Florida Glades.

In Key Marco painted wooden animal and bird heads, a human mask, and the figure of a kneeling cat-human were found in circumstances that suggested a ruined shrine. Recently carbon-14 dating of these items has confirmed a date of about 1000 CE. Although the heads are spare in details, the artists show a remarkable power of observation in reproducing the creatures they saw around them, such as the **PELICAN** in FIGURE **12–23**. The surviving head, neck, and breast of the pelican are made of carved wood, painted black, white, and gray (other images also had traces of pink and blue paint). The bird's outstretched wings were found nearby, but the wood shrank and disintegrated as it dried. Carved wooden wolf and deer heads were also found. Archaeologists think the heads might have been attached to ceremonial furniture or posts. Such images suggest the existence of a bird and animal cult or perhaps the use of birds and animals as clan symbols.

THE NORTH AMERICAN SOUTHWEST

Farming cultures were slower to arise in the arid American Southwest, which became home to three major early cultures. The Mimbres/Mogollon culture, located in the mountains of west-central New Mexico and east-central Arizona, flourished from about 200 to about 1250 CE. Potters made deep bowls with lively scenes of humans and animals inside. The Hohokam culture, centered in the central and southern parts of present-day Arizona, emerged around 200 BCE and endured until sometime around 1300 CE. The Hohokam built large-scale irrigation systems, multi-story residences, and ballcourts that demonstrate ties with Mesoamerica.

The third southwestern culture, the Ancestral Puebloans (formerly called Anasazi), emerged around 500 CE in the Four Corners region, where present-day Colorado, Utah, Arizona, and New Mexico meet. The Puebloans adopted the irrigation technology of the Hohokam and began building elaborate, multistoried, apartmentlike "great houses" with many rooms for specialized purposes, including communal food storage and ritual.

Ancestral Puebloan people found aesthetic expression in their pottery, an ancient craft refined over generations. Women were the potters in ancient Pueblo society. They developed a functional, aesthetically pleasing, coil-built earthenware, or low-fired ceramic. Ceramic traditions continue to be important today among the

serpent opening its jaws to swallow a huge egg. Perhaps the people who built it were responding to the spectacular astronomical display of Halley's Comet in 1066.

Mississippian peoples built a major urban center known as Cahokia, near the juncture of the Illinois, Missouri, and Mississippi rivers (now East St. Louis, Illinois). Although the site may have been inhabited as early as about 3000 BCE, most monumental construction at Cahokia took place between about 1000 and 1300 CE. At its height the city had a population of as many as 15,000 people, with another 10,000 in the surrounding countryside **(FIG. 12–22)**.

The most prominent feature of Cahokia is an enormous earth mound called Monk's Mound, covering 15 acres and originally 100 feet high. A small, rounded platform on its summit initially supported a wooden fence and a rectangular building. The mound is aligned with the sun at the equinox and may have had a special use during planting or harvest festivals. Smaller rectangular and rounded mounds in front of the principal mound surrounded a large, roughly rectangular plaza. The city's entire ceremonial center was protected by a stockade, or fence, of upright wooden posts. In all, the walled enclosure contained more than 100 mounds, platforms, wooden enclosures, and houses. The various earthworks functioned as tombs and bases for palaces and temples, and also served to make astronomical observations.

12-24 • SEED JAR
Ancestral Puebloan culture, c. 1150 CE. Earthenware and black-and-white pigment, diameter 14½" (36.9 cm). The St. Louis Art Museum, St. Louis, Missouri. Purchase: Funds given by the Children's Art Bazaar, St. Louis

Pueblo peoples of the Southwest. One type of vessel, a wide-mouthed **SEED JAR** with a globular body and holes near the rim (**FIG. 12–24**), would have been suspended from roof poles by thongs attached to the jar's holes, out of reach of voracious rodents. The example shown here is decorated with black-and-white dotted squares and zigzag patterns. The patterns conform to the body of the jar, and in spite of their angularity they enhance its curved shape.

CHACO CANYON. Chaco Canyon, a New Mexico canyon of about 30 square miles with nine great houses, or pueblos, was an important center of Ancestral Puebloan civilization. The largest known "great house" is **PUEBLO BONITO** (**FIG. 12–25**), which was built in stages between the tenth and mid thirteenth centuries. Eventually it comprised over 800 rooms in four or five stories, arranged in a D shape. Within the crescent part of the D, 32 **kivas** recall the round, semisubmerged pit houses of earlier Southwestern cultures. Here men performed religious rituals and instructed youths in their responsibilities. Interlocking pine logs formed a shallow, domelike roof with a hole in the center through which the men entered by climbing down a ladder. Inside the kiva, in the

12-25 • PUEBLO BONITO
Chaco Canyon, New Mexico. 830–1250 CE.

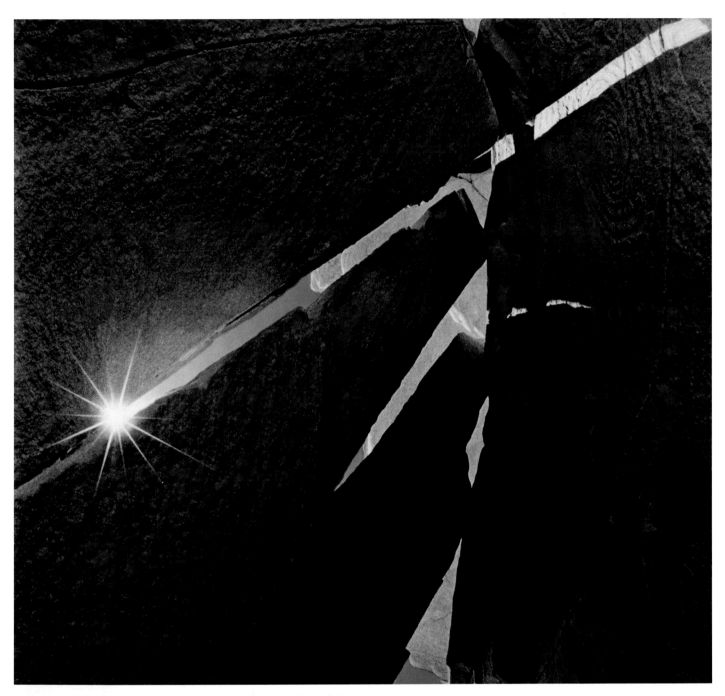

12–26 • SUN DAGGER SOLAR MARKER AT EQUINOX
Fajada Butte, Chaco Canyon, New Mexico. 850–1250 CE.

floor directly under the entrance and behind the fire pit, a small indentation—the "navel of the earth"—may have symbolized the place where the Ancestral Pueblo ancestors had emerged from the earth in the mythic "first times," based on analogies with later Pueblo beliefs. The top of the kivas formed the floor of the communal plaza.

Pueblo Bonito stood at the hub of a network of wide, straight roads that radiated out to some 70 other communities. Almost invisible today, the roads were discovered through aerial photography. They make no detour to avoid topographic obstacles; when they encounter cliffs, they become stairs. Their undeviating course

suggests that they were more than practical thoroughfares: They may have served as processional ways. Was Pueblo Bonito a gathering place for people in the entire region at specific times of year?

On the morning of the summer solstice a streak of light strikes a high cliff in Chaco Canyon. Slowly this "Sun Dagger" descends, and by noontime it pierces the heart of a large spiral engraved into the rock (**FIG. 12–26**; see also "Rock Art," page 400). The Ancestral Puebloans pecked out this spiral, along with a smaller one, on the face of the bluff. The shaft of light forming the dagger is created by openings between huge slabs of rock, which admit streaks of light that project on the wall. The light moves with

Rock Art

Rock art consists of pictographs, which are painted, and petroglyphs, which are pecked or engraved. While occurring in numerous distinctive styles, rock art images include humans, animals, and geometric figures, represented singly and in multi-figured compositions. Petroglyphs are often found in places where the dark brown bacterial growths and staining known as "**desert varnish**" streak down canyon walls (FIG. B). To create an image, the artist scrapes or pecks through the layer of varnish, exposing the lighter sandstone beneath.

In the Great Gallery of Horseshoe Canyon, Utah, the painted human figures have long, decorated rectangular bodies and knoblike heads (FIG. A). One large, wide-eyed figure (popularly known as the "Holy Ghost") is nearly 8 feet tall. Archaeologists have dated these paintings to as early as 1900 BCE and as recently as 300 CE; rock art is very difficult to date precisely.

In Nine Mile Canyon in central Utah, a large human hunter draws his bow and arrow on a flock of bighorn sheep. Other hunters and a large, rectangular armless figure wearing a horned headdress—perhaps a shaman—mingle with the animals. The scene gives rise to the same questions and arguments we have noted with regard to the prehistoric art discussed in Chapter 1: Is this a record of a successful hunt or is it part of some ritual activity to ensure success? The petroglyphs are attributed to the Fremont people (800–1300 CE), who were agriculturists as well as hunters.

A. ANTHROPOMORPHS, THE GREAT GALLERY, HORSESHOE (BARRIER) CANYON

Utah. c. 1900 BCE–300 CE. Largest figure about 8′ (2.44 m) tall.

The figures may represent shamans and are often associated with snakes, dogs, and other small energetic creatures. Big-eyed anthropomorphs may be rain gods. Painters used their fingers and yucca-fiber brushes to apply the reddish pigment made from hematite (iron oxide).

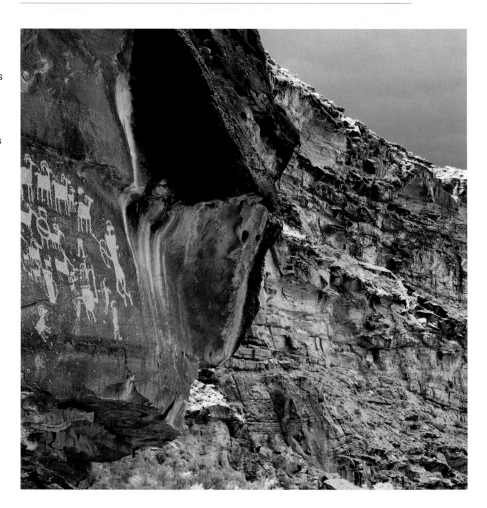

B. HUNTER'S MURAL

Nine Mile Canyon, Utah. Fremont people, 800–1300 CE.

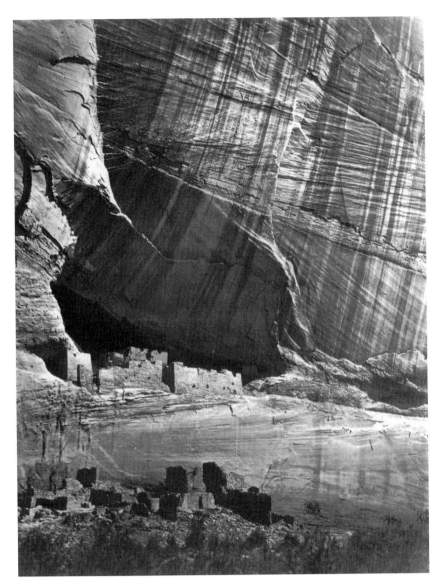

12-27 • Timothy O'Sullivan ANCIENT RUINS IN THE CANON DE CHELLEY
Arizona, 1873. Albumen print. National Archives, Washington, D.C.

While ostensibly a documentary photograph, Timothy O'Sullivan's depiction of "The White House," built by 12th-century Ancestral Puebloans, is both a valuable document for the study of architecture and an evocative photograph, filled with the Romantic sense of sublime melancholy.

River valleys. They built their new apartmentlike dwellings on ledges under sheltering cliffs (FIG. 12–27). Difficult as it must have been to live high on canyon walls and farm the valley below, the cliff communities had the advantage of being relatively secure. The rock shelters in the cliffs also acted as insulation, protecting the dwellings from extremes of heat and cold. Like a modern apartment complex, the many rooms housed an entire community comfortably. Communal solidarity and responsibility became part of the heritage of the Pueblo peoples.

Throughout the Americas, for the next several hundred years, artistic traditions would continue to emerge, develop, and be transformed as the indigenous peoples of various regions interacted. The sudden incursions of Europeans, beginning in the late fifteenth century, would have a dramatic and lasting impact on these civilizations and their art.

the seasonal motion of the sun. Only at the summer solstice in June does the great dagger appear. At the winter solstice two streaks frame the spiral petroglyph, and at both spring and fall equinoxes a small spike of light hits the center of the small spiral, and a large shaft cuts through the large spiral but misses its center. The rock formation that, together with the moving sun, creates the daggers of light is natural, but the two spirals were deliberately placed. Nature and art combine, as they do in the work of a modern environmental artist. Among Ancestral Puebloans spirals were signs for journeys, as well as for wind and water, serpents and snails. The later Zuni call the spiral a "journey in search of the Center." The clocklike workings of the spiral petroglyphs, together with their location on a high point distant from living areas in the canyon, have led to the speculation that the Sun Dagger was once a shrine.

Though no one knows for certain why the people of Chaco Canyon abandoned the site, the population declined during a severe drought in the twelfth century, and building at Pueblo Bonito ceased around 1250. The Pueblo population of Chaco Canyon may have moved to the Rio Grande and Mogollon

THINK ABOUT IT

12.1 Discuss the environmental challenges posed to the ancient peoples of the American Southwest and explain how they responded to them. Contrast this set of circumstances with that of another ancient people from Mesoamerica or South America, and explain how the respective circumstances impacted their art and culture.

12.2 Explain the original function of two ancient American objects from two different cultures. Discuss these objects within their larger sociocultural context.

12.3 Compare and contrast urban planning at Tikal and Teotihuacan. In your answer, make sure to give consideration to the issue of natural topography.

12.4 Explain how the Maya writing system functions, and discuss the impact this system had on the visual arts.

PRACTICE MORE: Compose answers to these questions, get flashcards for images and terms, and review chapter material with quizzes
www.myartslab.com

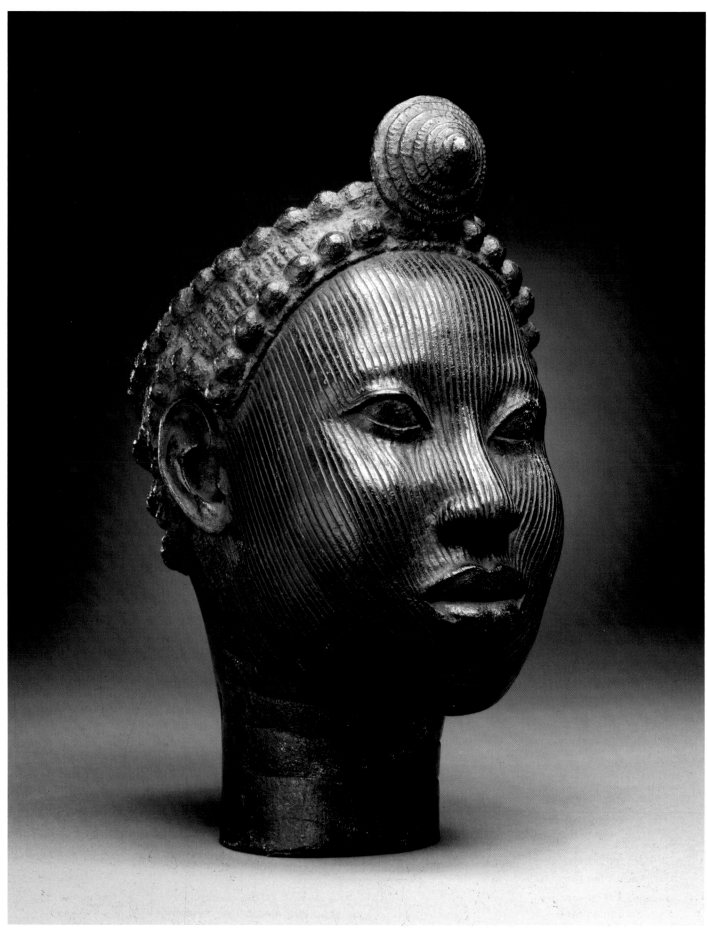

13-1 • CROWNED HEAD OF A KING   Ife, Yoruba. 12th–15th century CE.
Zinc brass, height 9⁷⁄₁₆" (24 cm). Museum of Ife Antiquities, Ife, Nigeria.

EARLY AFRICAN ART

The Yoruba people of southwestern Nigeria regard the city of Ife (also known as Ile-Ife) as the "navel of the world," the site of creation, the place where Ife's first ruler—the *oni* Oduduwa—came down from heaven to create earth and then to populate it. By the eleventh century CE, Ife was a lively metropolis. Today, every Yoruba city claims "descent" from Ife.

Ife was, and remains, the sacred city of the Yoruba people. A tradition of naturalistic sculpture began there about 1050 CE and flourished for some four centuries. Although the ancestral line of the Ife *oni* (king) has continued unbroken, knowledge of the precise purpose of these works has been lost.

A cast-bronze head (FIG. 13–1) shows the extraordinary artistry of ancient Ife. The modeling of the flesh is remarkably sensitive, especially the subtle transitions around the nose and mouth. The lips are full and delicate, and the eyes are strikingly similar in shape to those of some modern Yoruba. The face is covered with thin, parallel **scarification** patterns (decorations made by scarring). The head was cast of zinc brass using the lost-wax method.

The head was cast with a crown; its size and delicate features suggest it may represent a female *oni*. Although its precise use is not known, similar life-size heads have large holes in the neck, suggesting they may have been attached to wooden figures. Mannequins with naturalistic facial features have been documented at memorial services for deceased individuals among contemporary Yoruba peoples. The Ife mannequin was probably dressed in the *oni*'s robes; the head probably bore his crown. The head could also have been used to display a crown during annual purification and renewal rites.

There is debate as to whether the Ife heads are true portraits. Their realism gives an impression that they could be. The heads, however, all seem to represent individuals of the same age and embody a similar concept of physical perfection, suggesting they are idealized images representing both physical beauty and moral character. Idealized images of titled individuals are a common feature of sub-Saharan African sculpture, as they are among many cultures throughout the world.

The superb naturalism of Ife sculpture contradicted everything Europeans thought they knew about African art. The German scholar, Leo Frobenius, who "discovered" Ife sculpture in 1910 suggested that it was created not by Africans but by survivors from the legendary lost island of Atlantis. Later, there was speculation that influence from ancient Greece or Renaissance Europe must have reached Ife. Scientific study, however, finally put such prejudiced ideas to rest.

LEARN ABOUT IT

13.1 Identify and summarize the key roles that the visual arts play in sub-Saharan Africa.

13.2 Explore how African arts mediate and support communication between the temporal and the supernatural worlds of various spirit forces.

13.3 Specify how African visual arts are only fully realized in their context of use.

13.4 Contrast the role of African arts related to leadership as compared to the role of leadership arts in Western cultural traditions.

HEAR MORE: Listen to an audio file of your chapter **www.myartslab.com**

THE LURE OF ANCIENT AFRICA

"I descended [the Nile] with three hundred asses laden with incense, ebony, grain, panthers, ivory, and every good product." Thus the Egyptian envoy Harkhuf described his return from Nubia, the African land to the south of Egypt, in 2300 BCE. The riches of Africa attracted merchants and envoys in ancient times, and trade brought the continent in contact with the rest of the world. Egyptian relations with the rest of the African continent continued through the Hellenistic era and beyond. Phoenicians and Greeks founded dozens of settlements along the Mediterranean coast of North Africa between 1000 and 300 BCE to extend trade routes across the Sahara to the peoples of Lake Chad and the bend of the Niger River (MAP 13–1). When the Romans took control of North Africa, they continued this lucrative trans-Saharan trade. In the seventh and eighth centuries CE, the expanding empire of Islam swept across North Africa, and thereafter Islamic merchants were regular visitors to Bilad al-Sudan (the Land of the Blacks—sub-Saharan Africa). Islamic scholars chronicled the great West African empires of Ghana, Mali, and Songhay, and West African gold financed the flowering of Islamic culture.

East Africa, meanwhile, had been drawn since at least the beginning of the Common Era into the maritime trade that ringed the Indian Ocean and extended east to Indonesia and the South China Sea. Arab, Indian, and Persian ships plied the coastline. A new language, Swahili, evolved from centuries of contact between Arabic-speaking merchants and Bantu-speaking Africans, and great port cities such as Kilwa, Mombasa, and Mogadishu arose.

In the fifteenth century, Europeans ventured by ship into the Atlantic Ocean and down the coast of Africa. Finally rediscovering the continent firsthand, they were often astonished by what they found (see "The Myth of 'Primitive' Art," page 406). "Dear King My Brother," wrote a fifteenth-century Portuguese king to his new trading partner, the king of Benin in west Africa. The Portuguese king's respect was well founded—Benin was vastly more powerful and wealthier than the small European country that had just stumbled upon it.

As we saw in Chapter 3, Africa was home to one of the world's earliest great civilizations, that of ancient Egypt, and as we saw in Chapter 8, Egypt and the rest of North Africa contributed prominently to the development of Islamic art and culture. This chapter examines the artistic legacy of the rest of ancient Africa.

AFRICA—THE CRADLE OF ART AND CIVILIZATION

During the twentieth century, the sculpture of traditional African societies—wood carvings of astonishing formal inventiveness and power—found admirers the world over. While avidly collected, these works were much misunderstood. For the past 75 years, art historians and cultural anthropologists have studied African art firsthand, which has added to our overall understanding of art

making in many African cultures. However, except for a few isolated examples (such as in Nigeria and Mali), the historical depth of our understanding is still limited by the continuing lack of systematic archaeological research. Our understanding of traditions that are more than 100 years old is especially hampered by the fact that most African art was made from wood, which decays rapidly in sub-Saharan Africa. Consequently, few examples of African masks and sculpture remain from before the nineteenth century, and for the most part it is necessary to rely on contemporary traditions and oral histories to help extrapolate backward in time to determine what may have been the types, styles, and meaning of art made in the past. Nevertheless, the few ancient African artworks we have in such durable materials as terra cotta, stone, and bronze, and from an extensive record in rock art that has been preserved in sheltered places, bear eloquent witness to the skill of ancient African artists and the splendor of the civilizations in which they worked.

Twentieth-century archaeology has made it popular to speak of Africa as the cradle of human civilization. Certainly the earliest evidence for our human ancestors comes from southern Africa (see "Southern African Rock Art," page 408). Now evidence of the initial stirrings of artistic activity also comes from the southern tip of Africa. Recently, quantities of ocher pigment thought to have been used for ceremonial or decorative purposes, and perforated shells thought to have been fashioned into beads and worn as personal adornment, have been found in Blombos Cave on the Indian Ocean coast of South Africa, dating to approximately 77,000 years ago. Also discovered together with these were two small, ocher blocks that had been smoothed and then decorated with geometric arrays of carved lines (SEE FIG. 1.4 for an illustration of the decorated ocher). These incised abstract patterns predate any other findings of ancient art by more than 30,000 years, and they suggest a far earlier development of modern human behavior than had been previously recognized.

The earliest known figurative art works from the African continent are animal figures dating to about 25,000 BCE, painted in red and black pigment on flat stones found in a cave designated as Apollo 11, located in the desert mountains of Namibia. These figures are comparable to the better-known European cave drawings such as those from the Chauvet Cave (c. 32,000–30,000 BCE) and Lascaux Cave (c. 15,000–13,000 BCE) discussed in Chapter 1.

AFRICAN ROCK ART

Like the Paleolithic inhabitants of Europe, early Africans painted and inscribed images on the walls of caves and rock shelters. Rock art is found throughout the African continent in places where the environment has been conducive to preservation—areas ranging from small, isolated shelters to great cavernous formations. Distinct geographic zones of rock art can be identified broadly encompassing the northern, central, southern, and eastern regions of the continent. These rock paintings and engravings range in

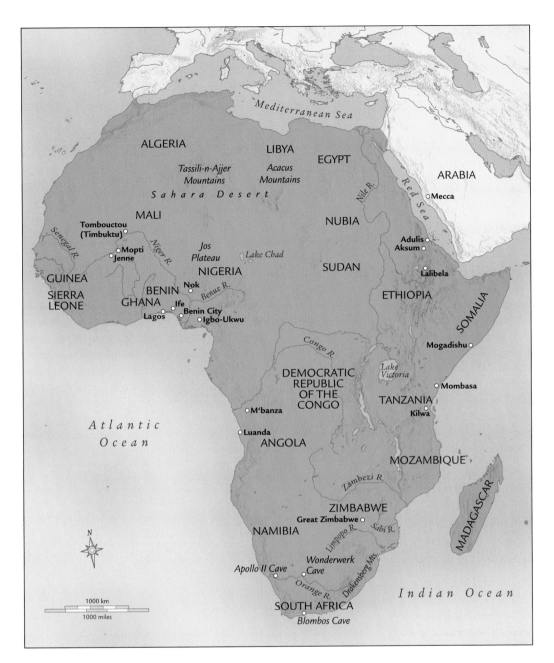

MAP 13-1 • ANCIENT AFRICA

Nearly 5,000 miles from north to south, Africa is the second-largest continent and was the home of some of the earliest and most advanced cultures of the ancient world.

form from highly abstract geometric designs to abstract and naturalistic representations of human and animal forms, including hunting scenes, scenes of domestic life, and costumed figures that appear to be dancing. The long record of rock art, extending over thousands of years in numerous places, charts dramatic environmental and social change in the deserts of Africa. Images depicting human subjects are also important evidence that the African artistic traditions of body decoration, mask-making and performance spring from ancient African roots.

SAHARAN ROCK ART

The mountains of the central Sahara—principally the Tassili-n-Ajjer range in the south of present-day Algeria and the Acacus Mountains in present-day Libya—contain images that span a period of thousands of years. They record not only the artistic and cultural development of the peoples who lived in the region, but also the transformation of the Sahara from a fertile grassland to the vast desert we know today.

The earliest images of Saharan rock art are thought to date from at least 8000 BCE, during the transition into a geological period known as the Makalian Wet Phase. At that time the Sahara was a grassy plain, perhaps much like the game-park reserves of modern east Africa. Vivid images of hippopotamus, elephant, giraffe, antelope, and other animals incised on rock surfaces attest to the abundant wildlife that roamed the region.

A variety of scenes found on rock walls in both southern Algeria and Libya depict men and women dancing or performing various ceremonial activities. The artists who created these works paid close attention to details of clothing, body decoration, and headdresses; in some examples the figures are depicted wearing

The Myth of "Primitive" Art

The word "primitive" was once used by Western art historians to categorize the art of Africa, the art of the Pacific islands, and the indigenous art of the Americas. The term itself means "early" or "first of its kind," but its use was meant to imply that these cultures were crude, simple, backward, and stuck in an early stage of development.

This attitude was accepted by Christian missionaries and explorers, who often described the peoples among whom they worked as "heathen," "barbaric," "ignorant," "tribal," "primitive," and other terms rooted in racism and colonialism. Such usages were extended to these peoples' creations, and "primitive art" became the conventional label for their cultural products.

Criteria that have been used to label a people "primitive" include the use of so-called Stone Age technology, the absence of written histories, and the failure to build great cities. Based on these criteria, however, the accomplishments of the peoples of Africa, to take just one example, contradict such prejudiced condescension: Africans south of the Sahara have smelted and forged iron since at least 500 BCE. Africans in many areas made and used high-quality steel for weapons and tools. Many African peoples have recorded their histories in Arabic since at least the tenth century CE. The first European visitors to Africa admired the style and sophistication of urban centers such as

Benin and Luanda, to name only two of the continent's great cities. Clearly, neither the cultures of ancient Africa nor the artworks they produced were "primitive" at all.

Until quite recently, Westerners tended to see Africa as a single country and not as an immense continent of vastly diverse cultures. Moreover, they perceived artists working in Africa as craftworkers bound to styles and images dictated by village elders and producing art that was anonymous and interchangeable. Over the past several decades, however, these misconceptions have crumbled. Art historians and anthropologists have now identified numerous African cultures and artists and compiled catalogs of their work. For example, the well-known Yoruba artist Olowe of Ise (see Chapter 28) was commissioned by rulers throughout the Yoruba region in the early twentieth century to create prestige objects such as palace veranda posts and palace doors or *tour-de-force* carvings such as magnificent lidded bowls supported by kneeling figures. Certainly we will never know the names of the vast majority of African artists of the past, just as we do not know the names of the sculptors responsible for the portrait busts of ancient Rome or the monumental reliefs of the Hindu temples of South Asia. But, as elsewhere, the greatest artists in Africa were famous and sought after, while innumerable others labored honorably and not at all anonymously.

---

masks that cover their faces. It is suggested that they are engaged in rituals intended to ensure adequate rainfall or success in hunting, or to honor their dead. These images, produced in a variety of styles, document the development of the complex ceremonial and ritual lives of the people who created them (FIG. 13–2).

By 4000 BCE the climate had become more arid, and hunting had given way to herding as the primary life-sustaining activity of the Sahara's inhabitants. Among the most beautiful and complex examples of Saharan rock art created in this period are scenes of sheep, goats, and cattle and of the daily lives of the people who tended them. Some scenes found at Tassili-n-Ajjer date from late in the herding period, about 5000–2000 BCE, and illustrate men and women gathered in front of round, thatched houses. As the men tend cattle, the women prepare a meal and care for children. Some scenes attempt to create a sense of depth and distance with over-lapping forms, and the placement of near figures lower and distant figures higher in the picture plane.

By 2500–2000 BCE the Sahara was drying and the great game had disappeared, but other animals were introduced that appear in the rock art. The horse was brought from Egypt by about 1500 BCE and is seen regularly in rock art over the ensuing millennia. The fifth-century BCE Greek historian Herodotus described a chariot-driving people called the Garamante, whose kingdom corresponds roughly to present-day Libya. Rock-art images of horse-drawn

chariots bear out his account. Around 600 BCE the camel was introduced into the region from the east, and images of camels were painted on and incised into the rock.

The drying of the Sahara coincided with the rise of Egyptian civilization along the Nile Valley to the east. Similarities can be noted between Egyptian and Saharan motifs, among them images of rams with what appear to be disks between their horns. These similarities have been interpreted as evidence of Egyptian influence on the less-developed regions of the Sahara. Yet in light of the great age of Saharan rock art, it seems just as plausible that the influence flowed the other way, carried by people who had migrated into the Nile Valley when the grasslands of the Sahara disappeared.

SUB-SAHARAN CIVILIZATIONS

Saharan peoples presumably migrated southward as well, into the Sudan, the broad belt of grassland that stretches across Africa south of the Sahara Desert. They brought with them knowledge of settled agriculture and animal husbandry. The earliest evidence of settled agriculture in the Sudan dates from about 3000 BCE. Toward the middle of the first millennium BCE, at the same time that iron technology was being developed elsewhere in Africa, knowledge of ironworking spread across the Sudan as well,

Nok sculpture was discovered in modern times by tin miners digging in alluvial deposits on the Jos plateau north of the confluence of the Niger and Benue rivers. Presumably, floods from centuries past had removed the sculptures from their original contexts, dragged and rolled them along, and then deposited them, scratched and broken, often leaving only the heads from what must have been complete human figures. Following archaeological convention, the name of a nearby village, Nok, was given to the culture that created these works. Nok-style works of sculpture have since been found in numerous sites over a wide area.

The Nok head shown (**FIG. 13–3**), slightly larger than life-size, probably formed part of a complete figure. The triangular or D-shaped eyes are characteristic of Nok style and appear also on sculptures of animals. Holes in the pupils, nostrils, and mouth allowed air to pass freely as the figure was fired. Each of the large buns of its elaborate hairstyle is pierced with a hole that may have held ornamental feathers. Other Nok figures were created displaying beaded necklaces,

13-2 • DANCERS IN CEREMONIAL ATTIRE
Section of rock-wall painting, Tassili-n-Ajjer, Algeria. c. 5000–2000 BCE.

enabling its inhabitants to create more effective weapons and farming tools. In the wake of these developments, larger and more complex societies emerged, especially in the fertile basins of Lake Chad in the central Sudan and the Niger and Senegal rivers to the west.

NOK

Some of the earliest evidence of iron technology in sub-Saharan Africa comes from the so-called Nok culture, which arose in the western Sudan, in present-day Nigeria, as early as 500 BCE. The Nok people were farmers who grew grain and oil-bearing seeds, but they were also smelters with the technology for refining ore. Slag and the remains of furnaces have been discovered, along with clay nozzles from the bellows used to fan the fires. The Nok people created the earliest known sculpture of sub-Saharan Africa, producing accomplished terra-cotta figures of human and animal subjects between about 500 BCE and 200 CE.

13-3 • HEAD
From Nok. c. 500 BCE–200 CE. Terra cotta, height 14¾₁₆″ (36 cm). National Museum, Lagos, Nigeria.

Southern African Rock Art

Rock painting and engraving from sites in southern Africa differ in terms of style and age from those discussed for the Sahara region. Some works of art predate those found in the Sahara, while others continued to be produced into the modern era. Early works include an engraved fragment found in dateable debris in Wonderwerk Cave, South Africa, which dates back to 10,000 years ago. Painted stone flakes found at a site in Zimbabwe suggest dates between 13,000 and 8000 BCE.

Numerous examples of rock painting are also found in South Africa in the region of the Drakensberg Mountains. Almost 600 sites have been located in rock shelters and caves, with approximately 35,000 individual images catalogued. It is believed the paintings were produced, beginning approximately 2,400 years ago, by the predecessors of San peoples who still reside in the region. Ethnographic research among the San and related peoples in southern Africa suggest possible interpretations for some of the paintings. For example, rock paintings depicting groups of dancing figures may relate to certain forms of San rituals that are still performed today to heal individuals or to cleanse communities. These may have been created by San ritual specialists or shamans to record their curing dances or trance experiences of the spirit world. San rock artists continued to create rock paintings into the late nineteenth century. These latter works depict the arrival of Afrikaner pioneers in the region as well as British soldiers brandishing guns used to hunt eland.

SECTION OF SAN ROCK-WALL PAINTING San peoples, n.d. Drakensberg Mountains, South Africa. Pigment and eland blood on rock.

armlets, bracelets, anklets, and other prestige ornaments. Nok sculpture may represent ordinary people dressed for special occasions or it may portray people of high status, thus reflecting social stratification in this early farming culture. In either case, the sculpture provides evidence of considerable technical accomplishment, which has led to speculation that Nok culture was built on the achievements of an earlier culture still to be discovered.

IGBO-UKWU

A number of significant sites were excavated in Nigeria in the mid twentieth century that increase our understanding of the development of art and culture in west Africa. This includes the archaeological site of Igbo-Ukwu in eastern Nigeria where Igbo peoples reside, numerically one of Nigeria's largest populations. The earliest-known evidence for copper alloy or bronze casting in sub-Saharan Africa is found at Igbo-Ukwu. This evidence dates to the ninth and tenth centuries CE. Igbo-Ukwu is also the earliest-known site containing an elite burial and shrine complex yet found in sub-Saharan Africa. Three distinct archaeological sites have been excavated at Igbo-Ukwu—one containing a burial chamber, another resembling a shrine or storehouse containing ceremonial objects, and the third an ancient pit containing ceremonial and prestige objects.

The **BURIAL CHAMBER (FIG. 13—4)** contained an individual dressed in elaborate regalia, placed in a seated position, and surrounded by emblems of his power and authority. These

13-4 • BURIAL CHAMBER
Igbo-Ukwu, showing the placement of the ruler
and artifacts in the chamber in the 10th century.
Reconstruction painting by Caroline Sassoon.

ornaments. Igbo-Ukwu's unique style consists of the representation in bronze of natural objects such as gourd bowls and snail shells whose entire outer surface is covered with elaborate raised and banded decorations. These decorations include linear, spiral, circular, and granular designs, sometimes with the addition of small animals or insects such as snakes, frogs, crickets, or flies applied to the decorated surface. Some castings are further enlivened with the addition of brightly colored beads.

A cast fly-whisk handle is topped with the representation of an equestrian figure whose face, like that of a pendant head also found during excavation, is represented scarified in a style similar to the patterning found on some of the terra-cotta and cast heads of rulers at Ife. These markings are similar to markings called *ichi*, which are still used by Igbo men as a symbol of high achievement.

A roped pot is among the most technically sophisticated castings found at Igbo-Ukwu (see "A Closer Look," page 411). It has been suggested that the vessel resembles a form of water-pot drum still used in this region of Nigeria. The vessel is filled with water and a flat mallet is struck across the surface of the water at the rim to create a percussive sound.

IFE

The naturalistic works of sculpture created by the artists of the city of Ife are among the most remarkable in art history. Ancient Ife, which arose in the southwestern forested part of Nigeria about 800 CE, was essentially circular in plan, with the *oni*'s palace at the center. Ringed by protective stone walls and moats, it was connected to other Yoruba cities by roads that radiated from the center, passing through the city walls at fortified gateways decorated with mosaics created from stones and pottery shards. From these elaborately patterned pavement mosaics, which covered much of Ife's open spaces, comes the name for Ife's most artistically cohesive historical period (c. 1000–1400), the Pavement period.

Just as the *oni*'s palace was located in a large courtyard in the center of Ife, so too were ritual spaces elsewhere in Ife located in paved courtyards with altars. In the center of such a sacred courtyard, outlined by rings of pavement mosaic, archaeologists

included three ivory tusks, thousands of imported beads that originally formed part of an elaborate necklace, other adornments, and a cast-bronze representation of a leopard skull. Elephants and leopards are still symbols of temporal and spiritual leadership in Africa today. Ethnographic research among the Nri, an Igbo-related people currently residing in the region, suggests that the burial site is that of an important Nri king or ritual leader (*eze*).

The second excavation uncovered a shrine or storehouse complex containing ceremonial and prestige objects. These copper alloy castings were made by the lost-wax technique (see "Lost-Wax Casting," page 413) in the form of elaborately decorated small bowls, fly-whisk handles, altar stands, staff finials (decorative tops), and

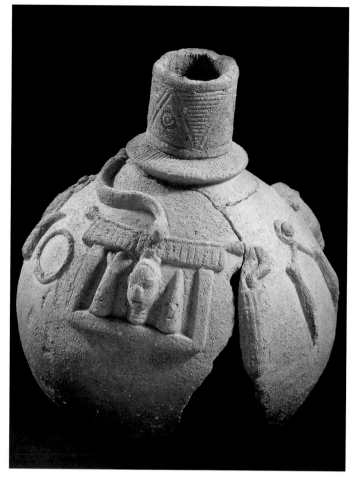

13-5 • RITUAL VESSEL
From Ife, Yoruba. 13th–14th century CE. Terra cotta, height 9¹³⁄₁₆″
(24.9 cm). University Art Museum, Obafemi, Awolowo University,
Ife, Nigeria.

excavated an exceptional terra-cotta vessel **(FIG. 13–5)**. The jar's
bottom had been ritually broken before it was buried, so that
liquid offerings (libations) poured into the neck opening would
flow into the earth. The objects depicted in relief on the surface of
the vessel include what looks like an altar platform with three
heads under it, the outer two quite abstract and the middle one
almost naturalistic in the tradition of free-standing Yoruba portrait
heads. The abstraction of the two outside heads may have been
a way of honoring or blessing the central portrait, a practice that
survives among Yoruba royalty today.

BENIN

Ife was probably the artistic parent of the great city-state of Benin,
which arose some 150 miles to the southeast. According to oral
histories, the earliest kings of Benin belonged to the Ogiso, or
Skyking, dynasty. After a long period of misrule, however, the
people of Benin asked the *oni* of Ife for a new ruler. The *oni* sent
Prince Oranmiyan, who founded a new dynasty in 1170. Some
two centuries later, the fourth king, or *oba*, of Benin decided to
start a tradition of memorial sculpture like that of Ife, and he sent

to Ife for a master metalcaster named Iguegha. The tradition of
casting memorial heads for the shrines of royal ancestors endures
among the successors of Oranmiyan to this day **(FIG. 13–6)**.

Benin came into contact with Portugal in the late fifteenth
century. The two kingdoms established cordial relations in 1485
and carried on an active trade, at first in ivory and forest products,
but eventually in slaves. Benin flourished until 1897, when, in
reprisal for the massacre of a party of trade negotiators, British
troops sacked and burned the royal palace, sending the *oba* into an
exile from which he did not return until 1914 (see Chapter 28,
pages 880–881). The palace was later rebuilt, and the present-day
oba continues the dynasty started by Oranmiyan.

The British invaders discovered shrines to deceased *oba*s
covered with brass heads, bells, and figures. They also found

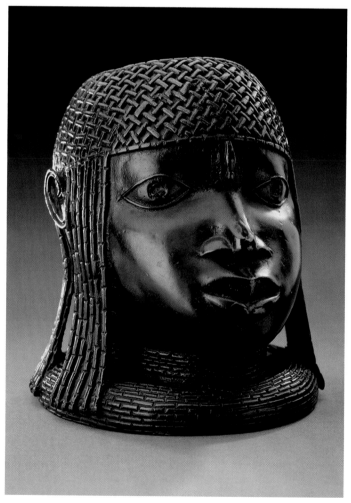

13-6 • MEMORIAL HEAD OF AN *OBA*
From Benin. Early Period, c. 16th century CE. Brass, height 9″ (23 cm).
The Nelson-Atkins Museum of Art, Kansas City, Missouri. Purchase:
Nelson Trust through the generosity of Donald J. and Adele C. Hall, Mr. and Mrs.
Herman Robert Sutherland, an anonymous donor, and the exchange of Nelson
Gallery Foundation properties (87-7)

This belongs to a small group of rare Early Period sculptures called
"rolled-collar" heads that are distinguished by the rolled collar that
serves as a firm base for the exquisitely rendered head.

A CLOSER LOOK

Roped Pot on a Stand ➤

From Igbo-Ukwu. 9th–10th century CE.
Leaded bronze, height 12¹¹⁄₁₆″ (32.3 cm). National Museum, Lagos.

Like a number of other objects excavated at Igbo-Ukwu, this vessel is a skeuomorph—an object created in a different material from the original but made to resemble the original form.

The flaring neck of the vessel just below the rim and the lower half of the pot stand were cast separately. Molten metal was then applied to the edges of the separate castings to join them together.

The knotted rope cage appears to be made from one continuous piece of "rope." Even the individual strands of the "rope" are replicated in leaded bronze.

Pot stands are used to support containers placed on sacred altars so that the water contained in the vessels should never touch the ground before its use in ritual ceremony.

The rope cage surrounding the pot and stand was cast separately and then positioned around the pot and upper part of the stand. The lower part of the knotted rope was then bent inward to grip the pot stand.

wooden rattles and enormous ivory tusks carved with images of kings, court attendants, and sixteenth-century Portuguese soldiers. The British appropriated the treasure as war booty, making no effort to note which head came from which shrine, thus destroying evidence that would have helped establish the relative age of the heads and determine a chronology for the evolution of Benin style. Nevertheless, it has been possible to piece together a chronology from other evidence.

The Benin heads, together with other objects, were originally placed on a semicircular platform or **ALTAR** and surmounted by large elephant tusks, another symbol of power (**FIG. 13–7**). Benin brass heads range from small, thinly cast, and naturalistic to large,

thickly cast, and highly stylized. Many scholars have concluded that the smallest, most naturalistic heads with only a few strands of beads around the neck were created during a so-called Early Period (1400–1550), when Benin artists were still heavily influenced by Ife. Heads grew heavier and increasingly stylized, and the strands of beads increased in number until they concealed the chin during the Middle Period (1550–1700). Heads from the ensuing Late Period (1700–1897) are very large and heavy, with angular, stylized features and an elaborate beaded crown. During the Late Period, the necklaces form a tall, cylindrical mass. In addition, broad, horizontal flanges, or projecting edges, bearing small images cast in low relief ring the base of the Late Period heads. The increase in size and weight of Benin memorial heads over time may reflect the growing power and wealth flowing to the *oba* from Benin's expanding trade with Europe.

At Benin, as in many other African cultures, the head is the symbolic center of a person's intelligence, wisdom, and ability to succeed in this world or to communicate with spiritual forces in the ancestral world. One of the honorifics used for the king is "Great Head": The head leads the body as the king leads the people. All of the memorial heads include representations of coral-beaded caps and necklaces and royal costume. Coral, enclosing the head and displayed on the body, is still the ultimate symbol of the *oba*'s power and authority.

The art of Benin is a royal art, for only the *oba* could commission works in brass (see "A Warrior Chief Pledging Loyalty," pages 414–415). Artisans who served the court were organized into guilds and lived in a separate quarter of the city. *Obas* also commissioned important works in ivory. One example is a beautiful ornamental mask **(FIG. 13–8)**. It represents an *iyoba* (queen mother—the *oba*'s mother), the senior female member of

13-8 • HIP MASK REPRESENTING AN *IYOBA*
("QUEEN MOTHER")
From Benin. Middle Period, c. 1550 CE. Ivory, iron, and copper, height 9⅜" (23.4 cm). Metropolitan Museum of Art, New York. The Michael C. Rockefeller Memorial Collection, Gift of Nelson A. Rockefeller, 1972 (1978.412.323)

TECHNIQUE | Lost-Wax Casting

In the **lost-wax casting** process a metal copy is produced from an original image made of wax. The usual metals for this casting process are bronze, an alloy of copper and tin, and brass, an alloy of copper and zinc. First, the sculptor models a wax original. Then the wax is invested in a heat-resistant mold. Next, the wax is melted, leaving an empty cavity into which molten metal is poured. After the metal cools and solidifies, the mold is broken away and the metal copy is chased and polished.

The progression of drawings here shows the steps used by the Benin sculptors of Africa. A heat-resistant "core" of clay (a) approximating the shape of the sculpture-to-be (and eventually becoming the hollow inside the sculpture) was covered by a layer of wax that had the thickness of the final sculpture. The sculptor carved

or modeled (b) the details in the wax. Rods and a pouring cup made of wax were attached (c) to the model. A thin layer of fine, damp sand was pressed very firmly into the surface of the wax model, and then model, rods, and cup were encased (d) in thick layers of clay. When the clay was completely dry, the mold was heated (e) to melt out the wax. The mold was then placed upside down in the ground to receive (f) the molten metal, heated to the point of liquefication. When the metal was completely cool, the outside clay cast and the inside core were broken up and removed (g), leaving the cast-brass sculpture. Details were polished to finish the piece, which could not be duplicated because the mold had been destroyed.

SEE MORE: View a video about the process of lost-wax casting www.myartslab.com

the royal court. The mask was carved as a belt ornament and was worn at the *oba*'s hip. Its pupils were originally inlaid with iron, as were the scarification patterns on the forehead. This particular belt ornament may represent Idia, who was the mother of Esigie, a powerful *oba* who ruled from 1504 to 1550. Idia is particularly remembered for raising an army and using magical powers to help her son defeat his enemies. Like Idia, the Portuguese helped Esigie

expand his kingdom. The necklace represents heads of Portuguese soldiers with beards and flowing hair. In the crown, more Portuguese heads alternate with figures of mudfish, which symbolize Olokun, the Lord of the Great Waters. Mudfish live near riverbanks, mediating between water and land, just as the *oba*, who is viewed as semidivine, mediates between the human world and the supernatural world of Olokun.

A Warrior Chief Pledging Loyalty

Produced during the sixteenth and seventeenth centuries, approximately 900 brass plaques, each averaging about 16 to 18 inches in height, once decorated the walls and pillars of the royal palace of the kingdom of Benin. Like the brass memorial heads and figure sculpture, the plaques were made following the lost-wax casting process. They illustrate a variety of subjects including ceremonial scenes at court, showing the *oba*, other court functionaries, and (at times) Portuguese soldiers. Modeled

in relief, the plaques depict one or more figures, with precise details of costume and regalia. Some figures are modeled in such high relief that they appear almost freestanding as they emerge from a textured surface background that often includes foliate patterning representing the leaves employed in certain healing rituals.

This plaque features a warrior chief in ceremonial attire. His rank is indicated by a necklace of leopard's teeth, and coral-decorated cap and collar. He also wears

an elaborately decorated skirt with a leopard mask on his hip. The chief is depicted holding a spear in one hand and an *eben* sword held above his head in the other hand. The *eben* sword, with its distinctive leaf-shaped blade made of iron with openwork surface decoration is a major symbol of high rank in Benin even today.

The plaque is organized in a hierarchal order with the warrior chief larger in size and in the center of the composition. The chief is

PLAQUE: WARRIOR CHIEF FLANKED BY WARRIORS AND ATTENDANTS
From Benin, Nigeria. Middle Period, c. 1550–1650 CE. Brass, height 14¾ × 15½" (37.5 × 39.4 cm).
The Nelson-Atkins Museum of Art, Kansas City, Missouri. (58-3)

Senior town chief supported by two attendants, one of them carries his *eben* sword.

flanked by two warriors holding shields and spears, and two smaller figures representing court attendants. One attendant is depicted playing a side-blown horn that announces the warrior chief's presence, while the other attendant carries a ceremonial box for conveying gifts to the *oba*. The scene is a ceremony of obeisance to the *oba*. The warrior chief's gesture of raising the *eben* sword is still performed at annual ceremonies in which chiefs declare their allegiance and loyalty to the *oba* by raising the sword and spinning it in the air. The kinetic movement of the sword spinning as it is held aloft certainly adds a degree of conviction and authority to the ceremony.

Oba Erediauwa wearing coral-beaded regalia and seated on a dais.

OTHER URBAN CENTERS

Ife and Benin were but two of the many cities that arose in ancient Africa. The first European visitors to the west African coast at the end of the fifteenth century were impressed not only by Benin, but also by the city of Mbanza Kongo, south of the mouth of the Congo River. Along the east African coastline, Europeans also happened upon cosmopolitan cities that had been busily carrying on long-distance trade across the Indian Ocean and as far away as China and Indonesia for hundreds of years.

Important centers also existed in the interior, especially across the central and western Sudan. There, cities and the states that developed around them grew wealthy from the trans-Saharan trade that had linked west Africa to the Mediterranean from at least the first millennium BCE. Indeed, the routes across the desert were probably as old as the desert itself. Among the most significant goods exchanged in this trade were salt from the north and gold from west Africa. Such fabled cities as Mopti, Timbuktu, and Jenné arose in the vast area of grasslands along the Niger River in the region known as the Niger Bend (present-day Mali), a trading crossroads as early as the first century BCE. They were great centers of commerce, where merchants from all over west Africa met

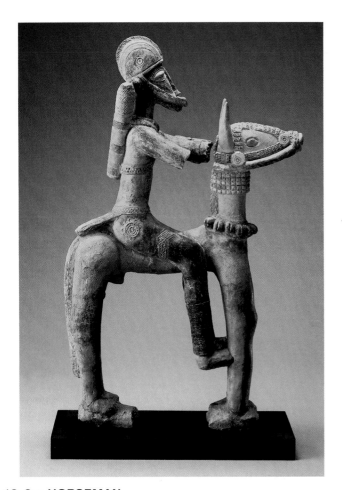

13-9 • HORSEMAN
From Old Jenné, Mali. 13th–15th century CE. Terra cotta, height 27¾″ (70.5 cm). National Museum of African Art, Smithsonian Institution, Washington, D.C. Museum Purchase (86-12-2)

caravans arriving from the Mediterranean. Eventually the trading networks extended across Africa from the Sudan in the east to the Atlantic coast in the west. In the twelfth century CE a Mande-speaking people formed the kingdom of Mali (Manden). The rulers adopted Islam, and by the fourteenth century they controlled the oases on which the traders' caravans depended. Mali prospered, and wealthy cities like Timbuktu and Jenné became famed as centers of Islamic learning.

At a site near Jenné known as Jenné-Jeno or Old Jenné, excavations (by both archaeologists and looters) have uncovered hundreds of terra-cotta figures dating from the thirteenth to the sixteenth centuries. The figures were polished, covered with a red clay slip, and fired at a low temperature. A **HORSEMAN**, armed with quiver, arrows, and a dagger, is a good example of the technique **(FIG. 13–9)**. Man and horse are formed of rolls of clay on which details of the face, clothing, and harness are carved, engraved, and painted. The rider has a long oval head and jutting chin, pointed oval eyes set in multiple framing lids, and a long straight nose. He wears short pants and a helmet with a chin strap, and his horse has an ornate bridle. Such elaborate trappings suggest that the horseman could be a guardian figure, hero, or even a deified ancestor. Similar figures have been found in sanctuaries. But, as urban life declined, so did the arts. The long tradition of ceramic sculpture came to an end in the fifteenth and sixteenth centuries, when rivals began to raid the Manden cities.

JENNÉ

In 1655, the Islamic writer al-Sadi wrote this description of Jenné:

> This city is large, flourishing, and prosperous; it is rich, blessed, and favoured by the Almighty…. Jenne [Jenné] is one of the great markets of the Muslim world. There one meets the salt merchants from the mines of Teghaza and merchants carrying gold from the mines of Bitou…. Because of this blessed city, caravans flock to Timbuktu from all points of the horizon…. The area around Jenne is fertile and well populated; with numerous markets held there on all the days of the week. It is certain that it contains 7,077 villages very near to one another.

(Translated by Graham Connah in *Connah*, page 97)

By the time al-Sadi wrote his account, Jenné already had a long history. Archaeologists have determined that the city was established by the third century CE, and that by the middle of the ninth century it had become a major urban center. Also by the ninth century, Islam was becoming an economic and religious force in west and north Africa, and the northern terminals of the trans-Saharan trade routes had already been incorporated into the Islamic empire.

When Koi Konboro, the 26th king of Jenné, converted to Islam in the thirteenth century, he transformed his palace into the first of three successive mosques in the city. Like the two that followed, the first mosque was built of adobe brick, a sun-dried mixture of clay and straw. With its great surrounding wall and tall towers, it was said to have been more beautiful and more lavishly decorated than the Kaaba, the central shrine of Islam, at Mecca. The mosque eventually attracted the attention of austere Muslim rulers who objected to its sumptuous furnishings. Among these was the early nineteenth-century ruler Sekou Amadou, who had it razed and a far more humble structure erected on a new site. This second mosque was in turn replaced by the current grand mosque, constructed between 1906 and 1907 on the ancient site in the style of the original. The reconstruction was supervised by the architect Ismaila Traoré, the head of the Jenné guild of masons.

The mosque's eastern, or "marketplace," façade boasts three tall towers, the center of which contains the *mihrab* **(FIG. 13–10)**. The finials, or crowning ornaments, at the top of each tower bear ostrich eggs, symbols of fertility and purity. The façade and sides of the mosque are distinguished by tall, narrow, engaged columns, which act as buttresses. These columns are characteristic of west African mosque architecture, and their cumulative rhythmic effect is one of great verticality and grandeur. The most unusual features of west African mosques are the **torons**, wooden beams projecting from the walls. Torons provide permanent supports for the

scaffolding erected each year so that the exterior of the mosque can be replastered.

Traditional houses resemble the mosque on a small scale. Adobe walls, reinforced by buttresses, rise above the roofline in conical turrets, emphasizing the entrance. Rooms open inward onto a courtyard. Extended upper walls mask a flat roof terrace that gives more private space for work and living.

GREAT ZIMBABWE

Thousands of miles from Jenné, in southeastern Africa, an extensive trade network developed along the Zambezi, Limpopo, and Sabi rivers. Its purpose was to funnel gold, ivory, and exotic skins to the coastal trading towns that had been built by Arabs and Swahili-speaking Africans. There, the gold and ivory were exchanged for prestige goods, including porcelain, beads, and other manufactured items. Between 1000 and 1500 CE, this trade was largely controlled from a site that was called Great Zimbabwe, home of the Shona people.

The word *zimbabwe* derives from the Shona term *dzimba dza mabwe* ("venerated houses" or "houses of stone"). The stone buildings at Great Zimbabwe were constructed by the ancestors of

13–10 • GREAT FRIDAY MOSQUE
Jenné, Mali, showing the eastern and northern façades. Rebuilding of 1907, in the style of 13th-century original.

The plan of the mosque is not quite rectangular. Inside, nine rows of heavy adobe columns, 33 feet (10 meters) tall and linked by pointed arches, support a flat ceiling of palm logs. An open courtyard on the west side (not seen here) is enclosed by a great double wall only slightly lower than the walls of the mosque itself. The main entrances to the prayer hall are in the north wall (to the right in the photograph).

the present-day people of this region. The earliest construction at the site took advantage of the enormous boulders abundant in the vicinity. Masons incorporated the boulders and used the uniform granite blocks that split naturally from them to build a series of tall enclosing walls high on a hilltop. Each enclosure defined a family's living space and housed dwellings made of adobe with conical, thatched roofs.

The largest building complex at Great Zimbabwe is located in a broad valley below the hilltop enclosures. Known as Imba Huru (the Great Enclosure), the complex is ringed by a masonry wall more than 800 feet long, up to 32 feet tall, and 17 feet thick at the base. Inside the great outer wall are numerous smaller stone enclosures and adobe platforms (FIG. 13–11). The buildings at Great Zimbabwe were built without mortar; for stability the walls are **battered**, or built so that they slope inward toward the top. Although some of the enclosures at Great Zimbabwe were built on hilltops, there is no evidence that they were constructed as fortresses. There are neither openings for weapons to be thrust through nor battlements for warriors to stand on. Instead, the walls and structures seem intended to reflect the wealth and power of the city's rulers. The Imba Huru was probably a royal residence, or palace complex, and other structures housed members of the ruler's family and court. The complex formed the nucleus of a city that radiated for almost a mile in all directions. Over the centuries, the builders grew more skillful, and the later additions are distinguished by dressed stones, or smoothly finished stones, laid in fine, even, level courses. One of these later additions is a structure known simply as the **CONICAL TOWER** (FIG. 13–12). Some 18 feet in diameter and 30 feet tall, the tower was originally capped with three courses of ornamental stonework. Constructed between the two walls and resembling a granary, it may have represented the good harvest and prosperity believed to result from allegiance to the ruler of Great Zimbabwe.

It is estimated that at the height of its power, in the fourteenth century, Great Zimbabwe and its surrounding city housed a population of more than 10,000 people. A large cache of goods containing items of such far-flung origin as Portuguese medallions, Persian pottery, and Chinese porcelain testify to the extent of its trade. Yet beginning in the mid fifteenth century Great Zimbabwe was gradually abandoned as control of the lucrative southeast African trade network passed to the Mwene Mutapa and Kami empires a short distance away.

13-11 • DRAWING OF GREAT ZIMBABWE

13-12 • CONICAL TOWER
Great Zimbabwe. c. 1200–1400 CE.
Height of tower 30′ (9.1 m).

AKSUM AND LALIBELA

In the second century BCE Aksumite civilization increased in importance in the Ethiopian highlands through the control of trade routes from the African interior to the Red Sea port of Adulis. Its exports included ivory, gold, slaves, frankincense, myrrh, and salt. In the mid fourth century CE the Aksumite king Ezana converted to Christianity, and soon gold and silver coinage minted at Aksum bore the Christian cross.

The archaeological remains at Aksum and Gondar speak of the splendor of the ancient kingdom. By the third century CE a series of stone palaces were built at Aksum. The elites also erected a number of monolithic granite stelae which date from the third and fourth centuries, the largest over 95 feet in height. Their outer surfaces were decorated with such carved architectural details as false doors, inset windows, and timber beams. The stelae served as commemorative markers among the tombs and burial sites of the elite.

The power and influence of the Aksumite state was diminished by the displacement of the Red Sea trade routes after the Persian conquest of south Arabia, and Aksum was conquered by the Zagwe from Ethiopia's western highlands. After its demise and abandonment, a new capital arose, the influence and prestige of which lasted until near the end of the thirteenth century.

The Zagwe king Lalibela, wishing to create a "new" Jerusalem (the holy city revered by Christians, Jews, and Muslims) in Ethiopia, founded a holy site named after himself in the highlands south of Aksum. The cultural embrace of Christianity by the populace during the thirteenth century is evidenced by the numerous rock-hewn sanctuaries that were created in Lalibela at this time. Rather than being built from the ground up, the churches and other structures were hewn from the living rock. A wide trench was first cut around the four sides of a block of volcanic tuff that would become the church. Stonemasons then carved out the exterior and interior of the sanctuaries with hammers and chisels. Each aspect of the structure had to be planned with precision before work could begin. The interior of the church was created with a hemispherical domed ceiling in the style of Byzantine churches: Ethiopian priests must have seen this form of architecture during their pilgrimages to Jerusalem.

The largest of the 11 churches is **BET GIORGIS** (Church of St. George) which was cut 40 feet down in the form of a modified cross **(FIG. 13–13)**. Most rock-cut sanctuaries have architectural details that appear to have been modeled in part from earlier Aksum palaces. However, Bet Giorgis has window details that are

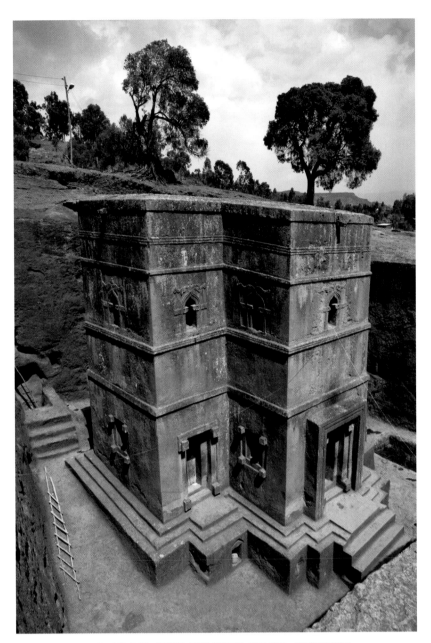

13-13 • BET GIORGIS (THE CHURCH OF ST. GEORGE), LALIBELA, ETHIOPIA

similar to the organic tendril forms found in later Ethiopian painted manuscripts. The origins of the rock-cut church are unknown. The churches at Lalibela may have been modeled on earlier Aksumite cave sanctuaries, but it has also been suggested that they have their origins in central and southern India where Buddhist and Hindu temples, shrines, and monasteries have been excavated from the living rock for over 2,000 years.

KONGO KINGDOM

As in other parts of sub-Saharan Africa, art-making traditions in the Kongo cultural region developed over thousands of years. However, as elsewhere on the African continent, the climate here is often not conducive to the survival of objects made from wood. Among the earliest known wooden artworks from central Africa is a wood

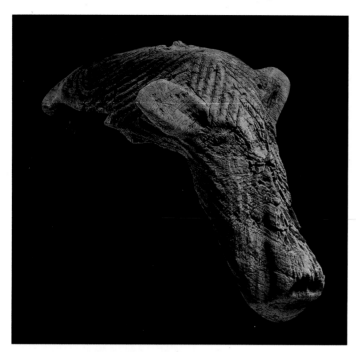

13-14 • ZOOMORPHIC HEAD
From Angola. c. 750 CE. Wood, 19⅞ × 6⅛" (50.5 × 15.5 cm).
Royal Museum of Central Africa, Tervuren, Belgium.

carving unearthed in Angola in 1928 (**FIG. 13–14**). This **ZOOMOR-PHIC HEAD** may have been created for use as a headdress or mask. Its elongated snout, pointed ears and geometric surface patterning resemble some masking traditions and sculptural practices that endured in the region well into the twentieth century.

The Portuguese first encountered Kongo culture in 1482 at approximately the same time contact was made with the royal court of Benin in present-day western Nigeria. They visited the capital of Mbanza Kongo (present-day M'banza Congo) and met the *manikongo* ("king"), who ruled over a kingdom that was remarkable in terms of its complex political organization and artistic sophistication. The kingdom, divided into six provinces, encompassed over 100,000 square miles of present-day north-western Angola and the western part of the Democratic Republic of the Congo. In 1491, King Nzinga aNkuwa converted to Christianity, as did his son and successor Afonso I, who established it as the state religion. The conversions helped to solidify trade relations with the Portuguese, and trade in copper, salt, ivory, cloth, and, later, slaves brought increased prosperity to the kingdom. Kongo's influence expanded until the mid seventeenth century when its trading routes were taken over by neighboring peoples, including the Lunda and Chokwe.

The increase in wealth brought a corresponding increase in the production of specialty textiles, baskets, and regalia for the nobility. Textiles in central Africa, as elsewhere in Africa, are of extreme importance in terms of their value as wealth. Textiles were used as forms of currency before European contact and figure prominently in funerary rituals even to the present day. Kongo decorated textiles were lauded by the Portuguese from first contact and were accepted as gifts or collected and found their way into European museum collections (**FIG. 13–15**).

Following Portuguese contact in the fifteenth century and Nzinga aNkuwa's conversion, Kongolese art increasingly absorbed Western influences. With the arrival of Catholic missionaries, who brought with them various religious objects—including the monstrance (a highly decorated vessel used to display the consecrated bread or "body" of Christ), figures of the Virgin Mary and various saints, and the **CRUCIFIX**—the crucifix became a potent symbol of both conversion and political authority. Cast in brass and copper alloy (**FIG. 13–16**) the forms mirror their European prototypes, but are often restated in African terms. The features of the crucified Christ, as well as his hands and feet and those of the supporting figures, suggest an African aesthetic, as does the placement of supporting figures above and below the central figure. Although the supporting figures appear to be praying, in Kongo iconography, as elsewhere in central Africa, the clapping of hands is a common gesture of respect for another person.

13-15 • DECORATED TEXTILE
From Kongo. Early 17th century CE. Raffia, 9½ × 18½" (24 × 47 cm).
Pitt Rivers Museum, University of Oxford, England.

13-16 • CRUCIFIX
From Kongo. Early 17th century CE. Bronze, height 10½″ (26.7 cm). Metropolitan Museum of Art. Collection of Ernst Anspach (1999.295.7)

13-17 • SAPI-PORTUGUESE STYLE HUNTING HORN
From Sierra Leone. Late 15th century CE, ivory, length 25″ (63.5 cm). National Museum of African Art, Smithsonian Institution. Walt Disney-Tishman African Art Collection (2005-6-9)

EXPORTING TO THE WEST

Shortly after initial contact with European explorers, merchants, and traders African artisans not only continued to fashion objects for their own consumption but also began to produce them for export to Europe. For example, by the late fifteenth century, artisans residing in present-day Sierra Leone (called Sapi by the Portuguese) and Nigeria (Bini) began to make objects such as ivory saltcellars, powder flasks, spoons and forks, as well as exquisitely carved oliphants, or horns (**FIG. 13–17**) for European patrons.

The form of the Sapi-Portuguese oliphant and virtually all its decorative motifs are European-inspired. The mouthpiece is at the narrow end rather than on the side as is typical for African horns. The various carvings on the horns, including the coat of arms of Portugal and Spain, the motto of Spain's Ferdinand V, and heraldic emblems and hunting scenes, were derived from illustrations found in European prayer books and other publications that were given to the artists as source material. However, not all of the designs found on some export ivories are derived from European sources. For example, some saltcellars depicting human subjects were carved in a style that resembles stone figures found locally that predate Portuguese contact with the west African coast. As Chapter 28 will show, the synthesis of Western and traditional influences continued to affect African art in both subtle and overt ways.

13.1 Select one three-dimensional artwork and one two-dimensional artwork discussed in the chapter, and identify and summarize the original purpose of each. What role did these works play in society?

13.2 What is the spiritual role of the *oba* in Benin? What is his relationship to the spirit world, and how is that relationship represented in one work discussed in the chapter?

13.3 Explain the original purpose of the Benin royal plaque (see "A Warrior Chief Pledging Loyalty," pages 410–411), and how the identity of the individuals on the plaque and their posture relate to hierarchy at the royal court and the glorification of Benin kingship.

13.4 Consider a representation of African royalty, such as FIGURE 13–1. How was this artwork used in the context of its culture? Explain differences between African portrayals of royalty and those of the West, such as the imperial portraits of ancient Rome studied in Chapter 6. Are the African heads *portraits*?

PRACTICE MORE: Compose answers to these questions, get flashcards for images and terms, and review chapter material with quizzes
www.myartslab.com

GLOSSARY

abacus (p. 108)   The flat slab at the top of a **capital**, directly under the **entablature**.

abbey church (p. 239)   An abbey is a religious community headed by an abbot or abbess. An abbey church often has an especially large choir to provide space for the monks or nuns.

absolute dating (p. 12)   A method of assigning a precise historical date to periods and objects, based on known and recorded events in the region, as well as technically extracted physical evidence (such as carbon-14 disintegration). See also **radiometric dating**, **relative dating**.

abstract, abstraction (p. 8)   Any art that does not represent observed aspects of nature or transforms visible forms into a stylized image. Also: the **formal** qualities of this process.

academy (p. 924)   A place of study, the word coming from the Greek name of a garden near Athens where Plato and, later, Platonic philosophers held discussions. Academies of fine arts, such as the Academy of Drawing or the Royal Academy of Painting, were created to foster the arts by teaching, by discussion, by exhibitions, and occasionally by financial aid.

acanthus (p. 110)   A Mediterranean plant whose leaves are reproduced in architectural ornament used on **moldings**, **friezes**, and **Corinthian capitals**.

acropolis (p. 129)   The citadel of an ancient Greek city, located at its highest point and housing temples, a treasury, and sometimes a royal palace. The most famous is the Acropolis in Athens.

acroterion (acroteria) (p. 110)   An ornament at the corner or peak of a roof.

adobe (p. 393)   Sun-baked blocks made of clay mixed with straw. Also: the buildings made with this material.

aedicula (p. 609)   A decorative architectural frame, usually found around a niche, door, or window. An aedicula is made up of a **pediment** and **entablature** supported by **columns** or **pilasters**.

agora (p. 138)   An open space in a Greek town used as a central gathering place or market. See also **forum**.

aisle (p. 228)   Passage or open corridor of a church, hall, or other building that parallels the main space, usually on both sides, and is delineated by a row, or **arcade**, of **columns** or **piers**. Called side aisles when they flank the **nave** of a church.

album (p. 795)   A book consisting of a series of painting or prints (album leaves) mounted into book form.

allegory (p. 625)   In a work of art, an image (or images) that symbolizes an idea, concept, or principle, often moral or religious.

alloy (p. 23)   A mixture of metals; different metals melted together.

amalaka (p. 301)   In Hindu architecture, the circular or square-shaped element on top of a spire (**shikhara**), often crowned with a **finial**, symbolizing the cosmos.

ambulatory (p. 228)   The passage (walkway) around the **apse** in a **basilican** church or around the central space in a **central-plan building**.

amphora (p. 101)   An ancient Greek jar for storing oil or wine, with an egg-shaped body and two curved handles.

aniconic (p. 262)   A symbolic representation without images of human figures, very often found in Islamic art.

animal interlace or style (p. 427)   Decoration made of interwoven animals or serpents, often found in Celtic and early medieval Northern European art.

ankh (p. 51)   A looped cross signifying life, used by ancient Egyptians.

appropriation (p. 1102)   Term used to describe the practice of some postmodern artists of adopting images in their entirety from other works of art or from visual culture for use in their own art. The act of recontextualizing the appropriated image allows the artist to critique both it and the time and place in which it was created.

apse, apsidal (p. 192)   A large semicircular or polygonal (and usually **vaulted**) niche protruding from the end wall of a building. In the Christian church, it contains the altar. Apsidal is an adjective describing the condition of having such a space.

arabesque (p. 263)   A type of linear surface decoration based on foliage and **calligraphic** forms, usually characterized by flowing lines and swirling shapes.

arcade (p. 172)   A series of **arches**, carried by **columns** or **piers** and supporting a common wall or **lintel**. In a **blind arcade**, the arches and supports are **engaged** (attached to the wall) and have a decorative function.

arch (p. 271)   In architecture, a curved structural element that spans an open space. Built from wedge-shaped stone blocks called **voussoirs**, which, when placed together and held at the top by a trapezoidal **keystone**, form an effective space-spanning and weight-bearing unit. Requires **buttresses** at each side to contain the outward **thrust** caused by the weight of the structure. **Corbel arch** (p. 16): an arch or **vault** formed by **courses** of stones, each of which projects beyond the lower course until the space is enclosed; usually finished with a **capstone**. **Horseshoe arch** (p. 268): an arch of more than a half-circle; typical of western Islamic architecture. **Round arch** (p. 271): arch that displaces most of its weight, or downward thrust along its curving sides, transmitting that weight to adjacent supporting uprights (door or window jambs, columns, or piers). Ogival arch: a pointed arch created by S-curves. Relieving arch: an arch built into a heavy wall just above a **post-and-lintel** structure (such as a gate, door, or window) to help support the wall above by transferring the load to the side walls. **Transverse arch** (p. 457): an arch that connects the wall **piers** on both sides of an interior space, up and over a stone vault.

Archaic smile (p. 114)   The curved lips of an ancient Greek statue, usually interpreted as a way of animating facial features.

architrave (p. 108)   The bottom element in an **entablature**, beneath the **frieze** and the **cornice**.

archivolt (p. 473)   A **molded** band framing an **arch**, or a series of stone blocks that rest directly on the **columns**.

ashlar (p. 99)   Highly finished, precisely cut block of stone. When laid in even courses, ashlar masonry creates a uniform face with fine joints. Often used as a facing on the visible exterior of a building, especially as a veneer for the **façade**. Also called **dressed stone**.

assemblage (p. 1026)   Artwork created by gathering and manipulating two- and/or three-dimensional found objects.

astragal (p. 110)   A thin convex decorative **molding**, often found on Classical **entablatures**, and usually decorated with a continuous row of beadlike circles.

atelier (p. 944)   The studio or workshop of a master artist or craftsperson, often including junior associates and apprentices.

atmospheric perspective (p. 562)   See **perspective**.

atrial cross (p. 941)   The cross placed in the **atrium** of a church. In Colonial America, used to mark a gathering and teaching place.

atrium (p. 160)   An unroofed interior courtyard or room in a Roman house, sometimes having a pool or garden, sometimes surrounded by **columns**. Also: the open courtyard in front of a Christian church; or an entrance area in modern architecture.

automatism (p. 1056)   A technique whereby the usual intellectual control of the artist over his or her brush or pencil is foregone. The artist's aim is to allow the subconscious to create the artwork without rational interference.

avant-garde (p. 971)   Term derived from the French military word meaning "before the group," or "vanguard." Avant-garde denotes those artists or concepts of a strikingly new, experimental, or radical nature for their time.

axis (p. xxxii)   An implied line around which the elements of a picture are organized.

axis-mundi (p. 297)   A concept of an "axis of the world," which marks sacred sites and denotes a link between the human and celestial realms. For example, in Buddhist art, the *axis mundi* can be marked by monumental freestanding decorative **pillars**.

bailey (p. 473)   The outermost walled courtyard of a castle.

baldachin (p. 467)   A canopy (whether suspended from the ceiling, projecting from a wall, or supported by **columns**) placed over an honorific or sacred space such as a throne or church altar.

bar tracery (p. 507)   See **tracery**.

barbarian (p. 151)   A term used by the ancient Greeks and Romans to label all foreigners outside their cultural orbit (e.g., Celts, Goths, Vikings). The word derives from an imitation of what the "barblings" of their language sounded like to those who could not understand it.

bargeboards (p. 870)   Boards covering the rafters at the gable end of a building; bargeboards are often carved or painted.

barrel vault (p. 188)   See **vault**.

base (p. 110)   Any support. Also: masonry supporting a statue or the shaft of a **column**.

basilica (p. 192)   A large rectangular building. Often built with a **clerestory**, side **aisles** separated from the center **nave** by **colonnades**, and an **apse** at one or both ends. Roman centers for administration, later adapted to Christian church use.

battered (p. 418)   An architectural design whereby walls are sloped inward toward the top to increase stability.

bay (p. 172)   A unit of space defined by architectural elements such as **columns, piers,** and walls.

beehive tomb (p. 98)   A **corbel-vaulted** tomb, conical in shape like a beehive, and covered by an earthen mound.

Benday dots (p. 1093)   In modern printing and typesetting, the individual dots that, together with many others, make up lettering and images. Often machine- or computer-generated, the dots are very small and closely spaced to give the effect of density and richness of tone.

bi (p. 333)   A jade disk with a hole in the center.

bilum (p. 863)   Netted bags made mainly by women throughout the central highlands of New Guinea. The bags can be used for everyday purposes or even to carry the bones of the recently deceased as a sign of mourning.

biomorphic (p. 1057)   A term used in the early twentieth century to denote the biologically or organically inspired shapes and forms that were routinely included in abstracted Modern art.

black-figure (p. 105) A style or technique of ancient Greek pottery in which black figures are painted on a red clay ground. See also **red-figure**.

blackware (p. 853) A **ceramic** technique that produces pottery with a primarily black surface with **matte** and glossy patterns on the surface.

blind arcade (p. 780) See **arcade**.

bodhisattva (p. 297) In Buddhism, a being who has attained enlightenment but chooses to remain in this world in order to help others advance spiritually. Also defined as a potential Buddha.

Book of Hours (p. 547) A private prayer book, containing a calendar, services for the canonical hours, and sometimes special prayers.

boss (p. 554) A decorative knoblike element that can be found in many places, such as at the intersection of a Gothic **rib vault** or in the buttonlike projections of metalwork.

bracket, bracketing (p. 335) An architectural element that projects from a wall to support a horizontal part of a building, such as beams or the eaves of a roof.

buon fresco (p. 87) See **fresco**.

burin (p. 590) A metal instrument used in **engraving** to cut lines into the metal plate. The sharp end of the burin is trimmed to give a diamond-shaped cutting point, while the other end is finished with a wooden handle that fits into the engraver's palm.

buttress, buttressing p. 172) A projecting support built against an external wall, usually to counteract the lateral **thrust** of a **vault** or **arch** within. In Gothic architecture, a **flying buttress** is an arched bridge above the **aisle** roof that extends from the upper **nave** wall, where the lateral thrust of the main vault is greatest, down to a solid **pier**.

cairn (p.17) A pile of stones or earth and stones that served both as a prehistoric burial site and as a marker of underground tombs.

calligraphy (p. 279) Handwriting as an art form.

calotype (p. 968) The first photographic process utilizing negatives and paper positives. It was invented by William Henry Fox Talbot in the late 1830s.

calyx krater (p. 118) See **krater**.

came (cames) (p. 497) A lead strip used in the making of leaded or **stained-glass windows**. Cames have an indented groove on the sides into which the separate pieces of glass are fitted to hold the composition together.

cameo (p. 178) Gemstone, clay, glass, or shell having layers of color, carved in **low relief** to create an image and ground of different colors.

camera obscura (p. 967) An early cameralike device used in the Renaissance and later for recording images of nature. Made from a dark box (or room) with a hole in one side (sometimes fitted with a lens), the camera obscura operates when bright light shines through the hole, casting an upside-down image of an object outside onto the inside wall of the box.

canon of proportions (p. 65) A set of ideal mathematical ratios in art based on measurements, as in the proportional relationships among the basic elements of the human body.

canopic jar (p. 56) Special jars used to store the major organs of a body before embalming, found in ancient Egyptian culture.

capital (p. 110) The sculpted block that tops a **column**. According to the **conventions** of the **orders**, capitals include different decorative elements. See **order**. A **historiated capital** is one displaying a figural composition of a **narrative** scene.

capriccio (p. 912) A painting or print of a fantastic, imaginary landscape, usually with architecture.

capstone (p. 99) The final, topmost stone in a **corbel arch** or **vault**, which joins the sides and completes the structure.

cartoon (p. 497) A full-scale drawing used to transfer or guide a design onto a surface (such as a wall, canvas, panel, or **tapestry**) to be painted, carved, or woven.

cartouche (p. 189) A frame for a **hieroglyphic** inscription formed by a rope design surrounding an oval space. Used to signify a sacred or honored name. Also: in architecture, a decorative device or plaque, usually with a plain center used for inscriptions or epitaphs.

caryatid (p. 107) A sculpture of a draped female figure acting as a **column** supporting an **entablature**.

cassone (cassoni) (p. 616) An Italian dowry chest often highly decorated with carvings, paintings, **inlaid** designs, and gilt embellishments.

catacomb (p. 219) A subterranean burial ground consisting of tunnels on different levels, having niches for urns and **sarcophagi** and often incorporating rooms (**cubiculae**).

cathedral (p. 222) The principal Christian church in a diocese, the bishop's administrative center and housing his throne (*cathedra*).

celadon (p. 352) A high-fired, transparent glaze of pale bluish-green hue whose principal coloring agent is an oxide of iron. In China and Korea, such glazes typically were applied over a pale gray **stoneware** body, though Chinese potters sometimes applied them over **porcelain** bodies during the Ming (1368–1644) and Qing (1644–1911) dynasties. Chinese potters invented celadon glazes and initiated the continuous production of celadon-glazed wares as early as the third century CE.

cella (p. 108) The principal interior room at the center of a Greek or Roman temple within which the cult statue was usually housed. Also called the **naos**.

celt (p. 377) A smooth, oblong stone or metal object, shaped like an axe-head.

cenotaph (p. 771) A funerary monument commemorating an individual or group buried elsewhere.

centering (p. 172) A temporary structure that supports a masonry **arch** and **vault** or **dome** during construction until the mortar is fully dried and the masonry is self-sustaining.

central-plan building (p. 228) Any structure designed with a primary central space surrounded by symmetrical areas on each side. For example, a **rotunda** or a Greek-cross plan (equal-armed cross).

ceramics (p. 22) A general term covering all types of wares made from fired clay, including **porcelain** and **terra cotta**.

chacmool (p. 390) In Mayan sculpture, a half-reclining figure probably representing an offering bearer.

chaitya (p. 302) A type of Buddhist temple found in India. Built in the form of a hall or **basilica**, a *chaitya* hall is highly decorated with sculpture and usually is carved from a cave or natural rock location. It houses a sacred shrine or **stupa** for worship.

chamfer (p. 780) The slanted surface produced when an angle is trimmed or beveled, common in building and metalwork.

chasing (p. 776) Ornamentation made on metal by **incising** or hammering the surface.

château (châteaux) (p. 691) A French country house or residential castle. A *château fort*, is a military castle incorporating defensive works such as towers and battlements.

chattri (chattris) (p. 779) A decorative pavilion with an umbrella-shaped **dome** in Indian architecture.

chevron (p. 350) A decorative or heraldic motif of repeated Vs; a zigzag pattern.

chiaroscuro (p. 634) An Italian word designating the contrast of dark and light in a painting, drawing, or print. *Chiaroscuro* creates spatial depth and volumetric forms through gradations in the intensity of light and shadow.

cista (cistae) (p. 166) **Cylindrical** containers used by wealthy women as a case for toiletry articles such as a mirror.

clerestory (p. 58) The topmost zone of a wall with windows in a **basilica** extending above the aisle roofs. Provides direct light into the central interior space (the **nave**).

cloister (p. 442) An open space within a monastery, surrounded by an **arcaded** or colonnaded walkway, often having a fountain and garden. The most important monastic buildings (e.g., dormitory, refectory) open off of it. Since members of a cloistered order do not leave the monastery or interact with outsiders, the cloister represents the center of their enclosed world.

codex (codices) (p. 243) A book, or a group of **manuscript** pages (folios), held together by stitching or other binding on one side.

coffer (p. 197) A recessed decorative panel that is used to reduce the weight of and to decorate ceilings or **vaults**. The use of coffers is called coffering.

coiling (p. 845) A technique in basketry. In coiled baskets a spiraling structure is held in place by another material.

collage (p. 1026) A composition made of cut and pasted scraps of materials, sometimes with lines or forms added by the artist.

colonnade (p. 69) A row of **columns**, supporting a straight **lintel** (as in a **porch** or **portico**) or a series of **arches** (an **arcade**).

colophon (p. 432) The data placed at the end of a book listing the book's author, publisher, **illuminator**, and other information related to its production. In East Asian **handscrolls**, the inscriptions which follow the painting are also called colophons.

column (p. 110) An architectural element used for support and/or decoration. Consists of a rounded or polygonal vertical **shaft** placed on a **base** and topped by a decorative **capital**. In Classical architecture, built in accordance with the rules of one of the architectural **orders**. Columns can be free-standing or attached to a background wall (**engaged**).

combine (p. 1085) Combinations of painting and sculpture using nontraditional art materials.

complementary color (p. 993) The primary and secondary colors across from each other on the color wheel (red and green, blue and orange, yellow and purple). When juxtaposed, the intensity of both colors increases. When mixed together, they negate each other to make a neutral gray-brown.

composite order (p. 163) See **order**.

composite pose or **image (p. 9)** Combining different viewpoints within a single representation of a subject.

composition (p. xxix) The overall arrangement, organizing design, or structure of a work of art.

conch (p. 234) A half-**dome**.

cong (p. 328) A square or octagonal jade tube with a cylindrical hole in the center. A symbol of the earth, it was used for ritual worship and astronomical observations in ancient China.

connoisseurship (p. 741) A term derived from the French word connoisseur, meaning "an expert," and signifying the study and evaluation of art based primarily on **formal**, visual, and stylistic analysis. A connoisseur studies the style and technique of an object to assess its relative quality and identify its maker through visual comparison with other works of secure authorship. See also **contextualism**; **formalism**.

contrapposto (p. 121) An Italian term meaning "set against," used to describe the pose that results from setting parts of the body in opposition to each other around a central **axis**.

convention (p. 51) A traditional way of representing forms.

corbel, corbeling (p. 16) An early roofing and arching technique in which each **course** of stone projects slightly beyond the previous layer (a corbel) until the uppermost corbels meet. Results in a high, almost pointed **arch** or **vault**.

corbeled vault (p. 99)   See **vault**.

Corinthian order (p. 108)   See **order**.

cornice (p. 110)   The uppermost section of a Classical **entablature**. More generally, a horizontally projecting element found at the top of a building wall or **pedestal**. A raking cornice is formed by the junction of two slanted cornices, most often found in **pediments**.

course (p. 99)   A horizontal layer of stone used in building.

crenellation (p. 44)   Alternating higher and lower sections along the top of a defensive wall, giving a stepped appearance and forming a permanent shield for defenders on top of a fortified building.

crocket (p. 585)   A stylized leaf used as decoration along the outer angle of spires, pinnacles, gables, and around **capitals** in Gothic architecture.

cruciform (p. 232)   A term describing anything that is cross-shaped, as in the cruciform plan of a church.

cubiculum (cubicula) (p. 224)   A small private room for burials in the **catacombs**.

cuneiform (p. 28)   An early form of writing with wedge-shaped marks impressed into wet clay with a **stylus**, primarily used by ancient Mesopotamians.

curtain wall (p. 1045)   A wall in a building that does not support any of the weight of the structure.

cyclopean construction (p. 93)   A method of building using huge blocks of rough-hewn stone. Any large-scale, monumental building project that impresses by sheer size. Named after the Cyclopes (sing. Cyclops) one-eyed giants of legendary strength in Greek myths.

cylinder seal (p. 32)   A small cylindrical stone decorated with **incised** patterns. When rolled across soft clay or wax, the resulting raised pattern or design (**relief**) served in Mesopotamian and Indus Valley cultures as an identifying signature.

dado (dadoes) (p. 163)   The lower part of a wall, differentiated in some way (by a molding or different coloring or paneling) from the upper section.

daguerreotype (p. 967)   An early photographic process that makes a positive print on a light-sensitized copperplate; invented and marketed in 1839 by Louis-Jacques-Mandé Daguerre.

demotic writing (p. 77)   The simplified form of ancient Egyptian **hieratic writing**, used primarily for administrative and private texts.

dendrochronology (p. xxxvi)   The dating of wood based on the patterns of the growth rings.

desert varnish (p. 400)   In southwestern North America, a substance that turned cliff faces into dark surfaces. Neolithic artists would draw images by scraping through the dark surface.

diptych (p. 215)   Two panels of equal size (usually decorated with paintings or **reliefs**) hinged together.

dogu (p. 356)   Small human figurines made in Japan during the Jomon period. Shaped from clay, the figures have exaggerated expressions and are in contorted poses. They were probably used in religious rituals.

dolmen (p. 17)   A prehistoric structure made up of two or more large upright stones supporting a large, flat, horizontal slab or slabs.

dome (p. 188)   A rounded **vault**, usually over a circular space. Consists of curved masonry and can vary in shape from hemispherical to bulbous to ovoidal. May use a supporting vertical wall (**drum**), from which the vault springs, and may be crowned by an open space (**oculus**) and/or an exterior **lantern**. When a dome is built over a square space, an intermediate element is required to make the transition to a circular drum. There are two systems: A dome on **pendentives** (spherical triangles) incorporates **arched**, sloping intermediate sections of wall that carry the weight and **thrust** of the dome to

heavily **buttressed** supporting **piers**. A dome on **squinches** uses an arch built into the wall (squinch) in the upper corners of the space to carry the weight of the dome across the corners of the square space below. A half-dome or **conch** may cover a semicircular space.

domino construction (p. 1045)   System of building construction introduced by the architect Le Corbusier in which reinforced concrete floor slabs are floated on six free-standing posts placed as if at the positions of the six dots on a domino playing piece.

Doric order (p. 108)   See **order**.

dressed stone (p. 85)   See **ashlar**.

drillwork (p. 190)   The technique of using a drill for the creation of certain effects in sculpture.

drum (p. 110)   The wall that supports a **dome**. Also: a segment of the circular **shaft** of a **column**.

drypoint (p. 748)   An **intaglio** printmaking process by which a metal (usually copper) plate is directly inscribed with a pointed instrument (**stylus**). The resulting design of scratched lines is inked, wiped, and printed. Also: the print made by this process.

earthenware (p. 22)   A low-fired, opaque **ceramic** ware that is fired in the range of 800 to 900 degrees Celsius. Earthenware employs humble clays that are naturally heat resistant; the finished wares remain porous after firing unless glazed. Earthenware occurs in a range of earth-toned colors, from white and tan to gray and black, with tan predominating.

earthwork (p. 1102)   Usually very large scale, outdoor artwork that is produced by altering the natural environment.

echinus (p. 110)   A cushionlike circular element found below the **abacus** of a **Doric capital**. Also: a similarly shaped molding (usually with egg-and-dart motifs) underneath the **volutes** of an **Ionic** capital.

electronic spin resonance (p. 12)   Method that uses magnetic field and microwave irradiation to date material such as tooth enamel and its surrounding soil.

elevation (p. 108)   The arrangement, proportions, and details of any vertical side or face of a building. Also: an architectural drawing showing an exterior or interior wall of a building.

emblema (emblemata) (p. 202)   In a **mosaic**, the elaborate central motif on a floor, usually a self-contained unit done in a more refined manner, with smaller **tesserae** of both marble and semiprecious stones.

embroidery (p. 484)   Stitches applied on top of an already-woven fabric ground.

encaustic (p. 79)   A painting medium using pigments mixed with hot wax.

engaged column (p. 173)   A column attached to a wall. See also **column**.

engraving (p. 590)   An **intaglio** printmaking process of inscribing an image, design, or letters onto a metal or wood surface from which a print is made. An engraving is usually drawn with a sharp implement (**burin**) directly onto the surface of the plate. Also: the print made from this process.

entablature (p. 108)   In the Classical **orders**, the horizontal elements above the **columns** and **capitals**. The entablature consists of, from bottom to top, an **architrave**, a **frieze**, and a **cornice**.

entasis (p. 108)   A slight swelling of the **shaft** of a Greek **column**. The optical illusion of entasis makes the column appear from afar to be straight.

etching (p. 748)   An **intaglio** printmaking process in which a metal plate is coated with acid-resistant resin and then inscribed with a **stylus** in a design, revealing the plate below. The plate is then immersed in acid, and the design of exposed metal is eaten away by the acid. The resin is removed, leaving the design etched permanently into the metal and the plate ready to be inked, wiped, and printed.

Eucharist (p. 222)   The central rite of the Christian Church, from the Greek word "thanksgiving." Also known as the Mass or Holy Communion, it is based on the Last Supper. According to traditional Catholic Christian belief, consecrated bread and wine become the body and blood of Christ; in Protestant belief, bread and wine symbolize the body and blood.

exedra (exedrae) (p. 199)   In architecture, a semicircular niche. On a small scale, often used as decoration, whereas larger exedrae can form interior spaces (such as an **apse**).

expressionism (p. 151)   Terms describing a work of art in which forms are created primarily to evoke subjective emotions rather than a rational response.

façade (p. 52)   The face or front wall of a building.

faience (p. 87)   Type of **ceramic** covered with colorful, opaque glazes that form a smooth, impermeable surface. First developed in ancient Egypt.

fang ding (p. 328)   A square or rectangular bronze vessel with four legs. The *fang ding* was used for ritual offerings in ancient China during the Shang dynasty.

femmage (p. 1101)   From "female" and "**collage**," the incorporation of fabric into painting.

fête galante (p. 908)   A subject in painting depicting well-dressed people at leisure in a park or country setting. It is most often associated with eighteenth-century French Rococo painting.

filigree (p. 87)   Delicate, lacelike ornamental work.

fillet (p. 110)   The flat ridge between the carved out **flutes** of a **column shaft**. See also fluting.

finial (p. 308)   A knoblike architectural decoration usually found at the top point of a spire, pinnacle, canopy, or gable. Also found on furniture; also the ornamental top of a staff.

flutes, fluted (p. 110)   In architecture, evenly spaced, rounded parallel vertical grooves incised on **shafts** of **columns** or columnar elements (such as **pilasters**).

flying buttress (p. 496)   See **buttress**.

flying gallop (p. 87)   Animals posed off the ground with legs fully extended backwards and forwards to signify that they are running.

foreshortening (p. 119)   The illusion created on a flat surface in which figures and objects appear to recede or project sharply into space. Accomplished according to the rules of perspective.

formal analysis (p. xxix)   An exploration of the visual character that artists bring to their works through the expressive use of elements such as line, form, color, and light, and through its overall structure or composition.

Formalism, formalist (p. 1073)   An approach to the understanding, appreciation, and valuation of art based almost solely on considerations of form. This approach tends to regard an artwork as independent of its time and place of making. In the 1940s, Formalism was most ardently proposed by critic Clement Greenberg. See also **connoisseurship**.

forum (p. 178)   A Roman town center; site of temples and administrative buildings and used as a market or gathering area for the citizens.

four-iwan mosque (p. 271)   See **iwan** and **mosque**.

fresco (p. 87)   A painting technique in which water-based pigments are applied to a surface of wet plaster (called **buon fresco**). The color is absorbed by the plaster, becoming a permanent part of the wall. **Fresco secco** is created by painting on dried plaster, and the color may flake off. Murals made by both these techniques are called frescoes.

fresco secco (p. 87)   See **fresco**.

frieze (p. 108)   The middle element of an **entablature**, between the **architrave** and the cornice. Usually decorated with sculpture, painting, or moldings. Also: any continuous flat band with **relief sculpture** or painted decorations.

frottage (p. 1056) A design produced by laying a piece of paper over a textured surface and rubbing with charcoal or other soft medium.

fusuma (p. 818) Sliding doors covered with paper, used in traditional Japanese construction. *Fusuma* are often highly decorated with paintings and colored backgrounds.

gallery (p. 236) In church architecture, the story found above the side **aisles** of a church, usually open to and overlooking the **nave**. Also: in secular architecture, a long room, usually above the ground floor in a private house or a public building used for entertaining, exhibiting pictures, or promenading. Also: a building or hall in which art is displayed or sold. Also: *galleria*.

garbhagriha (p. 301) From the Sanskrit word meaning "womb chamber," a small room or shrine in a Hindu temple containing a holy image.

genre painting (p. 712) A term used to loosely categorize paintings depicting scenes of everyday life, including (among others) domestic interiors, parties, inn scenes, and street scenes.

geoglyphs (p. 392) Earthen designs on a colossal scale, often created in a landscape as if to be seen from an aerial viewpoint.

gesso (p. 544) A ground made from glue, gypsum, and/or chalk forming the ground of a wood panel or the priming layer of a canvas. Provides a smooth surface for painting.

gilding (p. 87) The application of paper-thin **gold leaf** or gold pigment to an object made from another medium (for example, a sculpture or painting). Usually used as a decorative finishing detail.

giornata (giornate) (p. 537) Adopted from the Italian term meaning "a day's work," a giornata is the section of a **fresco** plastered and painted in a single day.

gold leaf (p. 47) Paper-thin sheets of hammered gold that are used in **gilding**. In some cases (such as Byzantine **icons**), also used as a ground for paintings.

gold foil (p. 87) A thin sheet of gold.

gopura (p. 775) The towering gateway to an Indian Hindu temple complex. A temple complex can have several different *gopuras*.

Grand Manner (p. 922) An elevated style of painting popular in the eighteenth century in which the artist looked to the ancients and to the Renaissance for inspiration; for portraits as well as history painting, the artist would adopt the poses, compositions, and attitudes of Renaissance and antique models.

Grand Tour (p. 911) Popular during the eighteenth and nineteenth centuries, an extended tour of cultural sites in France and Italy intended to finish the education of a young upper-class person primarily from Britain or North America.

granulation (p. 87) A technique of decoration in which metal granules, or tiny metal balls, are fused onto a metal surface.

graphic arts (p. xxiv) A term referring to those arts that are drawn or printed and that utilize paper as primary support.

grattage (p. 1056) A pattern created by scraping off layers of paint from a canvas laid over a textured surface. See also **frottage**.

grid (p. 64) A system of regularly spaced horizontally and vertically crossed lines that gives regularity to an architectural plan or in the composition of a work of art. Also: in painting, a grid is used to allow designs to be enlarged or transferred easily.

grisaille (p. 538) A style of monochromatic painting in shades of gray. Also: a painting made in this style.

groin vault (p. 188) See **vault**.

grozing (p. 497) In **stained-glass** windows, chipping away at the edges of a piece of glass to achieve the precise shape needed for inclusion in the composition.

hall church (p. 518) A church with a **nave** and **aisles** of the same height, giving the impression of a large, open hall.

handscroll (p. 337) A long, narrow, horizontal painting or text (or combination thereof) common in Chinese and Japanese art and of a size intended for individual use. A handscroll is stored wrapped tightly around a wooden pin and is unrolled for viewing or reading.

hanging scroll (p. 795) In Chinese and Japanese art, a vertical painting or text mounted within sections of silk. At the top is a semicircular rod; at the bottom is a round dowel. Hanging scrolls are kept rolled and tied except for special occasions, when they are hung for display, contemplation, or commemoration.

haniwa (p. 356) Pottery forms, including cylinders, buildings, and human figures, that were placed on top of Japanese tombs or burial mounds.

Happening (p. 1085) An art form developed by Allan Kaprow in the 1960s incorporating performance, theater, and visual images. A Happening was organized without a specific narrative or intent; with audience participation, the event proceeded according to chance and individual improvisation.

hemicycle (p. 508) A semicircular interior space or structure.

henge (p. 18) A circular area enclosed by stones or wood posts set up by Neolithic peoples. It is usually bounded by a ditch and raised embankment.

hieratic scale (p. 27) The use of different sizes for powerful or holy figures and for ordinary people to indicate relative importance. The larger the figure, the greater the importance.

hieroglyph (p. 52) Picture writing; words and ideas rendered in the form of pictorial symbols.

high relief (p. 304) See **relief sculpture**.

historiated capital (p. 479) See **capital**.

historicism (p. 963) The strong consciousness of and attention to the institutions, themes, styles, and forms of the past, made accessible by historical research, textual study, and archaeology.

history paintings (p. 924) Paintings based on historical, mythological, or biblical narratives. Once considered the noblest form of art, history paintings generally convey a high moral or intellectual idea and are often painted in a grand pictorial style.

horizon line A horizontal "line" formed by the implied meeting point of earth and sky. In **linear perspective**, the **vanishing point** or points are located on this "line."

horseshoe arch (p. 268) See **arch**.

hue (p. xxii) Pure color. The saturation or intensity of the hue depends on the purity of the color. Its value depends on its lightness or darkness.

hydria (p. 139) A large ancient Greek and Roman jar with three handles (horizontal ones at both sides and one vertical at the back), used for storing water.

hypostyle hall (p. 66) A large interior room characterized by many closely spaced columns that support its roof.

icon (p. 237) An image representing a sacred figure or event in the Byzantine, and later in the Orthodox, Church. Icons were venerated by the faithful, who believed them to have miraculous powers to transmit messages to God.

iconic image (p. 224) A picture that expresses or embodies an intangible concept or idea.

iconoclasm (p. 245) The banning or destruction of images, especially **icons** and religious art. Iconoclasm in eighth- and ninth-century Byzantium and sixteenth- and seventeenth-century Protestant territories arose from differing beliefs about the power, meaning, function, and purpose of imagery in religion.

iconography (p. xxxiii) Identifying and studying the subject matter and conventional motifs or symbols in works of art.

iconology (p. xxxv) Interpreting works of art as embodiments of cultural situation by placing them within broad social, political, religious, and intellectual contexts.

iconophile (p. 246) From the Greek for "lovers of images." In Byzantine art, iconophiles advocated for the continued use of **iconic images** in art.

iconostasis (p. 245) The partition screen in a Byzantine or Orthodox church between the **sanctuary** (where the Mass is performed) and the body of the church (where the congregation assembles). The iconostasis displays **icons**.

idealization (p. xxiv) A process in art through which artists strive to make their forms and figures attain perfection, based on pervading cultural values and/or their own personal ideals.

ideograph (p. 331) A written character or symbol representing an idea or object. Many Chinese characters are ideographs.

ignudi (p. 645) Heroic figures of nude young men.

illumination (p. 425) A painting on paper or parchment used as an illustration and/or decoration in **manuscripts** or **albums**. Usually richly colored, often supplemented by gold and other precious materials. The artists are referred to as illuminators. Also: the technique of decorating manuscripts with such paintings.

impasto (p. 748) Thick applications of pigment that give a painting a palpable surface texture.

impost block (p. 600) A block, serving to concentrate the weight above, imposed between the **capital** of a **column** and the springing of an **arch** above.

incising (p. 32) A technique in which a design or inscription is cut into a hard surface with a sharp instrument. Such a surface is said to be incised.

ink painting (p. 810) A monochromatic style of painting developed in China using black ink with gray washes.

inlay (p. 30) To set pieces of a material or materials into a surface to form a design. Also: material used in or decoration formed by this technique.

installation (p. 1087) Contemporary art created for a specific site, especially a gallery or outdoor area, that creates a complete and controlled environment.

intaglio (p. 590) Term used for a technique in which the design is carved out of the surface of an object, such as an **engraved seal** stone. In the **graphic arts**, intaglio includes **engraving**, **etching**, and **drypoint**—all processes in which ink transfers to paper from **incised**, ink-filled lines cut into a metal plate.

intarsia (p. 617) Decoration formed through wood **inlay**.

intuitive perspective (p. 184) See **perspective**.

Ionic order (p. 108) See **order**.

iwan (p. 71) A large, **vaulted** chamber in a **mosque** with a monumental **arched** opening on one side.

jamb (p. 473) In architecture, the vertical element found on both sides of an opening in a wall, and supporting an **arch** or **lintel**.

japonisme (p. 994) A style in French and American nineteenth-century art that was highly influenced by Japanese art, especially prints.

jasperware (p. 917) A fine-grained, unglazed, white **ceramic** developed by Josiah Wedgwood, often colored by metallic oxides with the raised designs remaining white.

jataka tales (p. 300) In Buddhism, stories associated with the previous lives of Shakyamuni, the historical Buddha.

joggled voussoirs (p. 272) Interlocking **voussoirs** in an **arch** or **lintel**, often of contrasting materials for colorful effect.

joined-block sculpture (p. 367) A method of constructing large-scale wooden sculpture developed in

Japan. The entire work is constructed from smaller hollow blocks, each individually carved, and assembled when complete. The joined-block technique allowed the production of larger sculpture, as the multiple joints alleviate the problems of drying and cracking found with sculpture carved from a single block.

kantharos (p. 117)   A type of Greek vase or goblet with two large handles and a wide mouth.

keep (p. 473)   The innermost and strongest structure or central tower of a medieval castle, sometimes used as living quarters, as well as for defense. Also called a donjon.

kente (p. 892)   A woven cloth made by the Ashanti peoples of Africa. Kente cloth is woven in long, narrow pieces in complex and colorful patterns, which are then sewn together.

key block (p. 826)   A key block is the master block in the production of a colored **woodblock print**, which requires different blocks for each color. The key block is a flat piece of wood upon which the outlines for the entire design of the print were first drawn on its surface and then all but these outlines were carved away with a knife. These outlines serve as a guide for the accurate **registration** or alignment of the other blocks needed to add colors to specific parts of a print.

keystone (p. 172)   The topmost **voussoir** at the center of an **arch**, and the last block to be placed. The pressure of this block holds the arch together. Often of a larger size and/or decorated.

kiln (p. 22)   An oven designed to produce enough heat for the baking, or firing, of clay.

kiva (p. 398)   A ceremonial enclosure, usually wholly or partly underground, used for ritual purposes by modern Pueblo peoples and Ancestral Puebloans. *Kivas* may be round or square, made of **adobe** or stone, and they usually feature a hearth and a small indentation in the floor behind it.

kondo (p. 360)   The main hall inside a Japanese Buddhist temple where the images of Buddha are housed.

korambo (p. 863)   A ceremonial or spirit house in Pacific cultures, reserved for the men of a village and used as a meeting place as well as to hide religious artifacts from the uninitiated.

kore (kourai) (p. 114)   An Archaic Greek statue of a young woman.

koru (p. 870)   A design depicting a curling stalk with a bulb at the end that resembles a young tree fern, and often found in Maori art.

kouros (kouroi) (p. 114)   An Archaic Greek statue of a young man or boy.

kowhaiwhai (p. 870)   Painted curvilinear patterns often found in Maori art.

krater (p. 99)   An ancient Greek vessel for mixing wine and water, with many subtypes that each have a distinctive shape. **Calyx krater**: a bell-shaped vessel with handles near the base that resemble a flower calyx. **Volute krater**: a type of krater with handles shaped like scrolls.

Kufic (p. 272)   An ornamental, angular Arabic script.

kylix (p. 124)   A shallow Greek cup, used for drinking, with a wide mouth and small handles near the rim.

lacquer (p. 22)   A type of hard, glossy surface varnish used on objects in East Asian cultures, made from the sap of the Asian sumac or from shellac, a resinous secretion from the lac insect. Lacquer can be layered and manipulated or combined with pigments and other materials for various decorative effects.

lakshana (p. 303)   Term used to designate the thirty-two marks of the historical Buddha. The *lakshana* include, among others, the Buddha's golden body, his long arms, the wheel impressed on his palms and the soles of his feet, and his elongated earlobes.

lamassu (p. 42)   Supernatural guardian-protector of ancient Near Eastern palaces and throne rooms, often represented sculpturally as a combination of the bearded head of a man, powerful body of a lion or bull, wings of an eagle, and the horned headdress of a god, usually possessing five legs.

lancet (p. 502)   A tall, narrow window crowned by a sharply pointed **arch**, typically found in Gothic architecture.

lantern (p. 458)   A turretlike structure situated on a roof, **vault**, or **dome**, with windows that allow light into the space below.

leythos (lekythoi) (p. 141)   A slim Greek oil vase with one handle and a narrow mouth.

linear perspective (p. 593)   See **perspective**.

linga shrine (p. 310)   A place of worship centered on an object or representation in the form of a phallus (the lingam), which symbolizes the power of the Hindu god Shiva.

lintel (p. 473)   A horizontal element of any material carried by two or more vertical supports to form an opening.

literati (p. 337)   The English word used for the Chinese *wenren* or the Japanese *bunjin*, referring to well educated artists who enjoyed literature, **calligraphy**, and painting as a pastime. Their paintings are termed **literati painting**.

literati painting (p. 791)   A style of painting that reflects the taste of the educated class of East Asian intellectuals and scholars. Aspects include an appreciation for the antique, small scale, and an intimate connection between maker and audience.

lithography (p. 951)   Process of making a print (lithograph) from a design drawn on a flat stone block with greasy crayon. Ink is applied to the wet stone and adheres only to the greasy areas of the design.

loggia (p. 532)   Italian term for a covered open-air **gallery**. Often used as a corridor between buildings or around a courtyard, loggias usually have **arcades** or **colonnades**.

logosyllabic (p. 385)   A writing system consisting of both logograms (symbols that represent words) and phonetic signs (symbols that represent sounds, in this case syllables). Cuneiform, Maya, and Japanese are examples of logosyllabic scripts.

longitudinal-plan building (p. 228)   Any structure designed with a rectangular shape. If a cross-shaped building, the main arm of the building would be longer then any arms that cross it. For example, **basilicas** or Latin-cross plan churches.

lost-wax casting (p. 413)   A method of casting metal, such as bronze, by a process in which a wax mold is covered with clay and plaster, then fired, melting the wax and leaving a hollow form. Molten metal is then poured into the hollow space and slowly cooled. When the hardened clay and plaster exterior shell is removed, a solid metal form remains to be smoothed and polished.

low relief (p. 39)   See **relief sculpture**.

lunette (p. 223)   A semicircular wall area, framed by an **arch** over a door or window. Can be either plain or decorated.

lusterware (p. 277)   **Ceramic** pottery decorated with metallic glazes.

madrasa (p. 271)   An Islamic institution of higher learning, where teaching is focused on theology and law.

maenad (p. 104)   In ancient Greece, a female devotee of the wine god Dionysos who participated in orgiastic rituals. She is often depicted with swirling drapery to indicate wild movement or dance. (Also called a Bacchante, after Bacchus, the Roman name of Dionysos.)

majolica (p. 571)   Pottery painted with a tin glaze that, when fired, gives a lustrous and colorful surface.

mandala (p. 299)   An image of the cosmos represented by an arrangement of circles or concentric geometric shapes containing diagrams or images. Used for meditation and contemplation by Buddhists.

mandapa (p. 301)   In a Hindu temple, an open hall dedicated to ritual worship.

mandorla (p. 474)   Light encircling, or emanating from, the entire figure of a sacred person.

manuscript (p. 242)   A handwritten book or document.

maqsura (p. 268)   An enclosure in a Muslim **mosque**, near the **mihrab**, designated for dignitaries.

martyrium (martyria) (p. 237)   In Christian architecture, a church, chapel, or shrine built over the grave of a martyr or the site of a great miracle.

mastaba (p. 53)   A flat-topped, one-story structure with slanted walls over an ancient Egyptian underground tomb.

matte (p. 571)   Term describing a smooth surface that is without shine or luster.

mausoleum (p. 177)   A monumental building used as a tomb. Named after the tomb of Mausolos erected at Halikarnassos around 350 BCE.

medallion (p. 225)   Any round ornament or decoration. Also: a large medal.

megalith (p. 17)   A large stone used in prehistoric building. Megalithic architecture employs such stones.

megaron (p. 93)   The main hall of a Mycenaean palace or grand house, having a columnar **porch** and a room with central fireplace surrounded by four **columns**.

memento mori (p. 907)   From Latin for "remember that you must die." An object, such as a skull or extinguished candle, typically found in a **vanitas** image, symbolizing the transience of life.

memory image (p. 8)   An image that relies on the generic shapes and relationships that readily spring to mind at the mention of an object.

menorah (p. 219)   A Jewish lamp-stand with seven or nine branches; the nine-branched menorah is used during the celebration of Hanukkah. Representations of the seven-branched menorah, once used in the Temple of Jerusalem, became a symbol of Judaism.

metope (p. 110)   The carved or painted rectangular panel between the **triglyphs** of a **Doric frieze**.

mihrab (p. 261)   A recess or niche that distinguishes the wall oriented toward Mecca (**qibla**) in a **mosque**.

millefiori (p. 428)   A term derived from the Italian for "a thousand flowers" that refers to a glass-making technique in which rods of differently-colored glass are fused in a long bundle then subsequently sliced to produce disks or beads with small-scale, multicolor patterns.

minaret (p. 267)   A tower on or near a **mosque**, varying extensively in form throughout the Islamic world, from which the faithful are called to prayer five times a day.

minbar (p. 261)   A high platform or pulpit in a **mosque**.

miniature (p. 243)   Anything small. In painting, miniatures may be illustrations within **albums** or **manuscripts** or intimate portraits.

mirador (p. 275)   In Spanish and Islamic palace architecture, a very large window or room with windows, and sometimes balconies, providing views to interior courtyards or the exterior landscape.

mithuna (p. 302)   The amorous male and female couples in Buddhist sculpture, usually found at the entrance to a sacred building. The *mithuna* symbolize the harmony and fertility of life.

moai (p. 859)   Statues found in Polynesia, carved from tufa, a yellowish brown volcanic stone, and depicting the human form. Nearly 1,000 of these statues have been found on the island of Rapa Nui but their significance has been a matter of speculation.

mobile (p. 1059)   A sculpture made with parts suspended in such a way that they move in a current of air.

modeling (p. xxix)   In painting, the process of creating the illusion of three-dimensionality on a two-dimensional surface by use of light and shade. In sculpture, the process of molding a three-dimensional form out of a malleable substance.

module (p. 341)   A segment or portion of a repeated design. Also: a basic building block.

molding (p. 315)   A shaped or sculpted strip with varying contours and patterns. Used as decoration on architecture, furniture, frames, and other objects.

mortise-and-tenon (p. 19)   A method of joining two elements. A projecting pin (tenon) on one element fits snugly into a hole designed for it (mortise) on the other. Such joints are very strong and flexible.

mosaic (p. 146)   Images formed by small colored stone or glass pieces (**tesserae**), affixed to a hard, stable surface.

mosque (p. 261)   An edifice used for communal Islamic worship.

Mozarabic (p. 433)   An eclectic style practiced in Christian medieval Spain while much of the Iberian peninsula was ruled by Muslim dynasties.

mudra (p. 304)   A symbolic hand gesture in Buddhist art that denotes certain behaviors, actions, or feelings.

mullion (p. 507)   A slender vertical element or colonnette that divides a window into subsidiary sections.

muqarna (p. 275)   Small nichelike components stacked in tiers to fill the transition between differing vertical and horizontal planes.

naos (p. 236)   The principal room in a temple or church. In ancient architecture, the **cella**. In a Byzantine church, the **nave** and **sanctuary**.

narrative image (p. 224)   A picture that recounts an event drawn from a story, either factual (e.g., biographical) or fictional.

narthex (p. 222)   The vestibule or entrance **porch** of a church.

nave (p. 192)   The central space of a **basilica**, two or three stories high and usually flanked by aisles.

necking (p. 110)   The molding at the top of the **shaft** of the **column**.

necropolis (p. 53)   A large cemetery or burial area; literally a "city of the dead."

negative space (p. 120)   Empty space, surrounded and shaped so that it acquires a sense of form or volume.

nemes headdress (p. 51)   The royal headdress of Egypt.

niello (p. 87)   A metal technique in which a black sulfur alloy is rubbed into fine lines **engraved** into metal (usually gold or silver). When heated, the **alloy** becomes fused with the surrounding metal and provides contrasting detail.

nishiki-e (p. 813)   A multicolored and ornate Japanese print.

oculus (p. 188)   In architecture, a circular opening. Oculi are usually found either as windows or at the apex of a **dome**. When at the top of a dome, an oculus is either open to the sky or covered by a decorative exterior **lantern**.

odalisque (p. 950)   Turkish word for "harem slave girl" or "concubine."

ogee (p. 551)   An S-shaped curve. See **arch**.

oinochoe (p. 128)   A Greek jug used for wine.

olpe (p. 105)   Any Greek vase or jug without a spout.

one-point perspective   See **perspective**.

orant (p. 222)   The representation of a standing figure praying with outstretched and upraised arms.

oratory (p. 232)   A small chapel.

order (p. 110)   A system of proportions in Classical architecture that includes every aspect of the building's plan, elevation, and decorative system. **Composite**: a combination of the **Ionic** and the **Corinthian** orders.

The **capital** combines **acanthus** leaves with **volute** scrolls. **Corinthian**: the most ornate of the orders, the Corinthian includes a **base**, a **fluted column shaft** with a capital elaborately decorated with acanthus leaf carvings. Its **entablature** consists of an **architrave** decorated with **moldings**, a **frieze** often containing sculptured **reliefs**, and a **cornice** with dentils. **Doric**: the column shaft of the Doric order can be fluted or smooth-surfaced and has no base. The Doric capital consists of an undecorated **echinus** and **abacus**. The Doric entablature has a plain architrave, a frieze with **metopes** and **triglyphs**, and a simple cornice. **Ionic**: the column of the Ionic order has a base, a fluted shaft, and a capital decorated with volutes. The Ionic entablature consists of an architrave of three panels and moldings, a frieze usually containing sculpted relief ornament, and a cornice with dentils. **Tuscan**: a variation of Doric characterized by a smooth-surfaced column shaft with a base, a plain architrave, and an undecorated frieze. A colossal order is any of the above built on a large scale, rising through several stories in height and often raised from the ground by a **pedestal**.

orientalism (p. 966)   The fascination with Middle Eastern cultures.

orthogonal (p. 140)   Any line running back into the represented space of a picture perpendicular to the imagined picture plane. In **linear perspective**, all orthogonals converge at a single **vanishing point** in the picture and are the basis for a **grid** that maps out the internal space of the image. An orthogonal plan is any plan for a building or city that is based exclusively on right angles, such as the grid plan of many major cities.

pagoda (p. 341)   An East Asian **reliquary** tower built with successively smaller, repeated stories. Each story is usually marked by an elaborate projecting roof.

painterly (p. xxiv)   A style of painting which emphasizes the techniques and surface effects of brushwork (also color, light, and shade).

palace complex (p. 41)   A group of buildings used for living and governing by a ruler and his or her supporters, usually fortified.

palazzo (p. 600)   Italian term for palace, used for any large urban dwelling.

palmette (p. 139)   A fan-shaped ornament with radiating leaves.

panel painting   Any painting executed on a wood support. The wood is usually planed to provide a smooth surface. A panel can consist of several boards joined together.

parapet (p. 138)   A low wall at the edge of a balcony, bridge, roof, or other place from which there is a steep drop, built for safety. A parapet walk is the passageway, usually open, immediately behind the uppermost exterior wall or battlement of a fortified building.

parchment (p. 243)   A writing surface made from treated skins of animals. Very fine parchment is known as **vellum**.

parish church (p. 239)   Church where local residents attend regular services.

parterre (p. 760)   An ornamental, highly regimented flowerbed. An element of the ornate gardens of seventeenth-century palaces and **châteaux**.

passage grave (p. 17)   A prehistoric tomb under a **cairn**, reached by a long, narrow, slab-lined access passageway or passageways.

pastel (p. 912)   Dry pigment, chalk, and gum in stick or crayon form. Also: a work of art made with pastels.

pedestal (p. 107)   A platform or **base** supporting a sculpture or other monument. Also: the block found below the base of a Classical **column** (or **colonnade**), serving to raise the entire element off the ground.

pediment (p. 108)   A triangular gable found over major architectural elements such as Classical Greek **porticoes**, windows, or doors. Formed by an **entablature** and the ends of a sloping roof or a raking **cornice**. A similar architectural element is often used decoratively

above a door or window, sometimes with a curved upper **molding**. A broken pediment is a variation on the traditional pediment, with an open space at the center of the topmost angle and/or the horizontal cornice.

pendentive (p. 236)   The concave triangular section of a **vault** that forms the transition between a square or polygonal space and the circular **base** of a **dome**.

peplos (p. 115)   A loose outer garment worn by women of ancient Greece. A cloth rectangle fastened on the shoulders and belted below the bust or at the waist.

Performance art (p. 1085)   An artwork based on a live, sometimes theatrical performance by the artist.

peristyle (p. 66)   A surrounding **colonnade** in Greek architecture. A peristyle building is surrounded on the exterior by a colonnade. Also: a peristyle court is an open colonnaded courtyard, often having a pool and garden.

perspective (p. 184)   A system for representing three-dimensional space on a two-dimensional surface. **Atmospheric perspective**: A method of rendering the effect of spatial distance by subtle variations in color and clarity of representation. **Intuitive perspective**: A method of giving the impression of recession by visual instinct, not by the use of an overall system or program. Oblique perspective: An intuitive spatial system in which a building or room is placed with one corner in the picture plane, and the other parts of the structure recede to an imaginary vanishing point on its other side. Oblique perspective is not a comprehensive, mathematical system. **One-point** and multiple-point perspective (also called **linear**, scientific or mathematical perspective): A method of creating the illusion of three-dimensional space on a two-dimensional surface by delineating a horizon line and multiple **orthogonal** lines. These recede to meet at one or more points on the horizon (called **vanishing points**), giving the appearance of spatial depth. Called scientific or mathematical because its use requires some knowledge of geometry and mathematics, as well as optics. Reverse perspective: A Byzantine perspective theory in which the orthogonals or rays of sight do not converge on a vanishing point in the picture, but are thought to originate in the viewer's eye in front of the picture. Thus, in reverse perspective the image is constructed with orthogonals that diverge, giving a slightly tipped aspect to objects.

photomontage (p. 1039)   A photographic work created from many smaller photographs arranged (and often overlapping) in a composition, which is then rephotographed.

pictograph (p. 331)   A highly stylized depiction serving as a symbol for a person or object. Also: a type of writing utilizing such symbols.

picture plane (p. 573)   The theoretical plane corresponding with the actual surface of a painting, separating the spatial world evoked in the painting from the spatial world occupied by the viewer.

picture stone (p. 436)   A medieval northern European memorial stone covered with figural decoration. See also **rune stone**.

picturesque (p. 917)   A term describing the taste for the familiar, the pleasant, and the agreeable, popular in the eighteenth and nineteenth centuries in Europe. Originally used to describe the "picture like" qualities of some landscape scenes. When contrasted with the **sublime**, the picturesque stood for the interesting but ordinary domestic landscape.

piece-mold casting (p. 328)   A casting technique in which the mold consists of several sections that are connected during the pouring of molten metal, usually bronze. After the cast form has hardened, the pieces of the mold are disassembled, leaving the completed object.

pier (p. 266)   A masonry support made up of many stones, or rubble and concrete (in contrast to a column **shaft** which is formed from a single stone or a series of **drums**), often square or rectangular in plan, and capable of carrying very heavy architectural loads.

pietà (p. 231) A devotional subject in Christian religious art. After the Crucifixion the body of Jesus was laid across the lap of his grieving mother, Mary. When others are present the subject is called the Lamentation.

pietra dura (p. 781) Italian for "hard stone." Semiprecious stones selected for color, variation, and cut in shapes to form ornamental designs such as flowers or fruit.

pietra serena (p. 600) A gray Tuscan limestone used in Florence.

pilaster (p. 160) An **engaged column**-like element that is rectangular in format and used for decoration in architecture.

pilgrimage church (p. 239) A site that attracts visitors wishing to venerate **relics** as well as attend services.

pillar (p. 219) In architecture, any large, free-standing vertical element. Usually functions as an important weight-bearing unit in buildings.

pilotis (p. 1045) Free-standing posts.

pinnacle (p. 499) In Gothic architecture, a steep pyramid decorating the top of another element such as a **buttress**. Also: the highest point.

plate tracery (p. 502) See **tracery**.

plinth (p. 163) The slablike base or **pedestal** of a **column**, statue, wall, building, or piece of furniture.

pluralism (p. 1106) A social structure or goal that allows members of diverse ethnic, racial, or other groups to exist peacefully within the society while continuing to practice the customs of their own divergent cultures, thus providing to artists a variety of valid contemporary styles.

podium (p. 138) A raised platform that acts as the foundation for a building, or as a platform for a speaker.

polychrome, polychromy (p. 521) The multi-colored painting decoration applied to any part of a building, sculpture, or piece of furniture.

polyptych (p. 564) An altarpiece constructed from multiple panels, sometimes with hinges to allow for movable wings.

porcelain (p. 22) A high-fired, vitrified, translucent, white **ceramic** ware that employs two specific clays—kaolin and petuntse—and is fired in the range of 1,300 to 1,400 degrees Celsius. The relatively high proportion of silica in the body clays renders the finished porcelains translucent. Like **stonewares**, porcelains are glazed to enhance their aesthetic appeal and to aid in keeping them clean. By definition, porcelain is white, though it may be covered with a glaze of bright color or subtle hue. Chinese potters were the first in the world to produce porcelain, which they were able to make as early as the eighth century.

porch (p. 108) The covered entrance on the exterior of a building. With a row of **columns** or **colonnade**, also called a **portico**.

portal (p. 39) A grand entrance, door, or gate, usually to an important public building, and often decorated with sculpture.

portico (p. 62) In architecture, a projecting roof or porch supported by **columns**, often marking an entrance. See also **porch**.

post-and-lintel (p. 16) An architectural system of construction with two or more vertical elements (posts) supporting a horizontal element (**lintel**).

potassium-argon dating (p. 12) Technique used to measure the decay of a radioactive potassium isotope into a stable isotope of argon, and inert gas.

potsherd (p. 22) A broken piece of **ceramic** ware.

poupou (p. 871) A house panel, often carved with designs and found in Pacific cultures.

Prairie Style (p. 1046) Style developed by a group of midwestern architects who worked together using the aesthetic of the Prairie and indigenous prairie plants for landscape design to design mostly domestic homes and small public buildings mostly in the midwest.

predella (p. 548) The base of an altarpiece, often decorated with small scenes that are related in subject to that of the main panel or panels.

primitivism (p. 1022) The borrowing of subjects or forms usually from non-European or prehistoric sources by Western artists. Originally practiced by Western artists as an attempt to infuse their work with the naturalistic and expressive qualities attributed to other cultures, especially colonized cultures.

pronaos (p. 108) The enclosed vestibule of a Greek or Roman temple, found in front of the **cella** and marked by a row of **columns** at the entrance.

proscenium (p. 150) The stage of an ancient Greek or Roman theater. In modern theater, the area of the stage in front of the curtain. Also: the framing **arch** that separates a stage from the audience.

psalter (p. 253) In Jewish and Christian scripture, a book containing the psalms, or songs, attributed to King David.

psykter (p. 127) A Greek vessel with an extended bottom allowing it to float in a larger krater; used to chill wine.

putto (putti) (p. 229) A plump, naked little boy, often winged. In Classical art, called a cupid; in Christian art, a cherub.

pylon (p. 66) A massive gateway formed by a pair of tapering walls of oblong shape. Erected by ancient Egyptians to mark the entrance to a temple complex.

qibla (p. 267) The **mosque** wall oriented toward Mecca indicated by the **mihrab**.

quatrefoil (p. 503) A four-lobed decorative pattern common in Gothic art and architecture.

quillwork (p. 845) A Native American decorative craft technique. The quills of porcupines and bird feathers are dyed and attached to materials in patterns.

radiometric dating (p. 12) A method of dating prehistoric works of art made from organic materials, based on the rate of degeneration of radiocarbons in these materials. See also **relative dating**, **absolute dating**.

raigo (p. 372) A painted image that depicts the Amida Buddha and other Buddhist deities welcoming the soul of a dying worshiper to paradise.

raku (p. 821) A type of **ceramic** pottery made by hand, coated with a thick, dark glaze, and fired at a low heat. The resulting vessels are irregularly shaped and glazed, and are highly prized for use in the Japanese tea ceremony.

readymade (p. 1037) An object from popular or material culture presented without further manipulation as an artwork by the artist.

red-figure (p. 118) A style and technique of ancient Greek vase painting characterized by red clay-colored figures on a black background. (The figures are reserved against a painted ground and details are drawn, not engraved, as in **black-figure style**.)

register (p. 30) A device used in systems of spatial definition. In painting, a register indicates the use of differing groundlines to differentiate layers of space within an image. In sculpture, the placement of self-contained bands of **reliefs** in a vertical arrangement. See **registration marks**.

registration marks (p. 826) In Japanese **woodblock printing**, these were two marks carved on the blocks to indicate proper alignment of the paper during the printing process. In multicolor printing, which used a separate block for each color, these marks were essential for achieving the proper position or registration of the colors.

relative dating (p. 12) See **radiometric dating**.

relic (p. 239) A venerated object associated with a saint or martyr.

relief sculpture (p. 5) A three-dimensional image or design whose flat background surface is carved away to a certain depth, setting off the figure. Called **high** or **low (bas) relief** depending upon the extent of projection of the image from the background. Called **sunken relief** when the image is carved below the original surface of the background, which is not cut away.

reliquary (p. 299) A container, often made of precious materials, used as a repository to protect and display sacred **relics**.

repoussé (p. 87) A technique of hammering metal from the back to create a protruding image. Elaborate **reliefs** are created with wooden armatures against which the metal sheets are pressed and hammered.

rhyton (p. 88) A vessel in the shape of a figure or an animal, used for drinking or pouring liquids on special occasions.

rib vault (p. 495) See **vault**.

ridgepole (p. 16) A longitudinal timber at the apex of a roof that supports the upper ends of the rafters.

roof comb (p. 386) In a Mayan building, a masonry wall along the apex of a roof that is built above the level of the roof proper. Roof combs support the highly decorated false façades that rise above the height of the building at the front.

rosettes (p. 105) A round or oval ornament resembling a rose.

rotunda (p. 197) Any building (or part thereof) constructed in a circular (or sometimes polygonal) shape, usually producing a large open space crowned by a **dome**.

round arch (p. 172) See **arch**.

roundel (p. 160) Any element with a circular format, often placed as a decoration on the exterior of architecture.

rune stone (p. 436) A stone used in early medieval northern Europe as a commemorative monument, which is carved or inscribed with runes, a writing system used by early Germanic peoples.

rustication (p. 600) In building, the rough, irregular, and unfinished effect deliberately given to the exterior facing of a stone edifice. Rusticated stones are often large and used for decorative emphasis around doors or windows, or across the entire lower floors of a building. Also, masonry construction with conspicuous, often beveled joints.

salon (p. 905) A large room for entertaining guests; a periodic social or intellectual gathering, often of prominent people; a hall or **gallery** for exhibiting works of art.

sanctuary (p. 102) A sacred or holy enclosure used for worship. In ancient Greece and Rome, consisted of one or more temples and an altar. In Christian architecture, the space around the altar in a church called the chancel or presbytery.

sarcophagus (p. 49) A stone coffin. Often rectangular and decorated with **relief sculpture**.

scarab (p. 51) In Egypt, a stylized dung beetle associated with the sun and the god Amun.

scarification (p. 403) Ornamental decoration applied to the surface of the body by cutting the skin for cultural and/or aesthetic reasons.

school of artists (p. 281) An art historical term describing a group of artists, usually working at the same time and sharing similar styles, influences, and ideals. The artists in a particular school may not necessarily be directly associated with one another, unlike those in a workshop or **atelier**.

scribe (p. 242) A writer; a person who copies texts.

scriptorium (scriptoria) (p. 242) A room in a monastery for writing or copying **manuscripts**.

scroll painting (p. 243) A painting executed on a rolled support. Rollers at each end permit the horizontal scroll to be unrolled as it is studied or the vertical scroll to be hung for contemplation or decoration.

sculpture in the round (p. 5)   Three-dimensional sculpture that is carved free of any background or block.

seals (p. 338)   Personal emblems usually carved of stone in **intaglio** or **relief** and used to stamp a name or legend onto paper or silk. In China, they traditionally employ the archaic characters appropriately known as "seal script," of the Zhou or Qin. Cut in stone, a seal may state a formal given name, or it may state any of the numerous personal names that China's painters and writers adopted throughout their lives. A treasured work of art often bears not only the seal of its maker but also those of collectors and admirers through the centuries. In the Chinese view, these do not disfigure the work but add another layer of interest.

serdab (p. 53)   In Egyptian tombs, the small room in which the *ka* statue was placed.

sfumato (p. 634)   Italian term meaning "smoky," soft, and mellow. In painting, the effect of haze in an image. Resembling the color of the atmosphere at dusk, *sfumato* gives a smoky effect.

sgraffito (p. 602)   Decoration made by **incising** or cutting away a surface layer of material to reveal a different color beneath.

shaft (p. 110)   The main vertical section of a **column** between the **capital** and the **base**, usually circular in cross section.

shaft grave (p. 98)   A deep pit used for burial.

shikhara (p. 301)   In the architecture of northern India, a conical (or pyramidal) spire found atop a Hindu temple and often crowned with an **amalaka**.

shoin (p. 819)   A term used to describe the various features found in the most formal room of upper-class Japanese residential architecture.

shoji (p. 819)   A standing Japanese screen covered in translucent rice paper and used in interiors.

siapo (p. 874)   A type of **tapa** cloth found in Samoa and still used as an important gift for ceremonial occasions.

silkscreen printing (p. 1091)   A technique of printing in which paint or ink is pressed through a stencil and specially prepared cloth to produce a previously designed image. Also called serigraphy.

sinopia (sinopie) (p. 537)   Italian word taken from "Sinope," the ancient city in Asia Minor that was famous for its red-brick pigment. In **fresco** paintings, a full-sized, preliminary sketch done in this color on the first rough coat of plaster or *arriccio*.

site-specific sculpture (p. 1102)   A sculpture commissioned and/or designed for a particular location.

slip (p. 120)   A mixture of clay and water applied to a ceramic object as a final decorative coat. Also: a solution that binds different parts of a vessel together, such as the handle and the main body.

spandrel (p. 172)   The area of wall adjoining the exterior curve of an **arch** between its springing and the **keystone**, or the area between two arches, as in an **arcade**.

spolia (p. 465)   Latin for "hide stripped from an animal." Term used for fragments of older architecture or sculpture reused in a secondary context.

springing (p. 172)   The point at which the curve of an **arch** or **vault** meets with and rises from its support.

squinch (p. 236)   An **arch** or **lintel** built across the upper corners of a square space, allowing a circular or polygonal dome to be more securely set above the walls.

stained glass (p. 464)   Molten glass stained with color using metallic oxides. Stained glass is most often used in windows, for which small pieces of different colors are precisely cut and assembled into a design, held together by lead **cames**. Additional details may be added with vitreous paint.

stave church (p. 436)   A Scandinavian wooden structure with four huge timbers (staves) at its core.

stele (stelae) (p. 27)   A stone slab placed vertically and decorated with inscriptions or reliefs. Used as a grave marker or memorial.

stereobate (p. 110)   A foundation upon which a Classical temple stands.

still life (p. xxxv)   A type of painting that has as its subject inanimate objects (such as food, dishes, fruit, or flowers).

stoa (p. 107)   In Greek architecture, a long roofed walk-way, usually having **columns** on one long side and a wall on the other.

stoneware (p. 22)   A high-fired, vitrified, but opaque **ceramic** that is fired in the range of 1,100 to 1,200 degrees Celsius. At that temperature, particles of silica in the clay bodies fuse together so that the finished vessels are impervious to liquids, even without glaze. Stoneware pieces are glazed to enhance their aesthetic appeal and to aid in keeping them clean (since unglazed ceramics are easily soiled). Stoneware occurs in a range of earth-toned colors, from white and tan to gray and black, with light gray predominating. Chinese potters were the first in the world to produce stoneware, which they were able to make as early as the Shang dynasty.

stringcourse (p. 499)   A continuous horizontal band, such as a **molding**, decorating the face of a wall.

studiolo (p. 617)   A room for private conversation and the collection of fine books and art objects. Also known as a study.

stupa (p. 298)   In Buddhist architecture, a bell-shaped or pyramidal religious monument, made of piled earth or stone, and containing sacred **relics**.

stylobate (p. 110)   In Classical architecture, the stone foundation on which a temple **colonnade** stands.

stylus (p. 28)   An instrument with a pointed end (used for writing and printmaking), which makes a delicate line or scratch. Also: a special writing tool for **cuneiform** writing with one pointed end and one triangular.

sublime (p. 955)   djective describing a concept, thing, or state of greatness or vastness with high spiritual, moral, intellectual or emotional value; or something awe-inspiring. The sublime was a goal to which many nineteenth-century artists aspired in their artworks.

sunken relief (p. 71)   See **relief sculpture**.

symposium (p. 118)   An elite gathering of wealthy and powerful men in ancient Greece that focused principally on wine, music, poetry, conversation, games, and love making.

syncretism (p. 222)   A process whereby artists assimilate images and ideas from other traditions or cultures and give them new meanings.

taotie (p. 328)   A mask with a dragon or animal-like face common as a decorative motif in Chinese art.

tapa (p. 874)   A type of cloth used for various purposes in Pacific cultures, made from tree bark stripped and beaten, and often bearing subtle designs from the mallets used to work the bark.

tapestry (p. 484)   Multicolored pictorial or decorative weaving meant to be hung on a wall or placed on furniture. Pictorial or decorative motifs are woven directly into the fabric of the cloth itself.

tatami (p. 819)   Mats of woven straw used in Japanese houses as a floor covering.

tempera (p. 141)   A painting medium made by blending egg yolks with water, pigments, and occasionally other materials, such as glue.

tenebrism (p. 724)   The use of strong **chiaroscuro** and artificially illuminated areas to create a dramatic contrast of light and dark in a painting.

terra cotta (p. 114)   A medium made from clay fired over a low heat and sometimes left unglazed. Also: the orange-brown color typical of this medium.

tessera (tesserae) (p. 146)   The small piece of stone, glass, or other object that is pieced together with many others to create a **mosaic**.

tetrarchy (p. 204)   Four-man rule, as in the late Roman Empire, when four emperors shared power.

thatch (p. 17)   Plant material such as reeds or straw tied over a framework of poles.

thermo-luminescence dating (p. 12)   A technique that measures the irradiation of the crystal structure of material such as flint or pottery and the soil in which it is found, determined by luminescence produced when a sample is heated.

tholos (p. 138)   A small, round building. Sometimes built underground, as in a Mycenaean tomb.

tholos tomb (p. 98)   See **tholos**.

thrust (p. 172)   The outward pressure caused by the weight of a **vault** and supported by **buttressing**. See **arch**.

tierceron (p. 554)   In vault construction, a secondary rib that arcs from a **springing** point to the rib that runs lengthwise through the **vault**, called the ridge rib.

tondo (p. 128)   A painting or **relief sculpture** of circular shape.

torana (p. 300)   In Indian architecture, an ornamented gateway **arch** in a temple, usually leading to the **stupa**.

torc (p. 151)   A circular neck ring worn by Celtic warriors.

toron (p. 417)   In West African **mosque** architecture, the wooden beams that project from the walls. Torons are used as support for the scaffolding erected annually for the replastering of the building.

tracery (p. 502)   Stonework or woodwork applied to wall surfaces or filling the open space of windows. In **plate tracery**, openings are cut through the wall. In **bar tracery**, **mullions** divide the space into vertical segments and form decorative patterns at the top of the opening or panel.

transept (p. 228)   The arm of a **cruciform** church, perpendicular to the **nave**. The point where the nave and transept cross is called the crossing. Beyond the crossing lies the **sanctuary**, whether **apse**, choir, or chevet.

transverse arch (p. 457)   An **arch** that connects the wall **piers** on both sides of an interior space, up and over a stone **vault**.

trefoil (p. 294)   An ornamental design made up of three rounded lobes placed adjacent to one another.

triforium (p. 502)   The element of the interior elevation of a church, found directly below the **clerestory** and consisting of a series of **arched** openings. The triforium can be made up of openings from a narrow wall passageway, or it can be attached directly to the wall.

triglyph (p. 110)   Rectangular block between the **metopes** of a **Doric frieze**. Identified by the three carved vertical grooves, which approximate the appearance of the end of a wooden beam.

triptych (p. 564)   An artwork made up of three panels. The panels may be hinged together so the side segments (wings) fold over the central area.

trompe l'oeil (p. 617)   A manner of representation in which the appearance of natural space and objects is re-created with the express intention of fooling the eye of the viewer, who may be convinced that the subject actually exists as three-dimensional reality.

trumeau (p. 473)   A **column**, **pier**, or post found at the center of a large **portal** or doorway, supporting the **lintel**.

tugra (p. 284)   A **calligraphic** imperial monogram used in Ottoman courts.

tukutuku (p. 871)   Lattice panels created by women from the Maori culture and used in architecture.

Tuscan order (p. 161)   See **order**.

twining (p. 845)   A basketry technique in which short rods are sewn together vertically. The panels are then joined together to form a vessel.

tympanum (p. 473)   In Classical architecture, the vertical panel of the **pediment**. In medieval and later architecture, the area over a door enclosed by an **arch** and a **lintel**, often decorated with sculpture or **mosaic**.

ukiyo-e (p. 994)   A Japanese term for a type of popular art that was favored from the sixteenth century, particularly in the form of color **woodblock prints**. *Ukiyo-e* prints often depicted the world of the common people in Japan, such as courtesans and actors, as well as landscapes and myths.

undercutting (p. 214)   A technique in sculpture by which the material is cut back under the edges so that the remaining form projects strongly forward, casting deep shadows.

underglaze (p. 799)   Color or decoration applied to a ceramic piece before glazing.

upeti (p. 874)   A carved wooden design tablet, used to create patterns in cloth by dragging the fabric across it, and found in Pacific cultures.

urna (p. 303)   In Buddhist art, the curl of hair on the forehead that is a characteristic mark of a buddha. The *urna* is a symbol of divine wisdom.

ushnisha (p. 303)   In Asian art, a round turban or tiara symbolizing royalty and, when worn by a buddha, enlightenment.

vanishing point (p. 608)   In a **perspective** system, the point on the **horizon line** at which orthogonals meet. A complex system can have multiple vanishing points.

vanitas (p. 751)   An image, especially popular in Europe during the seventeenth century, in which all the objects symbolize the transience of life. *Vanitas* paintings are usually of still lifes or genre subjects.

vault (p. 17)   An arched masonry structure that spans an interior space. **Barrel** or tunnel vault: an elongated or continuous semicircular vault, shaped like a half-cylinder.

Corbeled vault: a vault made by projecting **courses** of stone. **Groin** or cross vault: a vault created by the intersection of two barrel vaults of equal size which creates four side compartments of identical size and shape. Quadrant or half-barrel vault: as the name suggests a half-barrel vault. **Rib vault**: ribs (extra masonry) demarcate the junctions of a groin vault. Ribs may function to reinforce the groins or may be purely decorative. See also **corbeling**.

veduta (p. 913)   Italian for "vista" or "view." Paintings, drawings, or prints often of expansive city scenes or of harbors.

vellum (p. 243)   A fine animal skin prepared for writing and painting. See also **parchment**.

verism (p. 170)   style in which artists concern themselves with describing the exterior likeness of an object or person, usually by rendering its visible details in a finely executed, meticulous manner.

vihara (p. 301)   From the Sanskrit term meaning "for wanderers." A *vihara* is, in general, a Buddhist monastery in India. It also signifies monks' cells and gathering places in such a monastery.

volute (p. 110)   A spiral scroll, as seen on an **Ionic capital**.

votive figure (p. 31)   An image created as a devotional offering to a god or other deity.

voussoir (p. 172)   The oblong, wedge-shaped stone blocks used to build an arch. The topmost voussoir is called a **keystone**.

warp (p. 286)   The vertical threads in a weaver's loom. Warp threads make up a fixed framework that provides the structure for the entire piece of cloth, and are thus often thicker than weft threads. See also **weft**.

wattle and daub (p. 17)   A wall construction method combining upright branches, woven with twigs (wattles) and plastered or filled with clay or mud (daub).

weft (p. 286)   The horizontal threads in a woven piece of cloth. Weft threads are woven at right angles to and through the warp threads to make up the bulk of the decorative pattern. In carpets, the weft is often completely covered or formed by the rows of trimmed knots that form the carpet's soft surface. See also **warp**.

westwork (p. 439)   The monumental, west-facing entrance section of a Carolignian, Ottonian, or Romanesque church. The exterior consists of multiple stories between two towers; the interior includes an entrance vestibule, a chapel, and a series of **galleries** overlooking the nave.

white-ground (p. 141)   A type of ancient Greek pottery in which the background color of the object was painted with a **slip** that turns white in the firing process. Figures and details were added by painting on or **incising** into this slip. White-ground wares were popular in the Classical period as funerary objects.

woodblock print (p. 589)   A print made from one or more carved wooden blocks. In Japan, woodblock prints were made using multiple blocks carved in **relief**, usually with a block for each color in the finished print. See also **woodcut**.

woodcut (p. 590)   A type of print made by carving a design into a wooden block. The ink is applied to the block with a roller. As the ink remains only on the raised areas between the carved-away lines, these carved-away areas and lines provide the white areas of the print. Also: the process by which the woodcut is made.

yaksha, yakshi (p. 296)   The male (*yaksha*) and female (*yakshi*) nature spirits that act as agents of the Hindu gods. Their sculpted images are often found on Hindu temples and other sacred places, particularly at the entrances.

ziggurat (p. 28)   In Mesopotamia, a tall stepped tower of earthen materials, often supporting a shrine.

Susan V. Craig, updated by Carrie L. McDade

This bibliography is composed of books in English that are appropriate "further reading" titles. Most items on this list are available in good libraries, whether college, university, or public institutions. Recently published works have been emphasized so that the research information would be current. There are three classifications of listings: general surveys and art history reference tools, including journals and Internet directories; surveys of large periods that encompass multiple chapters (ancient art in the Western tradition, European medieval art, European Renaissance through eighteenth-century art, modern art in the West, Asian art, and African and Oceanic art, and art of the Americas); and books for individual Chapters 1 through 32.

General Art History Surveys and Reference Tools

Adams, Laurie Schneider. *Art across Time.* 4th ed. New York: McGraw-Hill, 2011.

Barnet, Sylvan. *A Short Guide to Writing about Art.* 10th ed. Upper Saddle River, NJ: Pearson/Prentice Hall, 2010.

Bony, Anne. *Design: History, Main Trends, Main Figures.* Edinburgh: Chambers, 2005.

Boström, Antonia. *Encyclopedia of Sculpture.* 3 vols. New York: Fitzroy Dearborn, 2004.

Broude, Norma, and Mary D. Garrard, eds. *Feminism and Art History: Questioning the Litany.* Icon Editions. New York: Harper & Row, 1982.

Chadwick, Whitney. *Women, Art, and Society.* 4th ed. New York: Thames & Hudson, 2007.

Chilvers, Ian, ed. *The Oxford Dictionary of Art.* 4th ed. New York: Oxford Univ. Press, 2009.

Curl, James Stevens. *A Dictionary of Architecture and Landscape Architecture.* 2nd ed. Oxford: Oxford Univ. Press, 2006.

Davies, Penelope J. E., et al. *Janson's History of Art: The Western Tradition.* 8th ed. Upper Saddle River, NJ: Prentice Hall, 2010.

The Dictionary of Art. Ed. Jane Turner. 34 vols. New York: Grove's Dictionaries, 1996.

Encyclopedia of World Art. 17 vols. New York: McGraw-Hill, 1959–84.

Frank, Patrick, Duane Preble, and Sarah Preble. *Prebles' Artforms.* 10th ed. Upper Saddle River, NJ: Pearson/Prentice Hall, 2008.

Gaze, Delia, ed. *Dictionary of Women Artists.* 2 vols. London: Fitzroy Dearborn, 1997.

Griffiths, Antony. *Prints and Printmaking: An Introduction to the History and Techniques.* 2nd ed. London: British Museum Press, 1996.

Hadden, Peggy. *The Quotable Artist.* New York: Allworth Press, 2002.

Hall, James. *Dictionary of Subjects and Symbols in Art.* 2nd ed. Boulder, CO: Westview Press, 2008.

Holt, Elizabeth Gilmore, ed. *A Documentary History of Art.* 3 vols. New Haven: Yale Univ. Press, 1986.

Honour, Hugh, and John Fleming. *The Visual Arts: A History.* 7th ed. rev. Upper Saddle River, NJ: Pearson/Prentice Hall, 2010.

Johnson, Paul. *Art: A New History.* New York: HarperCollins, 2003.

Kemp, Martin, ed. *The Oxford History of Western Art.* Oxford: Oxford Univ. Press, 2000.

Kleiner, Fred S. *Gardner's Art through the Ages.* Enhanced 13th ed. Belmont, CA: Thomson/Wadsworth, 2011.

Kostof, Spiro. *A History of Architecture: Settings and Rituals.* 2nd ed. Revised. Greg Castillo. New York: Oxford Univ. Press, 1995.

Mackenzie, Lynn. *Non-Western Art: A Brief Guide.* 2nd ed. Upper Saddle River, NJ: Pearson/Prentice Hall, 2001.

Marmor, Max, and Alex Ross, eds. *Guide to the Literature of Art History 2.* Chicago: American Library Association, 2005.

Onians, John, ed. *Atlas of World Art.* New York: Oxford Univ. Press, 2004.

Sayre, Henry M. *Writing about Art.* 6th ed. Upper Saddle River, NJ: Pearson/Prentice Hall, 2009.

Sed-Rajna, Gabrielle. *Jewish Art.* Trans. Sara Friedman and Mira Reich. New York: Abrams, 1997.

Slatkin, Wendy. *Women Artists in History: From Antiquity to the Present.* 4th ed. Upper Saddle River, NJ: Pearson/Prentice Hall, 2001.

Sutton, Ian. *Western Architecture: From Ancient Greece to the Present.* World of Art. New York: Thames & Hudson, 1999.

Trachtenberg, Marvin, and Isabelle Hyman. *Architecture, from Prehistory to Postmodernity.* 2nd ed. Upper Saddle River, NJ: Pearson/Prentice Hall, 2002.

Watkin, David. *A History of Western Architecture.* 4th ed. New York: Watson-Guptill, 2005.

Art History Journals: A Select List of Current Titles

African Arts. Quarterly. Los Angeles: Univ. of California at Los Angeles, James S. Coleman African Studies Center, 1967–.

American Art: The Journal of the Smithsonian American Art Museum. 3/year. Chicago: Univ. of Chicago Press, 1987–.

American Indian Art Magazine. Quarterly. Scottsdale, AZ: American Indian Art Inc., 1975–.

American Journal of Archaeology. Quarterly. Boston: Archaeological Institute of America, 1885–.

Antiquity: A Periodical of Archaeology. Quarterly. Cambridge: Antiquity Publications Ltd., 1927–.

Apollo: The International Magazine of the Arts. Monthly. London: Apollo Magazine Ltd., 1925–.

Architectural History. Annually. Farnham, UK: Society of Architectural Historians of Great Britain, 1958–.

Archives of American Art Journal. Quarterly. Washington, DC: Archives of American Art, Smithsonian Institution, 1960–.

Archives of Asian Art. Annually. New York: Asia Society, 1945–.

Ars Orientalis: The Arts of Asia, Southeast Asia, and Islam. Annually. Ann Arbor: Univ. of Michigan Dept. of Art History, 1954–.

Art Bulletin. Quarterly. New York: College Art Association, 1913–.

Art History: Journal of the Association of Art Historians. 5/year. Oxford: Blackwell Publishing Ltd., 1978–.

Art in America. Monthly. New York: Brant Publications Inc., 1913–.

Art Journal. Quarterly. New York: College Art Association, 1960–.

Art Nexus. Quarterly. Bogota, Colombia: Arte en Colombia Ltda, 1976–.

Art Papers Magazine. Bimonthly. Atlanta: Atlanta Art Papers Inc., 1976–.

Artforum International. 10/year. New York: Artforum International Magazine Inc., 1962–.

Artnews. 11/year. New York: Artnews LLC, 1902–.

Bulletin of the Metropolitan Museum of Art. Quarterly. New York: Metropolitan Museum of Art, 1905–.

Burlington Magazine. Monthly. London: Burlington Magazine Publications Ltd., 1903–.

Dumbarton Oaks Papers. Annually. Locust Valley, NY: J. J. Augustin Inc., 1940–.

Flash Art International. Bimonthly. Trevi, Italy: Giancarlo Politi Editore, 1980–.

Gesta. Semiannually. New York: International Center of Medieval Art, 1963–.

History of Photography. Quarterly. Abingdon, UK: Taylor & Francis Ltd., 1976–.

International Review of African American Art. Quarterly. Hampton, VA: International Review of African American Art, 1976–.

Journal of Design History. Quarterly. Oxford: Oxford Univ. Press, 1988–.

Journal of Egyptian Archaeology. Annually. London: Egypt Exploration Society, 1914–.

Journal of Hellenic Studies. Annually. London: Society for the Promotion of Hellenic Studies, 1880–.

Journal of Roman Archaeology. Annually. Portsmouth, RI: Journal of Roman Archaeology LLC, 1988–.

Journal of the Society of Architectural Historians. Quarterly. Chicago: Society of Architectural Historians, 1940–.

Journal of the Warburg and Courtauld Institutes. Annually. London: Warburg Institute, 1937–.

Leonardo: Art, Science and Technology. 6/year. Cambridge, MA: MIT Press, 1968–.

Marg. Quarterly. Mumbai, India: Scientific Publishers, 1946–.

Master Drawings. Quarterly. New York: Master Drawings Association, 1963–.

October. Cambridge, MA: MIT Press, 1976–.

Oxford Art Journal. 3/year. Oxford: Oxford Univ. Press, 1978–.

Parkett. 3/year. Zürich, Switzerland: Parkett Verlag AG, 1984–.

Print Quarterly. Quarterly. London: Print Quarterly Publications, 1984–.

Simiolus: Netherlands Quarterly for the History of Art. Quarterly. Apeldoorn, Netherlands: Stichting voor Nederlandse Kunsthistorische Publicaties, 1966–.

Woman's Art Journal. Semiannually. Philadelphia: Old City Publishing Inc., 1980–.

Internet Directories for Art History Information: A Selected List

ARCHITECTURE AND BUILDING,
http://www.library.unlv.edu/arch/rsrce/webresources/
A directory of architecture websites collected by Jeanne Brown at the Univ. of Nevada at Las Vegas. Topical lists include architecture, building and construction, design, history, housing, planning, preservation, and landscape architecture. Most entries include a brief annotation and the last date the link was accessed by the compiler.

ART HISTORY RESOURCES ON THE WEB,
http://witcombe.sbc.edu/ARTHLinks.html
Authored by Professor Christopher L. C. E. Witcombe of Sweet Briar College in Virginia, since 1995, the site includes an impressive number of links for various art historical eras as well as links to research resources, museums, and galleries. The content is frequently updated.

ART IN FLUX: A DIRECTORY OF RESOURCES FOR RESEARCH IN CONTEMPORARY ART,
http://www.boisestate.edu/art/artinflux/intro.html
Cheryl K. Shurtleff of Boise State Univ. in Idaho, has authored this directory, which includes sites selected according to their relevance to the study of national or international contemporary art and artists. The subsections include artists, museums, theory, reference, and links.

ARTCYCLOPEDIA: THE GUIDE TO GREAT ART ON THE INTERNET
http://www.artcyclopedia.com
With more than 2,100 art sites and 75,000 links, this is one of the most comprehensive web directories for artists and art topics. The primary search is by artist's name but access is also available by title of artwork, artistic movement, museums and galleries, nationality, period, and medium.

MOTHER OF ALL ART AND ART HISTORY LINKS PAGES
http://umich.edu/~motherha
Maintained by the Dept. of the History of Art at the Univ. of Michigan, this directory covers art history departments, art museums, fine arts schools and departments as well as links to research resources. Each entry includes annotations.

VOICE OF THE SHUTTLE,
http://vos.ucsb.edu
Sponsored by Univ. of California, Santa Barbara, this directory includes more than 70 pages of links to humanities and humanities-related resources on the Internet. The structured guide includes specific subsections on architecture, on art (modern and contemporary), and on art history. Links usually include a one-sentence explanation and the resource is frequently updated with new information.

ARTBABBLE
http://www.artbabble.org/
An online community created by staff at the Indianapolis Museum of Art to showcase art-based video content, including interviews with artists and curators, original documentaries, and art installation videos. Partners and contributors to the project include Art21, Los Angeles County Museum of Art, The Museum of Modern Art, The New York Public Library, San Francisco Museum of Modern Art, and Smithsonian American Art Museum.

YAHOO! ARTS>ART HISTORY,
http://dir.yahoo.com/Arts/Art_History/
Another extensive directory of art links organized into subdivisions with one of the most extensive being "Periods and

Movements." Links include the name of the site as well as a few words of explanation.

Asian Art, General

Addiss, Stephen, Gerald Groemer, and J. Thomas Rimer, eds. *Traditional Japanese Arts and Culture: An Illustrated Sourcebook*. Honolulu: Univ. of Hawai'i Press, 2006.

Barnhart, Richard M. *Three Thousand Years of Chinese Painting*. New Haven: Yale Univ. Press, 1997.

Blunden, Caroline, and Mark Elvin. *Cultural Atlas of China*. 2nd ed. New York: Checkmark Books, 1998.

Brown, Kerry, ed. *Sikh Art and Literature*. New York: Routledge in collaboration with the Sikh Foundation, 1999.

Chang, Léon Long-Yien, and Peter Miller. *Four Thousand Years of Chinese Calligraphy*. Chicago: Univ. of Chicago Press, 1990.

Chang, Yang-mo. *Arts of Korea*. Ed. Judith G. Smith. New York: Metropolitan Museum of Art, 1998.

Clark, John. *Modern Asian Art*. Honolulu: Univ. of Hawai'i Press, 1998.

Clunas, Craig. *Art in China*. 2nd ed. Oxford History of Art. Oxford: Oxford Univ. Press, 2009.

Coaldrake, William H. *Architecture and Authority in Japan*. London: Routledge, 1996.

Cohen, Warren I. *East Asian Art and American Culture: A Study in International Relations*. New York: Columbia Univ. Press, 1992.

Collcutt, Martin, Marius Jansen, and Isao Kumakura. *Cultural Atlas of Japan*. New York: Facts on File, 1988.

Craven, Roy C. *Indian Art: A Concise History*. Rev. ed. World of Art. New York: Thames & Hudson, 1997.

Dehejia, Vidya. *Indian Art. Art & Ideas*. London: Phaidon Press, 1997.

Fisher, Robert E. *Buddhist Art and Architecture*. World of Art. New York: Thames & Hudson, 1993.

Fu, Xinian. *Chinese Architecture*. Ed. & exp., Nancy S. Steinhardt. New Haven: Yale Univ. Press, 2002.

Hearn, Maxwell K., and Judith G. Smith, eds. *Arts of the Sung and Yüan: Papers Prepared for an International Symposium*. New York: Dept. of Asian Art, Metropolitan Museum of Art, 1996.

Heibonsha Survey of Japanese Art. 31 vols. New York: Weatherhill, 1972–80.

Hertz, Betti-Sue. *Past in Reverse: Contemporary Art of East Asia*. San Diego: San Diego Museum of Art, 2004.

Japanese Arts Library. 15 vols. New York: Kodansha International, 1977–87.

Kerlogue, Fiona. *Arts of Southeast Asia*. World of Art. New York: Thames & Hudson, 2004.

Khanna, Balraj, and George Michell. *Human and Divine: 2000 Years of Indian Sculpture*. London: Hayward Gallery, 2000.

Lee, Sherman E. *A History of Far Eastern Art*. 5th ed. Ed. Naomi Noble Richards. New York: Abrams, 1994.

———. *China, 5000 Years: Innovation and Transformation in the Arts*. New York: Solomon R. Guggenheim Museum, 1998.

Liu, Cary Y., and Dora C.Y. Ching, eds. *Arts of the Sung and Yüan: Ritual, Ethnicity, and Style in Painting*. Princeton: Art Museum, Princeton Univ., 1999.

McArthur, Meher. *The Arts of Asia: Materials, Techniques, Styles*. New York: Thames & Hudson, 2005.

———. *Reading Buddhist Art: An Illustrated Guide to Buddhist Signs and Symbols*. New York: Thames & Hudson, 2002.

Mason, Penelope. *History of Japanese Art*. 2nd ed. Upper Saddle River, NJ: Pearson/Prentice Hall, 2005.

Michell, George. *Hindu Art and Architecture*. World of Art. London: Thames & Hudson, 2000.

———. *The Penguin Guide to the Monuments of India*. 2 vols. New York: Viking, 1989.

Mitter, Partha. *Indian Art*. Oxford History of Art. Oxford: Oxford Univ. Press, 2001.

Murase, Miyeko. *Bridge of Dreams: The Mary Griggs Burke Collection of Japanese Art*. New York: Metropolitan Museum of Art, 2000.

Nickel, Lukas, ed. *Return of the Buddha: The Qingzhou Discoveries*. London: Royal Academy of Arts, 2002.

Pak, Youngsook, and Roderick Whitfield. *Buddhist Sculpture*. Handbook of Korean Art. London: Laurence King, 2003.

Sullivan, Michael. *The Arts of China*. 5th ed., rev. & exp. Berkeley: Univ. of California Press, 2008.

Thorp, Robert L., and Richard Ellis Vinograd. *Chinese Art & Culture*. New York: Abrams, 2001.

Topsfield, Andrew, ed. *In the Realm of Gods and Kings: Arts of India*. London: Philip Wilson, 2004.

Tucker, Jonathan. *The Silk Road: Art and History*. Chicago: Art Media Resources, 2003.

Tregear, Mary. *Chinese Art*. Rev. ed. World of Art. New York: Thames & Hudson, 1997.

Vainker S. J. *Chinese Pottery and Porcelain: From Prehistory to the Present*. New York: Braziller, 1991.

African and Oceanic Art and Art of the Americas, General

Anderson, Richard L., and Karen L. Field, eds. *Art in Small-Scale Societies: Contemporary Readings*. Upper Saddle River, NJ: Pearson/Prentice Hall, 1993.

Bacquart, Jean-Baptiste. *The Tribal Arts of Africa*. New York: Thames & Hudson, 1998.

Bassani, Ezio, ed. *Arts of Africa: 7000 Years of African Art*. Milan: Skira, 2005.

Benson, Elizabeth P. *Retratos: 2,000 Years of Latin American Portraits*. San Antonio, TX: San Antonio Museum of Art, 2004.

Berlo, Janet Catherine, and Lee Anne Wilson. *Arts of Africa, Oceania, and the Americas: Selected Readings*. Upper Saddle River, NJ: Prentice Hall, 1993.

Calloway, Colin G. *First Peoples: A Documentary Survey of American Indian History*. 3rd ed. Boston: Bedford/St. Martin's, 2008.

Coote, Jeremy, and Anthony Shelton, eds. *Anthropology, Art, and Aesthetics*. New York: Oxford Univ. Press, 1992.

Drewal, Henry, and John Pemberton III. *Yoruba: Nine Centuries of African Art and Thought*. New York: Center for African Art, 1989.

Evans, Susan Toby. *Ancient Mexico & Central America: Archaeology and Culture History*. 2nd ed. New York: Thames & Hudson, 2008.

———, and David L. Webster, eds. *Archaeology of Ancient Mexico and Central America: An Encyclopedia*. New York: Garland, 2001.

———, and Joanne Pillsbury, eds. *Palaces of the Ancient New World: A Symposium at Dumbarton Oaks, 10th and 11th October, 1998*. Washington, DC: Dumbarton Oaks Research Library and Collection, 2004.

Geoffroy-Schneiter, Bérénice. *Tribal Arts*. New York: Vendome Press, 2000.

Hiller, Susan, ed. & compiled. *The Myth of Primitivism: Perspectives on Art*. London: Routledge, 1991.

Mack, John, ed. *Africa, Arts and Cultures*. London: British Museum Press, 2000.

Mexico: Splendors of Thirty Centuries. New York: Metropolitan Museum of Art, 1990.

Nunley, John W., and Cara McCarty. *Masks: Faces of Culture*. New York: Abrams in assoc. with the Saint Louis Art Museum, 1999.

Perani, Judith, and Fred T. Smith. *The Visual Arts of Africa: Gender, Power, and Life Cycle Rituals*. Upper Saddle River, NJ: Pearson/Prentice Hall, 1998.

Phillips, Tom, ed. *Africa: The Art of a Continent*. New York: Prestel, 1995.

Price, Sally. *Primitive Art in Civilized Places*. 2nd ed. Chicago: Univ. of Chicago Press, 2001.

Rabineau, Phyllis. *Feather Arts: Beauty, Wealth, and Spirit from Five Continents*. Chicago: Field Museum of Natural History, 1979.

Schuster, Carl, and Edmund Carpenter. *Patterns that Connect: Social Symbolism in Ancient & Tribal Art*. New York: Abrams, 1996.

Scott, John F. *Latin American Art: Ancient to Modern*. Gainesville: Univ. Press of Florida, 1999.

Stepan, Peter. *Africa*. Trans. John Gabriel and Elizabeth Schwaiger. London: Prestel, 2001.

Visonà, Monica Blackmun, et al. *A History of Art in Africa*. 2nd ed. Upper Saddle River, NJ: Pearson/Prentice Hall, 2008.

Chapter 8 Islamic Art

Al-Faruqi, Isma'il R., and Lois Ibsen Al Faruqi. *Cultural Atlas of Islam*. New York: Macmillan, 1986.

Atil, Esin. *The Age of Sultan Suleyman the Magnificent*. Washington, DC: National Gallery of Art, 1987.

Baker, Patricia L. *Islam and the Religious Arts*. London: Continuum, 2004.

Barry, Michael A. *Figurative Art in Medieval Islam and the Riddle of Bihzâd of Herât (1465–1535)*. Paris: Flammarion, 2004.

Blair, Sheila S., and Jonathan Bloom. *The Art and Architecture of Islam 1250–1800*. Pelican History of Art. New Haven: Yale Univ. Press, 1995.

Denny, Walter B. *Iznik: The Artistry of Ottoman Ceramics*. New York: Thames & Hudson, 2004.

Dodds, Jerrilynn D., ed. *Al-Andalus: The Art of Islamic Spain*. New York: Metropolitan Museum of Art, 1992.

Ecker, Heather. *Caliphs and Kings: The Art and Influence of Islamic Spain*. Washington, DC: Arthur M. Sackler Gallery, Smithsonian Institution, 2004.

Ettinghausen, Richard, Oleg Grabar, and Marilyn Jenkins-Madina. *Islamic Art and Architecture, 650–1250*. 2nd ed. Pelican History of Art. New Haven: Yale Univ. Press, 2001.

Frishman, Martin, and Hasan-Uddin Khan. *The Mosque: History, Architectural Development and Regional Diversity*. London: Thames & Hudson, 1994.

Grabar, Oleg. *The Formation of Islamic Art*. Rev. and enlarged. New Haven: Yale Univ. Press, 1987.

———. *The Great Mosque of Isfahan*. New York: New York Univ. Press, 1990.

———. *Islamic Visual Culture, 1100–1800*. Burlington, VT: Ashgate, 2006.

———. *Mostly Miniatures: An Introduction to Persian Painting*. Princeton: Princeton Univ. Press, 2000.

———, Mohammad Al-Asad, Abeer Audeh, and Said Nuseibeh. *The Shape of the Holy: Early Islamic Jerusalem*. Princeton: Princeton Univ. Press, 1996.

Hillenbrand, Robert. *Islamic Art and Architecture*. World of Art. London: Thames & Hudson, 1999.

Irwin, Robert. *The Alhambra*. Cambridge, MA: Harvard Univ. Press, 2004.

Khalili, Nasser D. *Visions of Splendour in Islamic Art and Culture*. London: Worth Press, 2008.

Komaroff, Linda, and Stefano Carboni, eds. *The Legacy of Genghis Khan: Courtly Art and Culture in Western Asia, 1256–1353*. New York: Metropolitan Museum of Art, 2002.

Lentz, Thomas W., and Glenn D. Lowry. *Timur and the Princely Vision: Persian Art and Culture in the Fifteenth Century*. Los Angeles: Los Angeles County Museum of Art, 1989.

Necipolu, Gülru. *The Age of Sinan: Architectural Culture in the Ottoman Empire*. Princeton: Princeton Univ. Press, 2005.

Petruccioli, Attilio, and Khalil K. Pirani, eds. *Understanding Islamic Architecture*. New York: Routledge Curzon, 2002.

Roxburgh, David J., ed. *Turks: A Journey of a Thousand Years, 600–1600*. London: Royal Academy of Arts, 2005.

Sims, Eleanor, B. I. Marshak, and Ernst J. Grube. *Peerless Images: Persian Painting and Its Sources*. New Haven: Yale Univ. Press, 2002.

Stanley, Tim, Mariam Rosser-Owen, and Stephen Vernoit. *Palace and Mosque: Islamic Art from the Middle East*. London: V&A Publications, 2004.

Stierlin, Henri. *Islamic Art and Architecture*. New York: Thames & Hudson, 2002.

Tadgell, Christopher. *Four Caliphates: The Formation and Development of the Islamic Tradition*. London: Ellipsis, 1998.

Ward, R. M. *Islamic Metalwork*. New York: Thames & Hudson, 1993.

Watson, Oliver. *Ceramics from Islamic Lands*. New York: Thames & Hudson in assoc. with the al-Sabah Collection, Dar al-Athar al-Islamiyyah, Kuwait National Museum, 2004.

Chapter 9 Art of South and Southeast Asia before 1200

Atherton, Cynthia Packert. *The Sculpture of Early Medieval Rajasthan*. Studies in Asian Art and Archaeology, vol. 21. New York: Brill, 1997.

Behl, Benoy K. *The Ajanta Caves: Artistic Wonder of Ancient Buddhist India*. New York: Abrams, 1998.

Behrendt, Kurt A. *The Buddhist Architecture of Gandhara*. Handbook of Oriental Studies: Section Two: India, vol. 17. Boston: Brill, 2004.

Chakrabarti, Dilip K. *India, an Archaeological History: Palaeolithic Beginnings to Early Historic Foundations*. 2nd ed. New York: Oxford Univ. Press, 2009.

Craven, Roy C. *Indian Art: A Concise History*. Rev. ed. World of Art. New York: Thames & Hudson, 1997.

Czuma, Stanislaw J. *Kushan Sculpture: Images from Early India*. Cleveland: Cleveland Museum of Art, 1985.

Dehejia, Vidya. *Art of the Imperial Cholas*. New York: Columbia Univ. Press, 1990.

———. *The Sensuous and the Sacred: Chola Bronzes from South India*. New York: American Federation of Arts, 2002.

Dessai, Vishakha N., and Darielle Mason, eds. *Gods, Guardians, and Lovers: Temple Sculptures from North India, a.d. 700–1200*. New York: Asia Society Galleries, 1993.

Dhavalikar, Madhukar Keshav. *Ellora*. New York: Oxford Univ. Press, 2003.

Girard-Geslan, Maud. *Art of Southeast Asia*. Trans. J. A. Underwood. New York: Abrams, Inc., 1998.

Heller, Amy. *Early Himalayan Art*. Oxford: Ashmolean Museum, 2008.

Huntington, Susan L. *The Art of Ancient India: Buddhist, Hindu, Jain*. New York: Weatherhill, 1985.

———. *Leaves from the Bodhi Tree: The Art of Pala India (8th–12th Centuries) and Its International Legacy.* Dayton, OH: Dayton Art Institute, 1990.

Hutt, Michael. *Nepal: A Guide to the Art and Architecture of the Kathmandu Valley.* Boston: Shambhala, 1995.

Knox, Robert. *Amaravati: Buddhist Sculpture from the Great Stupa.* London: British Museum Press, 1992.

Khanna, Sucharita. *Dancing Divinities in Indian Art: 8th–12th Century a.d.* Delhi: Sharada Pub. House, 1999.

Kramrisch, Stella. *The Art of Nepal.* New York: Abrams, 1964.

———. The Presence of Siva. Princeton: Princeton Univ. Press, 1981.

Meister, Michael, ed. *Encyclopedia of Indian Temple Architecture.* 2 vols. in 7. Philadelphia: Univ. of Pennsylvania Press, 1983.

Michell, George. *Elephanta.* Bombay: India Book House, 2002.

———. *Hindu Art and Architecture.* World of Art. London: Thames & Hudson, 2000.

Mitter, Partha. *Indian Art.* Oxford History of Art. Oxford: Oxford Univ. Press, 2001.

Neumayer, Erwin. *Lines on Stone: The Prehistoric Rock Art of India.* New Delhi: Manohar, 1993.

Pal, Pratapaditya, ed. *The Ideal Image: The Gupta Sculptural Tradition and Its Influence.* New York: Asia Society, 1978.

Poster, Amy G. *From Indian Earth: 4,000 Years of Terracotta Art.* Brooklyn, NY: Brooklyn Museum, 1986.

Skelton, Robert, and Mark Francis. *Arts of Bengal: The Heritage of Bangladesh and Eastern India.* London: Whitechapel Art Gallery, 1979.

Stierlin, Henri. *Hindu India: From Khajuraho to the Temple City of Madurai.* Taschen's World Architecture. New York: Taschen, 1998.

Tadgell, Christopher. *India and South-East Asia: The Buddhist and Hindu Tradition.* New York: Whitney Library of Design, 1998.

Williams, Joanna G. *Art of Gupta India, Empire and Province.* Princeton: Princeton Univ. Press, 1982.

Chapter 10 Chinese and Korean Art before 1279

Ciarla, Roberto, ed. *The Eternal Army: The Terracotta Soldiers of the First Chinese Emperor.* Vercelli: White Star, 2005.

Fong, Wen, ed. *Beyond Representation: Chinese Painting and Calligraphy, 8th–14th Century.* Princeton Monographs in Art and Archaeology, 48. New York: Metropolitan Museum of Art, 1992.

Fraser, Sarah Elizabeth. *Performing the Visual: The Practice of Buddhist Wall Painting in China and Central Asia, 618–960.* Stanford, CA: Stanford Univ. Press, 2004.

James, Jean M. *A Guide to the Tomb and Shrine Art of the Han Dynasty 206 b.c.–a.d. 220.* Chinese Studies, 2. Lewiston, NY: Mellen Press, 1996.

Karetzky, Patricia Eichenbaum. *Court Art of the Tang.* Lanham, MD: Univ. Press of America, 1996.

Kim, Kumja Paik. *Goryeo Dynasty: Korea's Age of Enlightenment, 918–1392.* San Francisco: Asian Art Museum—Chong-Moon Lee Center for Asian Art and Culture in cooperation with the National Museum of Korea and the Nara National Museum, 2003.

Li, Jian, ed. *The Glory of the Silk Road: Art from Ancient China.* Dayton, OH: Dayton Art Institute, 2003.

Little, Stephen, and Shawn Eichman. *Taoism and the Arts of China.* Chicago: Art Institute of Chicago, 2000.

Liu, Cary Y., Dora C.Y. Ching, and Judith G. Smith, eds. *Character & Context in Chinese Calligraphy.* Princeton: Art Museum, Princeton Univ., 1999.

Luo, Zhewen. *Ancient Pagodas in China.* Beijing, China: Foreign Languages Press, 1994.

Ma, Chengyuan. *Ancient Chinese Bronzes.* Ed. Hsio-Yen Shih. Hong Kong: Oxford Univ. Press, 1986.

Murck, Alfreda. *Poetry and Painting in Song China: The Subtle Art of Dissent.* Harvard-Yenching Institute Monograph Series. Cambridge, MA: Harvard Univ. Asia Center for the Harvard-Yenching Institute, 2000.

Ortiz, Valérie Malenfer. *Dreaming the Southern Song Landscape: The Power of Illusion in Chinese Painting.* Studies in Asian Art and Archaeology, vol. 22. Boston: Brill, 1999.

Paludan, Ann. *Chinese Tomb Figurines.* Hong Kong: Oxford Univ. Press, 1994.

Portal, Jane. *Korea: Art and Archaeology.* New York: Thames & Hudson, 2000.

Rawson, Jessica. *Mysteries of Ancient China: New Discoveries from the Early Dynasties.* London: British Museum Press, 1996.

Rhie, Marylin M. *Early Buddhist Art of China and Central Asia.* 2 vols in 3. Handbuch der Orientalistik. Vierte Abteilung; China, 12. Leiden: Brill, 1999.

Scarpari, Maurizio. *Splendours of Ancient China.* London: Thames & Hudson, 2000.

So, Jenny F. ed. *Noble Riders from Pines and Deserts: The Artistic Legacy of the Qidan.* Hong Kong: Art Museum, Chinese Univ. of Hong Kong, 2004.

Sturman, Peter Charles. *Mi Fu: Style and the Art of Calligraphy in Northern Song.* New Haven: Yale Univ. Press, 1997.

Wang, Eugene Y. *Shaping the Lotus Sutra: Buddhist Visual Culture in Medieval China.* Seattle: Univ. of Washington Press, 2005.

Watson, William. *The Arts of China to a.d. 900.* Pelican History of Art. New Haven: Yale Univ. Press, 1995.

———. *The Arts of China 900–1620.* Pelican History of Art. New Haven: Yale Univ. Press, 2000. Reissue ed. 2003.

Watt, James C.Y. *China: Dawn of a Golden Age, 200–750 a.d..* New York: Metropolitan Museum of Art, 2004.

Whitfield, Susan, and Ursula Sims-Williams, eds. *The Silk Road: Trade, Travel, War and Faith.* Chicago: Serindia Publications, 2004.

Wu Hung. *Monumentality in Early Chinese Art and Architecture.* Stanford: Stanford Univ. Press, 1995.

Yang, Xiaoneng, ed. *The Golden Age of Chinese Archaeology: Celebrated Discoveries from the People's Republic of China.* Washington DC: National Gallery of Art, 1999.

Chapter 11 Japanese Art before 1333

Cunningham, Michael R. *Buddhist Treasures from Nara.* Cleveland: Cleveland Museum of Art, 1998.

Harris, Victor, ed. *Shinto: The Sacred Art of Ancient Japan.* London: British Museum Press, 2001.

Izutsu, Shinryu, and Shoryu Omori. *Sacred Treasures of Mount Koya: The Art of Japanese Shingon Buddhism.* Honolulu: Koyasan Reihokan Museum, 2002.

Kurata, Bunsaku. *Horyu-ji, Temple of the Exalted Law: Early Buddhist Art from Japan.* New York: Japan Society, 1981.

Levine, Gregory P.A., and Yukio Lippit. *Awakenings: Zen Figure Painting in Medieval Japan.* New York: Japan Society, 2007.

McCallum, Donald F. *The Four Great Temples: Buddhist Archaeology, Architecture, and Icons of Seventh-Century Japan.* Honolulu: Univ. of Hawai'i Press, 2009.

Mino, Yutaka. *The Great Eastern Temple: Treasures of Japanese Buddhist Art from Todai-ji.* Chicago: Art Institute of Chicago, 1986.

Mizoguchi, Koji. *An Archaeological History of Japan: 30,000 b.c. to a.d. 700.* Philadelphia: Univ. of Pennsylvania Press, 2002.

Murase, Miyeko. *The Tale of Genji: Legends and Paintings.* New York: Braziller, 2001.

Nishiwara, Kyotaro, and Emily J. Sano. *The Great Age of Japanese Buddhist Sculpture, a.d. 60–1300.* Fort Worth, TX: Kimbell Art Museum, 1982.

Pearson, Richard J. *Ancient Japan.* Washington, DC: Sackler Gallery, 1992.

Ten Grotenhuis, Elizabeth. *Japanese Mandalas: Representations of Sacred Geography.* Honolulu: Univ. of Hawai'i Press, 1999.

Washizuka, Hiromitsu, Park Youngbok, and Kang Woo-bang. *Transmitting the Forms of Divinity: Early Buddhist Art from Korea and Japan.* Ed. Naomi Noble Richard. New York: Japan Society, 2003.

Wong, Dorothy C., and Eric M. Field, eds. *Horyuji Reconsidered.* Newcastle: Cambridge Scholars, 2008.

Chapter 12 Art of the Americas before 1300

Benson, Elizabeth P., and Beatriz de la Fuente. *Olmec Art of Ancient Mexico.* Washington, DC: National Gallery of Art, 1996.

Berrin, Kathleen, ed. *Feathered Serpents and Flowering Trees: Reconstructing the Murals of Teotihuacan.* San Francisco: Fine Arts Museums of San Francisco, 1988.

Brody, J. J. *Anasazi and Pueblo Painting.* Albuquerque: Univ. of New Mexico Press, 1991.

———, Catherine J. Scott, and Steven A. LeBlanc. *Mimbres Pottery: Ancient Art of the American Southwest: Essays.* New York: Hudson Hills Press in assoc. with The American Federation of Arts, 1983.

Burger, Richard L. *Chavin and the Origins of Andean Civilization.* New York: Thames & Hudson, 1992.

Clark, John E., and Mary E. Pye, eds. *Olmec Art and Archaeology in Mesoamerica.* Studies in the History of Art, 58: Symposium Papers, 35. Washington, DC: National Gallery of Art, 2000.

Clayton, Lawrence A., Vernon J. Knight, and Edward Moore, eds. *The De Soto Chronicles: The Expedition of Hernando de Soto to North America, 1539–1543.* 2 vols. Tuscaloosa: Univ. of Alabama Press, 1993.

Coe, Michael D. and Rex Koontz. *Mexico: From the Olmecs to the Aztecs.* 5th ed. New York: Thames & Hudson, 2005.

———. *Breaking the Maya Code.* Rev. ed. New York: Thames & Hudson, 1999.

Donnan, Christopher. *Moche Portraits from Ancient Peru.* Austin: Univ. of Texas Press, 2003.

Fagan, Brian M. *Chaco Canyon: Archeologists Explore the Lives of an Ancient Society.* New York: Oxford Univ. Press, 2005.

Hall, Robert L. *An Archaeology of the Soul: North American Indian Belief and Ritual.* Urbana: Univ. of Illinois Press, 1997.

Heyden, Doris, and Paul Gendrop. *Pre-Columbian Architecture of Mesoamerica.* Trans. Judith Stanton. History of World Architecture. New York: Electa/Rizzoli, 1988.

Korp, Maureen. *The Sacred Geography of the American Mound Builders.* Native American Studies. Lewiston, NY: Mellen Press, 1990.

Kubler, George. *The Art and Architecture of Ancient America: The Mexican, Maya, and Andean Peoples.* 3rd ed. with updated bib. Pelican History of Art. New Haven: Yale Univ. Press, 1993.

Labbé, Armand J. *Shamans, Gods, and Mythic Beasts: Colombian Gold and Ceramics in Antiquity.* New York: American Federation of Arts, 1998.

Loendorf, Lawrence L., Christopher Chippindale, and David S. Whitley, eds. *Discovering North American Rock Art.* Tucson: Univ. of Arizona Press, 2005.

Martin, Simon, and Nikolai Grube. *Chronicle of the Maya Kings and Queens: Deciphering the Dynasties of the Ancient Maya.* 2nd ed. New York: Thames & Hudson, 2008.

Miller, Mary Ellen. *The Art of Mesoamerica: From Olmec to Aztec.* 4th ed. World of Art. London: Thames & Hudson, 2006.

———. *Maya Art and Architecture.* World of Art. London: Thames & Hudson, 1999.

———, and Simon Martin. *Courtly Art of the Ancient Maya.* San Francisco: Fine Arts Museums of San Francisco, 2004.

———, and Karl Taube. *The Gods and Symbols of Ancient Mexico and the Maya: An Illustrated Dictionary of Mesoamerican Religion.* London: Thames & Hudson, 1993.

Milner, George R. *The Moundbuilders: Ancient Peoples of Eastern North America.* Ancient Peoples and Places, 110. London: Thames & Hudson, 2004.

Noble, David Grant. *In Search of Chaco: New Approaches to an Archaeological Enigma.* Santa Fe, NM: School of American Research Press, 2004.

O'Connor, Mallory McCane. *Lost Cities of the Ancient Southeast.* Gainesville: Univ. Press of Florida, 1995.

Pasztory, Esther. *Teotihuacan: An Experiment in Living.* Norman: Univ. of Oklahoma Press, 1997.

Pillsbury, Joanne, ed. *Moche Art and Archaeology in Ancient Peru.* Studies in the History of Art, 63: Symposium Papers, 40. Washington, DC: National Gallery of Art, 2001.

Power, Susan C. *Early Art of the Southeastern Indians: Feathered Serpents & Winged Beings.* Athens: Univ. of Georgia Press, 2004.

Rohn, Arthur H., and William M. Ferguson. *Puebloan Ruins of the Southwest.* Albuquerque: Univ. of New Mexico Press, 2006.

Sharer, Robert J., and Loa P. Traxler. *The Ancient Maya.* 6th ed. Stanford, CA: Stanford Univ. Press, 2006.

Stierlin, Henri. *The Maya: Palaces and Pyramids of the Rainforest.* Köln: Taschen, 2001.

Stone-Miller, Rebecca. *Art of the Andes: From Chavin to Inca.* 2nd ed. World of Art. New York: Thames & Hudson, 2002.

———. *To Weave for the Sun: Ancient Andean Textiles.* New York: Thames & Hudson 1994.

Townsend, Richard F., and Robert V. Sharp, eds. *Hero, Hawk, and Open Hand: American Indian Art of the Ancient Midwest and South.* Chicago: Art Institute of Chicago, 2004.

Von Hagen, Adriana, and Craig Morris. *The Cities of the Ancient Andes.* New York: Thames and Hudson, 1998.

Chapter 13 Early African Art

Ben-Amos, Paula. *The Art of Benin.* Rev. ed. Washington, DC: Smithsonian Institution Press, 1995.

Berzock, Kathleen Bickford. *Benin: Royal Arts of a West African Kingdom.* Chicago: Art Institute of Chicago, 2008.

Blier, Suzanne Preston. *The Royal Arts of Africa: The Majesty of Form.* Perspectives. New York: Abrams, 1998.

Cole, Herbert M. *Igbo Arts: Community and Cosmos.* Los Angeles: Fowler Museum of Cultural History, Univ. of California, 1984.

Connah, Graham. *Forgotten Africa: An Introduction to Its Archaeology.* New York: Routledge, 2004.

Darish, Patricia J. *"Memorial Head of an Oba: Ancestral Time in Benin Culture."* In *Tempus Fugit, Time Flies,* edited by Jan Schall. Kansas City, MO: The Nelson Atkins Museum of Art, 2000: 290–297.

Eyo, Ekpo, and Frank Willett. *Treasures of Ancient Nigeria.* Ed. Rollyn O. Kirchbaum. New York: Knopf, 1980.

Garlake, Peter S. *Early Art and Architecture of Africa.* Oxford History of Art. Oxford: Oxford Univ. Press, 2002.

Grunne, Bernard de. *The Birth of Art in Africa: Nok Statuary in Nigeria.* Paris: A. Biro, 1998.

Huffman, Thomas N. *Symbols in Stone: Unravelling the Mystery of Great Zimbabwe.* Johannesburg: Witwatersrand Univ. Press, 1987.

LaViolette, Adria Jean. *Ethno-Achaeology in Jenné, Mali: Craft and Status among Smiths, Potters, and Masons.* Oxford: Archaeopress, 2000.

M'Bow, Babacar, and Osemwegie Ebohon. *Benin, a Kingdom in Bronze: The Royal Court Art.* Ft. Lauderdale, FL: African American Research Library and Cultural Center, Broward County Library, 2005.

Phillipson, D. W. *African Archaeology.* 3rd ed. Cambridge World Archaeology. New York: Cambridge Univ. Press, 2005.

Schädler, Karl-Ferdinand. *Earth and Ore: 2500 Years of African Art in Terra-Cotta and Metal.* Trans. Geoffrey P. Burwell. München: Panterra, 1997.

CREDITS

Chapter 8

8.1 Bibliothèque Nationale de France; 8.2 © Kazuyoshi Nomachi/Corbis. All Rights Reserved; Technique a AKG Images/François Guénet; Technique b Photo by Roya Marefat; Technique c Jan Boer; 8.7 AKG Images/Erich Lessing; Technique e Robert Ousterhout; Technique f Dede Fairchild Ruggles; Technique g © 2010 De Agostini Picture Library/Scala, Florence; 8.3 © Annie Griffiths Belt/Corbis. All Rights Reserved; 8.4 Dorling Kindersley; 8.5 Zev Radovan/Bibleland Pictures; 8.6 © Roger Wood/Corbis. All Rights Reserved; Object Speaks a, c Raffaello Bencini Fotografo; 8.8 B. O'Kane/Alamy; 8.9 After Robert Hillenbrand, *Islamic Architecture*, 1994, p. 195; Ch 8 Closer Look © Trustees of the British Museum; 8.10 © Achim Bednorz, Koln; 8.11 Peter Sanders Photography; 8.12 Scala, Florence/Art Resource, NY/The Metropolitan Museum of Art; 8.13 © 2010 Digital image Museum Associates/LACMA/Art Resource NY, Scala, Florence; 8.14 Scala, Florence/Art Resource, NY/Musée du Louvre; 8.15 Photograph © 1982 The Metropolitan Museum of Art; 8.16 © RMN/Frank Raux; 8.17 Musée du Louvre/RMN Réunion des Musées Nationaux, France. Scala/Art Resource, NY; 8.18 Photograph © 1994 The Metropolitan Museum of Art, New York, 1994. Scala, Florence/Art Resource, NY/The Metropolitan Museum of Art; 8.19 Bibliothèque Nationale de France; 8.20 National Library, Egypt; 8.21 By permission of The British Library; 8.22 Sonia Halliday Photographs; 8.23 Drawn by Christopher Woodward. From *A History of Ottoman Architecture* by Godfrey Goodwin, Thames & Hudson, London and New York; 8.24 Art Archive/Dagli Orti; 8.25 © Ruggero Vanni/Corbis; 8.26 Photograph © 1980 The Metropolitan Museum of Art; 8.27 Drawing by Keith Turner after Henri Stierlin © Aga Khan Visual Archive, MIT; 8.28 photo: Abbas Aminmansour; 8.29 Culture and Sport Glasgow (Museums); 8.30 V&A Images; 8.31 Courtesy of the architect/Aga Khan Trust for Culture

Chapter 9

9.1, 9.7, 9.9, 9.13, 9.18 Rick Asher; 9.2 a, b, c, d, e, f The Bridgeman Art Library/Giraudon; 9.3 Harrapa/J.M. Kenoyer; 9.4 © Mark Kenoyer Courtesy Department of Archaeology and Museums, Government of Pakistan; 9.5 National Museum of New Delhi; 9.6 Patna Museum; 9.8 © Adam Woolfitt/Robert Harding World Imagery/Corbis; 9.10 Richard Ashworth/Robert Harding; 9.11, 9.25 Dinodia Picture Agency; 9.12, 9.14 Richard Todd/National Museum of New Delhi; 9.15 Archaeological Museum, Sarnath. Asian Art Archives, University of Michigan; 9.16 Borromeo/Art Resource, NY; 9.17 © AAAUM, University of Michigan; 9.19 AKG-Images; 9.20 Asian Art Archives/University of Michigan; 9.21 Asian Art Archives/University of Michigan; 9.22 © Robert Gill; Papilio/Corbis. All Rights Reserved; Object Speaks Henri Stierlin/National Museum of India; Closer Look Rick Asher; 9.23 © David Cumming; Eye Ubiquitous/Corbis. All

Rights Reserved; 9.24 © Richard Ashworth/Robert Harding World Imagery/Corbis; 9.26 Benoy K. Behl; 9.27 Lynton Gardner; 9.28 The Norton Simon Foundation; 9.30 Borromeo/Art Resource, NY; 9.31 © AAAUM, University of Michigan; 9.32 Jean-Louis Nou/AKG Images; 9.33 © Kevin R. Morris/Corbis; 9.34 Robert Harding World Imagery

Chapter 10

10.1 National Geographic Image Collection; 10.2 Banpo Museum; 10.3 Line drawing illustrated in Michael Sullivan, *The Arts of China*, Berkeley: University of California Press, 2008, fig. 1-14, after Wenwu, no. 1 (1988), fig. 20.; 10.4 Shanghai Museum; 10.5 Photo: Michael A. Nedzweski © President and Fellows of Harvard College; 10.6, 10.7 Hubei Provincial Museum, Wuhan; 10.8, 10.14, 10.15, 10.16 Cultural Relics Publishing House; 10.9 The Nelson-Atkins Museum of Art, Kansas City, Missouri. Photograph by Jamison Miller; 10.10, 10.24 © Trustees of the British Museum; 10.11 National Palace Museum, Taipei, Taiwan, Republic of China; 10.12 © Corbis; 10.13 Photograph © 2008 Museum of Fine Arts, Boston; Object Speaks Cultural Relics Publishing House; 10.17 Photograph © 2008 Museum of Fine Arts, Boston; 10.18 Photo: Imaging Department © President and Fellows of Harvard College; 10.19 The Nelson-Atkins Museum of Art, Kansas City, Missouri. Photograph by Jamison Miller; 10.20 National Palace Museum, Taipei, Taiwan, Republic of China; 10.21, 10.23 The Nelson-Atkins Museum of Art, Kansas City, Missouri. Photograph by John Lamberton; 10.22 Palace Museum, Beijing; 10.25, 10.27 National Museum of Korea, Seoul, Republic of Korea; 10.26, 10.30 © 2006 President and Fellows of Harvard College. Photo: Photographic Services; 10.28 The Ancient Art & Architecture Collection Ltd; 10.29 Tokyo National Museum DNP Archives.Com Co., Ltd

Chapter 11

11.1 Mary and Jackson Burke Foundation, NY. Photo: Bruce Schwarz; 11.2 DNP Archives.Com Co., Ltd; 11.3 Kazuyoshi Miyoshi/Pacific Press Service; 11.4 Photo: Orion Press, Tokyo. Japan National Tourist Organization; 11.5 Japan National Tourist Organization. Horyu-ji Treasure House; 11.6 Japan National Tourist Organization; 11.7 Shosoin, Todaiji, Nara; Recovering the Past b Photo: Patricia Graham; 11.8 Benrido, Japan; 11.9 AKG-Images; 11.10 Sakamoto Manschichi Photo Research Library, Tokyo; Closer Look The Tokugawa Reimeikai Foundation; 11.11 Courtesy of the Freer Gallery of Art, Smithsonian Institution, Washington, D.C.; 11.12 Tokyo National Museum DNP Archives.Com Co., Ltd; 11.13 Photograph © Museum of Fine Arts, Boston; 11.14 Asanuma Photo Studios, Kyoto, Japan; 11.15 Photo Courtesy of Kyoto National Museum; Object Speaks a TNM Image Archives source http://TnmArchives.jp/; Object Speaks b Kenchoji, Kamakura

Chapter 12

12.1 The Art Archive/National Anthropological Museum Mexico/Gianni Dagli Orti; 12.2 © Scala, Florence/Art Resource, NY/The Metropolitan Museum of Art, NY; 12.3 Werner Forman/Art Resource, NY; 12.4 © Yann Arthus-Bertrand/Corbis; 12.6 Art Archive; 12.7 The Cleveland Museum of Art; 12.8 © ML Sinibaldi/Corbis; 12.9 The Museum of Modern Art/Licensed by Scala-Art Resource, NY; Closer Look © Philip Baird/www.anthroarcheart.org; 12.10 © Scala, Florence/Art Resource, NY; 12.11 © The Trustees of the British Museum; 12.12 Rollout photograph © Justin Kerr; 12.13 AKG-Images/Hedda Eid; 12.14 John Bigelow Taylor; 12.15 AKG-Images/Bildarchiv Steffens; 12.16 Photograph © Museum of Fine Arts, Boston; 12.17 © Kevin Schafer/Corbis; Technique Photograph © Museum of Fine Arts, Boston; 12.18 © 2005 Photo Scala, Florence/BPK, Bildagentur fuer Kunst, Kultur und Gechsichte, Berlin; 12.19 Fowler Museum at UCLA. Photo: Don Cole; 12.20 © Gilcrease Museum, Tulsa; 12.21 Tony Linck/ Ohio Dept. of Natural Resources; 12.22 William Iseminger, 'Reconstruction of Central Cahokia Mounds.' c. 1150 CE. Courtesy of Cahokia Mounds State Historic Site.; 12.23 University of Pennsylvania Museum of Archaeology and Anthropology; 12.24 Saint Louis Art Museum; 12.25 © Richard A. Cooke/Corbis; 12.26 Corson Hirschfeld; Object Speaks a Craig Law; Object Speaks b Fred Hirschmann Photography; 12.27 Timothy O'Sullivan/National Archives and Records Administration/Presidential Library

Chapter 13

13.1 © 1980 Dirk Bakker; 13.2 © Kazuyoshi Nomachi/Corbis; 13.3 © Werner Forman/Art Resource, NY; Art and its Contexts Neil Lee/Ringing Rocks Digitizing Laboratory/ www.SARADA.co.za/San Heritage Centre/Rock Art Research Centre/University of the Witwatersrand, Johannesburg; 13.4 From Thurstan Shaw, *Igbo-Ukwu: An Account of Archaeological Discoveries in Eastern Nigeria*. 2 vols. Evanston: Northwestern University Press, 1970; 13.5 Jerry Thompson; 13.6 The Nelson-Atkins Museum of Art. Photo: E. G. Schempf; Closer Look Photograph © 1979 Dirk Bakker; 13.7, 13.17 Eliot Elisofon Archives/National Museum of African Art/Smithsonian Institution; 13.8 Scala, Florence/Art Resource, NY/Photograph © 1995 The Metropolitan Museum of Art/; Object Speaks a The Nelson-Atkins Museum of Art, Kansas City, Missouri. Photo: Jamison Miller.; Object Speaks b, c Joseph Nevadomsky; 13.9 National Museum of African Art/Smithsonian Institution. Photo by Franko Khoury; 13.10 Getty Images, Inc.; 13.11 Source: Dorling Kindersley illustration from DK; 13.12 I Vanderharst/Robert Harding World Imagery; 13.13 Robert Harding Picture Library Ltd./Alamy; 13.15 The Pitt Rivers Museum/ University of Oxford. Photo by Heini Schneebeli; 13.16 © 2008 Image copyright The Metropolitan Museum of Art/Art Resource/ Scala, Florence

Page numbers in *italics* refer to illustrations and maps